The Jini™ Specifications

Second Edition

The Jini™ Technology Series

Lisa Friendly, Series Editor

Ken Arnold, Technical Editor

For more information see: http://java.sun.com/docs/books/jini/

This series, written by those who design, implement, and document the Jini™ technology, shows how to use, deploy, and create Jini applications. Jini technology aims to erase the hardware/software distinction, to foster spontaneous networking among devices, and to make pervasive a service-based architecture. In doing so, the Jini architecture is radically changing the way we think about computing. Books in **The Jini Technology Series** are aimed at serious developers looking for accurate, insightful, thorough, and practical material on Jini technology.

The Jini Technology Series web site contains detailed information on the Series, including existing and upcoming titles, updates, errata, sources, sample code, and other Series-related resources.

Eric Freeman, Susanne Hupfer, and Ken Arnold, *JavaSpaces™ Principles, Patterns, and Practice*
ISBN 0-201-30955-6

Jim Waldo and The Jini™ Technology, *The Jini™ Specifications, Second Edition, edited by Ken Arnold*
ISBN 0-201-72617-3

The Jini™ Specifications

Second Edition

Jim Waldo
The Jini™ Technology Team

Addison-Wesley

Boston • San Francisco • New York • Toronto • Montreal
London • Munich • Paris • Madrid
Capetown • Sydney • Tokyo • Singapore • Mexico City

Library of Congress Cataloging-in-Publication Data
The Jini™ specifications/edited by Ken Arnold, Jim Waldo.—2nd ed.
p. cm.—(Jini™ technology series)
Rev. ed of: The Jini™ specification. c1999.
Includes index.
ISBN 0-201-72617-3
1. Electronic data processing—Distributed processing. 2. Jini. I. Arnold, Ken, 1958- II. Waldo, Jim. III. Series.
QA76.9.D5 J56 2000
004'.36—dc21 00–048513

The publisher offers discounts on this book when ordered in quantity for special sales. For more information, please contact:

Pearson Education Corporate Sales Division
One Lake Street
Upper Saddle River, NJ 07458
(800) 382-3419
corpsales@pearsontechgroup.com

Text printed on recycled and acid-free paper

ISBN 0-201-72617-3
Text printed on recycled paper
1 2 3 4 5 6 7 8 9 10—MA—0403020100
First Printing, December 2000

This book is dedicated to the Jini team
without whom this book
would not have been necessary

Contents

PART 1 Overview and Examples

PART 2 Specifications

PART 3 Supplemental Material

Foreword

SECOND EDITION

THE emergence of the Internet has led computing into a new era. It is no longer what your computer can do that matters. Instead, your computer can have access to the power of everything that is connected to the network: The Network is the Computer™. This network of services is the computing environment of the future.

The Java™ programming language brought reliable object-oriented programs to the net. Its simplicity continues to allow programmers to become fully fluent, and allows debugged Java programs to be written in about a quarter the time it takes to write programs in C++. We believe that use of the Java platform is the key to the emergence of a "best practices" discipline in software construction to give us the reliability we need in our software systems as they become more and more widely used.

The Jini™ architecture is designed to bring reliability and simplicity to the construction of networked devices and services. The philosophy behind the Jini architecture is language-based systems: a network of Jini technology-enabled services—representing software and devices—is a collection of interacting Java programs, so you can understand the behavior of this Jini system completely by understanding the semantics of the Java programming language and the nature of the network—namely, that networks have limited bandwidth, inherent latency, and partial failure.

Because the Jini architecture focuses on a few simple principles, we can teach Java language programmers the full power of the Jini technology in a few days. To do this, we introduce remote objects (objects that have methods that throw a `RemoteException`), leasing (resources in a Jini system are of limited duration), distributed events (events over a network aren't as predictable as on a single machine), and the need for a two-phase commit mechanism (because the network is a world of partial failures). This small set of additional concepts allows distributed applications to be written, which we illustrate by a JavaSpaces™ service, also specified here. The rest of the specifications are for helper utilities and services that may help you with some of the more repeatable aspects of writing code under the Jini architecture.

For me, the Jini architecture represents the results of almost 20 years of yearning for a new substrate for distributed computing. Ever since I shipped the first widely used implementation of TCP/IP with the Berkeley UNIX system, I have wanted to raise the level of discourse on the network from the bits and bytes of TCP/IP to the level of objects. Objects have the enormous advantage of combining the data with the code that manipulates that data, greatly improving the reliability and integrity of systems. For me, the Jini architecture represents the culmination of this dream.

I would like to thank the entire Jini team for their continuing hard work and commitment. I would especially like to thank my longtime collaborator Mike Clary for helping to get the Jini project started and for directing the project; the Jini architects Jim Waldo, Ken Arnold, Bob Scheifler, and Ann Wollrath for designing and implementing such a simple and elegant system; Mark Hodapp for his excellent engineering management; and Samir Mitra for committing early to the Jini project, helping us understand how to explain it and what problems it would solve, and for driving the key business development that helped give Jini technology the momentum it has in the marketplace today. I would also like to thank Mark Tolliver, the head of the Consumer and Embedded Division, which the Jini project became part of, for his support.

Finally, I would like to thank Scott McNealy, with me a founder of Sun Microsystems™, Inc., and its longtime CEO. It is his continuing support of breakthrough technologies such as Java and Jini that makes them possible. As Machiavelli noted, it is hard to introduce new ideas, and support like Scott's is essential to our continuing success.

BILL JOY
ASPEN, COLORADO
OCTOBER, 2000

Preface

Perfection is reached, not when there is no longer anything to add,
but when there is no longer anything to take away.
—Antoine de Saint-Exupery

THE Jini architecture is designed for deploying and using services in a network. Networks are by nature dynamic: new things are added, old things are removed, existing things are changed, and parts of the network fail and are repaired. There are therefore problems unlike any that will appear in a single process or even multiple processes in a single machine.

These differences require an approach that takes them into account, makes changes apparent, and allows older parts to work with newer parts that are added. A distributed system must adapt as the network changes since the network *will* change. The Jini architecture is designed to be adaptable.

This book contains three parts. The first part gives an overview of the Jini architecture, its design philosophy, and its application. This overview sets up the following sections, which contain examples of programming in a Jini system. The first section of the introduction is also usable as a high-level overview for technical managers.

The sections of the introduction that contain examples are designed to orient you within the Jini technology and architecture. They are not a full tutorial: Think of them as a tour through the process of design and implementation in a Jini system. As with any tour, you can get the flavor of how things work and where you can start your own investigation.

The second part of the book contains the specifications themselves. Each specification has a brief introduction describing its place in the overall architecture.

The third part of the book contains supplementary material: a glossary that defines terms used in the specifications and in talking about Jini architecture, design, and technology, followed by two appendices. Appendix A is a reprint of

"A Note on Distributed Computing," which describes critical differences between local and remote programming. Appendix B contains the full source code for the examples in the introductory material.

History

The Jini architecture is the result of a rather extraordinary string of events. But then almost everything is. The capriciousness of life—and to the fortunate, its occasional serendipity—is always extraordinary. It is only in retrospect that we examine the causes and antecedents of something interesting and decide that, because they shaped that interesting result, we will call *them* "extraordinary." Other events, however remarkable, go unremarked because they are unexamined. Those of us who wrote the Jini architecture, along with the many who contributed to its growth, are lucky to have a reason to examine our particular history to savor its pleasures.

This is not the proper place for a long history of the project, but it seems appropriate to give a brief summary of the highlights. The project had its origins in Sun Microsystems Laboratories, where Jim Waldo ran the Large Scale Distribution research project. Jim Waldo and Ken Arnold had previously been involved with the Object Management Group's first CORBA specification while working for Hewlett-Packard. Jim brought that experience and a long-term background in distributed computing with him to Sun Labs.

After joining the Labs, Ann Wollrath joined Jim's team. Soon thereafter, observations about many common issues in the field of distributed computing led Jim, Ann, and other authors to write "A Note on Distributed Computing," which outlined critical distinctions between local and distributed design. Many people had been trying to hide those differences under the general rubric of "local/remote transparency." The "Note" argued that this was not possible. It has become the most cited Sun Laboratories technical report, and the lessons it distills are at the core of the design approach taken by our project.

At this time the project was using Modula 3 Network Objects for experiments in distributed computing. As Modula 3 ceased to be developed, the team looked around for a replacement language. At that time Oak, the language an internal Sun project, seemed a viable replacement with some interesting new properties. To a research project, the fact that Oak was commercially insignificant was irrelevant. It was at this time that Ken rejoined Jim on his new team.

Soon after, Oak was renamed "Java."

When it was still Oak, it had once had a remote method invocation mechanism, but that was removed when the mechanism failed—it, too, had fallen into the local/remote transparency trap. When Bill Joy and James Gosling wanted to create a working distributed computing mechanism, they asked Jim to lead the effort, which switched our team from the laboratories into the JavaSoft product group. As the first result of this effort, Ann, as the Java RMI architect, steered the team on an exploration of what could be done with a language-centric approach to distributed computing (most distributed computing systems are built on language-neutral approaches).

After RMI became part of the Java platform, Bill Joy asked the team to expand its horizons to include a platform for easier distributed computing, coining the name "Jini."[1] He convinced Sun management to put the RMI, JavaSpaces, and Jini projects into a separate unit. This new unit started with Jim, Ann, Ken, and Peter Jones, and was soon joined by Bob Scheifler who had extensive distributed computing experience from the X Windows project that he ran. This put together the original core architectural team: Jim, Ann, Ken, and Bob.

As the team grew, many people had a hand in the direction of various parts of the architecture, including Bryan O'Sullivan who took over the design of the lookup discovery protocol. Mike Clary took the project under his wing to give it time to grow. Mark Hodapp joined the team to manage its software development and run it in partnership with its technical leadership. Gary Holness, Zane Pan, Brian Murphy, John McClain, and Bob Resendes all reviewed the primary architecture documents and had responsibility for various parts of the tool design, implementation design, and the implementations themselves. Laird Dornin and Adrian Colley joined the RMI sub-team to continue and expand its development. Charlie Lamb joined the architectural team to oversee work with outside companies, starting with printing and storage service standards. Jen McGinn joined the team to document what we had done, later with the help of Susan Snyder on production support. Jimmy Torres started out as our release engineer and has changed to working on helping build our public developer community. Frank Barnaby took over the release engineering duties. Helen Leary joined early and kept our infrastructure humming along.

Our QA team was Mark Schuldenfrei and Anand Dhingra, managed by Brendan Daly. Alan Mortensen wrote the conformance tests and their infrastructure. Emily Suter and Theresa Lanowitz started out our marketing team, with Franc Romano, Donna Michael, Joan MacEachern, and Paula Kozak joining later. Jim Hurley started setting up our support organization, and Keith Thompson and Peter Marks joined to work on sales engineering. Samir Mitra led a marketing and business development team that included Jon Bostrom, Jaclyn Dahlby, Mike McNerny, Miko Matsamura, Darryl Mocek, Sharam Moradpour, and Vince Vasquez. Many others, too numerous to mention, did important work that made the Jini architecture possible and real.

---

[1] Jini is not an acronym. To remember this, think of it as standing for "Jini Is Not Initials." It is pronounced the same as "genie."

As the specifications were written, almost every member of the team made important contributions. Their names are listed above; we note the fact here to express our gratitude. A good idea and a dollar will buy a bad cup of espresso—you need people who will make that idea live, sand off any rough edges, and help you rework any bad parts of the idea into good ones. We had those people—some of the best we've ever worked with. Without them the Jini architecture would be some rather nice ideas on paper. Because of their commitment to adopt the vision as their own, to make it better, and to make it real, there are people (like you, the reader) who care about these ideas and can do something with them. We thank the entire team for what they have done to improve the Jini architecture and to help us write and release the Jini technology.

Bill Joy created the environment in which the Jini architecture could be developed and nurtured, and fed the architecture with his own reviews and ideas. His vision and support inside and outside of Sun made the project possible. This book itself is also his idea.

Bob Sproull gave the Large Scale Distribution project scope and support that has continued to this day, through all its many twists and turns, even after we were no longer were part of his Sun Labs organization. Mike Clary's protection and guidance was critical to fostering the creative atmosphere around the Jini project.

Jen McGinn and Susan Snyder did a lot of work to make this book possible, including hours in front of a screen converting the specification documents from their original form into that of the book. Jen also worked hard to improve the content of the specifications and introductory material during their creation, making them clearer and their English more correct. Dick Gabriel contributed to the content and organization of the *Jini Architecture Specification,* making it clearer and easier to use.

Many people reviewed the introductory material, making comments that improved it tremendously: Liz Blair, Charlie Lamb, John McClain, Bob Resendes, and Bob Sproull. Lisa Friendly has applied her experience as series editor with the Java Series to help us create this sibling Jini Series. We would also like to thank the people at Addison-Wesley's Professional Computing group who worked with us on this book and the series: Mike Hendrickson, Julie DeBaggis, Sarah Weaver, Marina Lang, and Diane Freed. And without Susan Stambaugh's help, communicating with Bill (and sometimes Mike) is not merely difficult, but probably theoretically impossible.

To these and many others too numerous to mention we give our thanks and appreciation for what they did to make these ideas and this book possible.

ACKNOWLEDGMENTS (SECOND EDITION)

As the team has grown, and public interest has grown faster, the number of people contributing to the Jini network architecture, its specifications, and its publication has grown. Most of the original team is still involved, and most of them continued to help with the creation of the specifications and this book. We first start these acknowledgements by re-thanking those who left for the firm foundation they helped us build, and those still with us for that and for staying to build more.

The community of people using the technology and architecture and pushing it to its limits have been both gratifying and frightening—it is formidable to think about continuing to keep them involved and interested. Not everyone can be mentioned, but some of the most important technical and moral support has come from Hellmuth Broda, Geoffry Clements, Danese Cooper, Cees de Groot, Keith Edwards, John Gage, Dan Hushon, Alan Kaminsky, John McKim, Tim O'Reilly, Aleta Ricciardi, Jerome Scheuring, Sylvia Scheuring, Iain Shigeoka, and Bill Venners. New team members helped with the specifications: Steven Harris, Brian Jeltema, and Mike Warres. Rosemary Michelle Simpson did our thorough and comprehensive index. And as usual, we couldn't think of doing anything more complex than tying our velcro-bound shoes without logistical support from Helen Leary.

Jennifer McGinn and Susan Snyder invested heroic and amazingly forbearing efforts to make this book and its contents intelligible, usable, and informative. Their work quite literally made this book possible.

Lisa Friendly gave much help in figuring out how to make this process actually work instead of thrash. As usual, this series depends on both her good advice and good humor. And the team from Addison-Wesley had most of the same dedicated folks—Mike Hendrickson, Julie DeBaggis, and Diane Freed—with the addition of Mamata Reddy and Julie Steele.

This is, of course, only a partial list of people who made this book and its contents possible in this second edition. The future of this work is in these and many other good hands.

Conception is so much more fun than delivery.
—Georges Pompidou

PART 1
Overview and Examples

The Jini Architecture: An Introduction

1 Overview

The man who sets out to carry a cat by its tail learns something that will always be useful and which never will grow dim or doubtful.
—Mark Twain

JINI technology is a simple infrastructure for providing services in a network, and for creating spontaneous interactions between programs that use these services. Services can join or leave the network in a robust fashion, and clients can rely upon the availability of visible services, or at least upon clear failure conditions. When you interact with a service, you do so through a Java object provided by that service. This object is downloaded into your program so that you can talk to the service even if you have never seen its kind before—the downloaded object knows how to do the talking.

That's the whole system in a nutshell. It's not very much to say (although you will learn a lot more about the details). But like many ideas that are relatively simple to explain, there is a lot of power in those few ideas. Together, they allow you to build systems that are dynamic, flexible, and robust, and to build them out of many parts, created independently by many providers.

This book contains the formal specifications for the Jini technology, preceded by this introductory part that gives you an overview of the design and basic usage. The specifications that follow give you the details that make this flexibility possible. Each specification has a brief introduction that places it in context.

In this section you will find discussion of several examples. Some of these will come from standard office environments and talk about printers, fax machines, and desktop systems. But others will come from less traditional networking environments: home entertainment systems, cars, and houses. These environments are quickly becoming networked, and Jini systems, with their relatively small size, are ideal for such use.

1.1 Goals

The Jini architecture is designed to allow a service on a network be available to anyone who can reach it, and to do so in a type-safe and robust way. The goals of the architecture are:

- **Network plug-and-work:** You should be able to plug a service into the network and have it be visible and available to those who want to use it. Plugging something into a network should be all or almost all you need to do to deploy the service.
- **Erase the hardware/software distinction:** You want a service. You don't particularly care what part of it is software and what part is hardware as long as it does what you need. A service on the network should be available in the same way under the same rules whether it is implemented in hardware, software, or a combination of the two.
- **Enable spontaneous networking:** When services plug into the network and are available, they can be discovered and used by clients and by other services. When clients and services work in a flexible network of services, they can organize themselves in the most appropriate way for the set of services that are actually available in the environment.
- **Promote service-based architecture:** With a simple mechanism for deploying services in a network, more products can be designed as services instead of stand-alone applications. Inside almost every application is a service or two struggling to get out. An application lets people who are in particular places (such as in front of a keyboard and monitor) use its underlying service. The easier it is to make the service itself available on the network, the more services you will find on the network.
- **Simplicity:** We are aesthetically driven to make things simple because simple systems please us. Much of our design time is spent trying to throw things out of a design. We try to throw out everything we can, and where we can't throw something out, we try to invent reusable pieces so that one idea can do duty in many places. You benefit because the resulting system is easier to learn to use and easier to provide systems in. Being a well-behaved Jini service is relatively simple, and much of what you need to do can be auto-

mated by other tools, leaving you with a few necessary pieces of work to do. Equally important, a large system built on simple principles is going to be more robust than a large complicated system.

1.2 Architecture

Each Jini system is built around one or more *lookup* services. The lookup service is where services advertise their availability so that you can find them. There may be one or more lookup services running in a network.

When a service is booted on the network, it uses a process called *discovery* to find the local lookup services. The service then registers its *proxy* object with each lookup service. The proxy object is a Java object, and its types—the interfaces it implements and its superclasses—define the service it is providing. For example, a proxy object for a printer will implement a `Printer` interface. If the printer is also capable of receiving faxes, the proxy object will also implement the `FaxReceiver` interface.

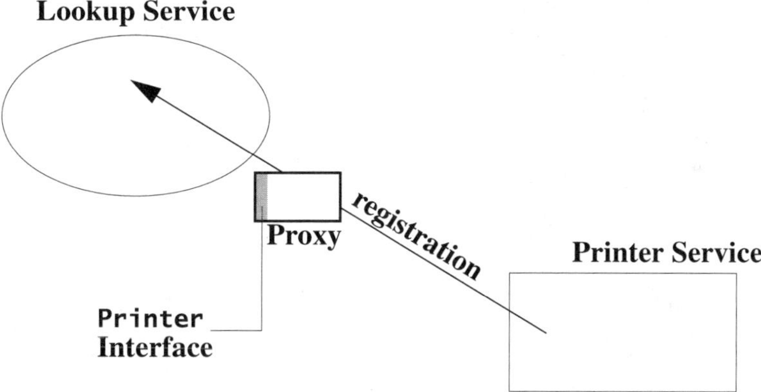

A client program asks for services by the Java language type the client will use. A client wanting a printer will ask the lookup service for a service that implements the `Printer` interface. When the lookup service returns the printer's proxy object, the client will automatically download the code for that object if it doesn't have it already.

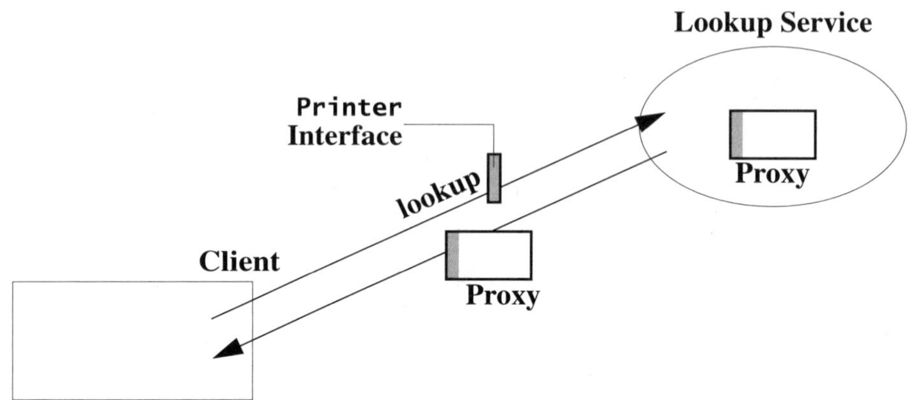

The client issues printer requests by invoking methods on the proxy object. The proxy communicates with the printer as it needs to in order to execute the requests. The Jini system does not define what the protocol between the proxy and its service should be; that is defined by the printer and its proxy object.

In fact, the proxy may talk to any number of remote systems to implement a single method, including zero. Whoever writes the proxy object determines when it talks to whom to get what, constrained, of course, by the security environment in which it executes. As long as the proxy object provides the services advertised by its interfaces and/or classes, the client will be satisfied. This encapsulation is one of the basic powers of object-oriented programming. The invoker of a method cares only that the method implementation does what is expected, not how it does it. The proxy object in a Jini system extends the benefits of this encapsulation to services on the network.

In effect, the proxy object is a driver for the printer that is downloaded on demand. This allows a client to speak to a kind of printer it has never before encountered without any human having to install the printer's driver on the client's computer. When the driver is needed, it is downloaded. When it is no longer needed, it can be disposed of automatically.

1.3 What the Jini Architecture Depends Upon

The Jini architecture relies upon several properties of the Java virtual machine:

- **Homogeneity:** The Java virtual machine provides a homogeneous platform—a single execution environment that allows downloaded code to behave the same everywhere.
- **A Single Type System:** This homogeneity results in types that mean the same thing on all platforms. The same typing system can be used for local and remote objects and the objects passed between them.
- **Serialization:** Java objects typically can be serialized into a transportable form that can later be deserialized.
- **Code Downloading:** Serialization can mark an object with a codebase: the place or places from which the object's code can be downloaded. Deserialization can then download the code for an object when needed.
- **Safety and Security:** The Java virtual machine protects the client machine from viruses that could otherwise come with downloaded code. Downloaded code is restricted to operations that the virtual machine's security allows.

Taken together, these properties mean that objects can be moved around the network in a consistent and trustable manner. These properties enable a system built on dynamic service proxies moving object state and implementation to the most useful parts of a system when they are needed. Such proxies are part of the foundation on which the Jini architecture is built.

1.4 The Value of a Proxy

The proxy object is central to the benefit of using a Jini system. The proxy defines a service type by being of a particular Java type. It implements that type in whatever way is appropriate for the service implementation that registered it. This is basic object-oriented philosophy: You know *what* the object does because you know its Java language type, but you don't know *how* it implements the methods defined by that type. The proxy is the part of the service that runs in the client's virtual machine.

This encapsulation allows the `Printer` interface to be designed as a good client API without requiring it to be a good network protocol for talking to a remote printer. The `Printer` interface should be designed at the abstraction level appropriate for client code. Each proxy object that implements the `Printer` interface does so in the right way for the particular printer, using that printer's network protocol. While it is very useful for everyone to agree on the design of the `Printer` interface, nobody needs to agree on the network protocol. The `Printer` interface's `printText` method would be implemented differently for a PostScript printer than for one that had a different printer language. The proxy object encapsulates such differences so the client can simply invoke the method.

And anyone can write a proxy object. If the printer manufacturer does not provide a Jini service proxy, you can write your own or buy one from someone else. As long as the proxy correctly implements the appropriate interface it is a valid proxy for the printer. If your use of a Jini system relies upon, say, a video camera, and the camera's manufacturer hasn't yet provided a proxy implementation you need, you can write it yourself or find someone else who has already done so. This works for integration of legacy services of any kind, not just devices. An existing database server can be made available through a Jini service's proxy, usually without modifying the server.

The service defines where the proxy code is loaded from. This allows the service to be its own HTTP server for its classes or to rely on an HTTP server somewhere else in the network. The service can, in fact, be unrelated to the hardware and software on which it is based. A service might, for example, be built from a server that monitors the network for some legacy hardware and when the hardware is present, registers a proxy on that hardware's behalf, unregistering the service when the hardware is disconnected. In such a model the service is completely uncoupled from the hardware on which it relies.

1.5 The Lookup Service

Each lookup service provides a list of available services, the proxy objects that know how to talk to the service, and attributes defined by either the local administrator or the service itself.

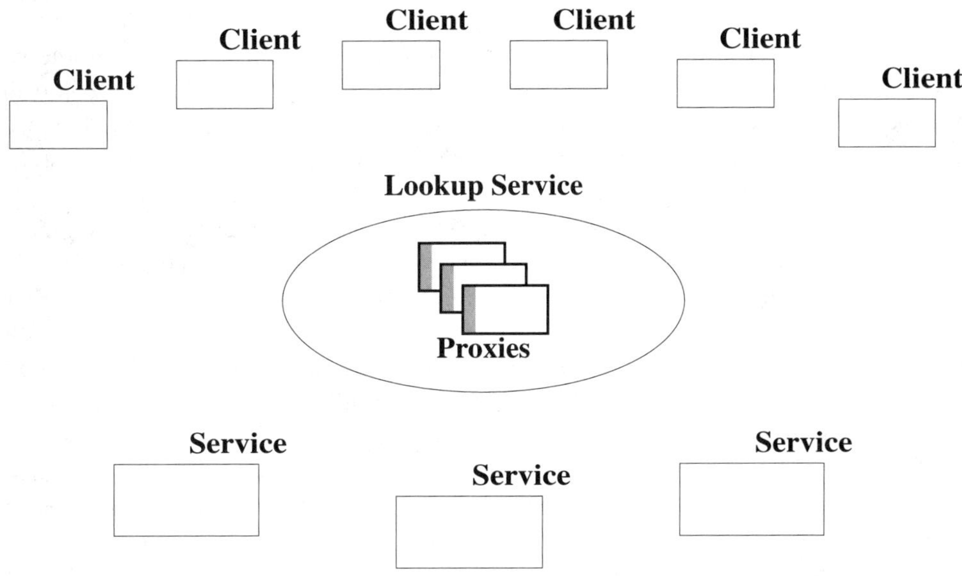

When a service is first booted up, it uses a *discovery* protocol to find local lookup services. This protocol will vary depending upon the kind of network, but its basic outline is:

- The service sends a "looking for lookup services" message to the local network. This is repeated for some period of time after initial startup.
- Each lookup service on the network responds with a proxy for itself.
- The service registers with each lookup service using its proxy by providing the service's proxy object and any desired initial attributes.

A client that wants a service goes through a matching protocol:

- The client sends a "looking for lookup services" message to the local network.
- Each lookup service in the network responds with a proxy for itself.

- The client searches for types of services it needs using the proxies of one or more lookup services. The lookup service returns one or more matching proxy objects, whose code is downloaded to the client if necessary.

The discovery protocol is how services and clients find nearby lookup services. A client or service can also be configured to locate specific lookup services as well as (or instead of) ones discovered on the local network. For example, when you plug in your laptop in a hotel, you might want not only to find the lookup service for your hotel room, but also to contact the lookup service in your home so you can interact with services there (such as programming the "Call Me" button on your home's telephone to call your hotel and ask for your room). Once a lookup service is located, rather than discovered, the registration and lookup steps are the same for service and client.

Matching in the lookup service is performed using standard Java language typing rules. If you ask for `Printer` objects, you will get only objects that implement the `Printer` interface. The actual object you get may also implement other interfaces, including subinterfaces of `Printer`, such as `ColorPrinter`. As with any other object you can check to see what types it supports. For example, you could check to see whether the `Printer` proxy implements the `ColorPrinter` interface, printing in color if it does, and otherwise printing in black and white.

Sometimes a service will be attached to a network when no lookup service can be found, for example in a broken network. The service's "looking for lookup services" message will therefore not reach the lookup service, and so the service cannot register. When the network is repaired, the service will be available but invisible. In order that this invisibility be temporary, each lookup service intermittently sends a "here I am" message to the network. When a service gets such a message, it registers with that lookup service if it isn't currently registered.

1.5.1 Attributes

When you look up an object by type, you will get an object with the capabilities you need, but it might not be the one you want. If you have two television sets in your house connected on one network, you will want to connect your VCR to the one you are about to watch. Both televisions will be `VideoDisplay` objects, so how do you distinguish between them?

Each proxy object in the lookup service can have *attributes.* These are objects that describe features relevant to distinguish one service from another in ways that are not reflected by the interfaces supported by the service. These often reflect ways to choose among services of the same type but are different in some way that is important to a human. In a home entertainment service, naming each television set by its location is probably enough—you can set the VCR to send its output to the `VideoDisplay` object with the `Name` attribute `"living room"`. In an office environment you might use `Location` attributes to help you choose the printer that is near your office, not at the other end of the hallway.

The Jini architecture does not define which attributes a service should have. The local administrator will decide which attributes are helpful in the local environment, and the service designer will decide which ones help users and clients find the right service. The Jini architecture does define a few example attributes in the package `net.jini.lookup.entry` as suggestions, but whether to use these, or others, or none, is up to service designers and local administrative policies.

An attribute is an object that is an *entry,* that is, it must implement the interface `net.jini.core.entry.Entry`, and have the associated semantics, which are:

- All non-static, non-transient, non-final fields must be public.
- Each field must be of an object type, not a primitive type (`int`, `char`, ...).
- The class must be public and have a public no-arg constructor.

An entry may have other kinds of fields, but they will not be saved when an attribute (entry) is stamped on a proxy or considered when matching attributes in lookup requests.

Attribute matching is done with simple expressions that use exact matching. You can say one of two things about an attribute: You require an attribute of that class (including a subclass) to be stamped on the proxy, or you don't care. Within each attribute you require, you can say a similar thing about each field: You require the field to have exactly some value or you don't care about its value. If you specify more than one attribute, the lookup service will return only proxies that match all the attributes you specify.

Attributes are properties of the service, not of its proxy in each individual lookup service. A service will have the same attributes in all lookup services in which it is registered (although network delays may allow you to see inconsistent sets of attributes in different lookup services while the service is updating its registrations).

1.5.2 Membership Management

When a service registers with a lookup service, it gets back (among other things) a *lease* on its presence in the lookup service. Leases are a programming model within the Jini architecture designed to allow providers of resources to clean up when the resource is no longer needed. In the lookup service case, for example, the lease keeps the list of available services fresh—as long as a service is up and running, it will renew its lease. If the service crashes or the network between the service and the lookup service breaks, the service will fail to renew its lease and thus be evicted from the lookup service.

This means that the list of services you find in a lookup service is a list of services that are available to you, modulo the time allowed by the lease. For example, if the lease time given to services by the lookup service (both initially and upon renewal) is five minutes, each service you see in the lookup service spoke to the lookup service within the last five minutes. Most lookup service implementations will let you tune this time to your required tolerances.

When combined with discovery of lookup services, the leased membership gives a powerful result: The list of services is current, self-healing, and self-replicating:

- It is current (modulo the lease times) because the leases make it so. Any network or host failure will force the removal of unreachable services.
- It is self-healing because if a network failure isolates a service from a lookup service, when the network is fixed, the service will receive a "here I am" message from the lookup service and rejoin.
- It is self-replicating because a service joins each lookup service it belongs to. If you want replication to increase robustness, just start another lookup service. All the services will simply register with both lookup services. If the only host running your lookup service crashes, just start a new one on a new host, and all the services will register with the new lookup service.

These features work together. If you run two lookup services on different hosts and the network between them fails, after the leases expire each will have the available services on its part of the network. When the network is fixed, each lookup service's "here I am" message will reconnect it with the services that were lost.

1.5.3 Lookup Groups

The discovery request may encounter many lookup services, but you might want a service to be visible in only a few of them. For example, if you have a lookup service that represents those services available to users of a conference room (fax machine, printer, projector, telephone, web server), you do not want those services available as default resources for the people who sit in offices next to the conference room. Nor do you want the people in the conference room to accidentally use a printer down the hall.

To limit a lookup service's scope, you place the lookup service in the conference room in its own *group* and configure each of the room's services to join only lookups in that group. The lookup discovery messages include the groups of the parties involved. Lookup services ignore discovery messages that are for groups they are not in, and services ignore "here I am" messages of lookup services in groups they are not configured to join. So when new services are added to the neighborhood, they will not be registered in the conference room's lookup service unless they are explicitly configured to join lookups in the right group.

1.5.4 Lookup Service Compared to Naming/Directory Services

A lookup service in a Jini system is the nexus where clients locate network services. In this sense its role is analogous to what are called naming or directory services in other distributed systems. The analogy is real, but it fails at some crucial junctures. In discussing the failures of the analogy we will use the term "naming services" to mean both naming and directory services, which are equivalent for this discussion.

In a directory system, services are stored by name, a human-readable string. The string is split up by conventional symbols that separate the components. For example, all printers may be stored under the directory `"/devices/printers"`. If you want to see the printers that are available in the directory service, you ask it for all the references to remote objects in this directory. Each installed printer will be placed in the directory when it is installed.

This system starts becoming unwieldy as you increase the number of services and their types. Color printers, for example, might be placed in the printers' directory, or possibly in a separate `"/devices/printers/color"` directory, or both so that people finding regular printers can find color printers, which after all can also be used as printers. Printers that are also fax machines would certainly be placed in at least two directories, since nobody would think to look for a fax machine in the printers' directory.

Also, note that the correlation between `"/devices/printers"` and print services is purely conventional. Should someone mistakenly place a fax service in the directory, clients will get very confused when the remote reference they get back is not actually a printer.

To find a service in a directory-based system, your client does the following:

1. Takes a string that is bound by convention to printers.
2. Asks the directory service what it has bound under that string.

3. Takes what it gets back and tries to use it as a `Printer` object (in the Java programming language this would be by casting it to the type `Printer` after checking, if you want a robust program, to be sure that it *is* a `Printer`).

Because the strings in a directory service are related only by convention to the type you need, failures to follow convention lead to errors for the client. The human-readable strings are actually of no value to the client except as a (risky) means to an end. The Jini Lookup service architecture gives your client a way to get at that end directly:

1. Asks the lookup service for a `Printer` object.
2. Takes the `Printer` object it gets back and uses it.

This directness also provides the benefits of object-oriented polymorphism: The object you get back will be at least a `Printer`, but it may in addition be something more: a `ColorPrinter`, possibly, or a `FaxSender`, `FaxReceiver`, or `Scanner`. You can use it as a `Printer` without regard to these extra capabilities, or you can test for their presence using the `instanceof` operator in the language.

People want to name things, of course. Most computers, printers, and other major systems in network are named. In a Jini system those names are attributes on the service that help humans distinguish between services. As attributes, names can be used to distinguish between services of identical type, but the primary mechanism a program uses to find services is the thing the program most cares about: the type of the service it will use.

1.6 Conclusion

The Jini architecture provides a platform for deploying services in a network. This platform is robust at many levels:

- It is robust in the face of network failures. The set of services automatically adapts the actual state of the network and service topology.
- It is robust in the face of changes in the implementation of services. As long as the service interface is implemented correctly, the details of the service implementation can change as you buy new equipment and as equipment generally becomes more capable.
- It is robust in the face of old services. It is relatively easy to incorporate old devices and servers seamlessly instead of leaving them as an impediment to progress.

- It is robust in the face of competition. The minimum standards necessary for cooperation are defined in the architecture—the definition of what defines a service (a Java language type) and how you find a service (in a lookup service)—and lets variation exist where it needs to. An industry can standardize on common ground (such as the basic `Printer` interface) and individual companies can add specific features in company-specific interfaces (such as `MyCompanysPrinter`) for clients that want to use them, without breaking generic clients that want only the common `Printer` functionality.
- It is robust in the face of scale. Jini services can be very large or very small, and can work with small devices via a supporting virtual machine.

The Jini architecture is not only robust, it is also flexible. Here are sketches of a few ways in which it can be used.

- You could design a kiosk that allowed the user to download information. For example, I might plug my PDA (personal digital assistant) into the kiosk and ask for directions to someplace. The kiosk can publish the information as a simple `TextPublisher` service which I would use to download the directions onto a text device such as a pager, as well as an `HTMLPublisher` service which I would use to download them onto a more capable device, such as a laptop computer.
- You could have expense sources (such as a taxi meter or credit card scanner) provide an `ExpenseSource` service that my PDA could use to download travel expense details. When I return to my office, my PDA could be its own `ExpenseSource` service that my spreadsheet or company expense report software could use as a source for expense report information.
- You could make sensors in a water supply system be Jini services and have several monitoring and report-generating applications adapt automatically to new sensors that are added to the network. Adding a new sensor would then be as simple as plugging it into the network: The monitoring applications would find the new service and incorporate it into the data flow. New "sensors" could be software services that aggregate and analyze information from sensors into higher-level data. The clients will be blissfully unaware of this hardware-software distinction.

These examples suggest the flavor of the benefits you can find using Jini technology. The example code that follows introduces you to the design of Jini clients and services. The specifications that come afterwards give you the details.

1.7 Notes on the Example Code

In the following two sections you will see an example service, an example client that uses that service, and two example implementations of that service. There are a few things you should know before we get started.

First, we have kept the examples as simple as possible. This means, for example, that we are using command line programs instead of graphical user interfaces. Graphical user interfaces require a good deal of programming, and explaining that part of the code would teach you nothing about using the Jini technology. We have also used very simple error-checking and handling except where more sophisticated techniques help us explain how you should use the Jini architecture.

We have also not shown some parts of the code that do not explain anything about programming in a Jini system—file system manipulation, string parsing, and so on. The full code for all the examples is in Appendix B.

1.7.1 Package Structure

The Jini technology is expressed in Java language interfaces and classes that live in three major package categories:

- `net.jini.core`: Standard interfaces and classes that are central ("core") to the Jini architecture live in subpackages of `net.jini.core`.
- `net.jini`: Interfaces and classes that are standards in the Jini architecture are in subpackages of `net.jini` (except the `net.jini.core` subpackage).
- `com.sun.jini`: Some interfaces and classes that are non-standard but potentially useful live in the subpackages of `com.sun.jini`. These packages may contain utility classes that help you write clients and services, example implementations of standard services, or utility classes used inside the example implementations.

As an example, here are three separate lookup-related packages:

- `net.jini.core.lookup`: The interfaces and class that comprise the lookup service that is at the heart of the Jini architecture.
- `net.jini.lookup`: Some standard tools to help you simplify code that interacts with a running lookup, and an interface (`DiscoveryAdmin`) that lookup services can support to allow administrators to configure which lookup groups the service will be a member of. These are advisory but stan-

dard: you need not use them, but they are common, traditional ways to accomplish these ends.

- `com.sun.jini.lookup.entry`: A utility class with some useful methods for operating on attributes, and a class to help you represent `ServiceType` attribtes on your service as resource bundles. These are used in some Sun code, and you are welcome to borrow it if you like, but they may not be supported in the future or may be changed as useful for future Sun code.

These packages progress from the core (the lookup service itself) to the standard (defined, though optional, ways to administer a lookup service) to the extended (useful utilities you may choose to use). Broken out these ways, the packages are:

- `net.jini.core.discovery`: A class (`LookupLocator`) that connects to a single lookup service
- `net.jini.core.entry`: The `Entry` interface that defines attributes
- `net.jini.core.event`: The interfaces and classes for distributed events
- `net.jini.core.lease`: The interfaces and classes for distributed leases
- `net.jini.core.lookup`: The interfaces and classes for the lookup service
- `net.jini.core.transaction`: The interfaces and classes for the clients of the transaction service
- `net.jini.core.transaction.server`: The interfaces and classes for the manager and participants in the transaction service
- `net.jini.admin`: Some standard administrative interfaces for services
- `net.jini.discovery`: Some standard utility classes that help clients and service implementations with the discovery protocol
- `net.jini.entry`: A useful base utility class (`AbstractEntry`) for entry (attribute) classes
- `net.jini.event`: The interfaces that define a mailbox service that can store event notifications for later retrieval
- `net.jini.lease`: The interfaces and classes that define a service that can manage leases on behalf of programs that may be occasionally disconnected from the network.
- `net.jini.lookup`: A standard administrative interface (`DiscoveryAdmin`) for lookup services
- `net.jini.lookup.entry`: Some standard attribute interfaces and classes you can use

- `net.jini.space`: The interfaces and classes that define the JavaSpaces technology
- `com.sun.jini.admin`: Interfaces for administering some common service necessities
- `com.sun.jini.lease`: Some abstract classes that may help your service manage the leases that it hands out
- `com.sun.jini.lease.landlord`: A particular instantiation of the abstract utility classes—the `LandlordLease`—and other server-side lease management tools.
- `com.sun.jini.lookup.entry`: Some classes to help you work with lookup service attributes.
- `com.sun.jini.start`: Utilities to help start up services, especially activatable services.

Other `com.sun.jini` classes exist. We have listed here the ones that you are most likely to find valuable in implementing your own clients and services.

As you will notice, we have taken a fine-grained approach to package structure—we make each package contain only related interfaces and classes. This leads to many well-focused packages instead of a few packages with many loosely related interfaces and classes. As the Jini architecture evolves, other packages will be added to this list. The notions of "core," "standard," and "extended" are currently mapped directly to package names. Future additions might not be able to follow this. For example, if a standard evolves that becomes core to the Jini architecture it could be viewed as "core" without renaming the package with a `net.jini.core` name. Such decisions are still in the future, and we cannot yet define a fixed policy until we have examples to consider.

You will see code from many of these packages in our example code. We will name the package of each Jini architecture interface or class when it first appears. The packages of the example classes themselves will be described at the beginning of the example. To keep the code to a reasonable size for the text, we will not show the import statements in the chapters. The full source (including import statements) is in Appendix B.

If computers get too powerful, we can organize them into a committee—
that will do them in.
—Braidley's Bromide

2 Writing a Client

A successful [software] tool is one that was used to do something undreamed of by its author.
—S.C. Johnson

LET'S make this architecture more concrete, first by showing how you would write a client that uses the Jini architecture. The next section will show how you would write two corresponding service implementations that are usable by this client. We will first describe the service being performed.

2.1 The MessageStream Interface

The example interface MessageStream provides an iterator through a stream of messages. It provides one method that returns the next message in the stream:

```
package message;

public interface MessageStream {
    Object nextMessage()
        throws EOFException, RemoteException;
}
```

The nextMessage method returns the next message as an object whose toString method prints out its default printed form. An EOFException signals the end of the stream. A RemoteException reflects failures in network messaging.

This simple interface could be used for many situations; in the next section we will show two: a "fortune cookie" service that returns a random saying, and a chat service whose messages are the utterances of the speakers in the discussion. Because the stream interface is general, the client that reads it can work with any type of message stream. The implementations of each stream will vary, but the client can do the same thing.

Our example client will simply find a user-specified stream and print out the requested number of messages. Other general clients could be fancier in many ways. In fact, many design features of our example client and service implementations are optimized for simplicity to keep the focus on the relevant Jini architecture and technology. You will see command line applications instead of graphical user interfaces, basic choices available rather than rich ones, and simple error handling. These simplifying choices help teaching by keeping the focus on the relevant parts of the code, even if they are sometimes unrealistic for product design (although simple choices for products are very often correct ones, too). The complete code for all examples is in Appendix B.

2.2 The Client

Now let's look at how you would write a client that finds and uses a message stream. Your users will need to give you enough information to pick the correct stream from among the available streams. Our example client allows the user to specify:

- Lookup groups that will be used in discovery or a specific lookup service
- The type of the service
- Attributes to use in selecting the service

The client bundles the service type and attribute information into a search template, queries the appropriate lookup services to find a matching service, and prints out one or more messages.

We will examine the client from the top down. Parts of the code that have little to do with learning the Jini architecture have been left out of the code presented here. The complete source to all examples is in Appendix B.

The command line syntax looks like this:

```
java [java-options] client.StreamReader [-c count]
     [groups|lookup-url] [stream-type|attributes ...]
```

The `java-options` will typically include setting a security policy file. The name of our client class is `client.StreamReader` (the `StreamReader` class in the `client` package). The `-c` option lets the user specify a count of messages to read; the default is one message. The user must choose from the set of lookup services by providing either a group specification for lookup discovery or an explicit lookup *locator,* which specifies a particular lookup service by its URL, which has the form `jini://host[:port]`. The user may also specify a type of stream, which must be a subtype of `MessageStream`, and/or a list of attributes. To simplify parsing, attributes are specified by either their type name, or their type name and a `String` parameter for the constructor. This means that only attributes with no-arg constructors or with single-argument `String` constructors can be used with `StreamReader` (a fancier client could let the user specify a richer set of attributes.)

A typical invocation might look like this:

```
java -Djava.security.policy=/policies/policy
     client.StreamReader "" fortune.FortuneStream
     fortune.FortuneTheme:General
```

In this invocation the group will be the empty string, which is the name of the public group; the type of the stream must be at least `fortune.FortuneStream`; and the registration in the lookup service must at least have an attribute of the type `fortune.FortuneTheme` that matches an attribute created with the string `"General"`. We will discuss the `fortune` package types when we show how the service is written.

When a user invokes the client command line, the `main` method of the class `client.StreamReader` will be invoked:

```
package client;

public class StreamReader
    implements ServiceDiscoveryListener
{
    private int count;
    private String[] groups = new String[0];
    private String lookupURL;
    private String[] typeArgs;

    public static void main(String[] args) throws Exception
    {
        StreamReader reader = new StreamReader(args);
        reader.execute();
    }

    //...
}
```

The `main` method simply creates a `StreamReader` object with the command line arguments and then invokes the object's `execute` method. The `StreamReader` constructor parses the command line to set the fields `count`, `groups`, `lookupURL`, and `typeArgs`. This parsing is shown only in the full source.

The execute method starts discovering lookup services:

```
private final static int MAX_WAIT = 5000;    // five seconds

public void execute() throws Exception {
    if (System.getSecurityManager() == null)
        System.setSecurityManager(new RMISecurityManager());

    LookupLocator[] locators = null;
    if (lookupURL != null) {
        LookupLocator loc = new LookupLocator(lookupURL);
        locators = new LookupLocator[] { loc };
    }

    DiscoveryManagement dm =          // lookups to search
        new LookupDiscoveryManager(groups, locators, null);
    ServiceDiscoveryManager sdm =    // services to look for
        new ServiceDiscoveryManager(dm, null);
    ServiceTemplate serviceTmpl = buildTmpl(typeArgs);
    sdm.createLookupCache(serviceTmpl, null, this);

    Thread.sleep(MAX_WAIT);
    exit(1, "No service found");
}
```

First we set a security manager to protect the client against misbehaving downloaded code. RMI requires a security manager to be in place during calls to ensure that you have thought about the security aspects of the code it will download. This code uses the RMISecurityManager, which is quite conservative about what it permits. Then we create the array of locators that will contain a URL if one was specified.

The next block of code sets up the mechanism we use for locating services in the network. The first question when looking for services in a Jini network is which lookup services to use. The DiscoveryManagement interface is an API that can maintain a set of service registrars (lookup services). Here we choose to use the LookupDiscoveryManager implementation of DiscoveryManagement, which maintains a set of services that match a particular set of groups and lookup locators (URLs). The final constructor parameter (which is null in this use) can be a listener that will be notified when the set of lookup services changes. When the constructor returns, the LookupDiscoveryManager object is off and running, watching for any relevant lookup services.

Having defined the set of lookup services in which we will look, we can now use the utility class ServiceDiscoveryManager to look within this set for the services we want. ServiceDiscoveryManager monitors the lookup services from the DiscoveryManager for relevant services. The second constructor parameter can provide a LeaseRenewalManager for managing any necessary leases, or null to ask the class to create its own. When this constructor returns, the ServiceDiscoveryManager has already started to watch for services.

There are several ways to use the ServiceDiscoveryManager. You can ask it to notify you when services arrive or query it when you are interested in the set of services. Here we use a lookup cache that stores only relevant services. We first use the method buildTmpl to create a ServiceTemplate object that describes the services we wish to search for (more on buildTmpl and service templates shortly). We then create the lookup cache, using that template as the first constructor parameter. Only services that match that template will be noticed by the cache. The second parameter allows you to specify a further filter to exclude services, typically for checks that can't be expressed by a ServiceTemplate. The final parameter can be an object that will be notified of changes to the cache contents. Here we are having it notify our StreamReader object. This notification will trigger reading the stream, as you will soon see.

All the work of ServiceDiscoveryManager happens in one or more independent threads, separate from the one that invoked execute. Once the service discovery is set up, the execute thread simply enforces the time limit on waiting for a usable service to arrive. The thread sleeps for that maximum time and then invokes exit, a method in the class the prints an message and exits with the given status (in this case 1, a non-zero exit status indicating a failure; the exit method is shown in the full source).

The next code of interest is buildTmpl. This takes the arguments given on the command line and turns them into a ServiceTemplate object that will match only services we're interested in:

```
private ServiceTemplate buildTmpl(String[] typeNames)
    throws ClassNotFoundException, IllegalAccessException,
           InstantiationException, NoSuchMethodException,
           InvocationTargetException
{
    Set typeSet = new HashSet();     // service types
    Set attrSet = new HashSet();     // attribute objects

    // MessageStream class is always required
    typeSet.add(MessageStream.class);
```

```
        for (int i = 0; i < typeNames.length; i++) {
            // break the type name up into name and argument
            StringTokenizer tokens =    // breaks up string
                new StringTokenizer(typeNames[i], ":");
            String typeName = tokens.nextToken();
            String arg = null;          // string argument
            if (tokens.hasMoreTokens())
                arg = tokens.nextToken();
            Class cl = Class.forName(typeName);

            // test if it is a type of Entry (an attribute)
            if (Entry.class.isAssignableFrom(cl))
                attrSet.add(attribute(cl, arg));
            else
                typeSet.add(cl);
        }

        // create the arrays from the sets
        Entry[] attrs = (Entry[])
            attrSet.toArray(new Entry[attrSet.size()]);
        Class[] types = (Class[])
            typeSet.toArray(new Class[typeSet.size()]);

        return new ServiceTemplate(null, types, attrs);
    }
```

The method loops through the type arguments given on the command line. The arguments can be either a type name or, in the case of attributes, a type name followed by a `String` argument to pass to the constructor, of the form *`type`*`(`*`arg`*`)`. The first part of the loop takes the name and checks to see whether it has an open parenthesis. If it does, it strips any closing parenthesis and remembers the argument in the variable `arg`, which is otherwise `null`. Once any argument has been stripped off from the class name in `cName`, we translate the name into a `Class` object for the type. If the type is assignable to `Entry` it is an attribute, and so an object is created of that attribute type, using `arg` if it was present—the method `attribute` (not shown) does this work. If it is not assignable to `Entry`, it must be a service type, and so we add its type to the types the service must support. When the loop is finished, `typeSet` contains all the required service types and `attrSet` contains all the required attribute templates. We then create appropriate arrays from the contents of these sets and pass the arrays to the `ServiceTemplate` constructor (the first `null` argument would be the service ID if we needed to match on a specific one).

At this point we've set up a cache that watches for services that we're interested in. When something changes the cache contents, it will tell the listener (our `StreamReader` object) via the methods of the `ServiceDiscoveryListener` interface. Our implementation of that interface in `StreamReader` looks like this:

```
public synchronized void
    serviceAdded(ServiceDiscoveryEvent ev)
{
    ServiceItem si = ev.getPostEventServiceItem();
    try {
        readStream((MessageStream) si.service);
        exit(0, null);
    } catch (RemoteException e) {
        return;     // ignore this one, try for another
    }
}

// stub these out -- we don't need them
public void serviceChanged(ServiceDiscoveryEvent ev) { }
public void serviceRemoved(ServiceDiscoveryEvent ev) { }
```

Of these three methods of `ServiceDiscoveryListener`, the only one of interest is `serviceAdded`, which tells us when a new matching service is found. The event parameter lets us look at the matching service item, from which we extract the stream service. We then use `readStream` to attempt to read from that service. If this succeeds we are done, and so we exit with a zero status to show success. If the reading fails, we return to await the next candidate or the expiration of our search time. The other two `ServiceDiscoveryListener` methods—`serviceChanged` and `serviceRemoved`—are of no interest to this code so they are stubbed out.

As you have seen, when `serviceAdded` finds a matching service, it tries to read the stream by invoking the `readStream` method:

```
private final static int MAX_RETRIES = 5;

public void readStream(MessageStream stream)
    throws RemoteException
{
    int errorCount = 0;      // # of errors seen this message
    int msgNum = 0;          // # of messages
    while (msgNum < count) {
```

```
            try {
                Object msg = stream.nextMessage();
                printMessage(msgNum, msg);
                msgNum++;                   // successful read
                errorCount = 0;             // clear error count
            } catch (EOFException e) {
                System.out.println("---EOF---");
                break;
            } catch (RemoteException e) {
                e.printStackTrace();
                if (++errorCount > MAX_RETRIES) {
                    if (msgNum == 0)    // got no messages
                        throw e;
                    else
                        exit(1, "too many errors");
                }
                try {
                    Thread.sleep(1000); // wait 1 second, retry
                } catch (InterruptedException ie) {
                    exit(1, "Interrupted");
                }
            }
        }
    }

    public void printMessage(int msgNum, Object msg) {
        if (msgNum > 0) // print separator
            System.out.println("---");
        System.out.println(msg);
    }
```

The `readStream` method will try to read the number of messages desired. If `readStream` gets a `RemoteException`, it retries up to `MAX_RETRIES` times, waiting one second (a thousand milliseconds) between each try. If it fails to read even a single message, it throws `RemoteException`, letting service discovery continue looking for a usable stream. If `readStream` reads at least one message, it prints out its failure and exits, so that the user will not see some messages from one stream and a few more from the next one should a failure occur before the desired number of messages are read.

2.3 In Conclusion

Let us revisit the example execution of `StreamReader` from page 21. If you use that command line, the client will look for a `fortune.FortuneStream` service (an interface that we will define in the next section) with an attribute that is of type `fortune.FortuneTheme` created with the string `"General"`. This search will be conducted in lookup services that manage the public group. If any such lookups are found, the `LookupDiscovery` utility object we created in `execute` will invoke our `discovered` method, which adds it to the list of known lookup services. The `searchDiscovered` method looks in each discovered lookup service for a matching stream, and invokes `readStream` to read one message from a stream and print it out. When all this is complete, you should (assuming there is an available matching fortune cookie service) have a fortune cookie message on your screen.

Again, notice that this client can work with any `MessageStream` service. The user specifies which particular service to use by the service's type and any desired attributes. Each message stream service implementation provides a proxy that works properly for the service's needs. The `StreamReader` client you have seen will print messages from any implementation of a message stream, using the proxy as an adaptor from the service definition (`MessageStream`) to the particular service that was matched (`FortuneStream`, `ChatStream`, or whatever). You will next see how to write two different message stream services that can be used by `StreamReader` or any other `MessageStream` client.

... After all, all [Shakespeare] did
was string together a lot of old, well-known quotations.
—H.L. Mencken

3 Writing a Service

Dare to be naïve.
—R. Buckminster Fuller

THE `MessageStream` interface is designed to work for many purposes. We will now show you two example implementations of a message stream service. The first will be a `FortuneStream` subinterface that returns randomly selected "fortune cookie" messages. The second will provide a chat stream that records a history of a conversation among several speakers. First, though, we must talk about what it means to be a Jini service.

A service differs from a client in that a service registers a proxy object with a lookup service, thereby advertising its services—the interfaces and classes that make up its type. A client finds one or more services in a lookup service that it wants to use. Of course, a service might rely on other services and therefore be both a service and a client of those other services.

3.1 Good Lookup Citizenship

To be a usable service, the service implementation must register with appropriate lookup services. In other words, it must be a good *lookup citizen,* which means:

- When starting, discovering lookup services of appropriate groups and registering with any that reply
- When running, listening for lookup service "here I am" messages and, after filtering by group, registering with any new ones
- Remembering its join configuration—the list of groups it should join and the lookup locators for specific lookup services
- Remembering all attributes stamped on it and informing all lookups of changes in those attributes
- Maintaining all leases in lookup services for as long as the service is available

- Remembering the service ID assigned to the service by the first lookup service, so that all registrations of the same service, no matter when made, will be under the same service ID

3.1.1 The JoinManager Utility

Although the work for these tasks is not a vast amount of labor, it is also more than trivial. Services may provide these behaviors in a number of ways. The utility class `net.jini.lookup.JoinManager` handles most of these tasks on a service's behalf, except for the management of storage for attributes and service IDs which the service implementation must provide.

Our example service implementations use `JoinManager` to manage lookup membership. You are not required to do so—you might find other mechanisms more to your liking, or you might want or need to invent your own.

3.2 The FortuneStream Service

Our first example service will extend `MessageStream` to provide a "fortune cookie" service, which returns a randomly selected message from a set of messages. Typically, such messages are intended to be amusing, informative, or inspiring. The collections are often broken up into various themes. The most general theme is to be amusing, but collections drawn from particular television shows, movie types, comic strips, or inspirational speakers also exist. Our `FortuneStream` interface looks like this:

```
package fortune;

interface FortuneStream extends MessageStream, Remote {
    String getTheme() throws RemoteException;
}
```

As with all the classes defined in this example, this interface is in the `fortune` package. The `FortuneStream` interface extends the `MessageStream` interface because it is a particular kind of message stream. `FortuneStream` extends the interface `Remote`, which indicates to RMI that objects implementing the `FortuneStream` interface are accessible remotely using RMI.

The `getTheme` method returns the theme of the particular stream. As you will see, the theme is primarily reflected as an attribute on the service so that a user can select a `FortuneStream` with a theme to their liking. The `getTheme` method is added here to allow queries after a stream has been selected.

Each fortune stream's theme is represented both in the interface via the `getTheme` method and as an attribute in the lookup service to help users find a stream that gives the types of fortunes they want:

```
public class FortuneTheme extends AbstractEntry
    implements ServiceControlled
{
    public String theme;

    public FortuneTheme() { }

    public FortuneTheme(String theme) {
        this.theme = theme;
    }
}
```

The `FortuneTheme` attribute is part of the service definition, and is independent of our particular implementation of `FortuneStream`—a different implementation of `FortuneStream` would use the same attribute type.

The `FortuneTheme` attribute fits the requirements for all entries: It has public object-typed fields and a public no-arg constructor. It adds another constructor for convenience. Each `FortuneStream` service expresses its theme as both a `FortuneTheme` attribute and a value returned by the `FortuneStream` class's `getTheme` method. This redundancy has a purpose—it allows a client of a fortune stream to be written independently of the code that finds the service. For example, it would be possible for a fortune stream client to display the theme of a stream it obtained without using a `FortuneTheme` attribute.

`FortuneTheme` extends `net.jini.entry.AbstractEntry`, which implements `Entry` and provides useful semantics for entry classes, specifically in defining semantics for the `equals`, `hashCode`, and `toString` methods. Using `AbstractEntry` is optional—we use it for convenience. `FortuneTheme` also implements `ServiceControlled`, which marks the attribute as one that is controlled by the service itself, as opposed to one placed on the service by an administrator. Any tools that let administrators modify attributes should not let `ServiceControlled` attributes be changed. Only attributes that are exclusively controlled by the service itself should be marked with this interface.

3.2.1 The Implementation Design

The overall fortune service implementation looks like this:

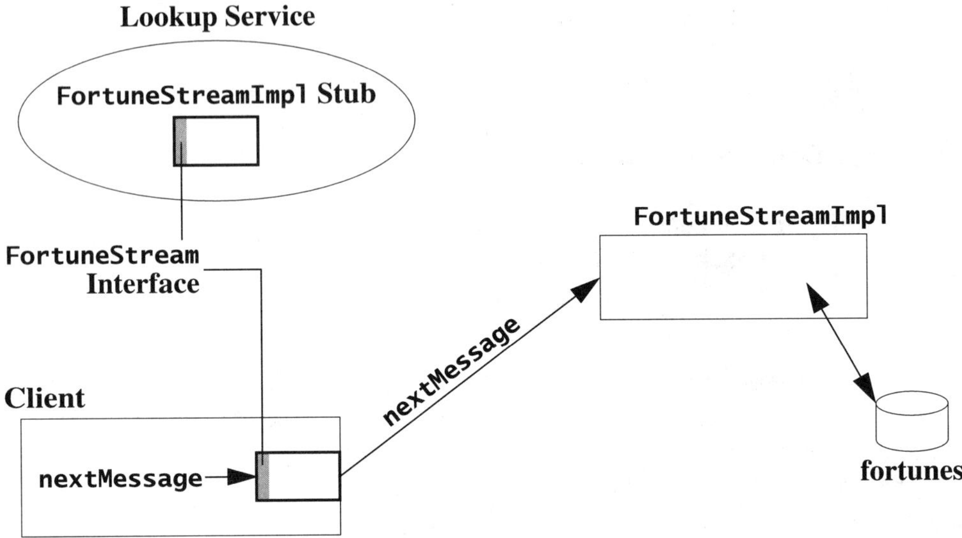

The running service is composed of three parts:

- A database of fortunes, consisting of the collection of fortunes and position offsets for the start of each fortune. The position information is built by reading the fortune collection.
- A server that runs on the same system that contains the database. This server reads the database, choosing a fortune at random each time it needs to return the next message.
- A proxy for the service. This proxy is the object installed in the lookup service to represent the fortune stream service in the Jini system. In this particular case, the proxy is simply a Java RMI stub that passes method invocations directly to the remote server.

3.2.2 Creating the Service

Our `FortuneStream` implementation is provided by the `FortuneStreamImpl` class, which is a Java RMI remote object. Requests for the next message in the stream will be sent directly to this remote object that will return a random fortune selected from its database.

The fortune database lives in a particular directory, which is set up by a separate FortuneAdmin program that creates the database of fortunes from the raw data. The FortuneAdmin program is run before the service is created to set up the database a running FortuneStream service will use. When the database is ready, you will run FortuneStreamImpl to get the service going.

The FortuneStreamAdmin command line looks like this:

```
java [java-options] fortune.FortuneAdmin database-dir
```

The *database-dir* parameter is the directory in which the database lives. This directory must initially contain a file named fortunes, which contains fortunes separated by lines that start with %%, as in:

```
"As an adolescent I aspired to lasting fame, I craved
factual certainty, and I thirsted for a meaningful vision
of human life -- so I became a scientist.  This is like
becoming an archbishop so you can meet girls."
                -- Matt Cartmill
%%
As far as the laws of mathematics refer to reality, they
are not certain, and as far as they are certain, they do
not refer to reality.
                -- Albert Einstein
%%
As far as we know, our computer has never had an undetected
error.
```

The FortuneAdmin program creates the position database in that directory if it does not already exist or if it is older than the fortune database file. The position database is stored in a file named pos. A typical invocation might look like this:

```
java fortune.FortuneAdmin /files/fortunes/general
```

FortuneAdmin will look in the directory /files/fortunes/general for a fortunes file and will read it to create a /files/fortunes/general/pos file.[1] The source to FortuneAdmin just manipulates files, so we will not describe it here.

---

[1] On a Windows system it would be something like C:\files\fortunes\general; on a MacOS system it would be more like Hard Disk:fortunes:general. We use POSIX-style paths in this book.

3.2.3 The Running Service

The fortune service is started by the `main` method of `FortuneStreamImpl`. The command line looks like this:

```
java [java-options] fortune.FortuneStreamImpl database-dir
     groups|lookup-url theme
```

The *java-options* must include a security policy file and the RMI server codebase URL. The *database-dir* should be the directory given to `FortuneAdmin`. The running service will join lookup services with the given groups or the specified lookup service, with a `FortuneTheme` attribute with the given name. A typical invocation might look like this:

```
java -Djava.security.policy=/file/policies/policy
     -Djava.rmi.server.codebase=http://server/fortune-dl.jar
     fortune.FortuneStreamImpl "" /files/fortunes/general
     General
```

Our implementation of the fortune stream service executes in the virtual machine this command creates, and therefore lives only as long as that virtual machine is running. Later you will see how to write services that live longer than the life of a single virtual machine.

Here is the code that starts the service running:

```
public class FortuneStreamImpl implements FortuneStream {
    private String[] groups = new String[0];
    private String lookupURL;
    private String dir;
    private String theme;
    private Random random = new Random();
    private long[] positions;
    private RandomAccessFile fortunes;
    private JoinManager joinMgr;

    public static void main(String[] args) throws Exception
    {
        FortuneStreamImpl f = new FortuneStreamImpl(args);
        f.execute();
    }

    // ...
}
```

The `main` method creates a `FortuneStreamImpl` object, whose constructor initializes the `groups`, `lookupURL`, `dir`, `theme`, and `initialAttrs` fields from the command line arguments. The rest of the work is done in the object's `execute` method:

```
private void execute() throws IOException {
    System.setSecurityManager(new RMISecurityManager());
    UnicastRemoteObject.exportObject(this);

    // set up the fortune database
    setupFortunes();

    // set our FortuneTheme attribute
    FortuneTheme themeAttr = new FortuneTheme(theme);
    Entry[] initialAttrs = new Entry[] { themeAttr };

    LookupLocator[] locators = null;
    if (lookupURL != null) {
        LookupLocator loc = new LookupLocator(lookupURL);
        locators = new LookupLocator[] { loc };
    }
    DiscoveryManagement dm =
        new LookupDiscoveryManager(groups, locators, null);
    joinMgr = new JoinManager(this, initialAttrs,
        (ServiceIDListener) null, dm, null);
}
```

First `execute` sets a security manager, as you saw done in the client. Next we export the `FortuneStreamImpl` object as an RMI object. Specifically, we export the object as a `UnicastRemoteObject`, which means that as long as this virtual machine is running, the object will be usable remotely. When the virtual machine dies, the remote object that it represents dies too. RMI provides a mechanism for activatable servers that will be restarted when necessary; most Jini software services are actually best written as activatable services. You will see an activatable service in the next example.

We then call `setupFortunes` to initialize this server's use of its fortune database. We do not show the code for that here because it is not relevant to the example; `setupFortunes` sets the `positions` and `fortunes` fields that are used by the implementation of `nextMessage`. The next two lines create the service-owned `FortuneTheme` attribute that will identify the theme of this fortune stream in the lookup service.

Then we create the JoinManager, which manages all the interactions with lookup services in the network. To do so, you must tell the JoinManager several things. The constructor that is used by execute (there are two available) takes the following parameters:

- The proxy object for the service. We use the this reference because RMI will convert this to the remote stub for the FortuneStreamImpl object, which is what we want in this case. (FortuneStreamImpl implements a Remote interface—FortuneStream extends Remote—so when a FortuneStreamImpl object is marshalled, it gets replaced by its stub.)
- An Entry array that is the initial set of attributes to be associated with the service. Here we provide an array that contains only our FortuneTheme.
- A net.jini.lookup.ServiceIDListener object. ServiceIDListener in an interface that defines a method to be called when the service's ID is assigned. This is a hook that lets the service store its ID persistently if it needs to. Because our particular service does not outlive its virtual machine, there is no need to store the ID. We therefore pass null, meaning that the service will not be notified. (The next example will show this feature in action.)
- A DiscoveryManagement object that the JoinManager object will use to manage discovered lookup services. As with the StreamReader client, we use a LookupDiscoveryManager to select the specified lookups. Multiple JoinManager objects could use the same DiscoveryManagement object if they were interested in the same set of lookup services.
- A net.jini.lease.LeaseRenewalManager object to manage renewing the leases returned by lookup services. We use null, which tells the JoinManager to create and use its own LeaseRenewalManager. In another situation (for example, exporting multiple services in the same virtual machine) you might want to specify this parameter so all the exported services can share this work.

When execute is finished we have a service ready to receive messages and, by virtue of its JoinManager, the service registers with all appropriate lookup services and will continue to register appropriately so as long as the service is running. In other words, at this point we have a running Jini service. When execute returns, so does main. RMI will keep the virtual machine running in another thread, waiting to receive requests.

The rest of the code implements nextMessage by picking a random fortune and getTheme by returning the theme field. Again, since these parts show no Jini service code, we leave them to Appendix B.

3.3 The `ChatStream` Service

For a more involved example, we provide a message stream whose messages are the utterances of people in a conversation, such as in a chat room. In this case there must be an order to the messages. The fortune stream was picking a message at random, so any message was as good as any other. For a conversation clients will want the messages in the order in which they were spoken.

Consider what happens when `nextMessage` is invoked and a network failure occurs. Either of two interesting situations may have occurred:

- The network failure prevented the request from getting to the remove server:

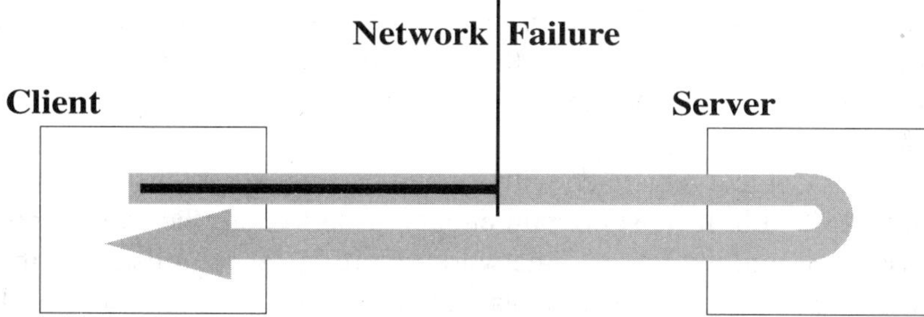

- The request made it to the remote server, but the network failure blocked the response:

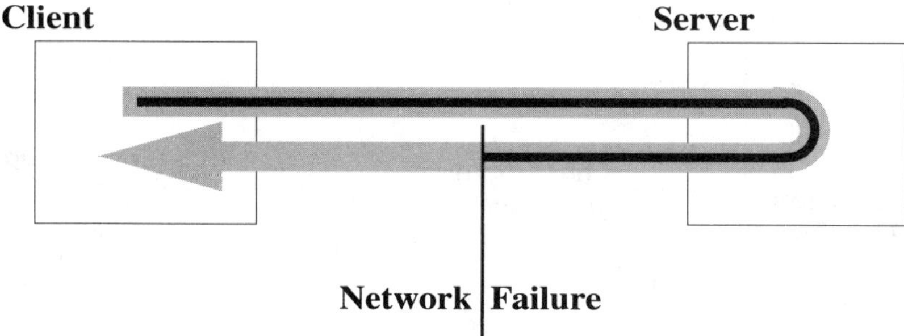

These are very different situations, but the client has no possible way to distinguish between the two cases. If the current position in the stream for each client was stored at the server, the next call to `nextMessage` by the client could return either message 29 (in the first case, in which the server never got the original, failed request) or message 30 (in the second case, in which the server thought it had returned message 29 but it didn't get to the client).

The nextMessage method of MessageStream is documented to be *idempotent*, that is, it can be re-invoked after an error to get the same result that would have come had there been no error. For FortuneStream idempotency was easy—the fortune was picked at random, so the next message will be equally random, no matter which of the failure situations actually happened.

But for ChatStream, this is not good enough. If the proxy was designed naïvely, an utterance might be skipped, and the utterance skipped could be the most important one of the discussion. If a call to nextMessage throws an exception because of a communication failure, the next time the client invokes nextMessage it should get the same message from the list that it would have gotten on the previous call had there been no failure. Suppose, for example, that we used the same strategy for a ChatStream proxy that we did for the FortuneStreamImpl proxy—an RMI stub. Then, after getting message number 28 from the server, a network exception is thrown when trying to get message number 29.

So the proxy object registered with lookup services for a ChatStream cannot be a simple RMI stub. It must contain enough state to help the service return the right message even in the face of a network failure. To accomplish this, the proxy object will implement the ChatStream interface for the client to use, but the server will have an implementation-specific interface that the proxy uses to tell the server which message should be next. It will look like this:

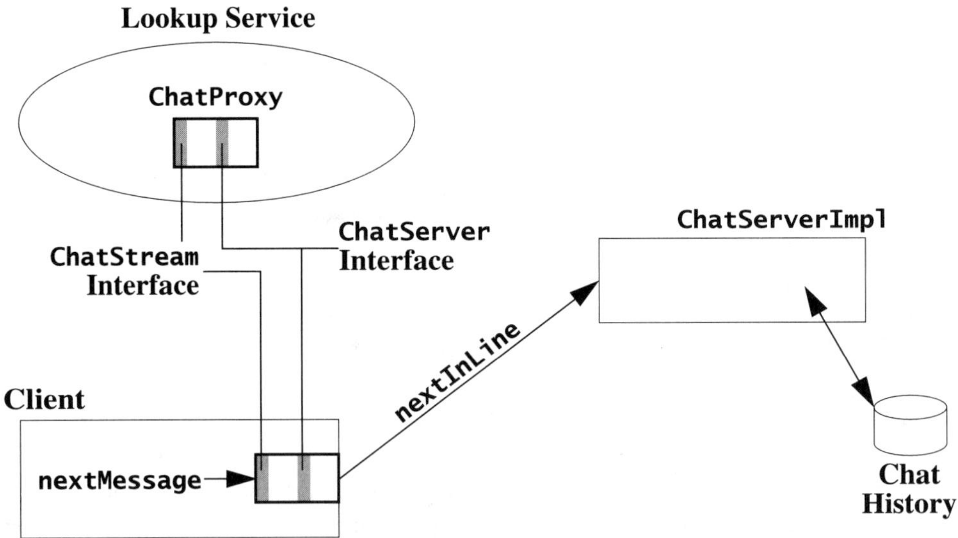

The proxy will use its internal stored state (the number of the last message successfully retrieved) as an argument to the `nextInLine` method of the `ChatServer` interface. That method is hidden from the client, and different implementations of the `ChatStream` service are welcome to use a different mechanism so long as they maintain the idempotency of `nextMessage`.

The `ChatStream` interface—the public service interface that the clients use—inherits `nextMessage` from the `MessageStream` interfaces, and adds a few methods of its own:

```
package chat;

public interface ChatStream extends MessageStream {
    public void add(String speaker, String[] message)
        throws RemoteException;
    public String getSubject() throws RemoteException;
    public String[] getSpeakers() throws RemoteException;
}
```

Like all the code in this example this class is part of the `chat` package. The `add` method lets people add new messages to the discussion. The `speaker` parameter is the name of the speaker; `message` is what they say. You can ask a `ChatStream` what the subject of the chat is, and for the names of the people who have spoken. These last two things are also stored as attributes of the service so they can be used to look up streams.

When a message is read, it will be a `ChatMessage` object:

```
public class ChatMessage implements Serializable {
    private String speaker;
    private String[] content;

    public ChatMessage(String speaker, String[] content) {
        this.speaker = speaker;
        this.content = content;
    }

    public String getSpeaker() { return speaker; }

    public String[] getContent() { return content; }

    public String toString() {
        StringBuffer buf = new StringBuffer(speaker);
        buf.append(": ");
```

```
            for (int i = 0; i < content.length; i++)
                buf.append(content[i]).append('\n');
            buf.setLength(buf.length() - 1); // strip newline
            return buf.toString();
        }
    }
```

ChatMessage has methods to pick out the pieces of the message—its speaker and the content—and its toString method prints out a reasonable default representation of the message.

When looking for a ChatStream, a user might want to choose the subject, so we define a ChatSubject attribute type:

```
public class ChatSubject extends AbstractEntry
    implements ServiceControlled
{
    public String subject;

    public ChatSubject() { }

    public ChatSubject(String subject) {
        this.subject = subject;
    }
}
```

A ChatStream service should mark itself as being on a certain subject—the same subject that getSubject would return. A user might also want to search for chats that had particular speakers, so a stream should also mark itself with a ChatSpeaker attribute for each speaker:

```
public class ChatSpeaker extends AbstractEntry
    implements ServiceControlled
{
    public String speaker;

    public ChatSpeaker() { }

    public ChatSpeaker(String speaker) {
        this.speaker = speaker;
    }
}
```

(Remember that we have chosen to use string-based attributes to simplify the examples in this text. Fields in attributes can be any serializable type, so when you design your own attributes, don't use the string-based nature of our examples with a requirement of attributes in general. Use the types you need, not just strings.)

3.3.1 "Service" versus "Server"

At this point it is important to discuss the difference between the word "service" and the word "server." A *service* is a logical notion that has at least one object—the object registered in the lookup service. It usually has other parts as well. Often at least one of those parts will be a *server*—a process running on a machine in the network.

Our fortune service is made up of a proxy object (the RMI stub), a fortune server (the `FortuneStreamImpl` object running on some host), and the underlying storage. A service may use one or more servers to provide its service. In both the fortune and chat examples, each service uses exactly one remote object, which in turn uses an underlying store. Other services might talk to no remote servers (doing all computation locally in the proxy) or several (combining the information from more than one server).

3.3.2 Creating the Service

As we stated before, the chat service's proxy (which runs on the client) needs to hold some state so that it can tell the server which message was last returned successfully. The communication between the proxy and the server must include this information. The `nextMessage` method has no way to impart that data, so the proxy will need a different way to talk to the server in order to pass it along. For this purpose the implementation of our service adds an internal, package-accessible interface:

```
interface ChatServer extends Remote {
    ChatMessage nextInLine(int lastIndex)
        throws EOFException, RemoteException;
    void add(String speaker, String[] msg)
        throws RemoteException;
    String getSubject() throws RemoteException;
    String[] getSpeakers() throws RemoteException;
}
```

The proxy will use the `nextInLine` method to get the message following the last successful one, which it represents by index. The message is returned to the client by the proxy's `nextMessage` method, and the new index is remembered for the next invocation. The other methods do not require any different treatment from those in the ChatStream interface, and so they are declared identically.

The proxy implementation is pretty simple: The proxy object contains an RMI reference to the server that implements ChatServer and the index of the last successfully returned message:

```
class ChatProxy implements ChatStream, Serializable {
    private final ChatServer server;
    private int lastIndex = -1;
    private transient String subject;

    ChatProxy(ChatServer server) {
        this.server = server;
    }

    public synchronized Object nextMessage()
        throws RemoteException, EOFException
    {
        ChatMessage msg = server.nextInLine(lastIndex);
        lastIndex++;
        return msg;
    }

    public void add(String speaker, String[] msg)
        throws RemoteException
    {
        server.add(speaker, msg);
    }

    public synchronized String getSubject()
        throws RemoteException
    {
        if (subject == null)
            subject = server.getSubject();
        return subject;
    }

    public String[] getSpeakers() throws RemoteException {
        return server.getSpeakers();
    }
```

```
    public boolean equals(Object other) {
      if (other instanceof ChatProxy)
          return server.equals(((ChatProxy) other).server);
      else
          return false;
    }

    public int hashCode() {
        return server.hashCode() + 1;
    }
}
```

When the client invokes `nextMessage`, the proxy invokes the remote server's `nextInLine` method, passing in the `lastIndex` field. If `nextInLine` returns successfully, it increments its notion of the last message index and then returns the message. If instead `nextInLine` throws an exception, the code following the invocation will not be executed, leaving the value of `lastIndex` unchanged. So in our example, even if a network failure happens after the request reaches the server, the client will get an exception and so the next invocation of `nextMessage` by the client will cause a `nextInLine` to be sent that gets the same message again.[2]

The proxy's `add` and `getSpeakers` methods simply forward the request along to the remote server. The proxy's `getSubject` method uses the fact that the subject of a single `ChatStream` never changes—once the proxy gets the subject it can be remembered to avoid a round trip to the server to get it again. Here again the proxy adds value.

3.3.3 The Chat Server

Now let us look at the server side. Our chat server implementation is decidedly simple to keep the example focused on the Jini service. We will allow an administrator to create a new chat service, which means creating a remotely accessible `ChatServerImpl` object that implements the `ChatServer` interface. This object registers a `ChatProxy` object with the lookup service, giving it the appropriate `ChatSubject` attribute and (initially) no `ChatSpeaker` attributes. The `ChatProxy` object contains a reference to its `ChatServerImpl` object.

---

[2] Note that the proxy's implementation of `nextMessage` is synchronized. This ensures that two threads in the same virtual machine invoking `nextMessage` at the same time on the same proxy object will not both use or modify `lastIndex` inconsistently.

The ChatServerImpl object will be *activatable,* that is, it will use the RMI activation mechanism to ensure that it is always available, even if the system it is running on crashes and reboots. The fortune service you saw before lives only as long as its virtual machine. Should the machine on which it runs die, it will die too. This may be acceptable for some services, but not others. Many Jini services will need to be activatable, or use some other mechanism to outlast reboots.

This service will be activatable, but this is not the place for a full tutorial on writing activatable services. We will give an overview, point out the places in the code where activation is visible, and provide the full code in Appendix B.

Activation works by having an *activation system* that starts virtual machines for remotely accessible objects when needed. Each activatable object is part of an *activation group*—remotely accessible objects that are part of the same group will always be activated in the same virtual machine, while objects that are in different groups will always be in different virtual machines.

An activatable object is created by registering it with the activation system, telling the system which group the object belongs to, providing a storage key that can be used by the object when it is activated to find its persistent state, and optionally a "keep active" flag. This registration returns a remote reference to a newly available remote object. The reference can be sent around the network like any other remote reference.

If the "keep active" flag is true, the activation system will always keep the object active when it can. For example, when a system is rebooted, the activation system will activate each "keep active" object. If the flag is false, the activation system will wait until it gets the first message for the object and then activate it. In our example we will set the "keep active" flag to be true so the active service can register with the lookup service and maintain its lease. Otherwise the service would be inactive, unable to renew its leases, and so would never be found by anyone looking for a chat stream.

Activation of an object is done via its *activation constructor*—a constructor with the following signature:

```
public ActivatableClass(ActivationID id,
                        MarshalledObject state)
{
    // ...
}
```

During activation the activation system first either creates a virtual machine to manage the group, or finds the existing virtual machine that is already doing so. It then has that virtual machine create a new local object of the correct class using its activation constructor.

An activatable class must extend `java.rmi.activation.Activatable`—in which case the activation constructor must invoke `super(id)`—or invoke the static method `java.rmi.activation.ActivatableObject.exportObject`. Either of these actions lets the activation system know that the object is ready to receive incoming messages.

Once the activation constructor returns, the activation system will tell clients of the remote object to talk directly to the running server object. This means that at most the first message from a client to an activatable object requires talking to the activation system (unless there is an intervening server crash). All subsequent requests go directly to the running service.

In our example we will provide a `ChatServerImpl` class that provides a `ChatStream` service by registration with the activation system. You create a new server with the following command:

```
java [java-options] chat.ChatServerAdmin directory subject
     [groups|lookup-url classpath codebase policy-file]
```

`ChatServerAdmin` is a class that creates an activatable `ChatServerImpl` object for the server. The *`java-options`* typically include the security policy file used during creation. The *`directory`* will define an activation group. If the directory does not exist it will be created; a new activation group will also be created and its information written into a file in that directory. If the directory does exist and contains such a file, that information will be used to place the new chat stream into the same activation group. A typical chat stream will not significantly occupy a single virtual machine, so grouping multiple activatable `ChatServerImpl` objects for different subjects into the same virtual machine will keep overall overhead low.

If you want to create a new activation group for the stream, you must give the last four parameters: the *`groups`* or *`lookup-url`* to specify the lookup services you want the chat registered with, and the *`classpath`*, *`codebase`*, and *`policy-file`* for the activated virtual machine. The classpath will be the one for the running server, the codebase will be where clients will download the remote parts of the service from, and the policy file will be the one used by the running server. This is different from the policy file provided in the *`java-options`*, which is the policy file used only during creation. The *`policy-file`* parameter defines the policy file that will be used by the activated virtual machine.

So a typical invocation to create a new chat stream in a new group would look like this:

```
java -Djava.security.policy=/policies/creation
     chat.ChatServerAdmin /files/chats/technical "Cats" ""
     /jars/chat.jar http://server/chat-dl.jar
     /policies/runtime
```

This invocation would create the /files/chats/technical directory (if necessary), create a new activation group, store the group information in it, and put the storage for the "Cats" chat in that directory. The service would register with the public group, "". The server would run using classes from /jars/chat.jar, clients would download code from the codebase http://server/chat-dl.jar, and the server's security policy file would be /policies/runtime. The subsequent command

```
java -Djava.security.policy=/policies/creation
     chat.ChatServerAdmin /files/chats/technical "Dogs"
```

would create a "Dogs" chat stream in the same activation group as the stream for the subject "Cats", and therefore with the same lookup group, classpath, codebase, and security policy because these are defined by the activation group—all objects sharing an activation group will, by virtue of sharing a single virtual machine, have the same lookup registration, classpath, codebase, and security policy.

Let us look at ChatServerAdmin.main:

```
public static void main(String[] args) throws Exception
{
    if (args.length != 2 && args.length != 6) {
        usage();            // print usage message
        System.exit(1);
    }

    File dir = new File(args[0]);
    String subject = args[1];

    ActivationGroupID group = null;
    if (args.length == 2)
        group = getGroup(dir);
    else {
        String[] groups = ParseUtil.parseGroups(args[2]);
        String lookupURL =
            (args[2].indexOf(':') > 0 ? args[2] : null);
        String classpath = args[3];
        String codebase = args[4];
        String policy = args[5];
        group = createGroup(dir, groups, lookupURL,
            classpath, codebase, policy);
    }
```

```
        File data = new File(dir, subject);
        MarshalledObject state = new MarshalledObject(data);
        ActivationDesc desc =
            new ActivationDesc(group, "chat.ChatServerImpl",
                               null, state, true);
        Remote newObj = Activatable.register(desc);
        ChatServer server = (ChatServer) newObj;
        String s = server.getSubject(); // force server up
        System.out.println("server created for " + s);
    }
```

The `main` method first figures out whether it is using an existing group or creating a new group, and gets the group accordingly. It then creates a `MarshalledObject` that contains the directory and subject; this `MarshalledObject` will be the one that is passed in to the activation constructor when each stream is activated, allowing it to recover its state, as you will see shortly.[3] With the group and startup information in hand, we can tell the activation system to register this new object. The `true` in the registration call is the "keep active" flag. We then invoke the `getSubject` method to force the chat stream to be active for the first time. Until this first call, the chat stream object will be inactive. Once `getSubject` forces the server to be active, it will start its discovery and registration.

This process of creation and subsequent activating is shown in Figure 3–1. When `main` invokes `createGroup`, the activation system remembers the group setup options. After `register`, the activation system has a record of a new object in that activation group. When `main` invokes `getSubject` on the newly registered stream, the activation system (1) starts up a new virtual machine using the settings given when the group was created; and then (2) tells the virtual machine (via a piece of its own code running in it) to create a new `ChatStreamImpl` object using its activation constructor, passing the persistent state `MarshalledObject` given to it when the object was registered. When the constructor invokes `exportObject`, the activation system views the object as ready for incoming messages. In the future, when the activation system starts up it will start up the object in the same way, but without requiring any method invocation to get things going.

The figure shows all this work being handled internally by the client's `ChatServerImpl` stub. A stub for an activatable object contains a direct reference

---

[3] A `java.rmi.MarshalledObject` stores an object in the same way as it would be marshalled to be passed as an argument in an RMI method call. Its `get` method returns the unmarshalled object. The activation system uses a `MarshalledObject` for the persistence parameter because it does not use the object—it just holds on to it and passes it back—so it has no need to download any required code for the persistence parameter.

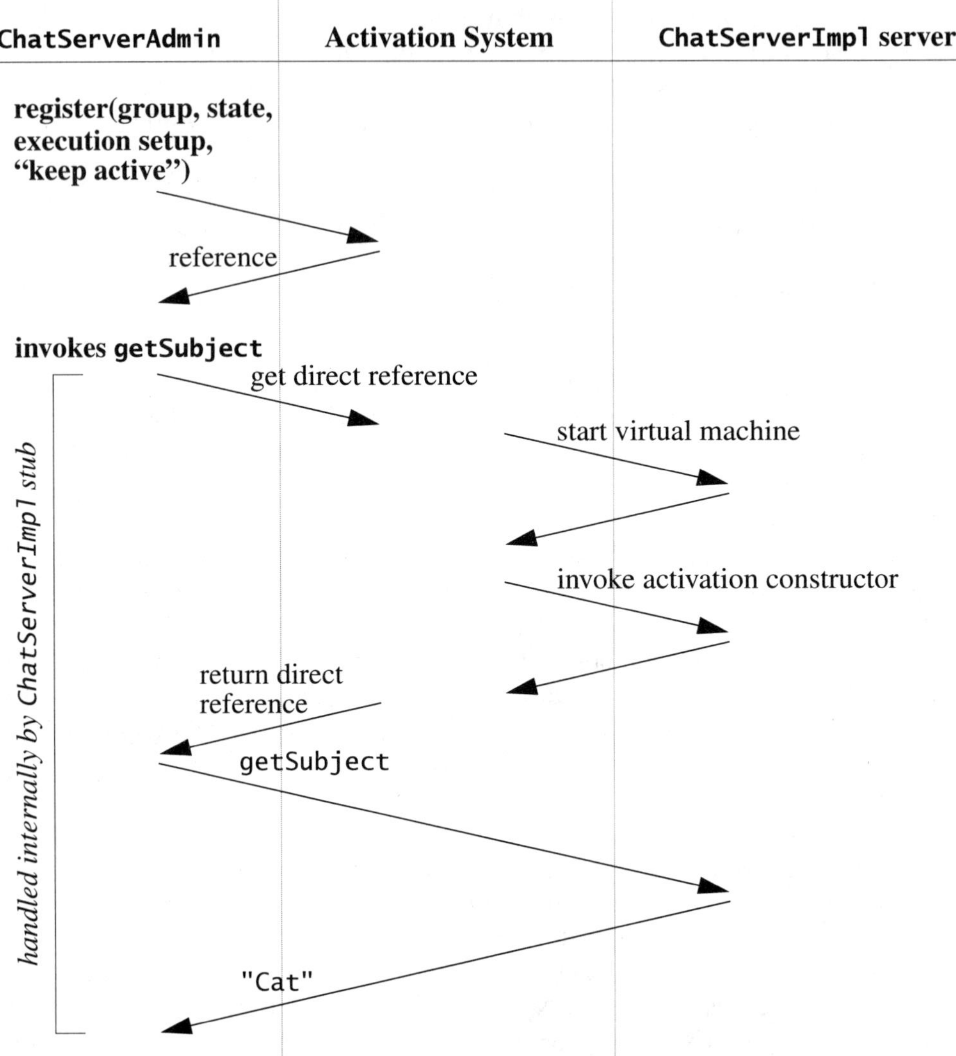

FIGURE 3–1: ***Registration and Activation in ChatAdmin***

to the remote service. When the stub is first used, it sets this reference by asking the activation system for a direct reference to the remote server. The activation system either activates the service to get a direct reference and then returns it or, if it is already active, simply returns the direct reference. The actual messages are sent directly to the service. Once the stub has a direct reference, it sends all future messages directly to the remote server without contacting the activation system.

The createGroup method creates the activation group, setting up the command line that will start the virtual machine to use the correct classpath, codebase, and policy file. It then serializes the group descriptor into a file so that future creations that want to share it can find it, adding the lookup groups and URL to the file for the server to use. The getGroup method finds an existing group by opening up the directory's group description file and returning the deserialized ActivationGroupID. The details of this activation and file work are in the full code in Appendix B.

When ChatServerAdmin.main invokes getSubject or when the activation system restarts, the ChatServerImpl class's activation constructor gets invoked to create the local object in the activated virtual machine:

```
public ChatServerImpl(ActivationID actID,
                      MarshalledObject state)
    throws IOException, ClassNotFoundException
{
    File dir = (File) state.get();
    store = new ChatStore(dir);
    ChatProxy proxy = new ChatProxy(this);

    LookupLocator[] locators = null;
    if (lookupURL != null) {
        LookupLocator loc = new LookupLocator(lookupURL);
        locators = new LookupLocator[] { loc };
    }
    DiscoveryManagement dm =
        new LookupDiscoveryManager(groups, locators, null);
    joinMgr = new JoinManager(proxy, getAttrs(), store,
                              dm, renewer);
    Activatable.exportObject(this, actID, 0);
}
```

The activation constructor uses the state object stored by ChatServerAdmin to find the directory in which the chat record is stored and to find its record within the directory (by the subject name).

The ChatStore object manages the server's persistent storage. When the server is first activated, the Jini service ID has not yet been assigned, so we want to know when the ID gets assigned. The JoinManager constructor allows us to provide a net.jini.lookup.ServiceIDListener object that will be notified when the identifier is assigned. ChatStore is an inner class of ChatServerImpl that implements this interface, adding the ID to the persistent store for future use. The relevant part of ChatStore looks like this:

```
class ChatStore extends LogHandler
    implements ServiceIDListener
{
    //...
    public void serviceIDNotify(ServiceID serviceID) {
        try {
            log.update(serviceID);
        } catch (IOException e) {
            unexpectedException(e);
        }
        ChatServerImpl.this.serviceID = serviceID;
    }
}
```

The serviceIDNotify method is invoked by the join manager when the service ID is first allocated. Our implementation stores it in the file system for future use. The log field and the LogHandler interface are part of a “reliable log” subsystem from the com.sun.jini.reliableLog package in the release of the Jini technology; the details are left for the full source in Appendix B.

3.3.4 Implementing nextInLine

The nextInLine method of the chat server takes the incoming message number, looks up the message associated with it, and returns it:

```
public synchronized ChatMessage nextInLine(int index) {
    try {
        int nextIndex = index + 1;
        while (nextIndex >= messages.size())
            wait();
        return (ChatMessage) messages.get(nextIndex);
    } catch (InterruptedException e) {
        unexpectedException(e);
        return null; // keeps the compiler happy
    }
}
```

If the next message isn't available yet, nextInLine waits until someone adds one:

```
public synchronized void add(String speaker, String[] lines)
{
    ChatMessage msg = new ChatMessage(speaker, lines);
    store.add(msg);
    addSpeaker(speaker);
    messages.add(msg);
    notifyAll();
}

private synchronized void addSpeaker(String speaker) {
    if (speakers.contains(speaker))
        return;
    speakers.add(speaker);
    Entry speakerAttr = new ChatSpeaker(speaker);
    attrs.add(speakerAttr);
    joinMgr.addAttributes(new Entry[] { speakerAttr });
}
```

When a new message is added, we create the `ChatMessage` object for the message and then store it in the log. We then add the speaker (`addSpeaker` ignores already known speakers), add the message to our in-memory list of messages, and notify any waiting `nextInLine` method that there is a new message to return.

If the speaker is a new one, `addSpeaker` creates a new `ChatSpeaker` attribute object and stamps it on itself by using the join manager's `addAttributes` method. The join manager will add this attribute to all current and future lookup service registrations.

We have not shown the `store.add` method because it consists only of file-system and data structure management, not Jini service implementation. The full code in Appendix B, of course, shows its implementation.

3.3.5 Notes on Improving `ChatServerImpl`

As shown `ChatServerImpl` works, but it does not scale to large systems well. Each client uses up a thread in the server virtual machine when `nextInLine` blocks waiting for a future message. If there are hundreds of observers of a discussion, the number of threads blocked in the server will also be hundreds as each client waits for its invocation of `nextInLine` to return. There are many possible solutions to this problem. The most interesting is to rewrite the proxy/server interaction to use event notification as described in the distributed event section of the core specification. The design would look something like this:

- The nextInLine method takes a RemoteEventListener. When no message are available, it returns an event registration instead of a message.
- When a new message is added, all registered listeners are notified.
- A proxy that gets an event registration will renew the registration's lease until it receives notification from the server that a new message is available. It will then resume asking for the nextInLine until it is blocked again.

We leave an actual implementation of this as an exercise to the reader, as well as other things that could be done to improve the service, such as:

- Making add idempotent.
- Handling the results of system crashes that result in partial creation of the service. The activation constructor should detect such corrupt data and unregister itself.
- A way to mark a chat as being completed so that people can see a record of it without adding to it. This might require adding methods to ChatStream.
- Administrative interfaces to allow users and administrators to add their own attributes to the service and to configure a running service as to which lookup groups and lookup URLs it will join. As an example, see the interface net.jini.admin.JoinAdmin.

Other improvements could be made as well. You might find it useful to get the existing source compiled and running, and then try adding one or more improvements to it to get a better feel for Jini service implementation.

3.3.6 The Clients

When a chat stream service is created, we will have a service that can be used anywhere in the network that can reach the relevant lookup services. The generic StreamReader client can read a chat discussion stream from the beginning. A more specialized client would let users add messages to the chat stream. The generic client has more limited functionality but can work across a broader array of services. A specialized chat client uses the extended features of a ChatStream. Both use the same service in different ways.

As an example of a specialized client, here is a Chatter client that will use a command line to provide access to a ChatStream:

```
package chatter;

public class Chatter extends StreamReader {
    public static void main(String[] args) throws Exception
    {
        String[] fullargs = new String[args.length + 3];
        fullargs[0] = "-c";
        fullargs[1] = String.valueOf(Integer.MAX_VALUE);
        System.arraycopy(args, 0, fullargs, 2, args.length);
        fullargs[fullargs.length - 1] = "chat.ChatStream";
        Chatter chatter = new Chatter(fullargs);
        chatter.execute();
    }

    private Chatter(String[] args) {
        super(args);
    }

    public void readStream(MessageStream msgStream)
        throws RemoteException
    {
        ChatStream stream = (ChatStream) msgStream;
        new ChatterThread(stream).start();
        super.readStream(stream);
    }

    public void printMessage(int msgNum, Object msg) {
        if (!(msg instanceof ChatMessage))
            super.printMessage(msgNum, msg);
        else {
            ChatMessage cmsg = (ChatMessage) msg;
            System.out.println(cmsg.getSpeaker() + ":");
            String[] lines = cmsg.getContent();
            for (int i = 0; i < lines.length; i++) {
                System.out.print("    ");
                System.out.println(lines[i]);
            }
        }
    }
}
```

All the client code in this section is in the chatter package. Chatter extends StreamReader (the generic client described in Section 2) to force an effectively infinite count of messages to read, and to require that the stream found be at least a ChatStream, not simply a MessageStream. It overrides readStream so that when the stream is found, a new thread will be created to read the user's input. The printMessage method is overridden to take advantage of the knowledge that the message object is a ChatMessage.

ChatterThread uses the stream's add method when the user types:

```
class ChatterThread extends Thread {
    private ChatStream stream;

    ChatterThread(ChatStream stream) {
        this.stream = stream;
    }

    public void run() {
        BufferedReader in = new BufferedReader(
            new InputStreamReader(System.in));
        String user = System.getProperty("user.name");
        List msg = new ArrayList();
        String[] msgArray = new String[0];
        for (;;) {
            try {
                String line = in.readLine();
                if (line == null)
                    System.exit(0);

                boolean more = line.endsWith("\\");
                if (more) {     // strip trailing backslash
                    int stripped = line.length() - 1;
                    line = line.substring(0, stripped);
                }
                msg.add(line);
                if (!more) {
                    msgArray = (String[])
                        msg.toArray(new String[msg.size()]);
                    stream.add(user, msgArray);
                    msg.clear();
                }
            } catch (RemoteException e) {
```

```
                    System.out.println("RemoteException:retry");
                    for (;;) {
                        try {
                            Thread.sleep(1000);
                            stream.add(user, msgArray);
                            msg.clear();
                            break;
                        } catch (RemoteException re) {
                            continue;        // try again
                        } catch (InterruptedException ie) {
                            System.exit(1);
                        }
                    }
                } catch (IOException e) {
                    System.exit(1);
                }
            }
        }
    }
```

The `run` method will be invoked by the virtual machine when the thread is started. It reads lines from the user to build up messages and uses `add` to add each message to the chat. Lines that end in \ (backslash) mean that the message continues on the next line. When the user types a line that doesn't end in backslash that line is put together with any preceding lines to create the message. The value defined in the `user.name` property (provided by the virtual machine) will be user's name in the chat. If `add` throws a `RemoteException` we retry adding the message until we succeed or until the user kills the application.

When the end of input has been reached, `readLine` returns `null`, and this thread will invoke `System.exit` to bring down the entire virtual machine, including the thread that is reading other speakers' messages.

"Multiply in your head" (ordered the compassionate Dr. Adams)
"365,365,365,365,365,365 by 365,365,365,365,365,365."
[Ten-year-old Truman Henry Safford] flew around the room like a top,
pulled his pantaloons over the tops of his boots,
bit his hands, rolled his eyes in their sockets,
sometimes smiling and talking, and then seeming to be in an agony,
until, in not more than one minute, said he,
"133,491,850,208,566,925,016,658,299,941,583,255!"
An electronic computer might do the job a little faster but it wouldn't be as much fun to watch.
—James R. Newman, *The World of Mathematics*

4 The Rest of This Book

A good question is never answered.
It is not a bolt to be tightened into place but a seed to be planted
and to bear more seed toward the hope of greening the landscape of idea.
—John Ciardi

BY now you should have an overview of how the Jini technology works and what it takes to write a client and service. The rest of this book contains the specifications of the Jini architecture. Each specification is prefaced by a short paragraph describing where it fits into the architecture. After the specifications you will find a glossary that defines terms used in the specifications. Appendix A is a reprint of "A Note on Distributed Computing," whose thinking undergirds the Jini architecture. Appendix B contains the full code for the examples. You can follow the Jini architecture and related technical discussions at `http://jini.org`.

Each specification has a two-letter code. For example, the *Jini Service Discovery Utilities Specification* has the code "SD." This provides a common identifier for the specification (such as SD.2.1) no matter what order the specifications are placed in. For example, in this book we have placed the specifications in a reasonable reading order. Another book might publish only relevant specifications, or publish them in a different order. The codes let you talk with others about specifications using the same section names no matter where each of you read the work. The code is shown at the beginning of each specification, in the specification's section and figure numbers, and on the thumb tabs at the edge of the right-hand pages. The core specification is the largest, containing several sections; to help keep track of these sections, each is also assigned a two-letter code.

This book is the first in a series that is "...from the source"— from those who design, implement, and document the Jini system. These books will all be written either by the originators of the work in question or by people who work closely with them to document the designs and technologies. Other good books and web sites are available from other sources. We hope that the Jini architecture and its designs prove useful to you both as user and as developer. At our series' web site `http://java.sun.com/docs/books/jini/` you will find related resources including a downloadable version of the source in the series' books (including this source from this book), errata, and other series-related information.

I have the simplest tastes.
I am always satisfied with the best.
—Oscar Wilde

PART 2
Specifications

The Jini Architecture Specification defines the top-level view of the Jini architecture, its components, and the systems on which the Jini architecture is layered. This will give you a high-level view of the architecture that will be filled out in the following specifications.

AR

The Jini Architecture Specification

AR.1 Introduction

THIS document describes the high-level architecture of system of Jini technology-enabled services and/or devices (Jini system), defines the different components that make up the system, characterizes the use of those components, discusses some of the component interactions, and gives an example. This document identifies those parts of the system that are necessary infrastructure, those that are part of the programming model, and those that are optional services that can live within the system.

AR.1.1 Goals of the System

A Jini system is a distributed system based on the idea of federating groups of users and the resources required by those users. The overall goal is to turn the network into a flexible, easily administered tool with which resources can be found by human and computational clients. Resources can be implemented as either hardware devices, software programs, or a combination of the two. The focus of the system is to make the network a more dynamic entity that better reflects the dynamic nature of the workgroup by enabling the ability to add and delete services flexibly.

A Jini system consists of the following parts:

- A set of components that provides an infrastructure for federating services in a distributed system

- A programming model that supports and encourages the production of reliable distributed services
- Services that can be made part of a federated Jini system and that offer functionality to any other member of the federation

Although these pieces are separable and distinct, they are interrelated, which can blur the distinction in practice. The components that make up the Jini technology infrastructure make use of the Jini technology programming model; services that reside within the infrastructure also use that model; and the programming model is well supported by components in the infrastructure.

The end goals of the system span a number of different audiences; these goals include the following:

- Enabling users to share services and resources over a network
- Providing users easy access to resources anywhere on the network while allowing the network location of the user to change
- Simplifying the task of building, maintaining, and altering a network of devices, software, and users

The Jini system extends the Java application environment from a single virtual machine to a network of machines. The Java application environment provides a good computing platform for distributed computing because both code and data can move from machine to machine. The environment has built-in security that allows the confidence to run code downloaded from another machine. Strong typing in the Java application environment enables identifying the class of an object to be run on a virtual machine even when the object did not originate on that machine. The result is a system in which the network supports a fluid configuration of objects that can move from place to place as needed and can call any part of the network to perform operations.

The Jini architecture exploits these characteristics of the Java application environment to simplify the construction of a distributed system. The Jini architecture adds mechanisms that allow fluidity of all components in a distributed system, extending the easy movement of objects to the entire networked system.

The Jini technology infrastructure provides mechanisms for devices, services, and users to join and detach from a network. Joining and leaving a Jini system are easy and natural, often automatic, occurrences. Jini systems are far more dynamic than is currently possible in networked groups where configuring a network is a centralized function done by hand.

AR.1.2 Environmental Assumptions

The Jini system federates computers and computing devices into what appears to the user as a single system. It relies on the existence of a network of reasonable speed connecting those computers and devices. Some devices require much higher bandwidth and others can do with much less—displays and printers are examples of extreme points. We assume that the latency of the network is reasonable.

We assume that each Jini technology-enabled device has some memory and processing power. Devices without processing power or memory may be connected to a Jini system, but those devices are controlled by another piece of hardware and/or software that presents the device to the Jini system and itself contains both processing power and memory. Architectures for devices not equipped with a Java virtual machine[1] (JVM) are explored more fully in the *Jini Device Architecture Specification.*

The Jini technology infrastructure is Java technology centered. The Jini architecture gains much of its simplicity from assuming that the Java programming language is the implementation language for components. The ability to dynamically download and run code is central to a number of the features of the Jini architecture. However, the Java technology-centered nature of the Jini architecture depends on the Java application environment rather than on the Java programming language. Any programming language can be supported by a Jini system if it has a compiler that produces compliant bytecodes for the Java programming language.

1 *As used in this document, the terms "Java virtual machine" or "JVM" mean a virtual machine for the Java platform.

AR.2 System Overview

AR.2.1 Key Concepts

THE purpose of the Jini architecture is to *federate* groups of devices and software components into a single, dynamic distributed system. The resulting federation provides the simplicity of access, ease of administration, and support for sharing that are provided by a large monolithic system while retaining the flexibility, uniform response, and control provided by a personal computer or workstation.

The architecture of a single Jini system is targeted to the workgroup. Members of the federation are assumed to agree on basic notions of trust, administration, identification, and policy. It is possible to federate Jini systems themselves for larger organizations.

AR.2.1.1 Services

The most important concept within the Jini architecture is that of a *service*. A service is an entity that can be used by a person, a program, or another service. A service may be a computation, storage, a communication channel to another user, a software filter, a hardware device, or another user. Two examples of services are printing a document and translating from one word-processor format to some other.

Members of a Jini system federate to share access to services. A Jini system should not be thought of as sets of clients and servers, users and programs, or even programs and files. Instead, a Jini system consists of services that can be collected together for the performance of a particular task. Services may make use of other services, and a client of one service may itself be a service with clients of its own. The dynamic nature of a Jini system enables services to be added or withdrawn from a federation at any time according to demand, need, or the changing requirements of the workgroup using the system.

Jini systems provide mechanisms for service construction, lookup, communication, and use in a distributed system. Examples of services include: devices such as printers, displays, or disks; software such as applications or utilities; information such as databases and files; and users of the system.

Services in a Jini system communicate with each other by using a *service protocol*, which is a set of interfaces written in the Java programming language. The set of such protocols is open ended. The base Jini system defines a small number of such protocols that define critical service interactions.

AR.2.1.2 Lookup Service

Services are found and resolved by a *lookup service*. The lookup service is the central bootstrapping mechanism for the system and provides the major point of contact between the system and users of the system. In precise terms, a lookup service maps interfaces indicating the functionality provided by a service to sets of objects that implement the service. In addition, descriptive entries associated with a service allow more fine-grained selection of services based on properties understandable to people.

Objects in a lookup service may include other lookup services; this provides hierarchical lookup. Further, a lookup service may contain objects that encapsulate other naming or directory services, providing a way for bridges to be built between a Jini lookup service and other forms of lookup service. Of course, references to a Jini lookup service may be placed in these other naming and directory services, providing a means for clients of those services to gain access to a Jini system.

A service is added to a lookup service by a pair of protocols called *discovery* and *join*—first the service locates an appropriate lookup service (by using the *discovery* protocol), and then it joins it (by using the *join* protocol).

AR.2.1.3 Java Remote Method Invocation (RMI)

Communication between services can be accomplished using *Java Remote Method Invocation* (RMI). The infrastructure to support communication between services is not itself a service that is discovered and used but is, rather, a part of the Jini technology infrastructure. RMI provides mechanisms to find, activate, and garbage collect object groups.

Fundamentally, RMI is a Java programming language-enabled extension to traditional remote procedure call mechanisms. RMI allows not only data to be passed from object to object around the network but full objects, including code. Much of the simplicity of the Jini system is enabled by this ability to move code around the network in a form that is encapsulated as an object.

AR.2.1.4 Security

The design of the security model for Jini technology is built on the twin notions of a *principal* and an *access control list*. Jini services are accessed on behalf of some entity—the principal—which generally traces back to a particular user of the system. Services themselves may request access to other services based on the identity of the object that implements the service. Whether access to a service is allowed depends on the contents of an access control list that is associated with the object.

AR.2.1.5 Leasing

Access to many of the services in the Jini system environment is *lease* based. A lease is a grant of guaranteed access over a time period. Each lease is negotiated between the user of the service and the provider of the service as part of the service protocol: A service is requested for some period; access is granted for some period, presumably taking the request period into account. If a lease is not renewed before it is freed—either because the resource is no longer needed, the client or network fails, or the lease is not permitted to be renewed—then both the user and the provider of the resource may conclude that the resource can be freed.

Leases are either exclusive or non-exclusive. Exclusive leases ensure that no one else may take a lease on the resource during the period of the lease; non-exclusive leases allow multiple users to share a resource.

AR.2.1.6 Transactions

A series of operations, either within a single service or spanning multiple services, can be wrapped in a *transaction*. The Jini transaction interfaces supply a service protocol needed to coordinate a *two-phase commit*. How transactions are implemented—and indeed, the very semantics of the notion of a transaction—is left up to the service using those interfaces.

AR.2.1.7 Events

The Jini architecture supports distributed *events*. An object may allow other objects to register interest in events in the object and receive a notification of the occurrence of such an event. This enables distributed event-based programs to be written with a variety of reliability and scalability guarantees.

AR.2.2 Component Overview

The components of the Jini system can be segmented into three categories: *infrastructure*, *programming model*, and *services*. The infrastructure is the set of components that enables building a federated Jini system, while the services are the entities within the federation. The programming model is a set of interfaces that enables the construction of reliable services, including those that are part of the infrastructure and those that join into the federation.

These three categories, though distinct and separable, are entangled to such an extent that the distinction between them can seem blurred. Moreover, it is possible to build systems that have some of the functionality of the Jini system with variants on the categories or without all three of them. But a Jini system gains its full power because it is a *system* built with the particular infrastructure and programming models described, based on the notion of a service. Decoupling the segments within the architecture allows legacy code to be changed minimally to take part in a Jini system. Nevertheless, the full power of a Jini system will be available only to new services that are constructed using the integrated model.

A Jini system can be seen as a network extension of the infrastructure, programming model, and services that made Java technology successful in the single-machine case. These categories along with the corresponding components in the familiar Java application environment are shown in Figure AR.2.1:

	Infrastructure	**Programming Model**	**Services**
Base Java	Java VM RMI Java Security	Java APIs JavaBeans ...	JNDI Enterprise Beans JTS ...
Java + Jini	Discovery/Join Distributed Security Lookup	Leasing Transactions Events	Printing Transaction Manager JavaSpaces Service ...

FIGURE AR.2.1: ***Jini Architecture Segmentation***

AR.2.2.1 Infrastructure

The Jini technology infrastructure defines the minimal Jini technology core. The infrastructure includes the following:

- A distributed security system, integrated into RMI, that extends the Java platform's security model to the world of distributed systems.
- The discovery and join protocols, service protocols that allow services (both hardware and software) to discover, become part of, and advertise supplied services to the other members of the federation.
- The lookup service, which serves as a repository of services. Entries in the lookup service are objects written in the Java programming language; these objects can be downloaded as part of a lookup operation and act as local proxies to the service that placed the code into the lookup service.

The discovery and join protocols define the way a service of any kind becomes part of a Jini system; RMI defines the base language within which the Jini technology-enabled services communicate; the distributed security model and its implementation define how entities are identified and how they get the rights to perform actions on their own behalf and on the behalf of others; and the lookup service reflects the current members of the federation and acts as the central marketplace for offering and finding services by members of the federation.

AR.2.2.2 Programming Model

The infrastructure both enables the programming model and makes use of it. Entries in the lookup service are leased, allowing the lookup service to reflect accurately the set of currently available services. When services join or leave a lookup service, events are signaled, and objects that have registered interest in such events get notifications when new services become available or old services cease to be active. The programming model rests on the ability to move code, which is supported by the base infrastructure.

Both the infrastructure and the services that use that infrastructure are computational entities that exist in the physical environment of the Jini system. However, services also constitute a set of interfaces which define communication protocols that can be used by the services and the infrastructure to communicate between themselves.

These interfaces, taken together, make up the distributed extension of the standard Java programming language model that constitutes the Jini programming model. Among the interfaces that make up the Jini programming model are the following:

- The leasing interface, which defines a way of allocating and freeing resources using a renewable, duration-based model
- The event and notification interfaces, which are an extension of the event model used by JavaBeans components to the distributed environment, enable event-based communication between Jini technology-enabled services
- The transaction interfaces, which enable entities to cooperate in such a way that either all of the changes made to the group occur atomically or none of them occur

The lease interface extends the Java programming language model by adding time to the notion of holding a reference to a resource, enabling references to be reclaimed safely in the face of network failures.

The event and notification interfaces extend the standard event models used by JavaBeans components and the Java application environment to the distributed case, enabling events to be handled by third-party objects while making various delivery and timeliness guarantees. The model also recognizes that the delivery of a distributed notification may be delayed.

The transaction interfaces introduce a lightweight, object-oriented protocol enabling applications using Jini technology to coordinate state changes. The transaction protocol provides two steps to coordinate the actions of a group of distributed objects. The first step is called the *voting phase,* in which each object "votes" whether it has completed its portion of the task and is ready to commit any changes it made. In the second step, a coordinator issues a "commit" request to each object.

The Jini transaction protocol differs from most transaction interfaces in that it does not assume that the transactions occur in a transaction processing system. Such systems define mechanisms and programming requirements that guarantee the correct implementation of a particular transaction semantics. The Jini transaction protocol takes a more traditional object-oriented view, leaving the correct implementation of the desired transaction semantics up to the implementor of the particular objects that are involved in the transaction. The goal of the transaction protocol is to define the interactions that such objects must have to coordinate such groups of operations.

The interfaces that define the Jini programming model are used by the infrastructure components where appropriate and by the initial Jini technology-enabled services. For example, the lookup service makes use of the leasing and event interfaces. Leasing ensures that services registered continue to be available, and events help administrators discover problems and devices that need configuration. The JavaSpaces service, one example of a Jini technology-enabled service, utilizes leasing and events, and also supports the Jini transaction protocol. The transaction manager can be used to coordinate the voting phase of a transaction for those objects that support transaction protocol.

The implementation of a service is not required to use the Jini programming model, but such services need to use that model for their interaction with the Jini technology infrastructure. For example, every service interacts with the Jini lookup service by using the programming model; and whether a service offers resources on a leased basis or not, the service's registration with the lookup service will be leased and will need to be periodically renewed.

The binding of the programming model to the services and the infrastructure is what makes such a federation a Jini system not just a collection of services and protocols. The combination of infrastructure, service, and programming model, all designed to work together and constructed by using each other, simplifies the overall system and unifies it in a way that makes it easier to understand.

AR.2.2.3 Services

The Jini technology infrastructure and programming model are built to enable services to be offered and found in the network federation. These services make use of the infrastructure to make calls to each other, to discover each other, and to announce their presence to other services and users.

Services appear programmatically as objects written in the Java programming language, perhaps made up of other objects. A service has an interface that defines the operations that can be requested of that service. Some of these interfaces are intended to be used by programs, while others are intended to be run by the receiver so that the service can interact with a user. The type of the service determines the interfaces that make up that service and also define the set of methods that can be used to access the service. A single service may be implemented by using other services.

Example Jini technology-enabled services include the following:

- A printing service, which can print from applications written in the Java programming language as well as legacy applications
- A JavaSpaces service, which can be used for simple communication and for storage of related groups of objects written in the Java programming language

- A transaction manager, which enables groups of objects to participate in the Jini transaction protocol defined by the programming model

AR.2.3 Service Architecture

Services form the interactive basis for a Jini system, both at the programming and user interface levels. The details of the service architecture are best understood once the Jini discovery and Jini lookup protocols are presented.

AR.2.3.1 Discovery and Lookup Protocols

The heart of the Jini system is a trio of protocols called *discovery*, *join*, and *lookup*. A pair of these protocols—discovery and join—occur when a device is plugged in. Discovery occurs when a service is looking for a lookup service with which to register. Join occurs when a service has located a lookup service and wishes to join it. Lookup occurs when a client or user needs to locate and invoke a service described by its interface type (written in the Java programming language) and possibly other attributes. Figure AR.2.2 outlines the discovery process.

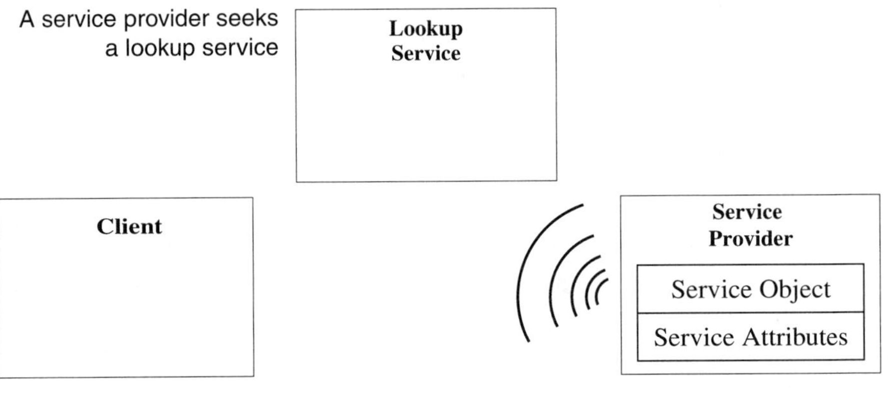

FIGURE AR.2.2: ***Discovery***

Jini discovery/join is the process of adding a service to a Jini system. A service provider is the originator of the service—a device or software, for example. First, the service provider locates a lookup service by multicasting a request on the local network for any lookup services to identify themselves (Figure AR.2.2).

Then, a service object for the service is loaded into the lookup service (Figure AR.2.3). This service object contains the Java programming language interface for the service, including the methods that users and applications will invoke to execute the service along with any other descriptive attributes.

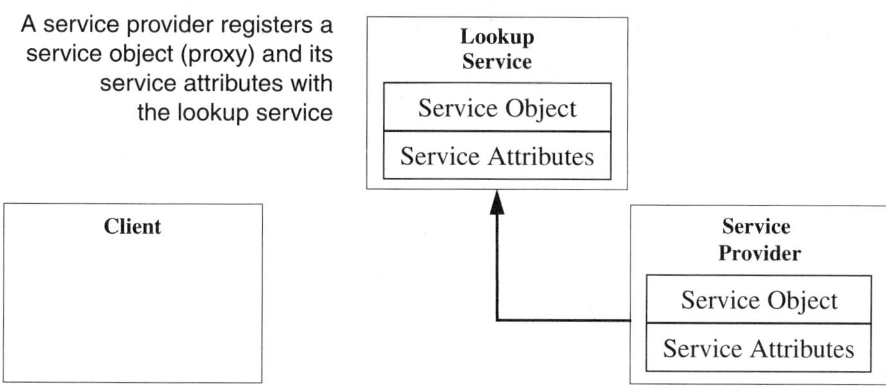

FIGURE AR.2.3: *Join*

Services must be able to find a lookup service; however, a service may delegate the task of finding a lookup service to a third party. The service is now ready to be looked up and used, as shown in the following diagram (Figure AR.2.4).

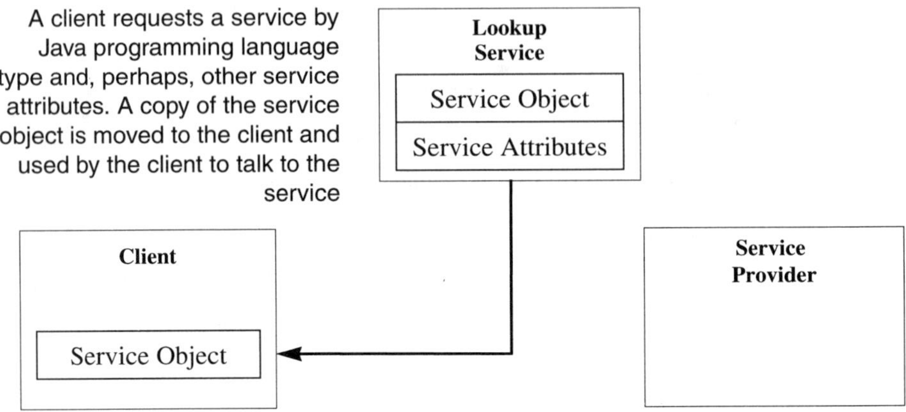

FIGURE AR.2.4: ***Lookup***

A client locates an appropriate service by its type—that is, by its interface written in the Java programming language—along with descriptive attributes that are used in a user interface for the lookup service. The service object is loaded into the client.

The final stage is to invoke the service, as shown in the following diagram (Figure AR.2.5).

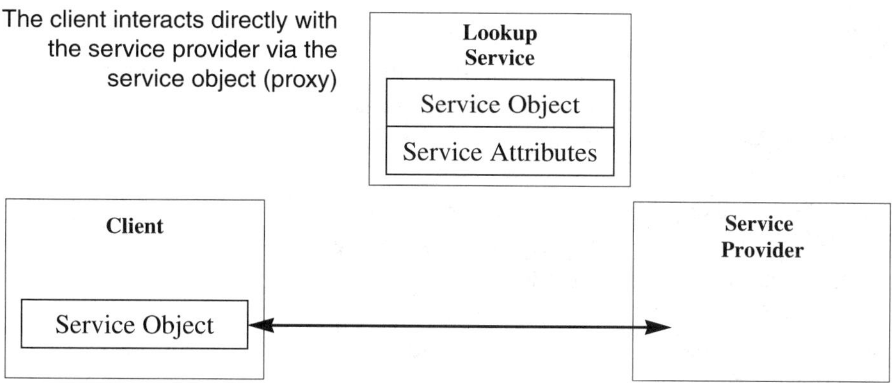

FIGURE AR.2.5: ***Client Uses Service***

The service object's methods may implement a private protocol between itself and the original service provider. Different implementations of the same service interface can use completely different interaction protocols.

The ability to move objects and code from the service provider to the lookup service and from there to the client of the service gives the service provider great freedom in the communication patterns between the service and its clients. This code movement also ensures that the service object held by the client and the service for which it is a proxy are always synchronized because the service object is supplied by the service itself. The client knows only that it is dealing with an implementation of an interface written in the Java programming language, so the code that implements the interface can do whatever is needed to provide the service. Because this code came originally from the service itself, the code can take advantage of implementation details of the service that are known only to the code.

The client interacts with a service via a set of interfaces written in the Java programming language. These interfaces define the set of methods that can be used to interact with the service. Programmatic interfaces are identified by the type system of the Java programming language, and services can be found in a lookup service by asking for those that support a particular interface. Finding a service this way ensures that the program looking for the service will know how to use that service, because that use is defined by the set of methods that are defined by the type.

Programmatic interfaces may be implemented either as RMI references to the remote object that implements the service, as a local computation that provides all of the service locally, or as some combination. Such combinations, called *smart proxies*, implement some of the functions of a service locally and the remainder through remote calls to a centralized implementation of the service.

A user interface can also be stored in the lookup service as an attribute of a registered service. A user interface stored in the lookup service by a Jini technology-enabled service is an implementation that allows the service to be directly manipulated by a user of the system.

In effect, a user interface for a service is a specialized form of the service interface that enables a program, such as a browser, to step out of the way and let the human user interact directly with a service.

In situations in which no lookup service can be found, a client could use a technique called *peer lookup* instead. In such situations, the client can send out the same identification packet that is used by a lookup service to request service providers to register. Service providers will then attempt to register with the client as though it were a lookup service. The client can select the services it needs from the registration requests it receives in response and drop or refuse the rest.

AR.2.3.2 Service Implementation

Objects that implement a service may be designed to run in a single address space with other, helper, objects especially when there are certain location or security-based requirements. Such objects make up an *object group*. An object group is guaranteed to always reside in a single address space or virtual machine when those objects are running. Objects that are not in the same object group are isolated from each other, typically by running them in a different virtual machine or address space.

A service may be implemented directly or indirectly by specialized hardware. Such devices can be contacted by the code associated with the interface for the service.

From the service client's point of view, there is no distinction between services that are implemented by objects on a different machine, services that are downloaded into the local address space, and services that are implemented in hardware. All of these services will appear to be available on the network, will appear to be objects written in the Java programming language, and, only as far as correct functioning is concerned, one kind of implementation could be replaced by another kind of implementation without change or knowledge by the client. (Note that security permissions must be properly granted.)

AR.3 An Example

THIS example shows how a Jini technology-enabled printing service might be used by a digital camera to print a high-resolution color image. It will start with the printer joining an existing Jini system, continue with its being configured, and end with printing the image.

AR.3.1 Registering the Printer Service

A printer that is either freshly connected to a Jini system or is powered up once it has been connected to a Jini system grouping needs to discover the appropriate lookup service and register with it. This is the *discovery* and *join* phase.

AR.3.1.1 Discovering the Lookup Service

The basic operations of discovering the lookup service are implemented by a Jini technology infrastructure software class. An instance of this class acts as a mediator between devices and services on one hand and the lookup service on the other. In this example the printer first registers itself with a local instance of this class. This instance then multicasts a request on the local network for any lookup services to identify themselves. The instance listens for replies and, if there are any, passes to the printer an array of objects that are proxies for the discovered lookup services.

AR.3.1.2 Joining the Lookup Service

To register itself with the lookup service, the printer needs first to create a service object of the correct type for printing services. This object provides the methods that users and applications will invoke to print documents. Also needed is an array of `LookupEntry` instances to specify the attributes that describe the printer, such as that it can print in color or black and white, what document formats it can print, possible paper sizes, and printing resolution.

The printer then calls the `register` method of the lookup service object that it received during the discovery phase, passing it the printer service object and the array of attributes. The printing service is now registered with the lookup service.

AR.3.1.3 Optional Configuration

At this point the printing service can be used, but the local system administrator might want to add additional information about the printer in the form of additional attributes, such as a local name for the service, information about its physical location, and a list of who may access the service. The system administrator might also want to register with the device to receive notifications for any errors that arise, such as when the printer is out of paper.

One way the system administrator could do this would be to use a special utility program to pass this additional information to the service. In fact this program might have received notification from the lookup service that a new service was being added and then alerted the system administrator.

AR.3.1.4 Staying Alive

When the printer registers with the Jini lookup service it receives a *lease*. Periodically, the printer will need to renew this lease with the lookup service. If the printer fails to renew the lease, then when the lease expires, the lookup service will remove the entry for it, and the printer service will no longer be available.

AR.3.2 Printing

Some services provide a user interface for interaction with them; others rely on an application to mediate such interaction. This example assumes that a person has a digital camera that has taken a picture they want to print on a high-resolution printer. The first thing that the camera needs to do after it is connected to the network is locate a Jini technology-enabled printing service. Once a printing service has been located and selected, the camera can invoke methods to print the image.

AR.3.2.1 Locate the Lookup Service

Before the camera can use a Jini technology-enabled service, it must first locate the Jini lookup service, just as the print service needed to do to register itself. The camera registers itself with a local instance of the Jini technology infrastructure class `LookupDiscovery`, which will notify the camera of all discovered lookup services.

AR.3.2.2 Search for Printing Services

Finding an appropriate service requires passing a template that is used to match and filter the set of existing services. The template specifies both the type of the required service, which is the first filter on possible services, and a set of attributes which is used to reduce the number of matching services if there are several of the right type. In this example, the camera supplies a template specifying the printer type and an array of attribute objects. The type of each object specifies the attribute type, and its fields specify values to be matched. For each attribute, fields that should be matched, such as color printing, are filled in; ones that don't matter are left null. The Jini lookup service is passed this template and returns an array of all of the printing services that match it. If there are several matching services, the camera may further filter them—in this case perhaps to ensure high print resolution—and present the user with the list of possible printers for choice. The final result is a single service object for the printing service.

At this point the printing service has been selected, and the camera and the printer service communicate directly with each other; the lookup service is no longer involved.

AR.3.2.3 Configuring the Printer

Before printing the image, the user might wish to configure the printer. This might be done directly by the camera invoking the service object's `configure` method; this method may display a dialog box on the camera's display with which the user may specify printer settings. When the image is printed, the service object sends the configuration information to the printer service.

AR.3.2.4 Requesting That the Image Be Printed

To print the image, the camera calls the print method of the service object, passing it the image as an argument. The service object performs any necessary preprocessing and sends the image to the printer service to be printed.

AR.3.2.5 Registering for Notification

If the user wishes to be notified when the image has been printed, the camera needs to register itself with the printer service using the service object. The camera might also wish to register to be notified if the printer encounters any errors.

AR.3.2.6 Receiving Notification

When the printer has finished printing the image or encounters an error, it signals an event to the camera. When the camera receives the event, it may notify the user that the image has been printed or that an error has occurred.

Architecture
(AR)

THE JINI TECHNOLOGY CORE PLATFORM SPECIFICATIONS defines A system of Jini™ technology-enabled services and/or devices is a Java™ technology-centered, distributed system designed for simplicity, flexibility, and federation. The Jini architecture provides mechanisms for machines or programs to enter into a federation where each machine or program offers resources to other members of the federation and uses resources as needed. The design of the Jini architecture exploits the ability to move Java programming language code from machine to machine and unifies, under the notion of a service, everything from the user of a system of Jini technology-enabled services and/or devices, to the software available on the machines, to the hardware components of the machines themselves.

Jini Technology Core Platform Specification

1 Introduction

THIS document is the 1.1 release of the Jini™ Technology Core Platform Specification. We have reordered the specifications with this release, combining the JCP specifications into a single specification. Chapter designations, for example, AR.1 as the Introduction chapter of the Jini™ Architecture Specification, have remained unchanged.

1.1 Dependencies

This document relies on the following other specifications:

- *The Java Remote Method Invocation Specification*
- *The Java Object Serialization Specification*

DJ

Discovery and Join

DJ.1 Introduction

ENTITIES that wish to start participating in a distributed a system of Jini technology-enabled services and/or devices, known as a *djinn*, must first obtain references to one or more Jini lookup services. The protocols that govern the acquisition of these references are known as the *discovery* protocols. Once these references have been obtained, a number of steps must be taken for entities to start communicating usefully with services in a djinn; these steps are described by the *join* protocol.

DJ.1.1 Terminology

A *host* is a single hardware device that may be connected to one or more networks. An individual host may house one or more Java virtual machines[1] (JVM).

Throughout this document we make reference to a *discovering entity*, a *joining entity,* or simply an *entity.*

- A *discovering entity* is simply one or more cooperating objects in the Java programming language on the same host that are about to start, or are in the process of, obtaining references to Jini lookup services.
- A *joining entity* comprises one or more cooperating objects in the Java programming language on the same host that have just received a reference to the lookup service and are in the process of obtaining services from, and possibly exporting them to, a djinn.

---

1 *As used in this document, the terms "Java virtual machine" or "JVM" mean a virtual machine for the Java platform.

- An *entity* may be a discovering entity, a joining entity, or an entity that is already a member of a djinn; the intended meaning should be clear from the context.
- A *group* is a logical name by which a group of djinns is identified.

Since all participants in a djinn are collections of one or more objects in the Java programming language, this document will not make a distinction between an entity that is a dedicated device using Jini technology or something running in a JVM that is hosted on a legacy system. Such distinctions will be made only when necessary.

DJ.1.2 Host Requirements

Hosts that wish to participate in a djinn must have the following properties:

- A functioning JVM, with access to all packages needed to run software written to the Jini specifications
- A properly configured network protocol stack

The properties required of the network protocol stack will vary depending on the network protocol(s) being used. Throughout this document we will assume that IP is being used, and highlight areas that might apply differently to other networking protocols.

DJ.1.2.1 Protocol Stack Requirements for IP Networks

Hosts that make use of IP for networking must have the following properties:

- An IP address. IP addresses may be statically assigned to some hosts, but we expect that many hosts will have addresses assigned to them dynamically. Dynamic IP addresses are obtained by hosts through use of DHCP.
- Support for unicast TCP and multicast UDP. The former is used by subsystems using Jini technology such as Java Remote Method Invocation (RMI); both are used during discovery.
- Provision of some mechanism (for example, a simple HTTP server) that facilitates the downloading of Java RMI stubs and other necessary code by remote parties. This mechanism does not have to be provided by the host itself, but the code must be made available by some cooperating party.

DJ.1.3 Protocol Overview

There are three related discovery protocols, each designed with different purposes:

- The *multicast request protocol* is employed by entities that wish to discover nearby lookup services. This is the protocol used by services that are starting up and need to locate whatever djinns happen to be close. It can also be used to support browsing of local lookup services.
- The *multicast announcement protocol* is provided to allow lookup services to advertise their existence. This protocol is useful in two situations. When a new lookup service is started, it might need to announce its availability to potential clients. Also, if a network failure occurs and clients lose track of a lookup service, this protocol can be used to make them aware of its availability after network service has been restored.
- The *unicast discovery protocol* makes it possible for an entity to communicate with a specific lookup service. This is useful for dealing with non-local djinns and for using services in specific djinns over a long period of time.

The discovery protocols require support for multicast or restricted-scope broadcast, along with support for reliable unicast delivery, in the transport layer. The discovery protocols make use of the Java platform's object serialization to exchange information in a platform-independent manner.

DJ.1.4 Discovery in Brief

This section provides a brief overview of the operation of the discovery protocols. For a detailed description suitable for use by implementors, see Section DJ.2 "The Discovery Protocols".

DJ.1.4.1 Groups

A group is an arbitrary string that acts as a name. Each lookup service has a set of zero or more groups associated with it. Entities using the multicast request protocol specify a set of groups they want to communicate with, and lookup services advertise the groups they are associated with using the multicast announcement protocol. This allows for flexibility in configuring entities: instead of maintaining a set of URLs for specific lookup services to contact, and that need to be changed if any of these services moves, an entity can maintain a set of group names.

Although group names are arbitrary strings, it is recommended that DNS-style names (for example, "eng.sun.com") be used to avoid name conflicts. One group name, represented by the empty string, is predefined as the *public* group. Unless otherwise configured, lookup services should default to being members of the public group, and discovering entities should attempt to find lookup services in the public group.

DJ.1.4.2 The Multicast Request Protocol

The multicast request protocol, shown in Figure AR.1.1, proceeds as follows:

1. The entity that wishes to discover a djinn establishes a TCP-based server that accepts references to the lookup service. This server is an instance of the *multicast response* service.
2. Lookup services listen for multicast requests for references to lookup services for the groups they manage. These listening entities are instances of the *multicast request* service. This is *not* an RMI-based service; the protocol is described in Section DJ.2 "The Discovery Protocols".
3. The discovering entity performs a multicast that requests references to lookup services; it provides a set of groups in which it is interested, and enough information to allow listeners to connect to its multicast response server.
4. Each multicast request server that receives the multicast will, if it is a member of a group for which it receives a request, connect to the multicast response server described in the request, and use the unicast discovery protocol to pass an instance of the lookup service's implementation of `net.jini.core.lookup.ServiceRegistrar`.

At this point, the discovering entity has one or more remote references to lookup services.

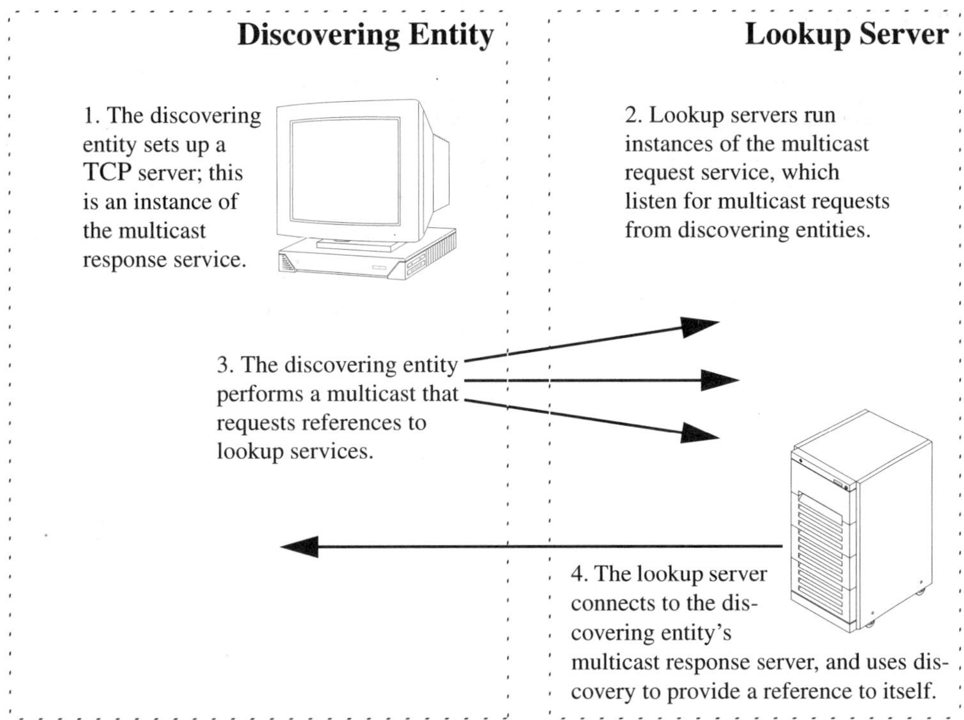

FIGURE DJ.1.1: ***The Multicast Request Protocol***

DJ.1.4.3 The Multicast Announcement Protocol

The multicast announcement protocol follows these steps:

1. Interested entities on the network listen for multicast announcements of the existence of lookup services. If an announcement of interest arrives at such an entity, it uses the unicast discovery protocol to contact the given lookup service.
2. Lookup services prepare to take part in the unicast discovery protocol (see below) and send multicast announcements of their existence at regular intervals.

DJ.1.4.4 The Unicast Discovery Protocol

The unicast discovery protocol works as follows:

1. The lookup service listens for incoming connections and, when a connection is made by a client, decodes the request and, if the request is correct, responds with a marshalled object that implements the `net.jini.core.lookup.ServiceRegistrar` interface.
2. An entity that wishes to contact a particular lookup service uses known host and port information to establish a connection to that service. It sends a discovery request and listens for a marshalled object as above in response.

DJ.2 The Discovery Protocols

THERE are three closely related discovery protocols: one is used to discover one or more lookup services on a local area network (LAN), another is used to announce the presence of a lookup service on a local network, and the last is used to establish communications with a specific lookup service over a wide-area network (WAN).

DJ.2.1 Protocol Roles

The multicast discovery protocols work together over time. When an entity is initially started, it uses the multicast request protocol to actively seek out nearby lookup services. After a limited period of time performing active discovery in this way, it ceases using the multicast request protocol and switches over to listening for multicast lookup announcements via the multicast announcement protocol.

DJ.2.2 The Multicast Request Protocol

The multicast request protocol allows an entity that has just been started, or that needs to provide browsing capabilities to a user, to actively discover nearby lookup services.

DJ.2.2.1 Protocol Participants

Several components take part in the multicast request protocol. Of these, two run on an entity that is performing multicast requests, and two run on the entity that listens for such requests and responds.

On the requesting side live the following components:

- A multicast request client performs multicasts to discover nearby lookup services.

- A multicast response server listens for responses from those lookup services.

These components are paired; they do not occur separately. Any number of pairs of such components may coexist in a single JVM at any given time.

The lookup service houses the other two participants:

- A multicast request server listens for incoming multicast requests.
- A multicast response client responds to callers, passing each a proxy that allows it to communicate with its lookup service.

Although these components are paired, as on the client side, only a single pair will typically be associated with each lookup service.

These local pairings apart, the remote client/server pairings should be clear from the above description and the diagram of protocol participants in Figure AR.2.1.

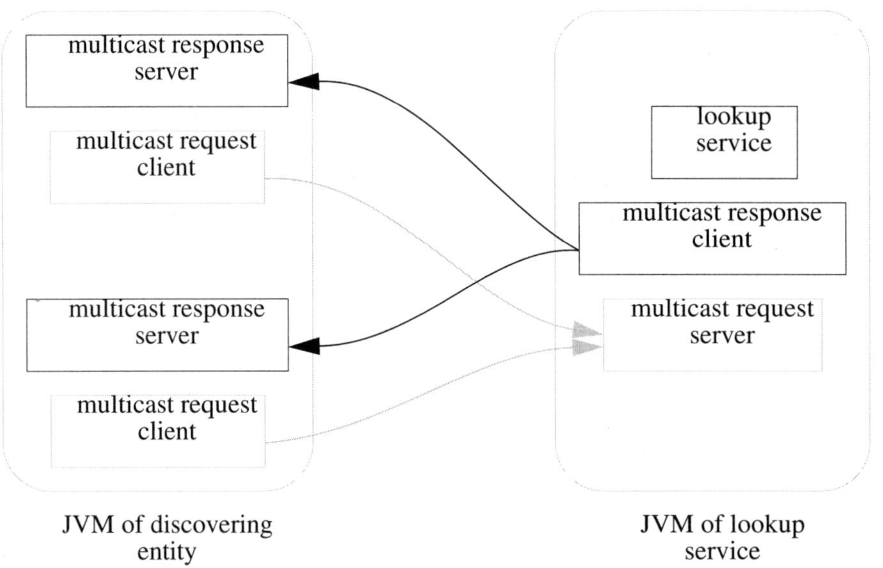

FIGURE DJ.2.1: ***Multicast Request Protocol Participants***

DJ.2.2.2 The Multicast Request Service

The multicast request service is not based on Java RMI; instead, it makes use of the multicast datagram facility of the networking transport layer to request that lookup services advertise their availability to a requesting host. In a TCP/IP environment the network protocol used is multicast UDP. Request datagrams are encoded as a sequence of bytes, using the data and object serialization facilities of the Java programming language to provide platform independence.

DJ.2.2.3 Request Packet Format

A multicast discovery request packet body must:

- Be 512 bytes in size or less, in order to fit into a single UDP datagram
- Encapsulate its parameters in a platform-independent manner
- Be straightforward to encode and decode

Accordingly, we define the packet format to be a contiguous series of bytes as would be produced by a `java.io.DataOutputStream` object writing into a `java.io.ByteArrayOutputStream` object. The contents of the packet, in order of appearance, are illustrated by the following fragment of pseudocode which generates the appropriate byte array:

```
int protoVersion;                          // protocol version
int port;                                  // port to contact
java.lang.String[] groups;                 // groups of interest
net.jini.core.lookup.ServiceID[] heard; // known lookups

java.io.ByteArrayOutputStream byteStr =
    new java.io.ByteArrayOutputStream();
java.io.DataOutputStream objStr =
    new java.io.DataOutputStream(byteStr);

objStr.writeInt(protoVersion);
objStr.writeInt(port);
objStr.writeInt(heard.length);
for (int i = 0; i < heard.length; i++) {
    heard[i].writeBytes(objStr);
}
objStr.writeInt(groups.length);
for (int i = 0; i < groups.length; i++) {
    objStr.writeUTF(groups[i]);
```

```
}

byte[] packetBody = byteStr.toByteArray(); // the final result
```

To elaborate on the roles of the variables above:

- The `protoVersion` variable contains an integer that indicates the version of the discovery protocol. This will permit interoperability between different protocol versions. For the current version of the discovery protocol, `protoVersion` must have the value 1.
- The `port` variable contains the TCP port respondents must connect to in order to continue the discovery process.
- The `groups` variable contains a set of strings (organized as an array) naming the groups the entity wishes to discover. This set may be empty, which indicates that all lookup services are being looked for.
- The `heard` variable contains a set of `net.jini.core.lookup.ServiceID` objects (organized as an array) that identify lookup services from which this entity has already heard and that do not need to respond to this request.
- The `packetBody` variable contains the marshalled discovery request in a form that is suitable for putting into a datagram packet or writing to an output stream.

The table below illustrates the contents of a multicast request packet body.

Count	Serialized Type	Description
1	`int`	protocol version
1	`int`	port to connect to
1	`int`	count of lookups heard
variable	`net.jini.core.lookup.ServiceID`	lookups heard
1	`int`	count of groups
variable	`java.lang.String`	groups

If the size of the packet body should exceed 512 bytes, the set of lookups from which an entity has heard must be left incomplete in the packet body, such that the size of the packet body will come to 512 bytes or less. How this is done is not specified. It is not permissible for implementations to simply truncate packets at 512 bytes.

Similarly, if the number of groups requested causes the size of a packet body to exceed 512 bytes, implementations must perform several separate multicasts, each with a disjoint subset of the full set of groups to be requested, until the entire set has been requested. Each request must contain the largest set of responses heard that will keep the size of the request below 512 bytes.

DJ.2.2.4 The Multicast Response Service

Unlike the multicast request service, the multicast response service is a normal TCP-based service. In this service the multicast response client contacts the multicast response server specified in a multicast request, after which unicast discovery is performed. The multicast response server to contact can be determined by using the source address of the request that has been received, along with the port number encapsulated in that request.

The only difference between the unicast discovery performed in this instance and the normal case is that the entity being connected to initiates unicast discovery, not the connecting entity. An alternative way of looking at this is that in both cases, once the connection has been established, the party that is looking for a lookup service proxy initiates unicast discovery.

DJ.2.3 Discovery Using the Multicast Request Protocol

Now we describe the discovery sequence for local area network (LAN)-based environments that use the multicast request protocol to discover one or more djinns.

DJ.2.3.1 Steps Taken by the Discovering Entity

The entity that wishes to discover a djinn takes the following steps:

1. It establishes a multicast request client, which will send packets to the well-known multicast network endpoint on which the multicast request service operates.
2. It establishes a TCP server socket that listens for incoming connections, over which the unicast discovery protocol is used. This server socket is the multicast response server socket.

3. It creates a set of `net.jini.core.lookup.ServiceID` objects. This set contains service IDs for lookup services from which it has already heard, and is initially empty.
4. It sends multicast requests at periodic intervals. Each request contains connection information for its multicast response server, along with the most recent set of service IDs for lookup services it has heard from.
5. For each response it receives via the multicast response service, it adds the service ID for that lookup service to the set it maintains.
6. The entity continues multicasting requests for some period of time. Once this point has been reached, it unexports its multicast response server and stops making multicast requests.
7. If the entity has received sufficient references to lookup services at this point, it is now finished. Otherwise, it must start using the multicast announcement protocol.

The interval at which requests are performed is not specified, though an interval of five seconds is recommended for most purposes. Similarly, the number of requests to perform is not mandated, but we recommend seven. Since requests may be broken down into a number of separate multicasts, these recommendations do not pertain to the number of packets to be sent.

DJ.2.3.2 Steps Taken by the Multicast Request Server

The system that hosts an instance of the multicast request service takes the following steps:

1. It binds a datagram socket to the well-known multicast endpoint on which the multicast request service lives so that it can receive incoming multicast requests.
2. When a multicast request is received, the discovery request server may use the service ID set from the entity that is sending requests to determine whether it should respond to that entity. If its own service ID is not in the set, and any of the groups requested exactly matches any of the groups it is a member of or the set of groups requested is empty, it must respond. Otherwise, it must not respond.
3. If the entity must be responded to, the request server connects to the other party's multicast response server using the information provided in the

request, and provides a lookup service registrar using the unicast discovery protocol.

DJ.2.3.3 Handling Responses from Multiple Djinns

What happens when there are several djinns on a network, and calls to an entity's discovery response service are made by principals from more than one of those djinns, will depend on the nature of the discovering entity. Possible approaches include the following:

If the entity provides a *finder*-style visual interface that allows a user to choose one or more djinns for their system to join, it should loop at step 4 in section DJ.2.3.1, and provide the ability to:

- Display the names and descriptions of the djinns it has found out about
- Allow the user to select zero or more djinns to join
- Continue to dynamically update its display, until the user has finished their selection
- Attempt to join all of those djinns the user selected

On the other hand, if the behavior of the entity is fully automated, it should follow the join protocol described in Section DJ.3 "The Join Protocol".

DJ.2.4 The Multicast Announcement Protocol

The multicast announcement protocol is used by Jini lookup services to announce their availability to interested parties within multicast radius. Participants in this protocol are the multicast announcement client, which resides on the same system as a lookup service, and the multicast announcement server, at least one instance of which exists on every entity that listens for such announcements.

The multicast announcement client is a long-lived process; it must start at about the same time as the lookup service itself and remain running as long as the lookup service is alive.

DJ.2.4.1 The Multicast Announcement Service

The multicast announcement service uses multicast datagrams to communicate from a single client to an arbitrary number of servers. In a TCP/IP environment the underlying protocol used is multicast UDP.

Multicast announcement packets are constrained by the same requirements as multicast request packets. The fields in a multicast announcement packet body are as follows:

Count	Serialized Type	Description
1	`int`	protocol version
1	`java.lang.String`	host for unicast discovery
1	`int`	port to connect to
1	`net.jini.core.lookup.ServiceID`	service ID of originator
1	`int`	count of groups
variable	`java.lang.String`	groups represented by originator

The fields have the following purposes:

- The protocol version field provides for possible future extensions to the protocol. For the current version of the multicast announcement protocol this field must contain the value 1. This field is written as if using the method `java.io.DataOutput.writeInt`.
- The host field contains the name of a host to be used by recipients to which they may perform unicast discovery. This field is written as if using the method `java.io.DataOutput.writeUTF`.
- The port field contains the TCP port of the above host at which to perform unicast discovery. This field is written as if using the method `java.io.DataOutput.writeInt`.
- The service ID field allows recipients to keep track of the services from which they have received announcements so that they will not need to unnecessarily perform unicast discovery. This field is written as if using the method `net.jini.core.lookup.ServiceID.writeBytes`.
- The count field indicates the number of groups of which the given lookup service is a member. This field is written as if using the method `java.io.DataOutput.writeInt`.
- This is followed by a sequence of strings equal in number to the count field, each of which is a group that the given lookup service is a member of. Each string is written as if using the method `java.io.DataOutput.writeUTF`.

If the size of the set of groups represented by a lookup service causes the size of a multicast announcement packet body to exceed 512 bytes, several separate packets must be multicast, each with a disjoint subset of the full set of groups, such that the full set of groups is represented by all packets.

DJ.2.4.2 The Protocol

The details of the multicast announcement protocol are simple. The entity that runs the lookup service takes the following steps:

1. It constructs a datagram socket object, set up to send to the well-known multicast endpoint on which the multicast announcement service operates.
2. It establishes the server side of the unicast discovery service.
3. It multicasts announcement packets at intervals. The length of the interval is not mandated, but 120 seconds is recommended.

An entity that wishes to listen for multicast announcements performs the following set of steps:

1. It establishes a set of service IDs of lookup services from which it has already heard, using the set discovered by using the multicast request protocol as the initial contents of this set.
2. It binds a datagram socket to the well-known multicast endpoint on which the multicast announcement service operates and listens for incoming multicast announcements.
3. For each announcement received, it determines whether the service ID in that announcement is in the set from which it has already heard. If so, or if the announcement is for a group that is not of interest, it ignores the announcement. Otherwise, it performs unicast discovery using the host and port in the announcement to obtain a reference to the announced lookup service, and then adds this service ID to the set from which it has already heard.

DJ.2.5 Unicast Discovery

While workgroup-level devices need to be able only to discover local djinns, a user might need to be able to access services in djinns that may be dispersed more widely (for example in offices in other cities or on other continents). To this end, the software at the user's fingertips must be able to obtain a reference to the lookup service of a remote djinn. This is done using the unicast discovery protocol.

The unicast Jini discovery protocol uses the underlying reliable unicast transport protocol provided by the network instead of the unreliable multicast transport. In the case of IP-based networks this means that the unicast discovery protocol uses unicast TCP instead of multicast UDP.

DJ.2.5.1 The Protocol

The unicast discovery protocol is a simple request-response protocol.

If an entity wishes to obtain a reference to a given djinn, the entity has a lookup locator object for that djinn and makes a TCP connection to the host and port specified by that lookup locator. It sends a unicast discovery request (see below), to which the remote host responds.

If a lookup service is responding to a multicast request, the request to which it is responding contains the address and port to respond to, and it makes a TCP connection to that address and port. The respondee sends a unicast discovery request, and the lookup service responds with a proxy.

The protocol diagram in Figure AR.2.2 illustrates the flow when unicast discovery is initiated by a discovering entity.

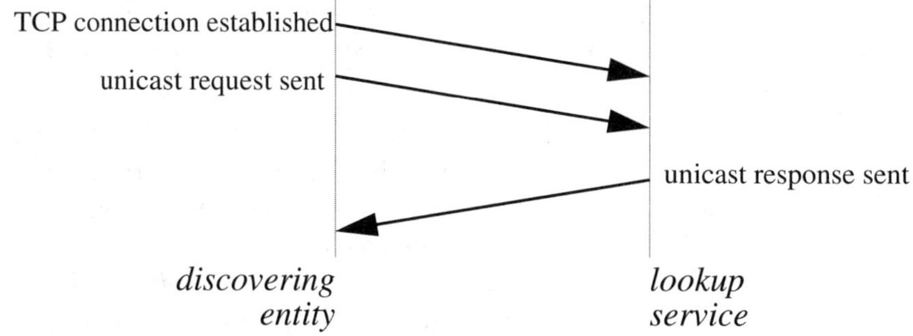

FIGURE DJ.2.2: ***Unicast Discovery Initiated by a Discovering Entity***

The protocol diagram in Figure AR.2.3 indicates the flow when a lookup service initiates unicast discovery in response to a multicast request.

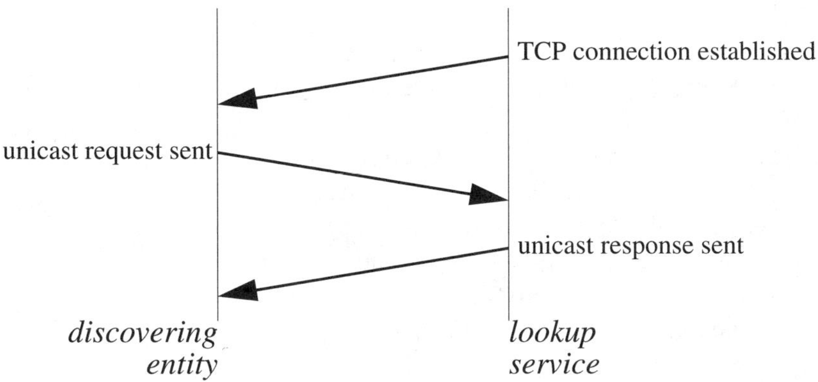

FIGURE DJ.2.3: ***Unicast Discovery Initiated by a Lookup Service***

DJ.2.5.2 Request Format

A discovery request consists of a stream of data as would be obtained by writing code similar to the following:

```
int protoVersion; // protocol version

java.io.ByteArrayOutputStream byteStr =
    new java.io.ByteArrayOutputStream();
java.io.DataOutputStream objStr =
    new java.io.DataOutputStream(byteStr);

objStr.writeInt(protoVersion);

byte[] requestBody = byteStr.toByteArray(); // final result
```

The `protoVersion` variable above must have a value of 1 for the current version of the unicast discovery protocol. The `requestBody` variable contains the discovery request as would be sent to the unicast discovery request service.

DJ.2.5.3 Response Format

The response to the above request consists of a stream of data as would be obtained by writing code similar to the following:

```
net.jini.core.lookup.ServiceRegistrar reg;
    String[] groups; // groups registrar will respond with

java.rmi.MarshalledObject obj =
    new java.rmi.MarshalledObject(reg);
java.io.ByteArrayOutputStream byteStr =
    new java.io.ByteArrayOutputStream();
java.io.ObjectOutputStream objStr = new
    java.io.ObjectOutputStream(byteStr);

objStr.writeObject(obj);
objStr.writeInt(groups.length);
for (int i = 0; i < groups.length; i++) {
    objStr.writeUTF(groups[i]);
}

byte[] responseBody = byteStr.toByteArray(); // final result
```

When the discovering entity receives this data stream, it can deserialize the `MarshalledObject` it has been sent and use the `get` method of that object to obtain a lookup service registrar for that djinn.

DJ.3 The Join Protocol

HAVING covered the discovery protocols, we continue on to describe the join protocol. This protocol makes use of the discovery protocols to provide a standard sequence of steps that services should perform when they are starting up and registering themselves with a lookup service.

DJ.3.1 Persistent State

A service must maintain certain items of state across restarts and crashes. These items are as follows:

- Its service ID. A new service will not have been assigned a service ID, so this will be not be set when a service is started for the first time. After a service has been assigned a service ID, it must continue to use it across all lookup services.
- A set of attributes that describe the service's lookup service entry.
- A set of groups in which the service wishes to participate. For most services this set will initially contain a single entry: the empty string (which denotes the public group).
- A set of specific lookup services to register with. This set will usually be empty for new services.

Note that by "new service" here, we mean one that has never before been started, not one that is being started again or one that has been moved from one network to another.

DJ.3.2 The Join Protocol

When a service initially starts up, it should pause a random amount of time (up to 15 seconds is a reasonable range). This will reduce the likelihood of a packet storm occurring if power is restored to a network segment that houses a large number of services.

D.J.3.2.1 Initial Discovery and Registration

For each member of the set of specific lookup services to register with, the service attempts to perform unicast discovery of each one and to register with each one. If any fails to respond, the implementor may choose to either retry or give up, but the non-responding lookup service should not be automatically removed from the set if an implementation decides to give up.

Joining Groups

If the set of groups to join is not empty, the service performs multicast discovery and registers with each of the lookup services that either respond to requests or announce themselves as members of one or more of the groups the service should join.

Order of Discovery

The unicast and multicast discovery steps detailed above do not need to proceed in any strict sequence. The registering service must register the same sets of attributes with each lookup service, and must use a single service ID across all registrations.

D.J.3.2.2 Lease Renewal and Handling of Communication Problems

Once a service has registered with a lookup service, it periodically renews the lease on its registration. A lease with a particular lookup service is cancelled only if the registering service is instructed to unregister itself.

If a service cannot communicate with a particular lookup service, the action it takes depends on its relation to that lookup service. If the lookup service is in the persistent set of specific lookup services to join, the service must attempt to reregister with that lookup service. If the lookup service was discovered using multicast discovery, it is safe for the registering service to forget about it and await a subsequent multicast announcement.

DJ.3.2.3 Making Changes and Performing Updates

Attribute Modification

If a service is asked to change the set of attributes with which it registers itself, it saves the changed set in a persistent store, then performs the requested change at each lookup service with which it is registered.

Registering and Unregistering with Lookup Services

If a service is asked to register with a specific lookup service, it adds that lookup service to the persistent set of lookup services it should join, and then registers itself with that lookup service as detailed above.

If a service is asked to unregister from a specific lookup service and that service is in the persistent set of lookup services to join, it should be removed from that set. Whether or not this step needs to be taken, the service cancels the leases for all entries it maintains at that lookup service.

DJ.3.2.4 Joining or Leaving a Group

If a service is asked to join a group, it adds the name of that group to the persistent set of groups to join and either starts or continues to perform multicast discovery using this augmented group.

If the service is requested to leave a group, the steps are a little more complex:

1. It removes that group from the persistent set of groups to join.
2. It removes all lookup services that match only that group in the set of groups it is interested in from the set it has discovered using multicast discovery, and unregisters from those lookup services.
3. It either continues to perform multicast discovery with the reduced set of groups or, if the set has been reduced to empty, ceases multicast discovery.

DJ.4 Network Issues

Now we will discuss various issues that pertain to the multicast network protocol used by the multicast discovery service. Much of the discussion centers on the Internet protocols, as the lookup discovery protocol is expected to be most heavily used on IP-based internets and intranets.

DJ.4.1 Properties of the Underlying Transport

The network protocol that is used to communicate between a discovering entity and an instance of the discovery request service is assumed to be unreliable and connectionless, and to provide unordered delivery of packets.

This maps naturally onto both IP multicast and local-area IP broadcast, but should work equally well with connection-oriented reliable multicast protocols.

DJ.4.1.1 Limitations on Packet Sizes

Since we assume that the underlying transport does not necessarily deliver packets in order, we must address this fact. Although we could mandate that request packets contain sequence numbers, such that they could be reassembled in order by instances of the discovery request service, this seems excessive. Instead, we require that discovery requests not exceed 512 bytes in size, including headers for lower-level protocols. This squeaks in below the lowest required MTU size that is required to be supported by IP implementations.

DJ.4.2 Bridging Calls to the Discovery Request Service

Whether or not calls to the discovery request service will need to be bridged across LAN or wide area network (WAN) segments will depend on the network protocol being used and the topology of the local network.

In an environment in which every LAN segment happens to host a Jini lookup service, bridging might not be necessary. This does not seem likely to be a typical scenario.

Where the underlying transport is multicast IP, intelligent bridges and routers must be able to forward packets appropriately. This simply requires that they support one of the multicast IP routing protocols; most router vendors already do so.

If the underlying transport were permitted to be local-area IP broadcast, some kind of intelligent broadcast relay would be required, similar to that described in the DHCP and BOOTP specifications. Since this would increase the complexity of the infrastructure needed to support the Jini discovery protocol, we mandate use of multicast IP instead of broadcast IP.

DJ.4.3 Limiting the Scope of Multicasts

In an environment that makes use of IP multicast or a similar protocol, the joining entity should restrict the scope of the multicasts it makes by setting the time-to-live (TTL) field of outgoing packets appropriately. The value of the TTL field is not mandated, but we recommend that it be set to 15.

DJ.4.4 Using Multicast IP as the Underlying Transport

If multicast IP is being used as the underlying transport, request packets are encapsulated using UDP (checksums must be enabled). A combination of a well-known multicast IP address and a well-known UDP port is used by instances of the discovery request service and joining entities.

DJ.4.5 Address and Port Mappings for TCP and Multicast UDP

The port number for Jini lookup discovery requests is `4160`. This applies to both the multicast and unicast discovery protocols. For multicast discovery the IP address of the multicast group over which discovery requests should travel is `224.0.1.85`. Multicast announcements should use the address `224.0.1.84`.

DJ.5 LookupLocator Class

THE LookupLocator class provides a simple interface for performing unicast discovery:

```
package net.jini.core.discovery;

import java.io.IOException;
import java.io.Serializable;
import java.net.MalformedURLException;
import net.jini.core.lookup.ServiceRegistrar;

public class LookupLocator implements Serializable {
    public LookupLocator(String host, int port) {...}
    public LookupLocator(String url)
        throws MalformedURLException {...}
    public String getHost() {...}
    public int getPort() {...}
    public ServiceRegistrar getRegistrar()
        throws IOException, ClassNotFoundException {...}
    public ServiceRegistrar getRegistrar(int timeout)
        throws IOException, ClassNotFoundException {...}
}
```

Each constructor takes parameters that allow the object to determine what IP address and TCP port number it should connect to. The first form takes a host name and port number. The second form takes what should be a *jini*-scheme URL. If the URL is invalid, it throws a java.net.MalformedURLException. Neither constructor performs the unicast discovery protocol, nor does either resolve the host name passed as argument.

The getHost method returns the name of the host with which this object attempts to perform unicast discovery, and the getPort method returns the TCP port at that host to which this object connects. The equals method returns true if both instances have the same host and port.

There are two forms of `getRegistrar` method. Each performs unicast discovery and returns an instance of the proxy for the specified lookup service, or throws either a `java.io.IOException` or a `java.lang.ClassNotFoundException` if a problem occurs during the discovery protocol. Each method performs unicast discovery every time it is called.

The form of this method that takes a `timeout` parameter will throw a `java.io.InterruptedIOException` if it blocks for more than `timeout` milliseconds while waiting for a response. A similar timeout is implied for the no-arg form of this method, but the value of the timeout in milliseconds may be specified globally using the `net.jini.discovery.timeout` system property, with a default equal to 60 seconds.

DJ.5.1 Jini Technology URL Syntax

While the Uniform Resource Locator (URL) specification merely demands that a URL be of the form `protocol:data`, standard URL syntaxes tend to take one of two forms:

- *protocol://host/data*
- *protocol://host:port/data*

The protocol component of a Jini technology URL is, not surprisingly, `jini`. The host name component of the URL is an ordinary DNS name or IP address. If the DNS name resolves to multiple IP addresses, it is assumed that a lookup service for the same djinn lives at each address. If no port number is specified, the default is 4160.[2]

The URL has no data component, since the lookup service is generally not searchable by name. As a result, a Jini technology URL ends up looking like

```
jini://example.org
```

with the port defaulting to 4160 since it is not provided explicitly, or, to indicate a non-default port,

```
jini://example.com:4162
```

---

[2] If you speak hexadecimal, you will notice that 4160 is the decimal representation of (CAFE – BABE).

DJ.5.2 Serialized Form

Class	serialVersionUID	Serialized Fields
LookupLocator	1448769379829432795L	String host int port

EN

Entry

EN.1 Entries and Templates

ENTRIES are designed to be used in distributed algorithms for which exact-match lookup semantics are useful. An entry is a typed set of objects, each of which may be tested for exact match with a template.

EN.1.1 Operations

A service that uses entries will support methods that let you use entry objects. In this document we will use the term "operation" for such methods. There are three types of operations:

- *Store operations*—operations that store one or more entries, usually for future matches.
- *Match operations*—operations that search for entries that match one or more templates.
- *Fetch operations*—operations that return one or more entries.

It is possible for a single method to provide more than one of the operation types. For example, consider a method that returns an entry that matches a given template. Such a method can be logically split into two operation types (match and fetch), so any statements made in this specification about either operation type would apply to the appropriate part of the method's behavior.

EN.1.2 Entry

An entry is a typed group of object references represented by a class that implements the marker interface net.jini.core.entry.Entry. Two different entries have the same type if and only if they are of the same class.

```
package net.jini.core.entry;

public interface Entry extends java.io.Serializable { }
```

For the purpose of this specification, the term "field" when applied to an entry will mean fields that are public, non-static, non-transient, and non-final. Other fields of an entry are not affected by entry operations. In particular, when an entry object is created and filled in by a fetch operation, only the public non-static, non-transient, and non-final fields of the entry are set. Other fields are not affected, except as set by the class's no-arg constructor.

Each Entry class must provide a public no-arg constructor. Entries may not have fields of primitive type (int, boolean, etc.), although the objects they refer to may have primitive fields and non-public fields. For any type of operation, an attempt to use a malformed entry type that has primitive fields or does not have a no-arg constructor throws IllegalArgumentException.

EN.1.3 Serializing Entry Objects

Entry objects are typically not stored directly by an entry-using service (one that supports one or more entry operations). The client of the service will typically turn an Entry into an implementation-specific representation that includes a serialized form of the entry's class and each of the entry's fields. (This transformation is typically not explicit but is done by a client-side proxy object for the remote service.) It is these implementation-specific forms that are typically stored and retrieved from the service. These forms are not directly visible to the client, but their existence has important effects on the operational contract. The semantics of this section apply to all operation types, whether the above assumptions are true or not for a particular service.

Each entry has its fields serialized separately. In other words, if two fields of the entry refer to the same object (directly or indirectly), the serialized form that is compared for each field will have a separate copy of that object. This is true only of different fields of an entry; if an object graph of a particular field refers to the same object twice, the graph will be serialized and reconstituted with a single copy of that object.

A fetch operation returns an entry that has been created by using the entry type's no-arg constructor, and whose fields have been filled in from such a serialized form. Thus, if two fields, directly or indirectly, refer to the same underlying object, the fetched entry will have independent copies of the original underlying object.

This behavior, although not obvious, is both logically correct and practically advantageous. Logically, the fields can refer to object graphs, but the entry is not itself a graph of objects and so should not be reconstructed as one. An entry (relative to the service) is a set of separate fields, not a unit of its own. From a practical standpoint, viewing an entry as a single graph of objects requires a matching service to parse and understand the serialized form, because the ordering of objects in the written entry will be different from that in a template that can match it.

The serialized form for each field is a `java.rmi.MarshalledObject` object instance, which provides an `equals` method that conforms to the above matching semantics for a field. `MarshalledObject` also attaches a codebase to class descriptions in the serialized form, so classes written as part of an entry can be downloaded by a client when they are retrieved from the service. In a store operation, the class of the entry type itself is also written with a `MarshalledObject`, ensuring that it, too, may be downloaded from a codebase.

EN.1.4 UnusableEntryException

A `net.jini.core.entry.UnusableEntryException` will be thrown if the serialized fields of an entry being fetched cannot be deserialized for any reason:

```
package net.jini.core.entry;

public class UnusableEntryException extends Exception {
    public Entry partialEntry;
    public String[] unusableFields;
    public Throwable[] nestedExceptions;
    public UnusableEntryException(Entry partial,
        String[] badFields, Throwable[] exceptions) {...}
    public UnusableEntryException(Throwable e) {...}
}
```

The `partialEntry` field will refer to an entry of the type that would have been fetched, with all the usable fields filled in. Fields whose deserialization caused an exception will be `null` and have their names listed in the `unusableFields` string array. For each element in `unusableFields` the corresponding element of `nestedExceptions` will refer to the exception that caused the field to fail deserialization.

If the retrieved entry is corrupt in such a way as to prevent even an attempt at field deserialization (such as being unable to load the exact class for the entry), `partialEntry` and `unusableFields` will both be `null`, and `nestedExceptions` will be a single element array with the offending exception.

The kinds of exceptions that can show up in `nestedExceptions` are:

- `ClassNotFoundException`: The class of an object that was serialized cannot be found.
- `InstantiationException`: An object could not be created for a given type.
- `IllegalAccessException`: The field in the entry was either inaccessible or `final`.
- `java.io.ObjectStreamException`: The field could not be deserialized because of object stream problems.
- `java.rmi.RemoteException`: When a `RemoteException` is the nested exception of an `UnusableEntryException`, it means that a remote reference in the entry's state is no longer valid (more below). Remote errors associated with a method that is a fetch operation (such as being unable to contact a remote server) are not reflected by `UnusableEntryException` but in some other way defined by the method (typically by the method throwing `RemoteException` itself).

Generally speaking, storing a remote reference to a non-persistent remote object in an entry is risky. Because entries are stored in serialized form, entries stored in an entry-based service will typically not participate in the garbage collection that keeps such references valid. However, if the reference is not persistent because the referenced server does not export persistent references, that garbage collection is the only way to ensure the ongoing validity of a remote reference. If a field contains a reference to a non-persistent remote object, either directly or indirectly, it is possible that the reference will no longer be valid when it is deserialized. In such a case the client code must decide whether to remove the entry from the entry-fetching service, to store the entry back into the service, or to leave the service as it is.

In the Java 2 platform, activatable object references fit this need for persistent references. If you do not use a persistent type, you will have to handle the above problems with remote references. You may choose instead to have your entries store information sufficient to look up the current reference rather than putting actual references into the entry.

EN.1.5 Templates and Matching

Match operations use entry objects of a given type, whose fields can either have *values* (references to objects) or *wildcards* (`null` references). When considering a template *T* as a potential match against an entry *E*, fields with values in *T* must be matched exactly by the value in the same field of *E*. Wildcards in *T* match any value in the same field of *E*.

The type of *E* must be that of *T* or be a subtype of the type of *T*, in which case all fields added by the subtype are considered to be wildcards. This enables a template to match entries of any of its subtypes. If the matching is coupled with a fetch operation, the fetched entry must have the type of *E*.

The values of two fields match if `MarshalledObject.equals` returns `true` for their `MarshalledObject` instances. This will happen if the bytes generated by their serialized form match, ignoring differences of serialization stream implementation (such as blocking factors for buffering). Class version differences that change the bytes generated by serialization will cause objects not to match. Neither entries nor their fields are matched using the `Object.equals` method or any other form of type-specific value matching.

You can store an entry that has a `null`-valued field, but you cannot match explicitly on a `null` value in that field, because `null` signals a wildcard field. If you have a field in an entry that may be variously `null` or not, you can set the field to `null` in your entry. If you need to write templates that distinguish between set and unset values for that field, you can (for example) add a `Boolean` field that indicates whether the field is set and use a `Boolean` value for that field in templates.

An entry that has no wildcards is a valid template.

Serialized Form

Class	`serialVersionUID`	Serialized Fields
`UnusableEntryException`	–2199083666668626172L	*all public fields*

LE

Distributed Leasing

LE.1 Introduction

THE purpose of the leasing interfaces defined in this document is to simplify and unify a particular style of programming for distributed systems and applications. This style, in which a resource is offered by one object in a distributed system and used by a second object in that system, is based on a notion of granting a use to the resource for a certain period of time that is negotiated by the two objects when access to the resource is first requested and given. Such a grant is known as a *lease* and is meant to be similar to the notion of a lease used in everyday life. As in everyday life, the negotiation of a lease entails responsibilities and duties for both the grantor of the lease and the holder of the lease. Part of this specification is a detailing of these responsibilities and duties, as well as a discussion of when it is appropriate to use a lease in offering a distributed service.

There is no requirement that the leasing notions defined in this document be the only time-based mechanism used in software. Leases are a part of the programmer's arsenal, and other time-based techniques such as time-to-live, ping intervals, and keep-alives can be useful in particular situations. Leasing is not meant to replace these other techniques, but rather to enhance the set of tools available to the programmer of distributed systems.

LE.1.1 Leasing and Distributed Systems

Distributed systems differ fundamentally from non-distributed systems in that there are situations in which different parts of a cooperating group are unable to communicate, either because one of the members of the group has crashed or because the connection between the members in the group has failed. This partial failure can happen at any time and can be intermittent or long-lasting.

The possibility of partial failure greatly complicates the construction of distributed systems in which components of the system that are not co-located provide resources or other services to each other. The programming model that is used most often in non-distributed computing, in which resources and services are granted until explicitly freed or given up, is open to failures caused by the inability to successfully make the explicit calls that cancel the use of the resource or system. Failure of this sort of system can result in resources never being freed, in services being delivered long after the recipient of the service has forgotten that the service was requested, and in resource consumption that can grow without bounds.

To avoid these problems, we introduce the notion of a lease. Rather than granting services or resources until that grant has been explicitly cancelled by the party to which the grant was made, a leased resource or service grant is time based. When the time for the lease has expired, the service ends or the resource is freed. The time period for the lease is determined when the lease is first granted, using a request/response form of negotiation between the party wanting the lease and the lease grantor. Leases may be renewed or cancelled before they expire by the holder of the lease, but in the case of no action (or in the case of a network or participant failure), the lease simply expires. When a lease expires, both the holder of the lease and the grantor of the lease know that the service or resource has been reclaimed.

Although the notion of a lease was originally brought into the system as a way of dealing with partial failure, the technique is also useful for dealing with another problem faced by distributed systems. Distributed systems tend to be long-lived. In addition, since distributed systems are often providing resources that are shared by numerous clients in an uncoordinated fashion, such systems are much more difficult to shut down for maintenance purposes than systems that reside on a single machine.

As a consequence of this, distributed systems, especially those with persistent state, are prone to accumulations of outdated and unwanted information. The accumulation of such information, which can include objects stored for future use and subsequently forgotten, may be slow, but the trend is always upward. Over the (comparatively) long life of a distributed system, such unwanted information can grow without upper bound, taking up resources and compromising the performance of the overall system.

A standard way of dealing with these problems is to consider the cleanup of unused resources to be a system administration task. When such resources begin to get scarce, a human administrator is given the task of finding resources that are no longer needed and deleting them. This solution, however, is error prone (since the administrator is often required to judge the use of a resource with no actual evidence about whether or not the resource is being used) and tends to happen only when resource consumption has gotten out of hand.

When such resources are leased, however, this accumulation of out-of-date information does not occur, and resorting to manual cleanup methods is not needed. Information or resources that are leased remain in the system only as long as the lease for that information or resource is renewed. Thus information that is forgotten (through either program error, inadvertence, or system crash) will be deleted after some finite time. Note that this is not the same as garbage collection (although it is related in that it has to do with freeing up resources), since the information that is leased is not of the sort that would generally have any active reference to it. Rather, this is information that is stored for (possible) later retrieval but is no longer of any interest to the party that originally stored the information.

This model of persistence is one that requires renewed proof of interest to maintain the persistence. Information is kept (and resources used) only as long as someone claims that the information is of interest (a claim that is shown by the act of renewing the lease). The interval for which the resource may be consumed without a proof of interest can vary, and is subject to negotiation by the party storing the information (which has expectations for how long it will be interested in the information) and the party in which the information is stored (which has requirements on how long it is willing to store something without proof that some party is interested).

The notion of persistence of information is not one of storing the information on stable storage (although it encompasses that notion). Persistent information, in this case, includes any information that has a lifetime longer than the lifetime of the process in which the request for storage originates.

Leasing also allows a form of programming in which the entity that reserves the information or resource is not the same as the entity that makes use of the information or resource. In such a model, a resource can be reserved (leased) by an entity on the expectation that some other entity will use the resource over some period of time. Rather than having to check back to see if the resource is used (or freed), a leased version of such a reservation allows the entity granted the lease to forget about the resource. Whether used or not, the resource will be freed when the lease has expired.

Leasing such information storage introduces a programming paradigm that is an extension of the model used by most programmers today. The current model is essentially one of infinite leasing, with information being removed from persistent stores only by the active deletion of such information. Databases and filesystems are perhaps the best known exemplars of such stores—both hold any information placed in them until the information is explicitly deleted by some user or program.

LE.1.2 Goals and Requirements

The requirements of this set of interfaces are:

- To provide a simple way of indicating time-based resource allocation or reservation
- To provide a uniform way of renewing and cancelling leases
- To show common patterns of use for interfaces using this set of interfaces

The goals of this chapter are:

- To describe the notion of a lease and show some of the applications of that notion in distributed computing
- To show the way in which this notion is used in a distributed system
- To indicate appropriate uses of the notion in applications built to run in a distributed environment

LE.2 Basic Leasing Interfaces

THE basic concept of leasing is that access to a resource or the request for some action is not open ended with respect to time, but granted only for some particular interval. In general (although not always), this interval is determined by some negotiation between the object asking for the leased resource (which we will call the lease holder) and the object granting access for some period (which we will call the lease grantor).

In its most general form, a lease is used to associate a mutually agreed upon time interval with an agreement reached by two objects. The kinds of agreements that can be leased are varied and can include such things as agreements on access to an object (references), agreements for taking future action (event notifications), agreements to supplying persistent storage (file systems, JavaSpaces systems), or agreements to advertise availability (naming or directory services).

While it is possible that a lease can be given that provides exclusive access to some resource, this is not required with the notion of leasing being offered here. Agreements that provide access to resources that are intrinsically sharable can have multiple concurrent lease holders. Other resources might decide to grant only exclusive leases, combining the notion of leasing with a concurrency control mechanism.

LE.2.1 Characteristics of a Lease

There are a number of characteristics that are important for understanding what a lease is and when it is appropriate to use one. Among these characteristics are:

- A lease is a time period during which the grantor of the lease ensures (to the best of the grantor's abilities) that the holder of the lease will have access to some resource. The time period of the lease can be determined solely by the lease grantor, or can be a period of time that is negotiated between the holder of the lease and the grantor of the lease. Duration negotiation need not be multi-round; it often suffices for the requestor to indicate the time desired and the grantor to return the actual time of grant.

- During the period of a lease, a lease can be cancelled by the entity holding the lease. Such a cancellation allows the grantor of the lease to clean up any resources associated with the lease and obliges the grantor of the lease to not take any action involving the lease holder that was part of the agreement that was the subject of the lease.
- A lease holder can request that a lease be renewed. The renewal period can be for a different time than the original lease, and is also subject to negotiation with the grantor of the lease. The grantor may renew the lease for the requested period or a shorter period or may refuse to renew the lease at all. However, when renewing a lease the grantor cannot, unless explicitly requested to do so, shorten the duration of the lease so that it expires before it would have if it had not been renewed. A renewed lease is just like any other lease and is itself subject to renewal.
- A lease can expire. If a lease period has elapsed with no renewals, the lease expires, and any resources associated with the lease may be freed by the lease grantor. Both the grantor and the holder are obliged to act as though the leased agreement is no longer in force. The expiration of a lease is similar to the cancellation of a lease, except that no communication is necessary between the lease holder and the lease grantor.

Leasing is part of a programming model for building reliable distributed applications. In particular, leasing is a way of ensuring that a uniform response to failure, forgetting, or disinterest is guaranteed, allowing agreements to be made that can then be forgotten without the possibility of unbounded resource consumption, and providing a flexible mechanism for duration-based agreement.

LE.2.2 Basic Operations

The `Lease` interface defines a type of object that is returned to the lease holder and issued by the lease grantor. The basic interface may be extended in ways that offer more functionality, but the basic interface is:

```
package net.jini.core.lease;

import java.rmi.RemoteException;

public interface Lease {
    long FOREVER = Long.MAX_VALUE;
    long ANY = -1;
```

```
    int DURATION = 1;
    int ABSOLUTE = 2;

    long getExpiration();
    void cancel() throws UnknownLeaseException,
                         RemoteException;
    void renew(long duration) throws LeaseDeniedException,
                                     UnknownLeaseException,
                                     RemoteException;
    void setSerialFormat(int format);
    int getSerialFormat();
    LeaseMap createLeaseMap(long duration);
    boolean canBatch(Lease lease);
}
```

Particular instances of the `Lease` type will be created by the grantors of a lease and returned to the holder of the lease as part of the return value from a call that allocates a leased resource. The actual implementation of the object, including the way (if any) in which the `Lease` object communicates with the grantor of the lease, is determined by the lease grantor and is hidden from the lease holder.

The interface defines two constants that can be used when requesting a lease. The first, `FOREVER`, can be used to request a lease that never expires. When granted such a lease, the lease holder is responsible for ensuring that the leased resource is freed when no longer needed. The second constant, `ANY`, is used by the requestor to indicate that no particular lease time is desired and that the grantor of the lease should supply a time that is most convenient for the grantor.

If the request is for a particular duration, the lease grantor is required to grant a lease of no more than the requested period of time. A lease may be granted for a period of time shorter than that requested.

A second pair of constants is used to determine the format used in the serialized form for a `Lease` object; in particular, the serialized form that is used to represent the time at which the lease expires. If the serialized format is set to the value `DURATION`, the serialized form will convert the time of lease expiration into a duration (in milliseconds) from the time of serialization. This form is best used when transmitting a `Lease` object from one address space to another (such as via an RMI call) where it cannot be assumed that the address spaces have sufficiently synchronized clocks. If the serialized format is set to `ABSOLUTE`, the time of expiration will be stored as an absolute time, calculated in terms of milliseconds since the beginning of the epoch.

The first method in the `Lease` interface, `getExpiration`, returns a `long` that indicates the time, relative to the current clock, that the lease will expire. Following the usual convention in the Java programming language, this time is represented as milliseconds from the beginning of the epoch and can be used to compare the expiration time of the lease with the result of a call to obtain the current time, `java.lang.System.currentTimeMillis`.

The second method, `cancel`, can be used by the lease holder to indicate that it is no longer interested in the resource or information held by the lease. If the leased information or resource could cause a callback to the lease holder (or some other object on behalf of the lease holder), the lease grantor should not issue such a callback after the lease has been cancelled. The overall effect of a `cancel` call is the same as lease expiration, but instead of happening at the end of a pre-agreed duration, it happens immediately. If the lease being cancelled is unknown to the lease grantor, an `UnknownLeaseException` is thrown. The method can also throw a `RemoteException` if the implementation of the method requires calling a remote object that is the lease holder.

The third method, `renew`, is used to renew a lease for an additional period of time. The length of the desired renewal is given, in milliseconds, in the parameter to the call. This duration is not added to the original lease, but is used to determine a new expiration time for the existing lease. This method has no return value; if the renewal is granted, this is reflected in the lease object on which the call was made. If the lease grantor is unable or unwilling to renew the lease, a `LeaseDeniedException` is thrown. If a renewal fails, the lease is left intact for the same duration that was in force prior to the call to `renew`. If the lease being renewed is unknown to the lease grantor, an `UnknownLeaseException` is thrown. The method can also throw a `RemoteException` if the implementation of the method requires calling a remote object that is the lease holder.

As with a call that grants a lease, the duration requested in a `renew` call need not be honored by the entity granting the lease. A renewal may not be for longer than the duration requested, but the grantor may decide to renew a lease for a period of time that is shorter than the duration requested. However, the new lease cannot have a duration that is shorter than the duration remaining on the lease being renewed unless a shorter duration is specifically requested.

Two methods are concerned with the serialized format of a `Lease` object. The first, `setSerialFormat`, takes an integer that indicates the appropriate format to use when serializing the lease. The current supported formats are a duration format which stores the length of time (from the time of serialization) before the lease expires, and an absolute format, which stores the time (relative to the current clock) that the lease will expire. The duration format should be used when serializing a `Lease` object for transmission from one machine to another; the absolute format should be used when storing a `Lease` object on stable store that will be read back later by the same process or machine. The default serialization format is durational. The second method, `getSerialFormat`, returns an integer indicating the format that will be used to serialize the `Lease` object.

The last two methods are used to aid in the batch renewal or cancellation of a group of `Lease` objects. The first of these, `createLeaseMap`, creates a `Map` object that can contain leases whose renewal or cancellation can be batched and adds the current lease to that map. The current lease will be renewed for the duration indicated by the argument to the method when all of the leases in the `LeaseMap` are renewed. The second method, `canBatch`, returns a boolean value indicating whether or not the lease given as an argument to the method can be batched (in `renew` and `cancel` calls) with the current lease. Whether or not two `Lease` objects can be batched is an implementation detail determined by the objects. However, if a `Lease` object can be batched with any other `Lease` object, the set of objects that can be batched must form an equivalence class. That is, the `canBatch` relationship must be reflexive, symmetric, and associative. This means that, for any three `Lease` objects `x`, `y`, and `z` that return `true` for any instance of the `canBatch` call, it will be the case that:

- `x.canBatch(x)` is `true`
- if `x.canBatch(y)` is `true` then `y.canBatch(x)` is `true`
- if `x.canBatch(y)` is `true` and `y.canBatch(z)` is `true`, then `x.canBatch(z)` is `true`

In addition to the above methods, an object that implements the `Lease` interface will probably need to override the `equals` and `hashcode` methods inherited from `Object`. It is likely that such leases, while appearing as local objects, will in fact contain remote references—either explicitly copied or passed via a method call—to implementation-specific objects in the address space of the lease grantor. These local references may even include their own state (such as the expiration time of the lease) that may, over time, vary from the actual expiration time of the lease to which they refer. Two such references should evaluate as equal (and have the same `hashcode` value) when they refer to the same lease in the grantor, which will not be reflected by the default implementation of the `equals` method.

Three types of `Exception` objects are associated with the basic lease interface. All of these are used in the `Lease` interface itself, and two can be used by methods that grant access to a leased resource.

The `RemoteException` is imported from the package `java.rmi`. This exception is used to indicate a problem with any communication that might occur between the lease holder and the lease grantor if those objects are in separate virtual machines. The full specification of this exception can be found in the *Java Remote Method Invocation Specification*.

The `UnknownLeaseException` is used to indicate that the `Lease` object used is not known to the grantor of the lease. This can occur when a lease expires or when a copy of a lease has been cancelled by some other lease holder. This exception is defined as:

```
package net.jini.core.lease;

public class UnknownLeaseException extends LeaseException {
    public UnknownLeaseException() {
        super();
    }
    public UnknownLeaseException(String reason) {
        super(reason);
    }
}
```

The final exception defined is the LeaseDeniedException, which can be thrown by either a call to renew or a call to an interface that grants access to a leased resource. This exception indicates that the requested lease has been denied by the resource holder. The exception is defined as:

```
package net.jini.core.lease;

public class LeaseDeniedException extends LeaseException {
    public LeaseDeniedException() {
        super();
    }
    public LeaseDeniedException(String reason) {
        super(reason);
    }
}
```

The LeaseException superclass is defined as:

```
package net.jini.core.lease;

public class LeaseException extends Exception {
    public LeaseException() {
        super();
    }
    public LeaseException(String reason) {
        super(reason);
    }
}
```

The final basic interface defined for leasing is that of a LeaseMap, which allows groups of Lease objects to be renewed or cancelled by a single operation. The LeaseMap interface is:

```
package net.jini.core.lease;

import java.rmi.RemoteException;

public interface LeaseMap extends java.util.Map {
    boolean canContainKey(Object key);
    void renewAll() throws LeaseMapException, RemoteException;
    void cancelAll() throws LeaseMapException,RemoteException;
}
```

A LeaseMap is an extension of the java.util.Map interface that associates a Lease object with a Long. The Long is the duration for which the lease should be renewed whenever it is renewed. Lease objects and associated renewal durations can be entered and removed from a LeaseMap by the usual Map methods. An attempt to add a Lease object to a map containing other Lease objects for which Lease.canBatch would return false will cause an IllegalArgumentException to be thrown, as will attempts to add a key that is not a Lease object or a value that is not a Long.

The first method defined in the LeaseMap interface, canContainKey, takes a Lease object as an argument and returns true if that Lease object can be added to the Map and false otherwise. A Lease object can be added to a Map if that Lease object can be renewed in a batch with the other objects in the LeaseMap. The requirements for this depend on the implementation of the Lease object. However, if a LeaseMap object, m, contains a Lease object, n, then for some Lease object o, n.canBatch(o) returns true if and only if m.canContainKey(o) returns true.

The second method, renewAll, will attempt to renew all of the Lease objects in the LeaseMap for the duration associated with the Lease object. If all of the Lease objects are successfully renewed, the method will return nothing. If some Lease objects fail to renew, those objects will be removed from the LeaseMap and will be contained in the thrown LeaseMapException.

The third method, cancelAll, cancels all the Lease objects in the LeaseMap. If all cancels are successful, the method returns normally and leaves all leases in the map. If any of the Lease objects cannot be cancelled, they are removed from the LeaseMap and the operation throws a LeaseMapException.

The LeaseMapException class is defined as:

```
package net.jini.core.lease;

import java.util.Map;

public class LeaseMapException extends LeaseException {
    public Map exceptionMap;
    public LeaseMapException(String s, Map exceptionMap) {
        super(s);
        this.exceptionMap = exceptionMap;
    }
}
```

Objects of type LeaseMapException contain a Map object that maps Lease objects (the keys) to Exception objects (the values). The Lease objects are the ones that could not be renewed or cancelled, and the Exception objects reflect the individual failures. For example, if a LeaseMap.renew call fails because one of the leases has already expired, that lease would be taken out of the original LeaseMap and placed in the Map returned as part of the LeaseMapException object with an UnknownLeaseException object as the corresponding value.

LE.2.3 Leasing and Time

The duration of a lease is determined when the lease is granted (or renewed). A lease is granted for a duration rather than until some particular moment of time, since such a grant does not require that the clocks used by the client and the server be synchronized.

The difficulty of synchronizing clocks in a distributed system is well known. The problem is somewhat more tractable in the case of leases, which are expected to be for periods of minutes to months, as the accuracy of synchronization required is expected to be in terms of minutes rather than nanoseconds. Over a particular local group of machines, a time service could be used that would allow this level of synchronization.

However, leasing is expected to be used by clients and servers that are widely distributed and might not share a particular time service. In such a case, clock drift of many minutes is a common occurrence. Because of this, the leasing specification has chosen to use durations rather than absolute time.

The reasoning behind such a choice is based on the observation that the accuracy of the clocks used in the machines that make up a distributed system is matched much more closely than the clocks on those systems. While there may be minutes of difference in the notion of the absolute time held by widely separated systems, there is much less likelihood of a significant difference over the rate of change of time in those systems. While there is clearly some difference in the notion of duration between systems (if there were not, synchronization for absolute time would be much easier), that difference is not cumulative in the way errors in absolute time are.

This decision does mean that holders of leases and grantors of leases need to be aware of some of the consequences of the use of durations. In particular, the amount of time needed to communicate between the lease holder and the lease grantor, which may vary from call to call, needs to be taken into account when renewing a lease. If a lease holder is calculating the absolute time (relative to the lease holder's clock) at which to ask for a renewal, that time should be based on the sum of the duration of the lease plus the time at which the lease holder requested the lease, not on the duration plus the time at which the lease holder received the lease.

LE.2.4 Serialized Forms

Class	`serialVersionUID`	Serialized Fields
`LeaseException`	–7902272546257490469L	*all public fields*
`UnknownLeaseException`	–2921099330511429288L	*none*
`LeaseDeniedException`	5704943735577343495L	*none*
`LeaseMapException`	–4854893779678486122L	*none*

LE.3 Example Supporting Classes

THE basic `Lease` interface allows leases to be granted by one object and handed to another as the result of a call that creates or provides access to some leased resource. The goal of the interface is to allow as much freedom as possible in implementation to both the party that is granting the lease (and thus is giving out the implementation that supports the `Lease` interface) and the party that receives the lease.

However, a number of classes can be supplied that can simplify the handling of leases in some common cases. We will describe examples of these supporting classes and show how these classes can be used with leased resources. Please note that complete specifications for such utilities and services do exist and may differ in some degree from these examples.

LE.3.1 A Renewal Class

One of the common patterns with leasing is for the lease holder to request a lease with the intention of renewing the lease until it is finished with the resource. The period of time during which the resource is needed is unknown at the time of requesting the lease, so the requestor wants the lease to be renewed until an undetermined time in the future. Alternatively, the lease requestor might know how long the lease needs to be held, but the lease holder might be unwilling to grant a lease for the full period of time. Again, the pattern will be to renew the lease for some period of time.

If the lease continues to be renewed, the lease holder doesn't want to be bothered with knowing about it, but if the lease is not renewed for some reason, the lease holder wants to be notified. Such a notification can be done by using the usual inter-address space mechanisms for event notifications, by registering a listener of the appropriate type. This functionality can be supplied by a class with an interface like the following:

```
class LeaseRenew {
    LeaseRenew(Lease toRenew,
               long renewTil,
               LeaseExpireListener listener) {…}
    void addRenew(Lease toRenew,
                  long renewTil,
                  LeaseExpireListener listener) {…}
    long getExpiration(Lease forLease)
        throws UnknownLeaseException {…}
    void setExpiration(Lease forLease,long toExpire)
        throws UnknownLeaseException {…}
    void cancel(Lease toCancel)
        throws UnknownLeaseException {…}
    void setLeaseExpireListener(Lease forLease,
                                LeaseExpireListener listener)
        throws UnknownLeaseException {…}
    void removeLeaseExpireListener(Lease forLease)
        throws UnknownLeaseException {…}
}
```

The constructor of this class takes a `Lease` object, presumably returned from some call that reserved a leased resource; an initial time indicating the time until which the lease should be renewed; and an object that is to be notified if a renewal fails before the time indicated in `renewTil`. This returns a `LeaseRenew` object, which will have its own thread of control that will do the lease renewals.

Once a `LeaseRenew` object has been created, other leases can be added to the set that are renewed by that object using the `addRenew` call. This call takes a `Lease` object, an expiration time or overall duration, and a listener to be informed if the lease cannot be renewed prior to the time requested. Internally to the `LeaseRenew` object, leases that can be batched can be placed into a `LeaseMap`.

The duration of a particular lease can be queried by a call to the method `getExpiration`. This method takes a `Lease` object and returns the time at which that lease will be allowed to expire by the `LeaseRenew` object. Note that this is different from the `Lease.getExpiration` method, which tells the time at which the lease will expire if it is not renewed. If there is no `Lease` object corresponding to the argument for this call being handled by the `LeaseRenew` object, an `UnknownLeaseException` will be thrown. This can happen either when no such `Lease` has ever been given to the `LeaseRenew` object, or when a `Lease` object that has been held has already expired or been cancelled. Notice that because this object is assumed to be in the same address space as the object that acquired the lease, we can also assume that it shares the same clock with that object, and hence can use absolute time rather than a duration-based system.

The `setExpiration` method allows the caller to adjust the expiration time of any `Lease` object held by the `LeaseRenew` object. This method takes as arguments the `Lease` whose time of expiration is to be adjusted and the new expiration time. If no lease is held by the `LeaseRenew` object corresponding to the first argument, an `UnknownLeaseException` will be thrown.

A call to `cancel` will result in the cancellation of the indicated `Lease` held by the `LeaseRenew` object. Again, if the lease has already expired on that object, an `UnknownLeaseException` will be thrown. It is expected that a call to this method will be made if the leased resource is no longer needed, rather than just dropping all references to the `LeaseRenew` object.

The methods `setLeaseExpireListener` and `removeLeaseExpireListener` allow setting and unsetting the destination of an event handler associated with a particular `Lease` object held by the `LeaseRenew` object. The handler will be called if the `Lease` object expires before the desired duration period is completed. Note that one of the properties of this example is that only one `LeaseExpireListener` can be associated with each `Lease`.

LE.3.2 A Renewal Service

Objects that hold a lease that needs to be renewed may themselves be activatable, and thus unable to ensure that they will be capable of renewing a lease at some particular time in the future (since they might not be active at that time). For such objects it might make sense to hand the lease renewal duty off to a service that could take care of lease renewal for the object, allowing that object to be deactivated without fear of losing its lease on some other resource.

The most straightforward way of accomplishing this is to hand the `Lease` object off to some object whose job it is to renew leases on behalf of others. This object will be remote to the objects to which it offers its service (otherwise it would be inactive when the others become inactive) but might be local to the machine; there could even be such services that are located on other machines.

The interface to such an object might look something like:

```
interface LeaseRenewService extends Remote {
    EventRegistration renew(Lease toRenew,
                            long renewTil,
                            RemoteEventListenter notifyBeforeDrop,
                            MarshalledObject returnOnNotify)
```

```
        throws RemoteException;
    void onRenewFailure(Lease toRenew,
                        RemoteEventListenter toNotify,
                        MarshalledObject returnOnNotify)
        throws RemoteException, UnknownLeaseException;
}
```

The first method, renew, is the request to the object to renew a particular lease on behalf of the caller. The Lease object to be renewed is passed to the LeaseRenewService object, along with the length of time for which the lease is to be renewed. Since we are assuming that this service might not be on the same machine as the object that acquired the original lease, we return to a duration-based time system, since we cannot assume that the two systems have synchronized clocks.

Requests to renew a Lease are themselves leased. The duration of the lease is requested in the duration argument to the renew method, and the actual time of the lease is returned as part of the EventRegistration return value. While it might seem odd to lease the service of renewing other leases, this does not cause an infinite regress. It is assumed that the LeaseRenewService will grant leases that are longer (perhaps significantly longer) than those in the leases that it is renewing. In this fashion, the LeaseRenewService can act as a concentrator for lease renewal messages.

The renew method also takes as parameters a RemoteEventListener and MarshalledObject objects to be passed to that RemoteEventListener. This is because part of the semantics of the renew call is to register interest in an event that can occur within the LeaseRenewService object. The registration is actually for a notification before the lease granted by the renewal service is dropped. This event notification can be directed back to the object that is the client of the renewal service, and will (if so directed) cause the object to be activated (if it is not already active). This gives the object a chance to renew the lease with the LeaseRenewService object before that lease is dropped.

The second method, onRenewFailure, allows the client to register interest in the LeaseRenewService being unable to renew the Lease supplied as an argument to the call. This call also takes a RemoteEventListener object that is the target of the notification and a MarshalledObject that will be passed as part of the notification. This allows the client to be informed if the LeaseRenewService is denied a lease renewal during the lease period offered to the client for such renewal. This call does not take a time period for the event registration, but instead will have the same duration as the leased renewal associated with the Lease object passed into the call, which should be the same as the Lease object that was supplied in a previous invocation of the method `renew`. If the `Lease` is not known to the `LeaseRenewService` object, an `UnknownLeaseException` will be thrown.

There is no need for a method allowing the cancellation of a lease renewal request. Since these requests are themselves leased, cancelling the lease with the `LeaseRenewService` will cancel both the renewing of the lease and any event registrations associated with that lease.

EV

Distributed Events

EV.1 Introduction

THE purpose of the distributed event interfaces specified in this document is to allow an object in one Java virtual machine (JVM) to register interest in the occurrence of some event occurring in an object in some other JVM, perhaps running on a different physical machine, and to receive a notification when an event of that kind occurs.

EV.1.1 Distributed Events and Notifications

Programs based on an object that is reacting to a change of state somewhere outside the object are common in a single address space. Such programs are often used for interactive applications in which user actions are modeled as events to which other objects in the program react. Delivery of such *local events* can be assumed to be well ordered, very fast, predictable, and reliable. Further, the entity that is interested in the event can be assumed to always want to know about the event as soon as the event has occurred.

The same style of programming is useful in distributed systems, where the object reacting to an event is in a different JVM, perhaps on a different physical machine, from the one on which the event occurred. Just as in the single-JVM case, the logic of such programs is often reactive, with actions occurring in response to some change in state that has occurred elsewhere.

A distributed event system has a different set of characteristics and requirements than a single-address-space event system. Notifications of events from remote objects may arrive in different orders on different clients, or may not arrive at all. The time it takes for a notification to arrive may be long (in comparison to the time for computation at either the object that generated the notification or the object interested in the notification). There may be occasions in which the object wishing the event notification does not wish to have that notification as soon as possible, but only on some schedule determined by the recipient. There may even be times when the object that registered interest in the event is not the object to which a notification of the event should be sent.

Unlike the single-address-space notion of an event, a distributed event cannot be guaranteed to be delivered in a timely fashion. Because of the possibilities of network delays or failures, the notification of an event may be delayed indefinitely and even lost in the case of a distributed system.

Indeed, there are times in a distributed system when the object of a notification may actively desire that the notification be delayed. In systems that allow object activation (such as is allowed by Java Remote Method Invocation (RMI) in the Java), an object might wish to be able to find out whether an event occurred but not want that notification to cause an activation of the object if it is otherwise quiescent. In such cases, the object receiving the event might wish the notification to be delayed until the object requests notification delivery, or until the object has been activated for some other reason.

Central to the notion of a distributed notification is the ability to place a third-party object between the object that generates the notification and the party that ultimately wishes to receive the notification. Such third parties, which can be strung together in arbitrary ways, allow ways of off-loading notifications from objects, implementing various delivery guarantees, storing of notifications until needed or desired by a recipient, and the filtering and rerouting of notifications. In a distributed system in which full applications are made up of components assembled to produce an overall application, the third party may be more than a filter or storage spot for a notification; in such systems it is possible that the third party is the final intended destination of the notification.

EV.1.2 Goals and Requirements

The requirements of this set of interfaces are to:

- Specify an interface that can be used to send a notification of the occurrence of the event
- Specify the information that must be contained in such a notification

In addition, the fact that the interfaces are designed to be used by objects in different virtual machines, perhaps separated by a network, imposes other requirements, including:

- Allowing various degrees of assurance on delivery of a notification

- Support for different policies of scheduling notification
- Explicitly allowing the interposition of objects that will collect, hold, filter, and forward notifications

Notice that there is no requirement for a single interface that can be used to register interest in a particular kind of event. Given the wide variety of kinds of events, the way in which interest in such events can be indicated may vary from object to object. This document will talk about a model that lies behind the system's notion of such a registration, but the interfaces that are used to accomplish such a registration are not open to general description.

EV.2 The Basic Interfaces

THE basic interfaces you are about to see define a protocol that can be used by one object to register interest in a kind of state change in another object, and to receive a notification of an occurrence of that kind of state change, either directly or through some third-party, that is specified by the object at the time of registration. The protocol is meant to be as simple as possible. No attempt is made to indicate the reliability or the timeliness of the notifications; such guarantees are not part of the protocol but instead are part of the implementation of the various objects involved.

In particular, the purpose of these interfaces is:

- To show the information needed in any method that allows registration of interest in the occurrence of a kind of event in an object
- To provide an example of an interface that allows the registration of interest in such events
- To specify an interface that can be used to send a notification of the occurrence of the event

Implicit in the event registration and notification is the idea that events can be classified into *kinds*. Registration of interest indicates the kind of event that is of interest, while a notification indicates that an instance of that kind of event has occurred.

EV.2.1 Entities Involved

An *event* is something that happens in an object, corresponding to some change in the abstract state of the object. Events are abstract occurrences that are not directly observed outside of an object, and might not correspond to a change in the *actual* state of the object that advertises the ability to register interest in the event. However, an object may choose to export an identification of a kind of event and allow other objects to indicate interest in the occurrence of events of that kind; this indi-

cates that the *abstract* state of the object includes the notion of this state changing. The information concerning what kinds of events occur within an object can be exported in a number of ways, including identifiers for the various events or methods allowing registration of interest in that kind of event.

An object is responsible for identifying the kinds of events that can occur within that object, allowing other objects to register interest in the occurrence of such events, and generating `RemoteEvent` objects that are sent as notifications to the objects that have registered interest when such events occur.

Registration of interest is not temporally open ended but is limited to a given duration using the notion of a lease. Full specification of the way in which leasing is used is contained in Section LE "Distributed Leasing".

The basic, concrete objects involved in a distributed event system are:

- The object that registers interest in an event
- The object in which an event occurs (referred to as the event generator)
- The recipient of event notifications (referred to as a remote event listener)

An *event generator* is an object that has some kinds of abstract state changes that might be of interest to other objects and allows other objects to register interest in those events. This is the object that will generate notifications when events of this kind occur, sending those notifications to the event listeners that were indicated as targets in the calls that registered interest in that kind of event.

A *remote event listener* is an object that is interested in the occurrence of some kinds of events in some other object. The major function of a remote event listener is to receive notifications of the occurrence of an event in some other object (or set of objects).

A *remote event* is an object that is passed from an event generator to a remote event listener to indicate that an event of a particular kind has occurred. At a minimum, a remote event contains information about the kind of event that has occurred, a reference to the object in which the event occurred, and a sequence number allowing identification of the particular instance of the event. A notification will also include an object that was supplied by the object that registered interest in the kind of event as part of the registration call.

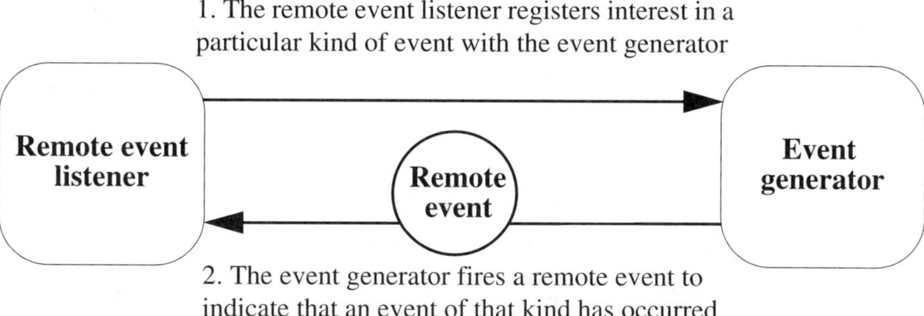

EV.2.2 Overview of the Interfaces and Classes

The event and notification interfaces introduced here define a single basic type of entity, a set of requirements on the information that needs to be handed to that entity, and some supporting interfaces and classes. All of the classes and interfaces defined in this specification are in the `net.jini.core.event` package.

The basic type is defined by the interface `RemoteEventListener`. This interface requires certain information to be passed in during the registration of interest in the kind of event that the notification is indicating. There is no single interface that defines how to register interest in such events, but the ways in which such information could be communicated will be discussed.

The supporting interfaces and classes define a `RemoteEvent` object, an `EventRegistration` object used as an identifier for registration, and a set of exceptions that can be generated.

The `RemoteEventListener` is the receiver of `RemoteEvents`, which signals that a particular kind of event has occurred. A `RemoteEventListener` is defined by an interface that contains a single method, `notify`, which informs interested listeners that an event has occurred. This method returns no value, and has parameters that contain enough information to allow the method call to be idempotent. In addition, this method will return information that was passed in during the registration of interest in the event, allowing the *registrant*, the object that registered interest with the event generator, to associate arbitrary information or actions with the notification.

The `RemoteEventListener` interface extends from the `Remote` interface, so the methods defined in `RemoteEventListener` are remote methods and objects supporting these interfaces will be passed by RMI, by reference. Other objects defined by the system will be local objects, passed by value in the remote calls.

The first of these supporting classes is `RemoteEvent`, which is sent to indicate that an event of interest has occurred in the event generator. The basic form of a `RemoteEvent` contains:

- An identifier for the kind of event in which interest has been registered
- A reference to the object in which the event occurred
- A sequence number identifying the instance of the event type
- An object that was passed in, as part of the registration of interest in the event by the registrant

These `RemoteEvent` notification objects are passed to a `RemoteEventListener` as a parameter to the `RemoteEventListener` `notify` method.

The `EventRegistration` class defines an object that returns the information needed by the registrant and is intended to be the return value of remote event registration calls. Instances of the `EventRegistration` class contain an identifier for the kind of event, the current sequence number of the kind of event, and a `Lease` object for the registration of interest.

Although there is no single interface that allows for the registration of event notifications, there are a number of requirements that would be put on any such interface if it wished to conform with the remote event registration model. In particular, any such interface should reflect:

- Event registrations are bounded in time in a way that allows those registrations to be renewed when necessary. This can easily be reflected by returning, as part of an event registration, a lease for that registration.
- Notifications need not be delivered to the entity that originally registered interest in the event. The ability to have third-party filters greatly enhances the functionality of the system. The easiest way to allow such functionality is to allow the specification of the `RemoteEventListener` to receive the notification as part of the original registration call.
- Notifications can contain a `MarshalledObject` supplied by the original registrant, allowing the passing of arbitrary information (including a closure that is to be run on notification) as part of the event notification, so the registration call should include a `MarshalledObject` that is to be passed as part of the `RemoteEvent`.

EV.2.3 Details of the Interfaces and Classes

EV.2.3.1 The RemoteEventListener Interface

The RemoteEventListener interface needs to be implemented by any object that wants to receive a notification of a RemoteEvent from some other object. The object supporting the RemoteEventListener interface does not have to be the object that originally registered interest in the occurrence of an event. To allow the notification of an event's occurrence to be sent to an entity other than the one that registered with the event generator, the registration call needs to accept a destination parameter that indicates the object to which the notification should be sent. This destination must be an object that implements the RemoteEventListener interface.

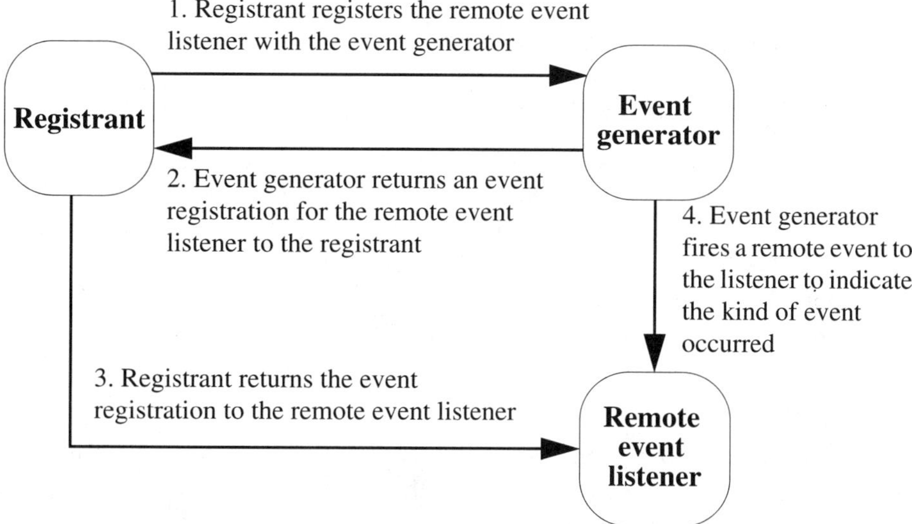

The RemoteEventListener interface extends the Remote interface (indicating that it is an interface to a Remote object) and the java.util.EventListener interface. This latter interface is used in the Java Abstract Window Toolkit (AWT) and JavaBeans components to indicate that an interface is the recipient of event

notifications. The `RemoteEventListener` interface consists of a single method, `notify`:

```
public interface RemoteEventListener extends Remote,
    java.util.EventListener
{
    void notify(RemoteEvent theEvent)
        throws UnknownEventException, RemoteException;
}
```

The `notify` method has a single parameter of type `RemoteEvent` that encapsulates the information passed as part of a notification. The `RemoteEvent` base class extends the class `java.util.EventObject` that is used in both JavaBeans components and AWT components to propagate event information. The `notify` method returns nothing but can throw exceptions.

EV.2.3.2 The RemoteEvent Class

The public part of the `RemoteEvent` class is defined as:

```
public class RemoteEvent extends java.util.EventObject {
    public RemoteEvent(Object source,long eventID,
                       long seqNum, MarshalledObject handback)
    public Object getSource () {...}
    public long getID() {...}
    public long getSequenceNumber() {...}
    public MarshalledObject getRegistrationObject() {...}
}
```

The abstract state contained in a `RemoteEvent` object includes: a reference to the object in which the event occurred, a `long` that identifies the kind of event relative to the object in which the event occurred, a `long` that indicates the sequence number of this instance of the event kind, and a `MarshalledObject` that is to be handed back when the notification occurs.

The combination of the event identifier and the object reference of the event generator obtained from the `RemoteEvent` object should uniquely identify the event type. If this type is not one in which the `RemoteEventListener` has registered interest (or in which someone else has registered interest on behalf of the `RemoteEventListener` object), an `UnknownEventException` may be generated as a return from the remote event listener's `notify` method.[1]

On receipt of an `UnknownEventException`, the caller of the `notify` method is allowed to cancel the lease for the combination of the `RemoteEventListener` instance and the kind of event that was contained in the `notify` call.

The sequence number obtained from the `RemoteEvent` object is an increasing value that can act as a hint to the number of occurrences of this event relative to some earlier sequence number. Any object that generates a `RemoteEvent` is required to ensure that for any two `RemoteEvent` objects with the same event identifier, the sequence number of those events differ if and only if the `RemoteEvent` objects are a response to different events. This guarantee is required to allow notification calls to be idempotent. A further guarantee is that if two `RemoteEvents`, *x* and *y*, come from the same source and have the same event identifier, then *x* occurred before *y* if and only if the sequence number of *x* is lower than the sequence number of *y*.

A stronger guarantee is possible for those generators of `RemoteEvents` that choose to support it. This guarantee states that not only do sequence numbers increase, but they are not skipped. In such a case, if `RemoteEvent` *x* and *y* have the same source and the same event identifier, and *x* has sequence number *m* and *y* has sequence number *n*, then if $m < n$ there were exactly $n–m–1$ events of the same event type between the event that triggered *x* and the event that triggered *y*. Such sequence numbers are said to be "fully ordered."

There are interactions between the generation of sequence numbers for a `RemoteEvent` object and the ability to see events that occur within the scope of a transaction. Those interactions are discussed in Section LEEV.2.4 "Sequence Numbers, Leasing and Transactions".

The common intent of a call to the `notify` method is to allow the recipient to find out that an occurrence of a kind of event has taken place. The call to the `notify` method is synchronous to allow the party making the call to know whether the call succeeded. However, it is not part of the semantics of the call that the notification return can be delayed while the recipient of the call reacts to the occurrence of the event. Simply put, the best strategy on the part of the recipient is to note the occurrence in some way and then return from the `notify` method as quickly as possible.

---

[1] There are cases in which the `UnknownEventException` may not be appropriate, even when the notification is for a combination of an event and a source that is not expected by the recipient. Objects that act as event mailboxes for other objects, for example, may be willing to accept any sort of notification from a particular source until explicitly told otherwise.

EV.2.3.3 The UnknownEventException

The UnknownEventException is thrown when the recipient of a RemoteEvent does not recognize the combination of the event identified and the source of the event as something in which it is interested. Throwing this exception has the effect of asking the sender to not send further notifications of this kind of event from this source in the future. This exception is defined as:

```
public class UnknownEventException extends Exception {
    public UnknownEventException() {
        super();
    }
    public UnknownEventException(String reason){
        super(reason);
    }
}
```

EV.2.3.4 An Example EventGenerator Interface

Registering interest in an event can take place in a number of ways, depending on how the event generator identifies its internal events. There is no single way of identifying the events that are reasonable for all objects and all kinds of events, and so there is no single way of registering interest in events. Because of this, there is no single interface for registration of interest.

However, the interaction between the event generator and the remote event listener does require that some initial information be passed from the registrant to the object that will make the call to its notify method.

The EventGenerator interface is an example of the kind of interface that could be used for registration of interest in events that can (logically) occur within an object. This is a remote interface that contains one method:

```
public interface EventGenerator extends Remote {
    public EventRegistration register(long evId,
                    MarshalledObject handback,
                    RemoteEventListener toInform,
                    long leaseLength)
        throws UnknownEventException, RemoteException;
}
```

The one method, register, allows registration of interest in the occurrence of an event inside the object. The method takes an evID that is used to identify the class of events, an object that is handed back as part of the notification, a reference to an

RemoteEventListener object, and a long integer indicating the leasing period for the interest registration.

The evID is a long that is obtained by a means that is not specified here. It may be returned by other interfaces or methods, or be defined by constants associated with the class or some interface implemented by the class. If an evID is supplied to this call that is not recognized by the EventGenerator object, an UnknownEventException is thrown. The use of a long to identify kinds of events is used only for illustrative purposes—objects may identify events by any number of mechanisms, including identifiers, using separate methods to allow registration in different events, or allowing various sorts of pattern matching to determine what events are of interest.

The second argument of the register method is a MarshalledObject that is to be handed back as part of the notification generated when an event of the appropriate type occurs. This object is known to the remote event listener and should contain any information that is needed by the listener to identify the event and to react to the occurrence of that event. This object will be passed back as part of the event object that is passed as an argument to the notify method. By passing a MarshalledObject into the register method, the re-creation of the object is postponed until the object is needed.

The ability to pass a MarshalledObject as part of the event registration should be common to all event registration methods. While there is no single method for identifying events in an object, the use of the pattern in which the remote event listener passes in an object that is passed back as part of the notification is central to the model of remote events presented here.

The third argument of the EventGenerator interface's register method is a RemoteEventListener implementation that is to receive event notifications. The listener may be the object that is registering interest, or it may be some other RemoteEventListener, such as a third-party event handler or notification "mailbox." The ability to specify some third-party object to handle the notification is also central to this model of event notification, and the capability of specifying the recipient of the notification is also common to all event registration interfaces.

The final argument to the register method is a long indicating the requested duration of the registration. This period is a request, and the period of interest actually granted by the event generator may be different. The actual duration of the registration lease is returned as part of the Lease object included in the EventRegistration object.

The register method returns an EventRegistration object. This object contains a long identifying the kind of event in which interest was registered (relative to the object granting the registration), a reference to the object granting the registration, and a Lease object.

EV.2.3.5 The `EventRegistration` Class

Objects of the class `EventRegistration` are meant to encapsulate the information the client needs to identify a notification as a response to a registration request and to maintain that registration request. It is not necessary for a method that allows event interest registration to return an `EventRegistration` object. However, the class does show the kind of information that needs to be returned in the event model.

The public parts of this class look like

```
public class EventRegistration implements java.io.Serializable
{
    public EventRegistration(long eventID,
                             Object eventSource,
                             Lease eventLease,
                             long seqNum) {...}
    public long getID() {...}
    public Object getSource() {...}
    public Lease getLease() {...}
    public long getSequenceNumber() {...}
}
```

The `getID` method returns the identifier of the event in which interest was registered. This, combined with the return value returned by `getSource`, will uniquely identify the kind of event. This information is needed to hand off to third-party repositories to allow them to recognize the event and route it correctly if they are to receive notifications of those events.

The result of the `EventRegistration.getID` method should be the same as the result of the `RemoteEvent.getID` method, and the result of the `EventRegistration.getSource` method should be the same as the `RemoteEvent.getSource` method.

The `getSource` method returns a reference to the event generator, which is used in combination with the result of the `getID` method to uniquely identify an event.

The `getLease` returns the `Lease` object for this registration. It is used in lease maintenance.

The `getSequenceNumber` method returns the value of the sequence number on the event kind that was current when the registration was granted, allowing comparison with the sequence number in any subsequent notifications.

EV.2.4 Sequence Numbers, Leasing and Transactions

There are cases in which event registrations are allowed within the scope of a transaction, in such a way that the notifications of these events can occur within the scope of the transaction. This means that other participants in the transaction may see some events whose visibility is hidden by the transaction from entities outside of the transaction. This has an effect on the generation of sequence numbers and the duration of an event registration lease.

An event registration that occurs within a transaction is considered to be scoped by that transaction. This means that any occurrence of the kind of event of interest that happens as part of the transaction will cause a notification to be sent to the recipients indicated by the registration that occurred in the transaction. Such events must have a separate event identification number (the `long` returned in the `RemoteEvent getID` method) to allow third-party store-and-forward entities to distinguish between an event that happens within a transaction and those that happen outside of the transaction. Notifications of these events will not be sent to entities that registered interest in this kind of event outside the scope of the transaction until and unless the transaction is committed.

Because of this isolation requirement of transactions, notifications sent from inside a transaction will have a different sequence number than the notifications of the same events would have outside of the transaction. Within a transaction, all `RemoteEvent` objects for a given kind of event are given a sequence number relative to the transaction, even if the event that triggered the `RemoteEvent` occurs outside of the scope of the transaction (but is visible within the transaction). One counter-intuitive effect of this is that an object could register for notification of some event *E* both outside a transaction and within a transaction, and receive two distinct `RemoteEvent` objects with different sequence numbers for the same event. One of the `RemoteEvent` objects would contain the event with a sequence number relative to the transaction, while the other would contain the event with a sequence number relative to the source object.

The other effect of transactions on event registrations is to limit the duration of a lease. A registration of interest in some kind of event that occurs within the scope of a transaction should be leased in the same way as other event interest registrations. However, the duration of the registration is the minimum of the length of the lease and the duration of the transaction. Simply put, when the transaction ends (either because of a commit or a rollback), the interest registration also ends. This is true even if the lease for the event registration has not expired and no call has been made to `cancel` the lease.

It is still reasonable to lease event interest registrations, even in the scope of a transaction, because the requested lease may be shorter than the transaction in

question. However, no such interest registration will survive the transaction in which it occurs.

EV.2.5 Serialized Forms

Class	serialVersionUID	Serialized Fields
RemoteEvent	1777278867291906446L	Object source long eventID long seqNum MarshalledObject handback
UnknownEventException	5563758083292687048L	*none*
EventRegistration	4055207527458053347L	Object source long eventID Lease lease long seqNum

EV.3 Third-Party Objects

ONE of the basic reasons for the event design is to allow the production of third-party objects, or "agents," that can be used to enhance a system built using distributed events and notifications. Now we will look at three examples of such agents, which allow various forms of enhanced functionality without changing the basic interfaces. Each of these agents may be thought of as *distributed event adapters*.

The first example we will look at is a *store-and-forward agent*. The purpose of this object is to act on behalf of the event generator, allowing the event generator to send the notification to one entity (the store-and-forward agent) that will forward the notification to all of the event listeners, perhaps with a particular policy that allows a failed delivery attempt to be retried at some later date.

The second example, which we will call a *notification filter*, is an object that may be local to either the event generator or the event listener. This agent gets the notification and spawns a thread that will respond, using a method supplied by the object that originally registered interest in events of that kind.

The final object is a *notification mailbox*. This mailbox will store notifications for another object (a remote event listener) until that object requests that the notifications be delivered. This design allows the listener object that registered interest in the event type to select the times at which a notification can be delivered without losing any notifications that would have otherwise have been delivered. Please note that complete specifications for such services do exist and may differ in some degree from this example.

EV.3.1 Store-and-Forward Agents

A store-and-forward agent enables the object generating a notification to hand off the actual notification of those who have registered interest to a separate object.

This agent can implement various policies for reliability. For example, the agent could try to deliver the notification once (or a small number of times) and, if that call fails, not try again. Or the agent could try and, on notification failure, try again at a preset or computed interval of time for some known period of time. Either way, the object in which the event occurred could avoid worrying about the

delivery of notifications, needing to notify only the store-and-forward agent (which might be on the same machine and hence more reliably available).

From the point of view of the remote event listener, there is no difference between the notification delivered by a store-and-forward agent and one delivered directly from the object in which the event that generated the original notification occurred. This transparency allows the decision to use a store-and-forward agent to be made by the object generating the notification, independent of the object receiving the notification. There is no need for distributed agreement; all that is required is that the object using the agent know about the agent.

A store-and-forward agent is used by an object that generates notifications. When an object registers interest in receiving notifications of a particular event type, the object receiving that registration will pass the registration along to the store-and-forward agent. This agent will keep track of which objects need to be notified of events that occur in the original object.

When an event of interest occurs in the original object, it need send only a single notification to the store-and-forward agent. This notification can return immediately, with processing further happening inside the store-and-forward agent. The object in which the event of interest occurred will now be freed from informing those that registered interest in the event.

Notification is taken over by the store-and-forward agent. This agent will now consult the list of entities that have registered interest in the occurrence of an event and send a notification to those entities. Note that these might not be the same as the objects that registered interest in the event; the object that should receive the event notification is specified during the event interest registration.

The store-and-forward agent might be able to make use of network-level multicast (assuming that the `RemoteEvent` object to be returned is identical for multiple recipients of the `notify` call), or might send a separate notification to each of the entities that have registered interest. Different store-and-forward agents could implement different levels of service, from a simple agent that sends a notification and doesn't care whether the notification is actually delivered (for example, one that simply caught `RemoteExceptions` and discards them) to agents that will repeatedly try to send the notification, perhaps using different fallback strategies, until the notification is known to be successful or some number of tries have been attempted.

The store-and-forward agent does not need to know anything about the kinds of events that are triggering the notifications that it stores and forwards. All that is needed is that the agent implement the `RemoteEventListener` interface and some interface that allows the object producing the initial notification to register with the agent. This combination of interfaces allows such a service to be offered to any number of different objects without having to know anything about the possible changes in abstract state that might be of interest in those objects.

Note that the interface used by the object generating the original notifications to register with the store-and-forward agent does not need to be standard. Different qualities of service concerning the delivery of notifications may require different registration protocols. Whether or not the relationship between the notification originator and the store-and-forward agent is leased or not is also up to the implementation of the agent. If the relationship is leased, lease renewal requests would need to be forwarded to the agent.

In fact, an expected pattern of implementation would be to place a store-and-forward agent on every machine on which objects were running that could produce events. This agent, which could be running in a separate JVM (on hardware that supported multiple processes) could off-load the notification-generating objects from the need to send those notifications to all objects that had registered interest. It would also allow for consistent handling of delivery guarantees across all objects on a particular machine. Since the store-and-forward agent is on the same machine as the objects using the agent, the possibilities of partial failure brought about by network problems (which wouldn't affect communication between objects on the same machine) and server machine failure (which would induce total, rather than partial, failure in this case) are limited. This allows the reliability of notifications to be off-loaded to these agents instead of being a problem that needs to be solved by all of the objects using the notification interfaces.

A store-and-forward agent does require an interface that allows the agent to know what notifications it is supposed to send, the destinations of those notifications, and on whose behalf those notifications are being sent. Since it is the store-and-forward agent that is directing notification calls to the individual recipients, the agent will also need to hold the `Object` (if any) that was passed in during interest registration to be returned as part of the `RemoteEvent` object.

In addition, the store-and-forward agent could be the issuer of `Lease` objects to the object registering interest in some event. This could offload any lease renewal calls from the original recipient of the registration call, which would need to know only when there were no more interest registrations of a particular event kind remaining in the store-and-forward agent.

EV.3.2 Notification Filters

Similar to a store-and-forward agent is a notification filter, which can be used by either the generator of a notification or the recipient to intercept notification calls, do processing on those calls, and act in accord with that processing (perhaps forwarding the notification, or even generating new notifications).

Again, such filters are made possible because of the uniform signature of the method used to send all notifications and because of the ability of an object to

indicate the recipient of a notification when registering for a notification. This uniformity and indirection allow the composition of third-party entities. A filter could receive events from a store-and-forward agent without the client of the original registration knowing about the store-and-forward agent or the server in which the notifications are generated knowing about the filter. This composition can be extended further; store-and-forward agents could use other store-and-forward agents, and filters can themselves receive notifications from other filters.

EV.3.2.1 Notification Multiplexing

One example of such a filter is one that can be used to concentrate notifications in a way to help minimize network traffic. If a number of different objects on a single machine are all interested in some particular kind of event, it could make sense to create a notification filter that would register interest in the event. When a notification was received by the filter, it would forward the notification to each of the (machine local) objects that had expressed interest.

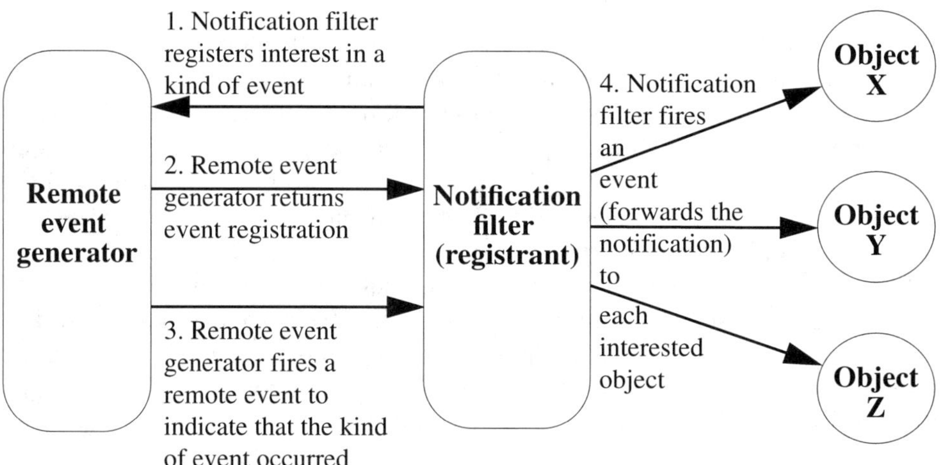

EV.3.2.2 Notification Demultiplexing

Another example of such a filter is an object that generates an event in response to a series of events that it has received. There might be an object that is interested only in some particular sequence of events in some other object or group of objects. This object could register interest in all of the different kinds of events, asking that the notifications be sent to a filter. The purpose of the filter is to receive the notifications and, when the notifications fit the desired pattern (as determined by some class passed in from the object that has asked the notifications be sent to the filter), generate some new notification that is delivered to the client object.

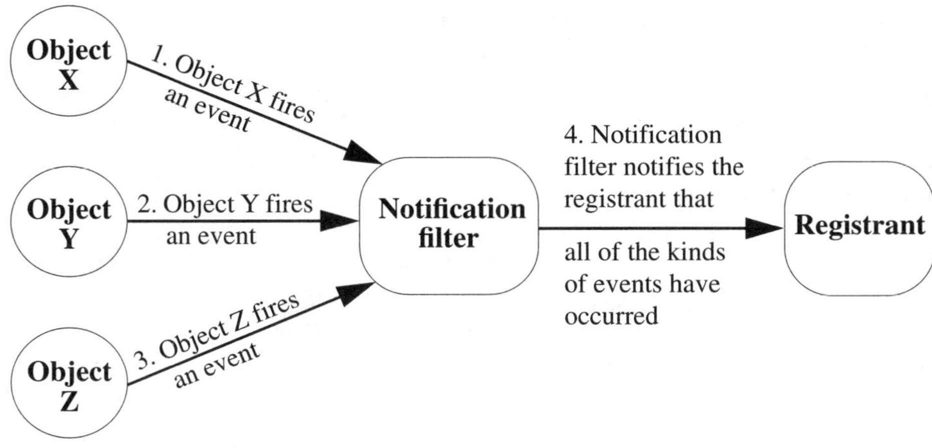

EV.3.3 Notification Mailboxes

The purpose of a notification mailbox is to store the notifications sent to an object until such time as the object for which the notifications were intended desires delivery.

Such delivery can be in a single batch, with the mailbox storing any notifications received after the last request for delivery until the next request is received. Alternatively, a notification mailbox can be viewed as a faucet, with notifications turned on (delivering any that have arrived since the notifications were last turned off) and then delivering any subsequent notifications to an object immediately, until told by that object to hold the notifications.

The ability to have notification mailboxes is important in a system that allows objects to be deactivated (for example, to be saved to stable storage in such a way that they are no longer taking up any computing resource) and re-activated. The usual mechanism for activating an object is a method call. Such activation can be expensive in both time and computing resources; it is often too expensive to be justified for the receipt of what would otherwise be an asynchronous event notification. An event mailbox can be used to ensure that an object will not be activated merely to handle an event notification.

Use of a mailbox is simple; the object registering interest in receiving an event notification simply gives the mailbox as the place to send the notifications. The mailbox can be made responsible for renewing leases while an object is inactive,

and for storing all (or the most recent, or the most recent and the count of other) notifications for each type of event of interest to the object. When the object indicates that it wishes to receive any notifications from the mailbox, those notifications can be delivered. Delivery can continue until the object requests storage to occur again, or storage can resume automatically.

Such a mailbox is a type of filter. In this case, however, the mailbox filters over time rather than over events. A pure mailbox need not be concerned with the kinds of notifications that it stores. It simply holds the `RemoteEvent` objects until they are wanted.

It is because of mailboxes and other client-side filters that the information returned from an event registration needs to include a way of identifying the event and the source of the event. Such client-side agents need a way of distinguishing between the events they are expected to receive and those that should generate an exception to the sender. This distinction cannot be made without some simple way of identifying the event and the object of origin.

EV.3.4 Compositionality

All of the above third-party entities work because of two simple features of the `RemoteEventListener` interface:

- There is a single method, `notify`, that passes a single type of object, `RemoteEvent` (or a subtype of that object) for all notifications
- There is a level of indirection in delivery allowed by the separate specification of a recipient in the registration method that allows the client of that call to specify a third-party object to contact for notifications

The first of these features allows the composition of notification handlers to be chained, beginning with the object that generates the notification. Since the ultimate recipient of the event is known to be expecting the event through a call to the single `notify` method, other entities can be composed and interposed in the call chain as long as they produce this call with the right `RemoteEvent` object (which will include a field indicating the object at which the notification originated). Because there is a single method call for all notifications, third-party handlers can be produced to accept notifications of events without having to know the kind of event that has occurred or any other detail of the event.

Compositionality in the other direction (driven by the recipient of the notification) is enabled by allowing the object registering interest to indicate the first in an arbitrary chain of third parties to receive the notification. Thus the recipient can build a chain of filters, mailboxes, and forwarding agents to allow any sort of delivery policy that object desires, and then register interest with an indication that all notifications should be delivered to the beginning of that chain. From the point of view of the object in which the notification originates, the series of objects the notification then goes through is unknown and irrelevant.

EV.4 Integration with JavaBeans Components

As we noted previously, distributed notification differs from local notification (such as the notification used in user interface programming) in a number of ways. In particular, a distributed notification may be delayed, dropped, or otherwise fail between the object in which the event occurred and the object that is the ultimate recipient of the notification of that event. Additionally, a distributed event notification may require handling by a number of third-party objects between the object that is interested in the notification and the object that generates the notification. These third-party objects need to be able to handle arbitrary events, and so from the point of view of the type system, all of the events must be delivered in the same fashion.

Although this model differs from the event model used for user interface tools such as the AWT or Java Foundation Classes (JFC), such a difference in model is to be expected. The event model for such user interface toolkits was never meant to allow the components that communicate using these local event notifications to be distributed across virtual or physical machines; indeed, such systems assume that the event delivery will be fast, reliable, and not open to the kinds of partial failures or delays that are common in the distributed case.

In between the requirements of a local event model and the distributed event model presented here is the event model used by software components to communicate changes in state. The delegation event model, which is the event model for JavaBeans components, written in the Java programming language, is built as an extension of the event model used for AWT and JFC. This is completely appropriate, as most JavaBeans components will be located in a single address space and can assume that the communication of events between components will meet the reliability and promptness requirements of that model.

However, it is also possible that JavaBeans components will be distributed across virtual, and even physical, machines. The assumption that the event propagation will be either fast or reliable can lead to subtle program errors that will not be found until the components are deployed (perhaps on a slow or unreliable network). In such case, an event and notification model such as that found in this specification is more appropriate.

One approach would be to add a second event model to the JavaBeans component specification that dealt only with distributed events. While this would have the advantage of exporting the difference between local and remote components to the component builder, it would also complicate the JavaBeans component model unnecessarily.

We will show how the current distributed event model can be fit into the existing Java platform's event model. While the mapping is not perfect (nor can it be, since there are essential differences between the two models), it will allow the current tools used to assemble JavaBeans components to be used when those components are distributed.

EV.4.1 Differences with the JavaBeans Component Event Model

The JavaBeans component event model is derived from the event model used in the AWT in the Java platform. The model is characterized by:

- Propagation of event notifications from sources to listeners by Java technology method invocations on the target listener objects
- Identification of the kind of event notification by using a different method in the listener being called for each kind of event
- Encapsulation of any state associated with an event notification in an object that inherits from `java.util.EventObject` and that is passed as the sole argument of the notification method
- Identification of event sources by the convention of those sources defining registration methods, one for each kind of event in which interest can be registered, that follow a particular design pattern

The distributed event and notification model that we have defined is similar in a number of ways:

- Distributed event propagation is accomplished by the use of `Remote` methods.
- State passed as part of the notification is encapsulated in an object that is derived from `java.util.EventObject` and is passed as the sole argument of the notification method.
- The `RemoteEventListener` interface extends the more basic interface `java.util.EventListener`.

However, there are also differences between the JavaBeans component event model and the distributed event model proposed here:

- Identification of the kind of event is accomplished by passing an identifier from the source of the notification to the listener; the combination of the object in which the event occurred and the identifier uniquely identifies the kind of event.
- Notifications are accomplished through a single method, `notify`, defined in the `RemoteEventListener` interface rather than by a different method for each kind of event.
- Registration of interest in a kind of event is for a (perhaps renewable) period of time, rather than being for a period of time bound by the active cancellation of interest.
- Objects registering interest in an event can, as part of that registration, include an object that will be passed back to the recipient of the notification when an event of the appropriate type occurs.

Most of these differences in the two models can be directly traced to the distributed nature of the events and notifications defined in this specification.

For example, as you have seen, reliability and recovery of the distributed notification model is based on the ability to create third-party objects that can provide those guarantees. However, for those third-party objects to be able to work in general cases, the signature for a notification must be the same for all of the event notifications that are to be handled by that third party. If we were to follow the JavaBeans component model of having a different method for each kind of event notification, third party objects would need to support every possible notification method, including those that had not yet been defined when the third-party object was implemented. This is clearly impossible.

Note that this is not a weakness in the JavaBeans component event model, merely a difference required by the different environments in which the event models are assumed to be used. The JavaBeans component event model, like the AWT model on which it is based, assumes that the event notification is being passed between objects in the same address space. Such notifications do not need various delivery and reliability guarantees—delivery can be considered to be (virtually) instantaneous and can be assumed to be fully reliable.

Being able to send event notifications through a single `Remote` method also requires that the events be identified in some way other than the signature of the notification delivery method. This leads to the inclusion of an event identifier in the event object. Since the generation of these event identifiers cannot be guaranteed to be globally unique across all of the objects in a distributed system, they

must be made relative to the object in which they are generated, thus requiring the combination of the object of origin and the event identifier to completely identify the kind of event.

The sequence number being included in the event object is also an outgrowth of the distributed nature of the interfaces. Since no distributed mechanism can guarantee reliability, there is always the possibility that a particular notification will not be delivered, or could be delivered more than once by some notification agent. This is not a problem in the single-address-space environment of AWT and JavaBeans components, but requires the inclusion of a sequence number in the distributed case.

EV.4.2 Converting Distributed Events to JavaBeans Component Events

Translating between the event models is fairly straightforward. All that is required is:

- Allow an event listener to map from a distributed event listener to the appropriate call to a notification method
- Allow creation of a `RemoteEvent` from the event object passed in the JavaBeans component event notification method
- Allow creation of a JavaBeans component event object from a `RemoteEvent` object without loss of information

Each of these is fairly straightforward and can be accomplished in a number of ways.

More complex matings of the two systems could be undertaken, including third-party objects that keep track of the interest registrations made by remote objects and implement the corresponding JavaBeans component event notification methods by making the remote calls to the `RemoteEventListener notify` method with properly constructed `RemoteEvent` objects. Such objects would need to keep track of the event sequence numbers and would need to deal with the additional failure modes that are inherent in distributed calls. However, their implementation would be fairly straightforward and would fit into the JavaBeans component model of event adapters.

TX

Transaction

TX.1 Introduction

TRANSACTIONS are a fundamental tool for many kinds of computing. A transaction allows a set of operations to be grouped in such a way that they either all succeed or all fail; further, the operations in the set appear from outside the transaction to occur simultaneously. Transactional behaviors are especially important in distributed computing, where they provide a means for enforcing consistency over a set of operations on one or more remote participants. If all the participants are members of a transaction, one response to a remote failure is to abort the transaction, thereby ensuring that no partial results are written.

Traditional transaction systems often center around transaction processing monitors that ensure that the correct implementation of transactional semantics is provided by all of the participants in a transaction. Our approach to transactional semantics is somewhat different. Within our system we leave it to the individual objects that take part in a transaction to implement the transactional semantics in the way that is best for that kind of object. What the system primarily provides is the coordination mechanism that those objects can use to communicate the information necessary for the set of objects to agree on the transaction. The goal of this system is to provide the *minimal* set of protocols and interfaces that *allow* objects to implement transaction semantics rather than the *maximal* set of interfaces, protocols, and policies that *ensure* the correctness of any possible transaction semantics. So the completion protocol is separate from the semantics of particular transactions.

This document presents this completion protocol, which consists of a two-phase commit protocol for distributed transactions. The two-phase commit protocol defines the communication patterns that allow distributed objects and resources to wrap a set of operations in such a way that they appear to be a single operation. The protocol requires a manager that will enable consistent resolution of the operations by a guarantee that all participants will eventually know whether they should commit the operations (roll forward) or abort them (roll backward). A participant can be any object that supports the participant contract by implementing the appropriate interface. Participants are not limited to databases or other persistent storage services.

Clients and servers will also need to depend on specific transaction semantics. The default transaction semantics for participants is also defined in this document.

The two-phase commit protocol presented here, while common in many traditional transaction systems, has the potential to be used in more than just traditional transaction processing applications. Since the semantics of the individual operations and the mechanisms that are used to ensure various properties of the meta-operation joined by the protocol are left up to the individual objects, variations of the usual properties required by transaction processing systems are possible using this protocol, as long as those variances can be resolved by this protocol. A group of objects could use the protocol, for example, as part of a process allowing synchronization of data that have been allowed to drift for efficiency reasons. While this use is not generally considered to be a classical use of transactions, the protocol defined here could be used for this purpose. Some variations will not be possible under these protocols, requiring subinterfaces and subclasses of the ones provided or entirely new interfaces and classes.

Because of the possibility of application to situations that are beyond the usual use of transactions, calling the two-phase commit protocol a transaction mechanism is somewhat misleading. However, since the most common use of such a protocol is in a transactional setting, and because we do define a particular set of default transaction semantics, we will follow the usual naming conventions used in such systems rather than attempting to invent a new, parallel vocabulary.

The classes and interfaces defined by this specification are in the packages `net.jini.core.transaction` and `net.jini.core.transaction.server`. In this document you will usually see these types used without a package prefix; as each type is defined, the package it is in is specified.

TX.1.1 Model and Terms

A transaction is created and overseen by a *manager*. Each manager implements the interface `TransactionManager`. Each *transaction* is represented by a `long` identifier that is unique with respect to the transaction's manager.

Semantics are represented by *semantic* transaction objects, such as the ones that represent the default semantics for services. Even though the manager needs to know only how to complete transactions, clients and participants need to share a common view of the semantics of the transaction. Therefore clients typically create, pass, and operate on semantic objects that contain the transaction identifier instead of using the transaction's identifier directly, and transactable services typically accept parameters of a particular semantic type, such as the `Transaction` interface used for the default semantics.

As shown in Figure AR.1.1, a *client* asks the manager to create a transaction, typically by using a semantic factory class such as `TransactionFactory` to create a semantic object. The semantic object created is then passed as a parameter when performing operations on a service. If the service is to accept this transaction and govern its operations thereby, it must *join* the transaction as a *participant.* Participants in a transaction must implement the `TransactionParticipant` interface. Particular operations associated with a given transaction are said to be *performed under* that transaction. The client that created the transaction might or might not be a participant in the transaction.

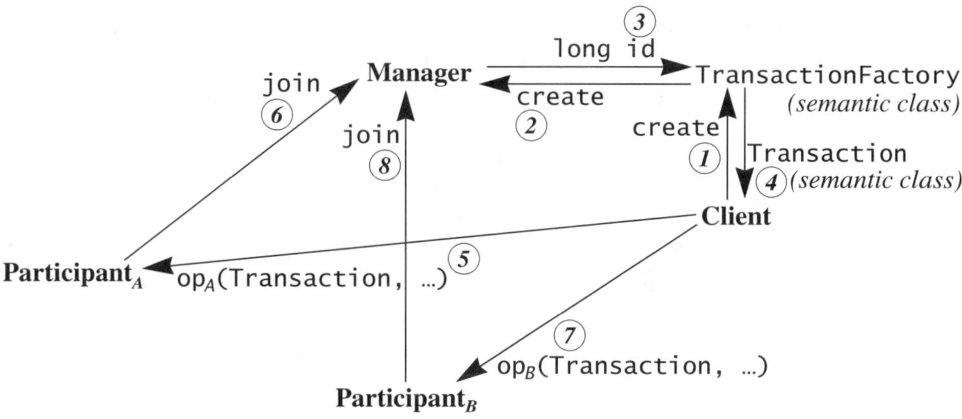

FIGURE TX.1.1: ***Transaction Creation and Use***

A transaction *completes* when any entity either *commits* or *aborts* the transaction. If a transaction commits successfully, then all operations performed under that transaction will complete. Aborting a transaction means that all operations performed under that transaction will appear never to have happened.

Committing a transaction requires each participant to *vote,* where a vote is either *prepared* (ready to commit), *not changed* (read-only), or *aborted* (the transaction should be aborted). If all participants vote "prepared" or "not changed," the transaction manager will tell each "prepared" participant to *roll forward,* thus committing the changes. Participants that voted "not changed" need do nothing more. If the transaction is ever aborted, the participants are told to *roll back* any changes made under the transaction.

TX.1.2 Distributed Transactions and ACID Properties

The two-phase commit protocol is designed to enable objects to provide ACID properties. The default transaction semantics define one way to preserve these properties. The ACID properties are:

- *Atomicity:* All the operations grouped under a transaction occur or none of them do. The protocol allows participants to discover which of these alternatives is expected by the other participants in the protocol. However, it is up to the individual object to determine whether it wishes to operate in concert with the other participants.
- *Consistency:* The completion of a transaction must leave the system in a consistent state. Consistency includes issues known only to humans, such as that an employee should always have a manager. The enforcement of consistency is outside of the realm of the transaction itself—a transaction is a tool to allow consistency guarantees and not itself a guarantor of consistency.
- *Isolation:* Ongoing transactions should not affect each other. Participants in a transaction should see only intermediate states resulting from the operations of their own transaction, not the intermediate states of other transactions. The protocol allows participating objects to know what operations are being done within the scope of a transaction. However, it is up to the individual object to determine if such operations are to be reflected only within the scope of the transaction or can be seen by others who are not participating in the transaction.
- *Durability:* The results of a transaction should be as persistent as the entity on which the transaction commits. However, such guarantees are up to the implementation of the object.

The dependency on the participant's implementation for the ACID properties is the greatest difference between this two-phase commit protocol and more traditional transaction processing systems. Such systems attempt to ensure that the ACID properties are met and go to considerable trouble to ensure that no participant can violate any of the properties.

This approach differs for both philosophical and practical reasons. The philosophical reason is centered on a basic tenet of object-oriented programming, which is that the implementation of an object should be hidden from any part of the system outside the object. Ensuring the ACID properties generally requires that an object's implementation correspond to certain patterns. We believe that if these properties are needed, the object (or, more precisely, the programmer implementing the object) will know best how to guarantee the properties. For this reason, the manager is solely concerned with completing transactions properly. Clients and participants must agree on semantics separately.

The practical reason for leaving the ACID properties up to the object is that there are situations in which only some of the ACID properties make sense, but that can still make use of the two-phase commit protocol. A group of transient objects might wish to group a set of operations in such a way that they appear atomic; in such a situation it makes little sense to require that the operations be durable. An object might want to enable the monitoring of the state of some long-running transactions; such monitoring would violate the isolation requirement of the ACID properties. Binding the two-phase commit protocol to all of these properties limits the use of such a protocol.

We also know that particular semantics are needed for particular services. The default transaction semantics provide useful general-purpose semantics built on the two-phase commit completion protocol.

Distributed transactions differ from single-system transactions in the same way that distributed computing differs from single-system computing. The clearest difference is that a single system can have a single view of the state of several services. It is possible in a single system to make it appear to any observer that all operations performed under a transaction have occurred or none have, thereby achieving isolation. In other words, no observer will ever see only part of the changes made under the transaction. In a distributed system it is possible for a client using two servers to see the committed state of a transaction in one server and the pre-committed state of the same transaction in another server. This can be prevented only by coordination with the transaction manager or the client that committed the transaction. Coordination between clients is outside the scope of this specification.

TX.1.3 Requirements

The transaction system has the following requirements:

- Define types and contracts that allow the two-phase commit protocol to govern operations on multiple servers of differing types or implementations.
- Allow participation in the two-phase commit protocol by any object in the Java programming language, where "participation" means to perform operations on that object under a given transaction.
- Each participant may provide ACID properties with respect to that participant to observers operating under a given transaction.

- Use standard Java programming language techniques and tools to accomplish these goals. Specifically, transactions will rely upon Java Remote Method Invocation (RMI) to communicate between participants.
- Define specific default transaction semantics for use by services.

TX.2 The Two-Phase Commit Protocol

THE two-phase commit protocol is defined using three primary types:

- `TransactionManager`: A transaction manager creates new transactions and coordinates the activities of the participants.
- `NestableTransactionManager`: Some transaction managers are capable of supporting nested transactions.
- `TransactionParticipant`: When an operation is performed under a transaction, the participant must join the transaction, providing the manager with a reference to a `TransactionParticipant` object that will be asked to vote, roll forward, or roll back.

The following types are imported from other packages and are referenced in unqualified form in the rest of this specification:

```
java.rmi.Remote
java.rmi.RemoteException
java.rmi.NoSuchObjectException
java.io.Serializable
net.jini.core.lease.LeaseDeniedException
net.jini.core.lease.Lease
```

All the methods defined to throw `RemoteException` will do so in the circumstances described by the RMI specification.

Each type is defined where it is first described. Each method is described where it occurs in the lifecycle of the two-phase commit protocol. All methods, fields, and exceptions that can occur during the lifecycle of the protocol will be specified. The section in which each method or field is specified is shown in a comment, using the § abbreviation for the word "section."

TX.2.1 Starting a Transaction

The `TransactionManager` interface is implemented by servers that manage the two-phase commit protocol:

```
package net.jini.core.transaction.server;

public interface TransactionManager
    extends Remote, TransactionConstants // §TX.2.4
{
    public static class Created implements Serializable {
        public final long id;
        public final Lease lease;
        public Created(long id, Lease lease) {…}
    }
    Created create(long leaseFor) // §TX.2.1
        throws LeaseDeniedException, RemoteException;
    void join(long id, TransactionParticipant part,
              long crashCount) // §TX.2.3
        throws UnknownTransactionException,
               CannotJoinException, CrashCountException,
               RemoteException;
    int getState(long id) // §TX.2.7
        throws UnknownTransactionException, RemoteException;
    void commit(long id) // §TX.2.5
        throws UnknownTransactionException,
               CannotCommitException,
               RemoteException;
    void commit(long id, long waitFor) // §TX.2.5
        throws UnknownTransactionException,
               CannotCommitException,
               TimeoutExpiredException, RemoteException;
    void abort(long id) // §TX.2.5
        throws UnknownTransactionException,
               CannotAbortException,
               RemoteException;
    void abort(long id, long waitFor) // §TX.2.5
        throws UnknownTransactionException,
               CannotAbortException,
               TimeoutExpiredException, RemoteException;
}
```

A client obtains a reference to a `TransactionManager` object via a lookup service or some other means. The details of obtaining such a reference are outside the scope of this specification.

A client creates a new transaction by invoking the manager's `create` method, providing a desired `leaseFor` time in milliseconds. This invocation is typically indirect via creating a semantic object. The time is the client's expectation of how long the transaction will last before it completes. The manager may grant a shorter lease or may deny the request by throwing `LeaseDeniedException`. If the granted lease expires or is cancelled before the transaction manager receives a `commit` or `abort` of the transaction, the manager will abort the transaction.

The purpose of the `Created` nested class is to allow the `create` method to return two values: the transaction identifier and the granted lease. The constructor simply sets the two fields from its parameters.

TX.2.2 Starting a Nested Transaction

The `TransactionManager.create` method returns a new *top-level* transaction. Managers that implement just the `TransactionManager` interface support only top-level transactions. *Nested* transactions, also known as *subtransactions*, can be created using managers that implement the `NestableTransactionManager` interface:

```
package net.jini.core.transaction.server;

public interface NestableTransactionManager
    extends TransactionManager
{
    TransactionManager.Created
        create(NestableTransactionManager parentMgr,
                long parentID, long leaseFor) // §TX.2.2
        throws UnknownTransactionException,
                CannotJoinException, LeaseDeniedException,
                RemoteException;
    void promote(long id, TransactionParticipant[] parts,
                 long[] crashCounts,
                 TransactionParticipant drop)
        throws UnknownTransactionException,
                CannotJoinException, CrashCountException,
                RemoteException; // §TX.2.7
}
```

The `create` method takes a *parent* transaction—represented by the manager for the parent transaction and the identifier for that transaction—and a desired lease time in milliseconds, and returns a new *nested* transaction that is *enclosed by* the specified parent along with the granted lease.

When you use a nested transaction you allow changes to a set of objects to abort without forcing an abort of the parent transaction, and you allow the commit of those changes to still be conditional on the commit of the parent transaction.

When a nested transaction is created, its manager joins the parent transaction. When the two managers are different, this is done explicitly via `join` (see Section TX.2.3 "Joining a Transaction"). When the two managers are the same, this may be done in a manager-specific fashion.

The `create` method throws `UnknownTransactionException` if the parent transaction is unknown to the parent transaction manager, either because the transaction ID is incorrect or because the transaction is no longer active and its state has been discarded by the manager.

```
package net.jini.core.transaction;

public class UnknownTransactionException
    extends TransactionException
{
    public UnknownTransactionException() {…}
    public UnknownTransactionException(String desc) {…}
}

public class TransactionException extends Exception {
    public TransactionException() {…}
    public TransactionException(String desc) {…}
}
```

The `create` method throws `CannotJoinException` if the parent transaction is known to the manager but is no longer active.

```
package net.jini.core.transaction;

public class CannotJoinException extends TransactionException
{
    public CannotJoinException() {…}
    public CannotJoinException(String desc) {…}
}
```

TX.2.3 Joining a Transaction

The first time a client tells a participant to perform an operation under a given transaction, the participant must invoke the transaction manager's `join` method with an object that implements the `TransactionParticipant` interface. This object will be used by the manager to communicate with the participant about the transaction.

```
package net.jini.core.transaction.server;

public interface TransactionParticipant
    extends Remote, TransactionConstants // §TX.2.4
{
    int prepare(TransactionManager mgr, long id) // §TX.2.6
        throws UnknownTransactionException, RemoteException;
    void commit(TransactionManager mgr, long id) // §TX.2.6
        throws UnknownTransactionException, RemoteException;
    void abort(TransactionManager mgr, long id) // §TX.2.6
        throws UnknownTransactionException, RemoteException;
    int prepareAndCommit(TransactionManager mgr, long id)
                                                  // §TX.2.7
        throws UnknownTransactionException, RemoteException;
}
```

If the participant's invocation of the `join` method throws `RemoteException`, the participant should not perform the operation requested by the client and should rethrow the exception or otherwise signal failure to the client.

The `join` method's third parameter is a *crash count* that uniquely defines the version of the participant's storage that holds the state of the transaction. Each time the participant loses the state of that storage (because of a system crash if the storage is volatile, for example) it must change this count. For example, the participant could store the crash count in stable storage.

When a manager receives a `join` request, it checks to see if the participant has already joined the transaction. If it has, and the crash count is the same as the one specified in the original `join`, the `join` is accepted but is otherwise ignored. If the crash count is different, the manager throws `CrashCountException` and forces the transaction to abort.

```
package net.jini.core.transaction.server;

public class CrashCountException extends TransactionException
{
```

```
        public CrashCountException() {…}
        public CrashCountException(String desc) {…}
    }
```

The participant should reflect this exception back to the client. This check makes `join` idempotent when it should be, but forces an abort for a second `join` of a transaction by a participant that has no knowledge of the first `join` and hence has lost whatever changes were made after the first `join`.

An invocation of `join` can throw `UnknownTransactionException`, which means the transaction is unknown to the manager, either because the transaction ID was incorrect, or because the transaction is no longer active and its state has been discarded by the manager. The `join` method throws `CannotJoinException` if the transaction is known to the manager but is no longer active. In either case the `join` has failed, and the method that was attempted under the transaction should reflect the exception back to the client. This is also the proper response if `join` throws a `NoSuchObjectException`.

TX.2.4 Transaction States

The `TransactionConstants` interface defines constants used in the communication between managers and participants.

```
package net.jini.core.transaction.server;

public interface TransactionConstants {
    int ACTIVE = 1;
    int VOTING = 2;
    int PREPARED = 3;
    int NOTCHANGED = 4;
    int COMMITTED = 5;
    int ABORTED = 6;
}
```

These correspond to the states and votes that participants and managers go through during the lifecycle of a given transaction.

TX.2.5 Completing a Transaction: The Client's View

In the client's view, a transaction goes through the following states:

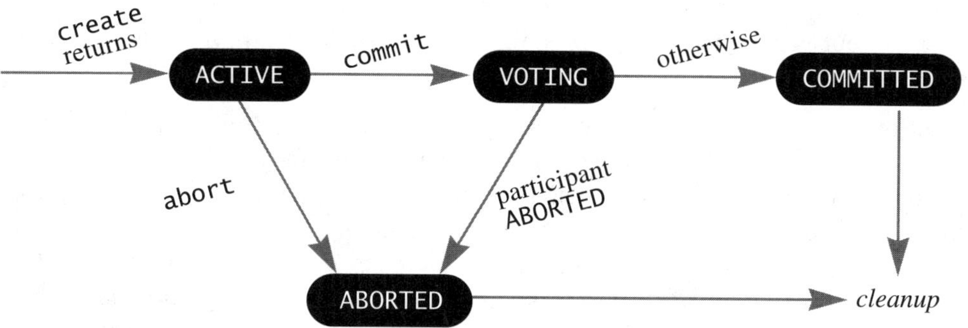

For the client, the transaction starts out `ACTIVE` as soon as `create` returns. The client drives the transaction to completion by invoking `commit` or `abort` on the transaction manager, or by cancelling the lease or letting the lease expire (both of which are equivalent to an `abort`).

The one-parameter `commit` method returns as soon as the transaction successfully reaches the `COMMITTED` state, or if the transaction is known to have previously reached that state due to an earlier `commit`. If the transaction reaches the `ABORTED` state, or is known to have previously reached that state due to an earlier `commit` or `abort`, then `commit` throws `CannotCommitException`.

```
package net.jini.core.transaction;

public class CannotCommitException
    extends TransactionException
{
    public CannotCommitException() {...}
    public CannotCommitException(String desc) {...}
}
```

The one-parameter `abort` method returns as soon as the transaction successfully reaches the `ABORTED` state, or if the transaction is known to have previously reached that state due to an earlier `commit` or `abort`. If the transaction is known to have previously reached the `COMMITTED` state due to an earlier `commit`, then `abort` throws `CannotAbortException`.

```
package net.jini.core.transaction;

public class CannotAbortException extends TransactionException
{
    public CannotAbortException() {...}
    public CannotAbortException(String desc) {...}
}
```

Both `commit` and `abort` can throw `UnknownTransactionException`, which means the transaction is unknown to the manager. This may be because the transaction ID was incorrect, or because the transaction has proceeded to *cleanup* due to an earlier commit or abort, and has been forgotten.

Overloads of the `commit` and `abort` methods take an additional `waitFor` timeout parameter specified in milliseconds that tells the manager to wait until it has successfully notified all participants about the outcome of the transaction before the method returns. If the timeout expires before all participants have been notified, a `TimeoutExpiredException` will be thrown. If the timeout expires before the transaction reaches the `COMMITTED` or `ABORTED` state, the manager must wait until one of those states is reached before throwing the exception. The `committed` field in the exception is set to `true` if the transaction committed or to `false` if it aborted.

```
package net.jini.core.transaction;

public class TimeoutExpiredException extends
            TransactionException
{
    public boolean committed;
    public TimeoutExpiredException(boolean committed) {...}
    public TimeoutExpiredException(String desc,
                                   boolean committed) {...}
}
```

TX.2.6 Completing a Transaction: A Participant's View

In a participant's view, a transaction goes through the following states:

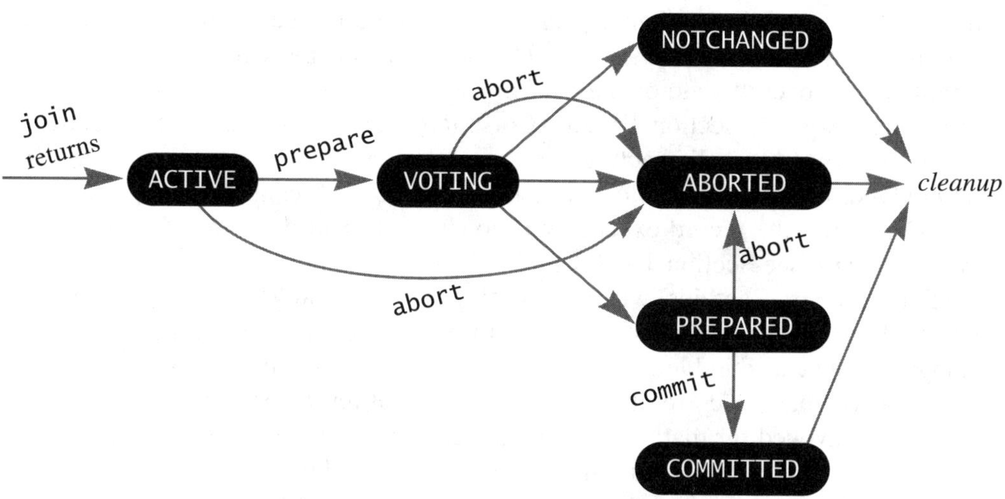

For the participant, the transaction starts out `ACTIVE` as soon as `join` returns. Any operations attempted under a transaction are valid only if the participant has the transaction in the `ACTIVE` state. In any other state, a request to perform an operation under the transaction should fail, signaling the invoker appropriately.

When the manager asks the participant to `prepare`, the participant is `VOTING` until it decides what to return. There are three possible return values for `prepare`:

- The participant had no changes to its state made under the transaction—that is, for the participant the transaction was read-only. It should release any internal state associated with the transaction. It must signal this with a return of `NOTCHANGED`, effectively entering the `NOTCHANGED` state. As noted below, a well-behaved participant should stay in the `NOTCHANGED` state for some time to allow idempotency for `prepare`.
- The participant had its state changed by operations performed under the transaction. It must attempt to prepare to roll those changes forward in the event of a future incoming `commit` invocation. When the participant has successfully prepared itself to roll forward (see Section TX.2.8 "Crash Recovery"), it must return `PREPARED`, thereby entering the `PREPARED` state.
- The participant had its state changed by operations performed under the transaction but is unable to guarantee a future successful roll forward. It

must signal this with a return of ABORTED, effectively entering the ABORTED state.

For top-level transactions, when a participant returns PREPARED it is stating that it is ready to roll the changes forward by saving the necessary record of the operations for a future commit call. The record of changes must be at least as durable as the overall state of the participant. The record must also be examined during recovery (see Section TX.2.8 "Crash Recovery") to ensure that the participant rolls forward or rolls back as the manager dictates. The participant stays in the PREPARED state until it is told to commit or abort. It cannot, having returned PREPARED, drop the record except by following the "roll decision" described for crash recovery (see Section TX.2.8.1 "The Roll Decision").

For nested transactions, when a participant returns PREPARED it is stating that it is ready to roll the changes forward into the parent transaction. The record of changes must be as durable as the record of changes for the parent transaction.

If a participant is currently executing an operation under a transaction when prepare is invoked for that transaction, the participant must either: wait until that operation is complete before returning from prepare; know that the operation is guaranteed to be read-only, and so will not affect its ability to prepare; or abort the transaction.

If a participant has not received any communication on or about a transaction over an extended period, it may choose to invoke getState on the manager. If getState throws UnknownTransactionException or NoSuchObjectException, the participant may safely infer that the transaction has been aborted. If getState throws a RemoteException the participant may choose to believe that the manager has crashed and abort its state in the transaction—this is not to be done lightly, since the manager may save state across crashes, and transient network failures could cause a participant to drop out of an otherwise valid and committable transaction. A participant should drop out of a transaction only if the manager is unreachable over an extended period. However, in no case should a participant drop out of a transaction it has PREPARED but not yet rolled forward.

If a participant has joined a nested transaction and it receives a prepare call for an enclosing transaction, the participant must complete the nested transaction, using getState on the manager to determine the proper type of completion.

If a participant receives a prepare call for a transaction that is already in a post-VOTING state, the participant should simply respond with that state.

If a participant receives a prepare call for a transaction that is unknown to it, it should throw UnknownTransactionException. This may happen if the participant has crashed and lost the state of a previously active transaction, or if a previous NOTCHANGED or ABORTED response was not received by the manager and the participant has since forgotten the transaction.

Note that a return value of NOTCHANGED may not be idempotent. Should the participant return NOTCHANGED it may proceed directly to clean up its state. If the manager receives a RemoteException because of network failure, the manager will likely retry the prepare. At this point a participant that has dropped the information about the transaction will throw UnknownTransactionException, and the manager will be forced to abort. A well-behaved participant should stay in the NOTCHANGED state for a while to allow a retry of prepare to again return NOTCHANGED, thus keeping the transaction alive, although this is not strictly required. No matter what it voted, a well-behaved participant should also avoid exiting for a similar period of time in case the manager needs to re-invoke prepare.

If a participant receives an abort call for a transaction, whether in the ACTIVE, VOTING, or PREPARED state, it should move to the ABORTED state and roll back all changes made under the transaction.

If a participant receives a commit call for a PREPARED transaction, it should move to the COMMITTED state and roll forward all changes made under the transaction.

The participant's implementation of prepareAndCommit must be equivalent to the following:

```
public int prepareAndCommit(TransactionManager mgr, long id)
    throws UnknownTransactionException, RemoteException
{
    int result = prepare(mgr, id);
    if (result == PREPARED) {
        commit(mgr, id);
        result = COMMITTED;
    }
    return result;
}
```

The participant can often implement prepareAndCommit much more efficiently than shown, but it must preserve the above semantics. The manager's use of this method is described in the next section.

TX.2.7 Completing a Transaction: The Manager's View

In the manager's view, a transaction goes through the following states:

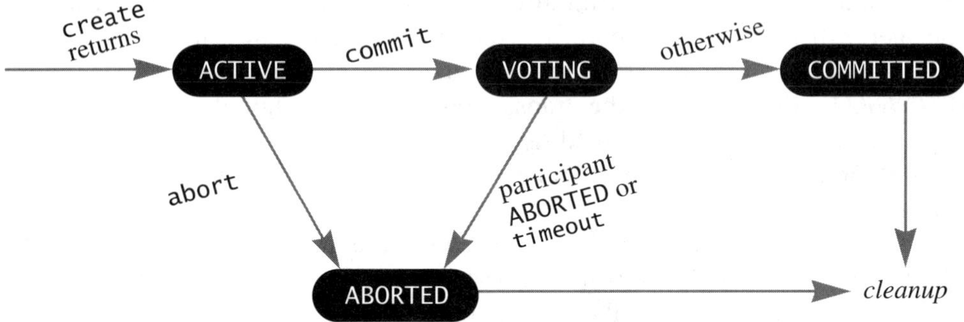

When a transaction is created using `create`, the transaction is `ACTIVE`. This is the only state in which participants may `join` the transaction. Attempting to join the transaction in any other state throws a `CannotJoinException`.

Invoking the manager's `commit` method causes the manager to move to the `VOTING` state, in which it attempts to complete the transaction by rolling forward. Each participant that has joined the transaction has its `prepare` method invoked to vote on the outcome of the transaction. The participant may return one of three votes: `NOTCHANGED`, `ABORTED`, or `COMMITTED`.

If a participant votes `ABORTED`, the manager must abort the transaction. If `prepare` throws `UnknownTransactionException` or `NoSuchObjectException`, the participant has lost its state of the transaction, and the manager must abort the transaction. If `prepare` throws `RemoteException`, the manager may retry as long as it wishes until it decides to abort the transaction.

To abort the transaction, the manager moves to the `ABORTED` state. In the `ABORTED` state, the manager should invoke `abort` on all participants that have voted `PREPARED`. The manager should also attempt to invoke `abort` on all participants on which it has not yet invoked `prepare`. These notifications are not strictly necessary for the one-parameter forms of `commit` and `abort`, since the participants will eventually abort the transaction either by timing out or by asking the manager for the state of the transaction. However, informing the participants of the abort can speed up the release of resources in these participants, and so attempting the notification is strongly encouraged.

If a participant votes `NOTCHANGED`, it is dropped from the list of participants, and no further communication will ensue. If all participants vote `NOTCHANGED` then the entire transaction was read-only and no participant has any changes to roll forward. The transaction moves to the `COMMITTED` state and then can immediately move to *cleanup*, in which resources in the manager are cleaned up. There is no behavioral difference to a participant between a NOTCHANGED transaction and one that has completed the notification phase of the COMMITTED state.

If no participant votes ABORTED and at least one participant votes PREPARED, the transaction also moves to the COMMITTED state. In the COMMITTED state the manager must notify each participant that returned PREPARED to roll forward by invoking the participant's commit method. When the participant's commit method returns normally, the participant has rolled forward successfully and the manager need not invoke commit on it again. As long as there exists at least one participant that has not rolled forward successfully, the manager must preserve the state of the transaction and repeat attempts to invoke commit at reasonable intervals. If a participant's commit method throws UnknownTransactionException, this means that the participant has already successfully rolled the transaction forward even though the manager did not receive the notification, either due to a network failure on a previous invocation that was actually successful or because the participant called getState directly.

If the transaction is a nested one and the manager is prepared to roll the transaction forward, the members of the nested transaction must become members of the parent transaction. This *promotion* of participants into the parent manager must be atomic—all must be promoted simultaneously, or none must be. The multi-participant promote method is designed for this use in the case in which the parent and nested transactions have different managers.

The promote method takes arrays of participants and crash counts, where crashCounts[i] is the crash count for parts[i]. If any crash count is different from a crash count that is already known to the parent transaction manager, the parent manager throws CrashCountException and the parent transaction must abort. The drop parameter allows the nested transaction manager to drop itself out of the parent transaction as it promotes its participants into the parent transaction if it no longer has any need to be a participant itself.

The manager for the nested transaction should remain available until it has successfully driven each participant to completion and promoted its participants into the parent transaction. If the nested transaction's manager disappears before a participant is positively informed of the transaction's completion, that participant will not know whether to roll forward or back, forcing it to vote ABORTED in the parent transaction. The manager may cease commit invocations on its participants if any parent transaction is aborted. Aborting any transaction implicitly aborts any uncommitted nested transactions. Additionally, since any committed nested transaction will also have its results dropped, any actions taken on behalf of that transaction can be abandoned.

Invoking the manager's abort method, cancelling the transaction's lease, or allowing the lease to expire also moves the transaction to the ABORTED state as described above. Any transactions nested inside that transaction are also moved directly to the ABORTED state.

The manager may optimize the VOTING state by invoking a participant's prepareAndCommit method if the transaction has only one participant that has not yet been asked to vote and all previous participants have returned NOTCHANGED. (Note that this includes the special case in which the transaction has exactly one participant.) If the manager receives an ABORTED result from prepareAndCommit, it proceeds to the ABORTED state. In effect, a prepareAndCommit moves through the VOTING state straight to operating on the results.

A getState call on the manager can return any of ACTIVE, VOTING, ABORTED, NOTCHANGED, or COMMITTED. A manager is permitted, but not required, to return NOTCHANGED if it is in the COMMITTED state and all participants voted NOTCHANGED.

TX.2.8 Crash Recovery

Crash recovery ensures that a top-level transaction will consistently abort or roll forward in the face of a system crash. Nested transactions are not involved.

The manager has one *commit point,* where it must save state in a durable fashion. This is when it enters the COMMITTED state with at least one PREPARED participant. The manager must, at this point, commit the list of PREPARED participants into durable storage. This storage must persist until all PREPARED participants successfully roll forward. A manager may choose to also store the list of PREPARED participants that have already successfully rolled forward or to rewrite the list of PREPARED participants as it shrinks, but this optimization is not required (although it is recommended as good citizenship). In the event of a manager crash, the list of participants must be recovered, and the manager must continue acting in the COMMITTED state until it can successfully notify all PREPARED participants.

The participant also has one commit point, which is prior to voting PREPARED. When it votes PREPARED, the participant must have durably recorded the record of changes necessary to successfully roll forward in the event of a future invocation of commit by the manager. It can remove this record when it is prepared to successfully return from commit.

Because of these commitments, manager and participant implementations should use durable forms of RMI references, such as the Activatable references introduced in the Java 2 platform. An unreachable manager causes much havoc and should be avoided as much as possible. A vanished PREPARED participant puts a transaction in an untenable permanent state in which some, but not all, of the participants have rolled forward.

TX.2.8.1 The Roll Decision

If a participant votes `PREPARED` for a top-level transaction, it must guarantee that it will execute a recovery process if it crashes between completing its durable record and receiving a `commit` notification from the manager. This recovery process must read the record of the crashed participant and make a *roll decision*—whether to roll the recorded changes forward or roll them back.

To make this decision, it invokes the `getState` method on the transaction manager. This can have the following results:

- `getState` returns `COMMITTED`: The recovery should move the participant to the `COMMITTED` state.
- `getState` throws either an `UnknownTransactionException` or a `NoSuchObjectException`: The recovery should move the participant to the `ABORTED` state.
- `getState` throws `RemoteException`: The recovery should repeat the attempt after a pause.

TX.2.9 Durability

Durability is a commitment, but it is not a guarantee. It is impossible to guarantee that any given piece of stable storage can *never* be lost; one can only achieve decreasing probabilities of loss. Data that is force-written to a disk may be considered durable, but it is less durable than data committed to two or more separate, redundant disks. When we speak of "durability" in this system it is always used relative to the expectations of the human who decided which entities to use for communication.

With multi-participant transactions it is entirely possible that different participants have different durability levels. The manager may be on a tightly replicated system with its durable storage duplicated on several host systems, giving a high degree of durability, while a participant may be using only one disk. Or a participant may always store its data in memory, expecting to lose it in a system crash (a database of people currently logged into the host, for example, need not survive a system crash). When humans make a decision to use a particular manager and set of participants for a transaction they must take into account these differences and be aware of the ramifications of committing changes that may be more durable on one participant than another. Determining, or even defining and exposing, varying levels of durability is outside the scope of this specification.

TX.3 Default Transaction Semantics

THE two-phase commit protocol defines how a transaction is created and later driven to completion by either committing or aborting. It is neutral with respect to the semantics of locking under the transaction or other behaviors that impart semantics to the use of the transaction. Specific clients and servers, however, must be written to expect specific transaction semantics. This model is to separate the completion protocol from transaction semantics, where transaction semantics are represented in the parameters and return values of methods by which clients and participants interact.

This chapter defines the default transaction semantics of services. These semantics preserve the traditional ACID properties (you will find a brief description of the ACID properties in Section TX.1.2 "Distributed Transactions and ACID Properties"). The semantics are represented by the `Transaction` and `NestableTransaction` interfaces and their implementation classes `ServerTransaction` and `NestableServerTransaction`. Any participant that accepts as a parameter or returns any of these types is promising to abide by the following definition of semantics for any activities performed under that transaction.

TX.3.1 `Transaction` and `NestableTransaction` Interfaces

The client's view of transactions is through two interfaces: `Transaction` for top-level transactions and `NestableTransaction` for transactions under which nested transactions can be created. First, the `Transaction` interface:

```
package net.jini.core.transaction;

public interface Transaction {
    public static class Created implements Serializable {
        public final Transaction transaction;
        public final Lease lease;
        Created(Transaction transaction, Lease lease) {…}
```

```
    }
    void commit() // §TX.2.5
        throws UnknownTransactionException,
               CannotCommitException,
               RemoteException;
    void commit(long waitFor) // §TX.2.5
        throws UnknownTransactionException,
               CannotCommitException,
               TimeoutExpiredException, RemoteException;
    void abort() // §TX.2.5
        throws UnknownTransactionException,
               CannotAbortException,
               RemoteException;
    void abort(long waitFor) // §TX.2.5
        throws UnknownTransactionException,
               CannotAbortException,
               TimeoutExpiredException, RemoteException;
}
```

The `Created` nested class is used in a factory `create` method for top-level transactions (defined in the next section) to hold two return values: the newly created `Transaction` object and the transaction's lease, which is the lease granted by the transaction manager. The `commit` and `abort` methods have the same semantics as discussed in Section TX.2.5 "Completing a Transaction: The Client's View".

Nested transactions are created using `NestableTransaction` methods:

```
package net.jini.core.transaction;

public interface NestableTransaction extends Transaction {
    public static class Created implements Serializable {
        public final NestableTransaction transaction;
        public final Lease lease;
        Created(NestableTransaction transaction, Lease lease)
            {...}
    }
    Created create(long leaseFor) // §TX.2.2
        throws UnknownTransactionException,
               CannotJoinException, LeaseDeniedException,
               RemoteException;
    Created create(NestableTransactionManager mgr,
                   long leaseFor) // §TX.2.2
        throws UnknownTransactionException,
```

```
            CannotJoinException, LeaseDeniedException,
            RemoteException;
}
```

The `Created` nested class is used to hold two return values: the newly created `Transaction` object and the transaction's lease, which is the lease granted by the transaction manager. In both `create` methods, `leaseFor` is the requested lease time in milliseconds. In the one-parameter `create` method the nested transaction is created with the same transaction manager as the transaction on which the method is invoked. The other `create` method can be used to specify a different transaction manager to use for the nested transaction.

TX.3.2 `TransactionFactory` Class

The `TransactionFactory` class is used to create top-level transactions.

```
package net.jini.core.transaction;

public class TransactionFactory {
    public static Transaction.Created
        create(TransactionManager mgr, long leaseFor)
                                                   // §TX.2.1
        throws LeaseDeniedException, RemoteException {…}
    public static NestableTransaction.Created
        create(NestableTransactionManager mgr,long leaseFor)
                                                   // §TX.2.2
        throws LeaseDeniedException, RemoteException {…}
}
```

The first `create` method is usually used when nested transactions are not required. However, if the manager that is passed to this method is in fact a `NestableTransactionManager`, then the returned `Transaction` can in fact be cast to a `NestableTransaction`. The second `create` method is used when it is known that nested transactions need to be created. In both cases, a `Created` instance is used to hold two return values: the newly created transaction object and the granted lease.

TX.3.3 `ServerTransaction` and `NestableServerTransaction` Classes

The `ServerTransaction` class exposes functionality necessary for writing participants that support top-level transactions. Participants can cast a `Transaction` to a `ServerTransaction` to obtain access to this functionality.

```
public class ServerTransaction
    implements Transaction, Serializable
{
    public final TransactionManager mgr;
    public final long id;
    public ServerTransaction(TransactionManager mgr, long id)
        {…}
    public void join(TransactionParticipant part,
                     long crashCount) // §TX.2.3
        throws UnknownTransactionException,
               CannotJoinException, CrashCountException,
               RemoteException {…}
    public int getState() // §TX.2.7
        throws UnknownTransactionException, RemoteException
        {…}
    public boolean isNested() {…} // §TX.3.3
}
```

The `mgr` field is a reference to the transaction manager that created the transaction. The `id` field is the transaction identifier returned by the transaction manager's `create` method.

The constructor should not be used directly; it is intended for use by the `TransactionFactory` implementation.

The methods `join`, `commit`, `abort`, and `getState` invoke the corresponding methods on the manager, passing the transaction identifier. They are provided as a convenience to the programmer, primarily to eliminate the possibility of passing an identifier to the wrong manager. For example, given a `ServerTransaction` object `tr`, the invocation

```
tr.join(participant, crashCount);
```

is equivalent to

```
tr.mgr.join(tr.id, participant, crashCount);
```

The `isNested` method returns `true` if the transaction is a nested transaction (that is, if it is a `NestableServerTransaction` with a non-`null` parent) and `false` otherwise. It is provided as a method on `ServerTransaction` for the convenience of participants that do not support nested transactions.

The `hashCode` method returns the `id` cast to an `int` XORed with the result of `mgr.hashCode()`. The `equals` method returns `true` if the specified object is a `ServerTransaction` object with the same manager and transaction identifier as the object on which it is invoked.

The `NestableServerTransaction` class exposes functionality that is necessary for writing participants that support nested transactions. Participants can cast a `NestableTransaction` to a `NestableServerTransaction` to obtain access to this functionality.

```
package net.jini.core.transaction.server;

public class NestableServerTransaction
    extendsServerTransaction implements NestableTransaction
{
    public final NestableServerTransaction parent;
    public NestableServerTransaction(
            NestableTransactionManager mgr, long id,
            NestableServerTransaction parent) {...}
    public void promote(TransactionParticipant[] parts,
                        long[] crashCounts,
                        TransactionParticipant drop)
                                                        // §TX.2.7
        throws UnknownTransactionException,
               CannotJoinException, CrashCountException,
               RemoteException {...}
    public boolean enclosedBy(NestableTransaction enclosing)
        {...}
}
```

The `parent` field is a reference to the parent transaction if the transaction is nested (see Section TX.2.2 “Starting a Nested Transaction”) or `null` if it is a top-level transaction.

The constructor should not be used directly; it is intended for use by the `TransactionFactory` and `NestableServerTransaction` implementations.

Given a `NestableServerTransaction` object `tr`, the invocation

```
tr.promote(parts, crashCounts, drop)
```

is equivalent to

```
((NestableTransactionManager)tr.mgr).promote(tr.id, parts,
                                        crashCounts, drop)
```

The `enclosedBy` method returns `true` if the specified transaction is an enclosing transaction (parent, grandparent, etc.) of the transaction on which the method is invoked; otherwise it returns `false`.

TX.3.4 CannotNestException Class

If a service implements the default transaction semantics but does not support nested transactions, it usually needs to throw an exception if a nested transaction is passed to it. The `CannotNestException` is provided as a convenience for this purpose, although a service is not required to use this specific exception.

```
package net.jini.core.transaction;

public class CannotNestException extends TransactionException
{
    public CannotNestException() {...}
    public CannotNestException(String desc) {...}
}
```

TX.3.5 Semantics

Activities that are performed as pure transactions (all access to shared mutable state is performed under transactional control) are subject to sequential ordering, meaning the overall effect of executing a set of sibling (all at the same level, whether top-level or nested) pure transactions concurrently is always equivalent to some sequential execution.

Ancestor transactions can execute concurrently with child transactions, subject to the locking rules below.

Transaction semantics for objects are defined in terms of strict two-phase locking. Every transactional operation is described in terms of acquiring locks on objects; these locks are held until the transaction completes. The most typical locks are read and write locks, but others are possible. Whatever the lock types are, conflict rules are defined such that if two operations do not commute, then they acquire conflicting locks. For objects using standard read and write locks, read locks do not conflict with other read locks, but write locks conflict with both read locks and other write locks. A transaction can acquire a lock if the only conflicting locks are those held by ancestor transactions (or itself). If a necessary lock cannot be acquired and the operation is defined to proceed without waiting for that lock, then serializability might be violated. When a subtransaction commits, its locks are inherited by the parent transaction.

In addition to locks, transactional operations can be defined in terms of object creation and deletion visibility. If an object is defined to be created under a transaction, then the existence of the object is visible only within that transaction and its inferiors, but will disappear if the transaction aborts. If an object is defined to be deleted under a transaction, then the object is not visible to any transaction (including the deleting transaction) but will reappear if the transaction aborts. When a nested transaction commits, visibility state is inherited by the parent transaction.

Once a transaction reaches the `VOTING` stage, if all execution under the transaction (and its subtransactions) has finished, then the only reasons the transaction can abort are:

- The manager crashes (or has crashed)
- One or more participants crash (or have crashed)
- There is an explicit abort

Transaction deadlocks are not guaranteed to be prevented or even detected, but managers and participants are permitted to break known deadlocks by aborting transactions.

An active transaction is an *orphan* if it or one of its ancestors is guaranteed to abort. This can occur because an ancestor has explicitly aborted or because some participant or manager of the transaction or an ancestor has crashed. Orphans are not guaranteed to be detected by the system, so programmers using transactions must be aware that orphans can see internally inconsistent state and take appropriate action.

Causal ordering information about transactions is not guaranteed to be propagated. First, given two sibling transactions (at any level), it is not possible to tell whether they were created concurrently or sequentially (or in what order). Second, if two transactions are causally ordered and the earlier transaction has completed, the outcome of the earlier transaction is not guaranteed to be known at every participant used by the later transaction, unless the client is successful in using the variant of `commit` or `abort` that takes a timeout parameter. Programmers using non-blocking forms of operations must take this into account.

As long as a transaction persists in attempting to acquire a lock that conflicts with another transaction, the participant will persist in attempting to resolve the outcome of the transaction that holds the conflicting lock. Attempts to acquire a lock include making a blocking call, continuing to make non-blocking calls, and registering for event notification under a transaction.

TX.3.6 Serialized Forms

Class	`serialVersionUID`	Serialized Fields
`Transaction.Created`	–5199291723008952986L	*all public fields*
`NestableTransaction.Created`	–2979247545926318953L	*all public fields*
`TransactionManager.Created`	–4233846033773471113L	*all public fields*
`ServerTransaction`	4552277137549765374L	*all public fields*
`NestableServerTransaction`	–3438419132543972925L	*all public fields*
`TransactionException`	–5009935764793203986L	*none*
`CannotAbortException`	3597101646737510009L	*none*
`CannotCommitException`	–4497341152359563957L	*none*
`CannotJoinException`	5568393043937204939L	*none*
`CannotNestException`	3409604500491735434L	*none*
`TimeoutExpiredException`	3918773760682958000L	*all public fields*
`UnknownTransactionException`	443798629936327009L	*none*
`CrashCountException`	4299226125245015671L	*none*

LU

Lookup Service

LU.1 Introduction

THE Jini lookup service is a fundamental part of the federation infrastructure for a *djinn,* the group of devices, resources, and users that are joined by the Jini technology infrastructure. The *lookup service* provides a central registry of services available within the djinn. This lookup service is a primary means for programs to find services within the djinn, and is the foundation for providing user interfaces through which users and administrators can discover and interact with services in the djinn.

Although the primary purpose of this specification is to define the interface to the djinn's central service registry, the interfaces defined here can readily be used in other service registries.

LU.1.1 The Lookup Service Model

The lookup service maintains a flat collection of *service items*. Each service item represents an instance of a service available within the djinn. The item contains the RMI stub (if the service is implemented as a remote object) or other object (if the service makes use of a local proxy) that programs use to access the service, and an extensible collection of attributes that describe the service or provide secondary interfaces to the service.

When a new service is created (for example, when a new device is added to the djinn), the service registers itself with the djinn's lookup service, providing an initial collection of attributes. For example, a printer might include attributes indicating speed (in pages per minute), resolution (in dots per inch), and whether duplex printing is supported. Among the attributes might be an indicator that the service is new and needs to be configured.

An administrator uses the event mechanism of the lookup service to receive notifications as new services are registered. To configure the service, the administrator might look for an attribute that provides an applet for this purpose. The administrator might also use an applet to add new attributes, such as the physical location of the service and a common name for it; the service would receive these attribute change requests from the applet and respond by making the changes at the lookup service.

Programs (including other services) that need a particular type of service can use the lookup service to find an instance. A match can be made based on the specific data types for the Java programming language implemented by the service as well as the specific attributes attached to the service. For example, a program that needs to make use of transactions might look for a service that supports the type `net.jini.core.transaction.server.TransactionManager` and might further qualify the match by desired location.

Although the collection of service items is flat, a wide variety of hierarchical views can be imposed on the collection by aggregating items according to service types and attributes. The lookup service provides a set of methods to enable incremental exploration of the collection, and a variety of user interfaces can be built by using these methods, allowing users and administrators to browse. Once an appropriate service is found, the user might interact with the service by loading a user interface applet, attached as another attribute on the item.

If a service encounters some problem that needs administrative attention, such as a printer running out of toner, the service can add an attribute that indicates what the problem is. Administrators again use the event mechanism to receive notification of such problems.

LU.1.2 Attributes

The attributes of a service item are represented as a set of attribute sets. An individual *attribute set* is represented as an instance of some class for the Java platform, each attribute being a public field of that class. The class provides strong typing of both the set and the individual attributes. A service item can contain multiple instances of the same class with different attribute values, as well as multiple instances of different classes. For example, an item might have multiple instances of a `Name` class, each giving the common name of the service in a different language, plus an instance of a `Location` class, an `Owner` class, and various service-specific classes. The schema used for attributes is not constrained by this specification, but a standard foundation schema for Jini technology-enabled systems is defined in the *Jini Lookup Attribute Schema Specification*.

Concretely, a set of attributes is implemented with a class that correctly implements the interface `net.jini.core.entry.Entry`, as described in Section DJ "Entry". Operations on the lookup service are defined in terms of template matching, using the same semantics as in Section DJ "Entry", but the definition is augmented to deal with sets of entries and sets of templates. A set of entries matches a set of templates if there is at least one matching entry for every template (with every entry usable as the match for more than one template).

LU.2 The ServiceRegistrar

THE types defined in this specification are in the `net.jini.core.lookup` package. The following types are imported from other packages and are referenced in unqualified form in the rest of this specification:

```
java.rmi.MarshalledObject
java.rmi.RemoteException
java.rmi.UnmarshalException
java.io.Serializable
java.io.DataInput
java.io.DataOutput
java.io.IOException
net.jini.core.discovery.LookupLocator
net.jini.core.entry.Entry
net.jini.core.lease.Lease
net.jini.core.event.RemoteEvent
net.jini.core.event.EventRegistration
net.jini.core.event.RemoteEventListener
```

LU.2.1 ServiceID

Every service is assigned a universally unique identifier (UUID), represented as an instance of the `ServiceID` class.

```
public final class ServiceID implements Serializable {
    public ServiceID(long mostSig, long leastSig) {...}
    public ServiceID(DataInput in) throws IOException {...}
    public void writeBytes(DataOutput out) throws IOException
        {...}
    public long getMostSignificantBits() {...}
    public long getLeastSignificantBits() {...}
}
```

A service ID is a 128-bit value. Service IDs are equal (using the `equals` method) if they represent the same 128-bit value. For simplicity and reliability, service IDs are intended to be generated only by lookup services, not by clients. As such, the `ServiceID` constructor merely takes 128 bits of data, to be computed in an implementation-dependent manner by the lookup service. The `writeBytes` method writes out 16 bytes in standard network byte order. The second constructor reads in 16 bytes in standard network byte order.

The most significant long can be decomposed into the following unsigned fields:

```
0xFFFFFFFF00000000        time_low
0x00000000FFFF0000        time_mid
0x000000000000F000        version
0x0000000000000FFF        time_hi
```

The least significant long can be decomposed into the following unsigned fields:

```
0xC000000000000000        variant
0x3FFF000000000000        clock_seq
0x0000FFFFFFFFFFFF        node
```

The `variant` field must be 0x2. The `version` field must be either 0x1 or 0x4. If the `version` field is 0x4, then the most significant bit of the `node` field must be set to 1, and the remaining fields are set to values produced by a cryptographically strong pseudo-random number generator. If the `version` field is 0x1, then the `node` field is set to an IEEE 802 address, the `clock_seq` field is set to a 14-bit random number, and the `time_low`, `time_mid`, and `time_hi` fields are set to the least, middle, and most significant bits (respectively) of a 60-bit timestamp measured in 100-nanosecond units since midnight, October 15, 1582 UTC.

The `toString` method returns a 36-character string of six fields separated by hyphens, each field represented in lowercase hexadecimal with the same number of digits as in the field. The order of fields is: `time_low`, `time_mid`, `version` and `time_hi` treated as a single field, `variant` and `clock_seq` treated as a single field, and `node`.

LU.2.2 ServiceItem

Items are stored in the lookup service using instances of the `ServiceItem` class.

```
public class ServiceItem implements Serializable {
    public ServiceItem(ServiceID serviceID,
                       Object service,
```

```
                              Entry[] attributeSets) {…}
        public ServiceID serviceID;
        public Object service;
        public Entry[] attributeSets;
    }
```

The constructor simply assigns each parameter to the corresponding field.

Each `Entry` represents an attribute set. The class must have a public no-arg constructor, and all non-static, non-final, non-transient public fields must be declared with reference types, holding serializable objects. Each such field is serialized separately as a `MarshalledObject`, and field equality is defined by `MarshalledObject.equals`. The only relationship constraint on attribute sets within an item is that exact duplicates are eliminated; other than that, multiple attribute sets of the same type are permitted, multiple attribute set types can have a common superclass, and so on.

The `net.jini.core.entry.UnusableEntryException` is not used in the lookup service; alternate semantics for individual operations are defined later in this section.

LU.2.3 `ServiceTemplate` and Item Matching

Items in the lookup service are matched using instances of the `ServiceTemplate` class.

```
    public class ServiceTemplate implements Serializable {
        public ServiceTemplate(ServiceID serviceID,
                               Class[] serviceTypes,
                               Entry[] attributeSetTemplates) {…}
        public ServiceID serviceID;
        public Class[] serviceTypes;
        public Entry[] attributeSetTemplates;
    }
```

The constructor simply assigns each parameter to the corresponding field. A service item (`item`) matches a service template (`tmpl`) if:

- `item.serviceID` equals `tmpl.serviceID` (or if `tmpl.serviceID` is `null`), and
- `item.service` is an instance of every type in `tmpl.serviceTypes`, and
- `item.attributeSets` contains at least one matching entry for each entry template in `tmpl.attributeSetTemplates`.

An entry matches an entry template if the class of the template is the same as, or a superclass of, the class of the entry, and every non-null field in the template equals the corresponding field of the entry. Every entry can be used to match more than one template. For both service types and entry classes, type matching is based simply on fully qualified class names. Note that in a service template, for serviceTypes and attributeSetTemplates, a null field is equivalent to an empty array; both represent a wildcard.

LU.2.4 Other Supporting Types

The ServiceMatches class is used for the return value when looking up multiple items.

```
public class ServiceMatches implements Serializable {
    public ServiceMatches(ServiceItem[] items,
                          int totalMatches) {...}
    public ServiceItem[] items;
    public int totalMatches;
}
```

The constructor simply assigns each parameter to the corresponding field.

A ServiceEvent extends RemoteEvent with methods to obtain the service ID of the matched item, the transition that triggered the event, and the new state of the matched item.

```
public abstract class ServiceEvent extends RemoteEvent {
    public ServiceEvent(Object source,
                        long eventID,
                        long seqNum,
                        MarshalledObject handback,
                        ServiceID serviceID,
                        int transition) {...}
    public ServiceID getServiceID() {...}
    public int getTransition() {...}
    public abstract ServceItem getServiceItem() {...}
}
```

The getServiceID and getTransition methods return the value of the corresponding constructor parameter. The remaining constructor parameters are the same as in the RemoteEvent constructor.

The rest of the semantics of both these classes is explained in the next section.

LU.2.5 ServiceRegistrar

The ServiceRegistrar defines the interface to the lookup service. The interface is not a remote interface; each implementation of the lookup service exports proxy objects that implement the ServiceRegistrar interface local to the client, using an implementation-specific protocol to communicate with the actual remote server. All of the proxy methods obey normal RMI remote interface semantics except where explicitly noted. Two proxy objects are equal (using the equals method) if they are proxies for the same lookup service.

Methods are provided to register service items, find items that match a template, receive event notifications when items are modified, and incrementally explore the collection of items along the three major axes: entry class, attribute value, and service type.

```
public interface ServiceRegistrar {
    ServiceRegistration register(ServiceItem item,
                                 long leaseDuration)
        throws RemoteException;

    Object lookup(ServiceTemplate tmpl)
        throws RemoteException;

    ServiceMatches
        lookup(ServiceTemplate tmpl, int maxMatches)
        throws RemoteException;

    int TRANSITION_MATCH_NOMATCH = 1 << 0;
    int TRANSITION_NOMATCH_MATCH = 1 << 1;
    int TRANSITION_MATCH_MATCH = 1 << 2;

    EventRegistration notify(ServiceTemplate tmpl,
                             int transitions,
                             RemoteEventListener listener,
                             MarshalledObject handback,
                             long leaseDuration)
        throws RemoteException;

    Class[] getEntryClasses(ServiceTemplate tmpl)
        throws RemoteException;

    Object[] getFieldValues(ServiceTemplate tmpl,
```

```
                                     int setIndex,
                                     String field)
         throws NoSuchFieldException, RemoteException;

    Class[] getServiceTypes(ServiceTemplate tmpl,
                                     String prefix)
         throws RemoteException;

    ServiceID getServiceID();
    LookupLocator getLocator() throws RemoteException;

    String[] getGroups() throws RemoteException;
}
```

Every method invocation on ServiceRegistrar and ServiceRegistration is atomic with respect to other invocations.

The register method is used to register a new service and to re-register an existing service. The method is defined so that it can be used in an idempotent fashion. Specifically, if a call to register results in a RemoteException (in which case the item might or might not have been registered), the caller can simply repeat the call to register with the same parameters, until it succeeds.

To register a new service, item.serviceID should be null. In that case, if item.service does not equal (using MarshalledObject.equals) any existing item's service object, then a new service ID will be assigned and included in the returned ServiceRegistration (described in the next section). The service ID is unique over time and space with respect to all other service IDs generated by all lookup services. If item.service does equal an existing item's service object, the existing item is first deleted from the lookup service (even if it has different attributes) and its lease is cancelled, but that item's service ID is reused for the newly registered item.

To re-register an existing service, or to register the service in any other lookup service, item.serviceID should be set to the same service ID that was returned by the initial registration. If an item is already registered under the same service ID, the existing item is first deleted (even if it has different attributes or a different service instance) and its lease is cancelled by the lookup service. Note that service object equality is not checked in this case, to allow for reasonable evolution of the service (for example, the serialized form of the stub changes or the service implements a new interface).

Any duplicate attribute sets that are included in a service item are eliminated in the stored representation of the item. The lease duration request (specified in milliseconds) is not exact; the returned lease is allowed to have a shorter (but not longer) duration than what was requested. The registration is persistent across restarts (crashes) of the lookup service until the lease expires or is cancelled.

The single-parameter form of `lookup` returns the service object (that is, just `ServiceItem.service`) from an item matching the template or `null` if there is no match. If multiple items match the template, it is arbitrary as to which service object is returned by the invocation. If the returned object cannot be deserialized, an `UnmarshalException` is thrown with the standard RMI semantics.

The two-parameter form of `lookup` returns at most `maxMatches` items matching the template and the total number of items that match the template. The return value is never `null`, and the returned items array is `null` only if `maxMatches` is zero. For each returned item, if the service object cannot be deserialized, the `service` field of the item is set to `null` and no exception is thrown. Similarly, if an attribute set cannot be deserialized, that element of the `attributeSets` array is set to `null` and no exception is thrown.

The `notify` method is used to register for event notification. The registration is leased; the lease duration request (specified in milliseconds) is not exact. The registration is persistent across restarts (crashes) of the lookup service until the lease expires or is cancelled. The event ID in the returned `EventRegistration` is unique at least with respect to all other active event registrations at this lookup service with different service templates or transitions.

While the event registration is in effect, a `ServiceEvent` is sent to the specified listener whenever a `register`, lease cancellation or expiration, or attribute change operation results in an item changing state in a way that satisfies the template and transition combination. The `transitions` parameter is the bitwise OR of any non-empty set of transition values:

- `TRANSITION_MATCH_NOMATCH`: An event is sent when the changed item matches the template before the operation, but doesn't match the template after the operation (this includes deletion of the item).
- `TRANSITION_NOMATCH_MATCH`: An event is sent when the changed item doesn't match the template before the operation (this includes not existing), but does match the template after the operation.
- `TRANSITION_MATCH_MATCH`: An event is sent when the changed item matches the template both before and after the operation.

The `getTransition` method of `ServiceEvent` returns the singleton transition value that triggered the match.

The `getServiceItem` method of `ServiceEvent` returns the new state of the item (the state after the operation) or `null` if the item was deleted by the operation. Note that this method is declared `abstract`; a lookup service uses a subclass of `ServiceEvent` to transmit the new state of the item however it chooses.

Sequence numbers for a given event ID are strictly increasing. If there is no gap between two sequence numbers, no events have been missed; if there is a gap, events might (but might not) have been missed. For example, a gap might occur if the lookup service crashes, even if no events are lost due to the crash.

As mentioned earlier, users are allowed to explore a collection of items down each of the major axes: entry class, attribute value, and service type.

The getEntryClasses method looks at all service items that match the specified template, finds every entry (among those service items) that either doesn't match any entry templates or is a subclass of at least one matching entry template, and returns the set of the (most specific) classes of those entries. Duplicate classes are eliminated, and the order of classes within the returned array is arbitrary. A null reference (not an empty array) is returned if there are no such entries or no matching items. If a returned class cannot be deserialized, that element of the returned array is set to null and no exception is thrown.

The getFieldValues method looks at all service items that match the specified template, finds every entry (among those service items) that matches tmpl.attributeSetTemplates[setIndex], and returns the set of values of the specified field of those entries. Duplicate values are eliminated, and the order of values within the returned array is arbitrary. a null reference (not an empty array) is returned if there are no matching items. If a returned value cannot be deserialized, that element of the returned array is set to null and no exception is thrown. NoSuchFieldException is thrown if field does not name a field of the entry template.

The getServiceTypes method looks at all service items that match the specified template and, for every service item, finds the most specific type (class or interface) or types the service item is an instance of that are neither equal to, nor a superclass of, any of the service types in the template and that have names that start with the specified prefix, and returns the set of all such types. Duplicate types are eliminated, and the order of types within the returned array is arbitrary. A null reference (not an empty array) is returned if there are no such types. If a returned type cannot be deserialized, that element of the returned array is set to null and no exception is thrown.

Every lookup service assigns itself a service ID when it is first created; this service ID is returned by the getServiceID method. (Note that this does not make a remote call.) A lookup service is always registered with itself under this service ID, and if a lookup service is configured to register itself with other lookup services, it will register with all of them using this same service ID.

The getLocator method returns a LookupLocator that can be used if necessary for unicast discovery of the lookup service. The definition of this class is given in Section DJ "Discovery and Join".

The getGroups method returns the set of groups that this lookup service is currently a member of. The semantics of these groups is defined in Section DJ "Discovery and Join".

LU.2.6 ServiceRegistration

A registered service item is manipulated using a ServiceRegistration instance.

```
public interface ServiceRegistration {
    ServiceID getServiceID();
    Lease getLease();
    void addAttributes(Entry[] attrSets)
        throws UnknownLeaseException, RemoteException;
    void modifyAttributes(Entry[] attrSetTemplates,
                          Entry[] attrSets)
        throws UnknownLeaseException, RemoteException;
    void setAttributes(Entry[] attrSets)
        throws UnknownLeaseException, RemoteException;
}
```

Like ServiceRegistrar, this is not a remote interface; each implementation of the lookup service exports proxy objects that implement this interface local to the client. The proxy methods obey normal RMI remote interface semantics.

The getServiceID method returns the service ID for this service. (Note that this does not make a remote call.)

The getLease method returns the lease that controls the service registration, allowing the lease to be renewed or cancelled. (Note that getLease does not make a remote call.)

The addAttributes method adds the specified attribute sets (those that aren't duplicates of existing attribute sets) to the registered service item. Note that this operation has no effect on existing attribute sets of the service item and can be repeated in an idempotent fashion. UnknownLeaseException is thrown if the registration lease has expired or been cancelled.

The modifyAttributes method is used to modify existing attribute sets. The lengths of the attrSetTemplates and attrSets arrays must be equal, or IllegalArgumentException is thrown. The service item's attribute sets are modified as follows. For each array index i: if attrSets[i] is null, then every entry that matches attrSetTemplates[i] is deleted; otherwise, for every non-null field in attrSets[i], the value of that field is stored into the corresponding field of every entry that matches attrSetTemplates[i]. The class of attrSets[i] must be the same as, or a superclass of, the class of attrSetTemplates[i], or

IllegalArgumentException is thrown. If the modifications result in duplicate entries within the service item, the duplicates are eliminated. An UnknownLeaseException is thrown if the registration lease has expired or been cancelled.

Note that it is possible to use modifyAttributes in ways that are not idempotent. The attribute schema should be designed in such a way that all intended uses of this method can be performed in an idempotent fashion. Also note that modifyAttributes does not provide a means for setting a field to null; it is assumed that the attribute schema is designed in such a way that this is not necessary.

The setAttributes method deletes all of the service item's existing attributes and replaces them with the specified attribute sets. Any duplicate attribute sets are eliminated in the stored representation of the item. UnknownLeaseException is thrown if the registration lease has expired or been cancelled.

LU.2.7 Serialized Forms

Class	serialVersionUID	Serialized Fields
ServiceID	–7803375959559762239L	long mostSig long leastSig
ServiceItem	717395451032330758L	*all public fields*
ServiceTemplate	7854483807886483216L	*all public fields*
ServiceMatches	–5518280843537399398L	*all public fields*
ServiceEvent	1304997274096842701L	ServiceID serviceID int transition

Lookup
Service
(LU)

THE JINI™ TECHNOLOGY EXTENDED PLATFORM SPECIFICATIONS define a set of standard Jini technology infrastructure software utilities and services that extend the Jini Technology Core Platform. These utilities and services encapsulate desirable behaviors in the form of a set of reusable components that can be used to help simplify the process of developing clients and services for the Jini technology application environment. Employing these utilities and services to build such desirable behavior into a Jini client or service can help to avoid poor design and implementation decisions, greatly simplifying the development process.

JINI™

US

Introduction to Helper Utilities and Services

US.1 Summary

WHEN developing clients and services that will participate in the application environment for Jini technology, there are a number of behaviors that the developer may find desirable to incorporate in the client or service. Some of these behaviors may satisfy requirements described in the specifications of various Jini technology components; some behaviors may simply represent design practices that are desirable and should be encouraged. Examples of the sort of behavior that is required or desirable include the following:

- It is a requirement of the Jini discovery protocols that a service must continue to listen for and act on announcements from lookup services in which the service has registered interest.
- It is a requirement of the Jini discovery protocols that, until successful, a service must continue to attempt to join the specific lookup services with which it has been configured to join.
- Under many conditions, a Jini technology-enabled client (*Jini client*) or service will wish to regularly renew leases that it holds. For example, when a Jini technology-enabled service (*Jini service*) registers with a Jini lookup service, the service is requesting residency in the lookup service. Residency in a lookup service is a leased resource. Thus, when the requested residency is granted, the lookup service also imposes a lease on that residency. Typically, such a registered service will wish to extend the lease on its residency

beyond the original expiration time, resulting in a need to renew the lease on a regular basis.

- Many Jini services will need to maintain a dormant (inactive) state, becoming active only when needed.
- Many Jini clients and services will need to have a mechanism for finding and managing Jini services.
- Many Jini clients and services will find it desirable to employ a separate service that will handle events, in some useful way, on behalf of the participant.

To help simplify the process of developing clients and services for the application environment for Jini technology (*Jini application environment*), several specifications in this document collection define reusable components that encapsulate behaviors such as those outlined above. Employing such utilities and services to build such desirable behavior into a Jini client or service can help to avoid poor design and implementation decisions, greatly simplifying the development process.

What is presented first is terminology that may be helpful when analyzing these specifications. Following the section on terminology, brief summaries of the content of each of the current helper utilities and services specifications are provided. Finally, the other specifications on which these specifications depend are listed for reference.

US.2 Terminology

THIS section defines terms and discusses concepts that may be referenced throughout the helper utilities and services specifications. While the terms and concepts that appear in this section are general in nature and may apply to multiple components specified in this collection, each specification may define additional terms and concepts to further facilitate the understanding of a particular component. Each specification may also present supplemental information about some of the terms defined in this section and their relationship with the component being specified.

Because this document makes use of a number of terms defined in the *"Jini Technology Glossary"*, reviewing the glossary is recommended. A number of the terms defined in the glossary are also defined in this section to provide easy reference because those terms are used extensively in the helper utilities and services specifications. Additionally, this section augments the definitions of some of the terms from the glossary with details relevant to those specifications.

In addition to the glossary, the *Jini Technology Core Platform Specification* (referred to as the *core specification*) presents detailed definitions of a number of terms and concepts appearing both in this section and throughout the helper utilities and services specifications. When appropriate, the relevant specification will be referenced.

US.2.1 Terms Related to Discovery and Join

The Jini Technology Core Platform Specification, "Discovery and Join", defines a *discovering entity* as one or more cooperating software objects written in the Java programming language (*Java software objects*), executing on the same host, that are in the process of obtaining references to Jini lookup services. That specification also defines a *joining entity* as one or more cooperating Java software objects, on the same host, that have received a reference to a lookup service and are in the process of obtaining services from, and possibly exporting services to, a federation of Jini technology-enabled services and/or devices and Jini lookup services referred to as a *djinn*. The lookup services comprising a djinn may be organized into one or more sets known as *groups*. Multiple groups may or may not be disjoint. Each group of lookup services is identified by a logical name represented by a `String` object.

The Jini Technology Core Platform Specification, "Discovery and Join" defines two protocols used in the discovery process: the *multicast discovery protocol* and the *unicast discovery protocol*.

When a discovering entity employs the multicast discovery protocol to discover lookup services that are members of one or more groups belonging to a set of groups, that discovery process is referred to as *group discovery*.

The utility class `net.jini.core.discovery.LookupLocator` is defined in *The Jini Technology Core Platform Specification,* "Discovery and Join". Any instance of that class is referred to as a *locator*. When a discovering entity employs the unicast discovery protocol to discover specific lookup services, each corresponding to an element in a set of locators, that discovery process is referred to as *locator discovery*.

US.2.2 Jini Clients and Services

For the purposes of the helper utilities and services specifications, a *Jini client* is defined as a discovering entity that can retrieve a service (or a remote reference to a service) registered with a discovered lookup service and invoke the methods of the service to meet the entity's requirements. An entity that acts only as a client never registers with (requests residency in) a lookup service.

A *Jini service* is defined as both a discovering and a joining entity containing methods that may be of use to some other Jini client or service, and which registers with discovered lookup services to provide access to those methods. Note that a Jini service can also act as a Jini client.

The term *client-like entity* may be used, in general, when referring to Jini clients and Jini services that act as clients.

Note that when the term *entity* is used, that term may be referring to a discovering entity, a joining entity, a client-like entity, a service, or some combination of these types of entities. Whenever that general term is used, it should be clear from the context what type of entity is being discussed.

US.2.3 Helper Service

A Jini technology-enabled *helper service* is defined in this document as an interface or set of interfaces, with an associated implementation, that encapsulates behavior that is either required or highly desirable in service entities that adhere to the Jini technology programming model (or simply the *Jini programming model*). A helper service is a Jini service that can be registered with any number of lookup services and whose methods can execute on remote hosts.

In general, a helper service should be of use to more than one type of entity participating in the Jini application environment and should provide a significant reduction in development complexity for developers of such entities.

US.2.4 Helper Utility

This document distinguishes between a helper *utility* and a helper *service*. Helper utilities are programming components that can be used during the construction of Jini services and/or clients. Helper utilities are *not* remote and do not register with a lookup service. Helper utilities are instantiated locally by entities wishing to employ them.

US.2.5 Managed Sets

When performing discovery duties, entities will often maintain references to discovered lookup services in a set referred to as the *managed set of lookup services*. The entity may also maintain two other notable sets: the *managed set of groups* and the *managed set of locators*.

Each element of the managed set of groups is a name of a group whose members are lookup services that the entity wishes to be discovered via group discovery. The managed set of groups is typically represented as a `String` array, or a `Collection` of `String` elements.

Each element of the managed set of locators corresponds to a specific lookup service that the entity wishes to be discovered via locator discovery. Typically, this set is represented as an array of `net.jini.core.discovery.LookupLocator` objects or some other `Collection` type whose elements are `LookupLocator` objects.

Note that when the general term *managed set* is used, it should be clear from the context whether groups, locators, or lookup services are being discussed.

US.2.6 What Exceptions Imply about Future Behavior

When interacting with a remote object, an entity may call methods that result in exceptions. The specification of those methods should define what each possible exception implies (if anything) about the current state of the object. One important aspect of an object's state is whether or not further interactions with the object are likely to be fruitful. Throughout the helper utilities and services specifications, the following general terms may be used to classify what a given exception implies about the probability of success of future operations on the object that threw the exception:

- Bad object exception: If a method invocation on an object throws a *bad object exception,* it can be assumed that any further operations on that object will also fail.
- Bad invocation exception: If a method invocation on an object throws a *bad invocation exception,* it can be assumed that any retries of the *same* method with the *same* arguments that are expected to return the *same* value will also fail. No new assertions can be made about the probability of success of any future invocation of that method with different arguments or if a different return value is expected, nor can any new assertions be made about the probability of success of invocations of the object's other methods.
- Indefinite exception: If a method invocation on an object throws an *indefinite exception*, no new assertions can be made about the probability of success of any future invocation of that method, regardless of the arguments used or return value expected, nor can any new assertions be made about the probability of success of any *other* operation on the same object.

Unless otherwise noted, the throwing of a bad object, bad invocation, or indefinite exception by one object does not imply anything about the state of another object, even if both objects are associated with the same remote entity.

These terms can be used in the specification of a method to describe the meaning of exceptions that might be thrown, as well as in the specification of what a given utility or service will, may, or should do when it receives an exception in the course of interacting with a given object.

If a specification does not say otherwise, the following classification is used to categorize each `RuntimeException`, `Error`, or `java.rmi.RemoteExceptions` as a bad object, bad invocation, or indefinite exception:

- Bad object exceptions:
  - Any `java.lang.RuntimeException`
  - Any `java.lang.Error` *except* one that is a `java.lang.LinkageError` or `java.lang.OutOfMemoryError`
  - Any `java.rmi.NoSuchObjectException`

- Any `java.rmi.ServerError` with a `detail` field that is a bad object exception
- Any `java.rmi.ServerException` with a `detail` field that is a bad object exception

◆ Bad invocation exceptions:

- Any `java.rmi.MarshalException` with a `detail` field that is a `java.io.ObjectStreamException`
- Any `java.rmi.UnmarshalException` with a `detail` field that is a `java.io.ObjectStreamException`
- Any `java.rmi.ServerException` with a `detail` field that is a bad invocation exception

◆ Indefinite exceptions

- Any `java.lang.OutOfMemoryError`
- Any `java.lang.LinkageError`
- Any `java.rmi.RemoteException` *except* those that can be classified as either a bad invocation or bad object exception

US.2.7 Unavailable Lookup Services

While interacting (or attempting to interact) with a lookup service, an entity may encounter one of the exception types described in the previous section. When the entity does receive such an exception, what may be concluded about the state of the lookup service is dependent on the type of exception encountered.

If an entity encounters a bad object exception while interacting with a lookup service, the entity can usually conclude that the associated proxy it holds can no longer be used to interact with the lookup service. This can be due to any number of reasons. For example, if the lookup service is administratively destroyed, the old proxy will never be capable of communicating with any new incarnations of the lookup service, allowing the entity to dispose of the old proxy since it is no longer of any use to the entity.

If an indefinite exception occurs while interacting with a lookup service, the entity can interpret such an occurrence as a communication failure that may or may not be only temporary.

Finally, entities that encounter a bad invocation exception while interacting with a lookup service should view the lookup service as being in an unknown, possibly corrupt state, and should discontinue further interaction with that lookup service until the problem is resolved.

Whenever an entity receives any of these exceptions while interacting with a lookup service, the affected lookup service is referred to as *unavailable* or *unreachable*. For most entities the unavailability of a particular lookup service should not prevent the entity from continuing its processing, although in other situations an entity might consider at least some of these exceptional conditions unrecoverable. In general, when an entity encounters an unreachable lookup service, the exception or error indicating that the lookup service is unavailable should be caught and handled, usually by requesting that the lookup service be *discarded* (see the next section), and the entity should continue its processing.

US.2.8 Discarding a Lookup Service

When an already discovered lookup service is removed from the managed set of lookup services, it is said to be *discarded*. The process of discarding a lookup service is initiated either directly or indirectly by the discovering entity itself or by the utility that the entity employs to perform the actual discovery duties.

Whenever a lookup service is discarded by a utility employed by the entity, the utility sends to all of the entity's discovery listeners, a notification event referencing both the discarded lookup service and the member groups to which the lookup service belongs. This event is referred to as a *discarded event*. It may be useful to note that discarded events can be classified by two characteristics:

- Whether the event was generated as a direct consequence of an explicit request made by the entity itself (*active*) or as a consequence of a determination made by some utility employed by the entity (*passive*)
- Whether the event is related to communication problems or to the entity losing interest in discovering the affected lookup services

US.2.8.1 Active Communication Discarded Event

When the occurrence of exceptional conditions causes an entity to conclude that a lookup service is unreachable, the entity typically will request that the lookup service be discarded. When the entity itself requests that such an unreachable lookup service be discarded, the resulting discarded event may be referred to as an *active communication discarded event*. The term *active* is used because the entity takes specific action to request that the lookup service be discarded. Because the entity cannot communicate with the unreachable lookup service, the event is associated with *communication*.

US.2.8.2 Active No-Interest Discarded Event

Whenever the entity makes a request that results in the removal of an element from the relevant managed set of groups or locators, one or more of the lookup services associated with the removed groups or locators may be discarded—even though the lookup services are still reachable. The lookup services may be discarded in this situation because the contents of the sets of groups and locators the entity wishes to discover may have changed in such a way that one or more of the previously discovered lookup services are no longer of interest to the entity. In this case, if any already discovered lookup service is found to belong to none of the groups in the new managed set of groups or if its locator no longer belongs to the entity's new managed set of locators, a discarded event is generated and sent to all of the entity's discovery listeners. This type of discarded event may be referred to as an *active no-interest discarded event* (active because the entity itself executed an action that resulted in the discarding of one or more lookup services).

US.2.8.3 Passive Communication Discarded Event

If the utility that the entity uses to perform group (multicast) discovery determines that one of the previously discovered lookup services has stopped sending multicast announcements, that utility may discard the lookup service. That is, the utility may remove the lookup service from the managed set and send a discarded event to notify the entity that the lookup service is unavailable. The discarded event sent in this situation is often referred to as a *passive communication discarded event*.

US.2.8.4 Passive No-Interest Discarded Event

If the utility that the entity uses to perform group discovery determines that the member groups of one of the previously discovered lookup services has changed, the utility may discard that lookup service. The lookup service may be discarded in this situation because the lookup service may no longer be a member of any of the groups the entity wishes to discover; that is, the lookup service is no longer of interest to the entity. In this case, the utility sends a discarded event to all of the entity's discovery listeners. This type of discarded event may be referred to as a *passive no-interest discarded event* (passive because the entity itself did not explicitly request that the lookup service be discarded).

If a lookup service is discarded because it was found to be unreachable (associated with a communication discarded event), that lookup service will be made eligible for rediscovery. In this case, the process of discarding a lookup service—either actively or passively—can be viewed as a mechanism for the removal of stale entries in the managed set of lookup services. Discarding such a lookup service removes the need for operations such as lease renewal attempts on a lookup service that is currently unavailable. Upon rediscovery of the discarded lookup service, the entity typically processes the rediscovered lookup service as if it were discovered for the first time.

Any lookup service corresponding to a no-interest discarded event is no longer eligible for discovery until one of the following occurs:

- The entity changes its managed set of locators or its managed set of groups to include, either the discarded lookup service's locator or at least one of its member groups respectively.
- The set of member groups of the discarded lookup service is changed to include one or more of the groups the entity is currently interested in discovering.

US.2.8.5 Changed Event

An event related to the discarded event is referred to as a *changed event*. This event notifies the entity of changes in the contents of the member groups of one or more of the lookup services in the managed set. If the entity registers interest in such an event and if the utility that the entity uses to perform group discovery determines that one or more of those member group sets has indeed changed, then a changed event is sent.

US.2.8.6 Remote Objects, Stubs, and Proxies

The *"Jini Technology Glossary"* defines a *remote object* as an object whose methods can be invoked from a Java virtual machine (JVM)[1], potentially on a different host. Furthermore, the glossary states that such an object is described by one or more *remote interfaces*.

When invoking methods remotely through Java Remote Method Invocation (RMI), it is useful to think of the invocation as consisting of two components: a client component and a server component. When the client component initiates a

---

1 The terms "Java virtual machine" or "JVM" mean a virtual machine for the Java platform.

remote method call, the server component carries out the execution of the remote method, and RMI facilitates the necessary communication between the two parties. Note that in discussing concepts related to RMI, the term *server* (or *remote server*) is sometimes used in place of the term *remote object*.

To initiate an invocation of a remote method, the client must have access to an object referred to as the *stub* of the remote object. The stub is an object local to the client that acts as the "representative" of the remote object. The stub implements the same set of remote interfaces that the remote object implements. From the point of view of the client, the stub *is* the remote object. When the client invokes a method on the local stub, communication with the remote object occurs, resulting in the execution of the corresponding method in the remote object's JVM.

The term *proxy* is used extensively throughout the helper utilities and services specifications. With respect to remote objects in general, and entities operating within a Jini application environment in particular, a proxy is simply an intermediary object through which one entity (the client) may request the invocation of the methods provided by another entity (the remote object or the service).

Proxies can take a number of different forms. A *smart proxy* typically consists of a set of local methods and a set of one or more remote object references (stubs). Clients invoke one or more of the local methods to access the methods of the remote objects referenced in the proxy.

Another form that a proxy can take is that of the stub of a remote object. That is, all stubs are simply proxies to their corresponding remote objects. Except for the local methods `equals` and `hashCode`, this type of proxy consists of remote methods only.

Some proxies are implemented as *strictly local*. Proxies of this form consist of only local methods, each executing in the client's JVM. Unlike smart proxies, no remote invocations result when any method of a strictly local proxy is invoked.

Typically, Jini services provide a proxy that has one of the forms described above. When a service registers with a lookup service, the service's proxy is copied (through serialization) into the lookup service. When a client looks up the service, the service's proxy is downloaded to the client. The client can then invoke the methods contained in the service's proxy. If the invoked method is a local method, then execution will occur in the JVM of the client. If the invoked method is a remote method (or results in a remote invocation), then execution is initiated in the client's JVM, but ultimately occurs in the JVM of the service.

Note that the term *front-end proxy* (or simply *front end*) is often used interchangeably with the term *proxy*. Similarly, the term *back-end server* (or simply, *back end*) is often used interchangeably with the term *remote object*. Thus, the back end of a service is the part of the service's implementation that satisfies the contract advertised in the service's remote interface.

US.2.9 Activation

The glossary defines *active object* as a remote object that is instantiated and exported in a JVM on some system. Remote objects can be implemented with the ability to change their state from inactive to active, or from active to inactive; the process of doing so is referred to as *activation* or *deactivation*, respectively. Many Jini services that wish to conserve computational resources may find this capability desirable. When the back end of any Jini service is implemented with the ability to activate and deactivate, the service is referred to as an *activatable service*. Refer to the *Java Remote Method Invocation Specification* for the details of activation.

US.3 Introduction to the Helper Utilities

US.3.1 The Discovery Utilities

THE *Jini Discovery Utilities Specification* defines a set of general-purpose utility interfaces collectively referred to as the discovery management interfaces. Those interfaces define the policies to apply when implementing helper utilities that manage an entity's discovery duties. Currently, the set of discovery management interfaces consists of the following three interfaces:

- `DiscoveryManagement`
- `DiscoveryGroupManagement`
- `DiscoveryLocatorManagement`

Because the discovery management interfaces provide a uniform way to define utility classes that perform discovery-related management duties on behalf of an entity, the discovery utilities specification defines a number of helper utility classes that implement one or more of these interfaces. Those classes are:

- `LookupDiscovery`
- `LookupLocatorDiscovery`
- `LookupDiscoveryManager`

The discovery utilities specification closes with a discussion of a set of low-level utility classes that can be useful when applying the discovery management policies to build higher-level helper utilities for discovery. Those classes are:

- `Constants`
- `OutgoingMulticastRequest`
- `IncomingMulticastRequest`
- `OutgoingMulticastAnnouncement`

- IncomingMulticastAnnouncement
- OutgoingUnicastRequest
- IncomingUnicastRequest
- OutgoingUnicastResponse
- IncomingUnicastResponse

US.3.1.1 The DiscoveryManagement Interface

The DiscoveryManagement interface defines methods related to the discovery event mechanism and discovery process termination. Through this interface an entity can register or unregister DiscoveryListener objects to receive discovery events, retrieve proxies to the currently discovered lookup services, discard a lookup service so that it is eligible for rediscovery, or terminate the discovery process.

US.3.1.2 The DiscoveryGroupManagement Interface

The DiscoveryGroupManagement interface defines methods and constants related to the management of the set containing the names of the groups whose members are the lookup services that are to be discovered via group discovery. The methods of this interface define how an entity retrieves or modifies the managed set of groups to discover.

US.3.1.3 The DiscoveryLocatorManagement Interface

The DiscoveryLocatorManagement interface defines methods related to the management of the set of LookupLocator objects corresponding to the specific lookup services that are to be discovered via locator discovery. The methods of this interface define how an entity retrieves or modifies the managed set of locators to discover.

US.3.1.4 The LookupDiscovery Helper Utility

The LookupDiscovery helper utility encapsulates the functionality required of an entity that wishes to employ multicast discovery to discover a lookup service located within the entity's *multicast radius*. This utility provides an implementation that makes the process of acquiring lookup service instances, based on no information other than group membership, which is much simpler for both services and clients.

US.3.1.5 The `LookupLocatorDiscovery` Helper Utility

The `LookupLocatorDiscovery` helper utility encapsulates the functionality required of an entity that wishes to employ the unicast discovery protocol to discover a lookup service. This utility provides an implementation that makes the process of finding specific instances of a lookup service much simpler for both services and clients.

US.3.1.6 The `LookupDiscoveryManager` Helper Utility

The `LookupDiscoveryManager` is a helper utility class that organizes and manages all discovery-related activities on behalf of a Jini client or service. Rather than providing its own facility for coordinating and maintaining all of the necessary state information related to group names, locators, and listeners, such an entity can employ this class to provide those facilities on its behalf.

US.3.1.7 The `Constants` Class

The `Constants` class provides easy access to defined constants that may be useful when participating in the discovery process.

US.3.1.8 The `OutgoingMulticastRequest` Utility

The `OutgoingMulticastRequest` class provides facilities for marshalling multicast discovery requests into a form suitable for transmission over a network to announce one's interest in discovering a lookup service.

US.3.1.9 The `IncomingMulticastRequest` Utility

The facilities provided by the `IncomingMulticastRequest` class encapsulate the details of the process of unmarshalling received multicast discovery requests into a form in which the individual parameters of the request may be easily accessed.

US.3.1.10 The OutgoingMulticastAnnouncement Utility

The `OutgoingMulticastAnnouncement` class encapsulates the details of the process of marshalling multicast discovery announcements into a form suitable for transmission over a network to announce the availability of a lookup service to interested parties.

US.3.1.11 The IncomingMulticastAnnouncement Utility

The `IncomingMulticastAnnouncement` class encapsulates the details of the process of unmarshalling multicast discovery announcements into a form in which the individual parameters of the announcement may be easily accessed.

US.3.1.12 The OutgoingUnicastRequest Utility

The `OutgoingUnicastRequest` class encapsulates the details of the process of marshalling unicast discovery requests into a form suitable for transmission over a network to attempt discovery of a specific lookup service.

US.3.1.13 The IncomingUnicastRequest Utility

The `IncomingUnicastRequest` class encapsulates the details of the process of unmarshalling unicast discovery requests into a form in which the individual parameters of the request may be easily accessed.

US.3.1.14 The OutgoingUnicastResponse Utility

The `OutgoingUnicastResponse` class encapsulates the details of the process of marshalling a unicast discovery response into a form suitable for transmission over a network to respond to a unicast discovery request.

US.3.1.15 The IncomingUnicastResponse Utility

The `IncomingUnicastResponse` class encapsulates the details of the process of unmarshalling a unicast discovery response into a form in which the individual parameters of the request may be easily accessed.

US.3.2 The Lease Utilities

The *Jini Lease Utilities Specification* defines helper utility classes, along with supporting interfaces and supporting classes, that encapsulate functionality which provides for the coordination, systematic renewal, and overall management of a set of leases associated with some object on behalf of another object. Currently, this specification defines only one helper utility class:

- `LeaseRenewalManager`

US.3.2.1 The `LeaseRenewalManager` Helper Utility

The `LeaseRenewalManager` is a helper utility class that organizes and manages all of the activities related to the renewal of the leases granted to a Jini client or service by another Jini service. Rather than providing its own facility for coordinating and maintaining all of the necessary state information related to lease renewal, such an entity can employ this class to provide those facilities on its behalf.

US.3.3 The Join Utilities

The *Jini Join Utilities Specification* defines helper utility classes, supporting interfaces, and supporting classes, that encapsulate functionality related to discovery and registration interactions that a well-behaved Jini service will typically have with a lookup service. Currently, this specification defines only one helper utility class:

- `JoinManager`

US.3.3.1 The `JoinManager` Helper Utility

The `JoinManager` is a helper utility class that performs all of the functions related to lookup service discovery, joining, lease renewal, and attribute management, functions that the programming model requires of a well-behaved Jini service. Rather than providing its own facility for providing such functions, a Jini service can employ this class to provide those facilities on its behalf.

US.3.4 The Service Discovery Utilities

The *Jini Service Discovery Utilities Specification* defines helper utility classes (with supporting interfaces and classes) that encapsulate functionality that aids a Jini service or client in acquiring services of interest, registered with the various lookup services with which the service or client wishes to interact. Currently, the service discovery utilities specification defines only one helper utility class:

- `ServiceDiscoveryManager`

US.3.4.1 The `ServiceDiscoveryManager` Helper Utility

The `ServiceDiscoveryManager` class is a helper utility class that any entity can use to create and populate a cache of service references, and with which the entity can register for notification of the availability of services of interest. Although the `ServiceDiscoveryManager` performs lookup discovery event handling for clients and services, the primary functionality the `ServiceDiscoveryManager` provides is service discovery and management.

The `ServiceDiscoveryManager` class can be asked to "discover" services an entity is interested in using and to cache the references to those services as each is found. The cache can be viewed as a set of services that the entity can access through a set of public, non-remote methods. The `ServiceDiscoveryManager` class also provides a mechanism for an entity to request notification when a service of interest is discovered for the first time or has encountered a state change (such as removal from all lookup services or attribute set changes).

For convenience, the `ServiceDiscoveryManager` class also provides versions of a method named `lookup`, which employs invocation semantics similar to the semantics of the `lookup` method of the `ServiceRegistrar` interface, specified in *The Jini Technology Core Platform Specification,* "Lookup Service". Entities needing to find services on only an infrequent basis, or in which the cost of making a remote call is outweighed by the overhead of maintaining a local cache (for example, because of limited resources), may find this method useful.

All three mechanisms described above—local queries on the cache, service discovery notification, and remote lookups—employ the same template-matching scheme as that described in *The Jini Technology Core Platform Specification,* "Lookup Service". Additionally, each mechanism allows the entity to supply an action object referred to as a *filter.* Such an object is a non-remote object that defines additional matching criteria that will be applied when searching for the entity's services of interest. This filtering facility is particularly useful to entities that wish to extend the capabilities of the standard template-matching scheme.

US.4 Introduction to the Helper Services

US.4.1 The Lookup Discovery Service

UNDER certain circumstances, a discovering entity may find it useful to allow a third party to perform the entity's discovery duties. For example, an activatable entity that wishes to deactivate may wish to employ a separate helper service to perform discovery duties on the entity's behalf. Such an entity may wish to deactivate for various reasons, one being to conserve computational resources. While the entity is deactivated, the helper service, running on the same or a separate host, would employ the discovery protocols to find lookup services in which the entity has expressed interest and would notify the entity when a previously unavailable lookup service becomes available. Such a helper service is referred to as a *lookup discovery service*.

The `LookupDiscoveryService` interface defines the lookup discovery helper service. Through that interface, other Jini services and clients may request that discovery processing be performed on their behalf.

US.4.2 The Lease Renewal Service

The *lease renewal service*—defined by the `net.jini.lease.LeaseRenewalService` interface—is a helper service that can be employed by both Jini clients and services to perform all lease renewal duties on their behalf. Services that wish to remain inactive until they are needed may find the lease renewal service quite useful. Such a service can request that the lease renewal service take on the responsibility of renewing the leases granted to the service, and then safely deactivate without risking the loss of access to the resources corresponding to the leases being renewed.

Entities that have continuous *access* to a network but that cannot be continuously *connected* to that network (for example, a cell phone), may also find this service useful. By allowing a lease renewal service (which can be continuously connected) to renew the leases on the resources acquired by the entity, the entity may remain disconnected until needed. This lease renewal service removes the need to perform the discovery and lookup process each time the entity reconnects to the network, potentially resulting in a significant increase in efficiency.

US.4.3 The Event Mailbox Service

The *event mailbox service* defined by the `net.jini.event.EventMailbox` interface is a helper service that can be employed by entities to store event notifications on their behalf. When an entity registers with the event mailbox service, that service will collect events intended for the registered entity until the entity initiates delivery of the events.

A service such as the event mailbox service can be particularly useful to entities that desire more control over the delivery of the events sent to them. Some entities operating in a distributed system may find it undesirable or inefficient to be contacted solely for the purpose of having an event delivered, preferring to defer the delivery to a time that is more convenient, as determined by the entity itself.

For example, an entity wishing to deactivate or detach from a network may wish to have its events stored until the entity is available to retrieve them. Additionally, some entities may wish to batch process event notifications for efficiency. In both scenarios, the entities described may find the event mailbox service useful in achieving their respective event delivery goals.

US.5 Dependencies

THE helper utilities and services specifications rely on one or more of the following specifications:

- *Java Remote Method Invocation Specification*
- *Java Object Serialization Specification*
- *Jini Technology Glossary*
- *Jini Technology Core Platform Specification*
    - Section DJ "Discovery and Join"
    - Section LE "Distributed Leasing"
    - Section TX "Transaction"
    - Section LU "Lookup Service"
- *Jini Lookup Attribute Schema Specification*

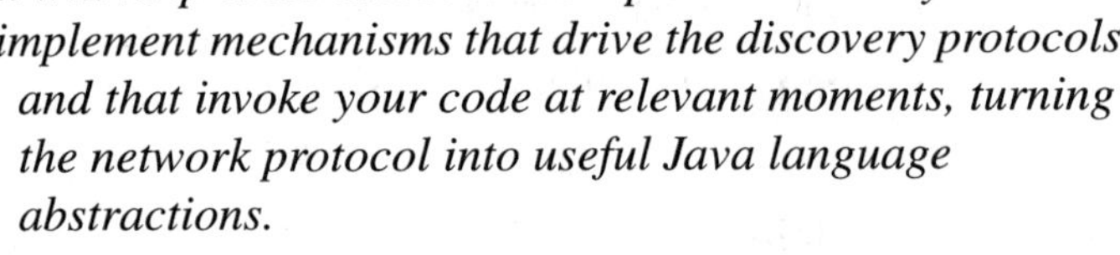
THE JINI DISCOVERY UTILITIES SPECIFICATION describes a set of utility classes and interfaces that will help users discover lookup services. They implement mechanisms that drive the discovery protocols and that invoke your code at relevant moments, turning the network protocol into useful Java language abstractions.

DU

Jini Discovery Utilities Specification

DU.1 Introduction

EACH discovering entity in a Java virtual machine (JVM)[1] on a given host is independently responsible for obtaining references to lookup services. In this specification we first cover a set of *discovery management interfaces* that define the policies to apply when implementing helper utilities that manage an entity's discovery duties: in particular, the management of multicast (group) discovery and unicast (locator) discovery. After the discovery management interfaces are defined, a set of standard helper utility classes that implement one or more of those interfaces is presented. This specification closes with a discussion of a set of lower-level utility classes that can be useful when applying the discovery management policies to build higher-level helper utilities for discovery.

DU.1.1 Dependencies

This specification relies on the following other specifications:

- *Java Object Serialization Specification*
- *The Jini Technology Core Platform Specification,* "Lookup Service"
- *The Jini Technology Core Platform Specification,* "Discovery and Join"

---

[1] The terms "Java virtual machine" and "JVM" mean a virtual machine for the Java platform.

DU.2 The Discovery Management Interfaces

DU.2.1 Overview

DISCOVERY is one behavior that is common to all entities wishing to interact with a Jini lookup service. Whether an entity is a client, a service, or a service acting as a client, the entity must first discover a lookup service, before the entity can begin interacting with that lookup service.

The interfaces collectively referred to as the *discovery management* interfaces specify sets of methods that define a mechanism that may be used to manage various aspects of the discovery duties of entities that wish to participate in an application environment for Jini technology (a *Jini application environment*). These interfaces provide a uniform way to define utility classes that perform the necessary discovery-related management duties on behalf of a client or service. Currently, there are three discovery management interfaces belonging to the package `net.jini.discovery`:

- `DiscoveryManagement`
- `DiscoveryGroupManagement`
- `DiscoveryLocatorManagement`

The `DiscoveryManagement` interface defines semantics for methods related to the discovery event mechanism and discovery process termination. Through this interface, an entity can register or un-register for discovery events, discard a lookup service, or terminate the discovery process.

The `DiscoveryGroupManagement` interface defines methods related to the management of the sets of lookup services that are to be discovered using the multicast discovery protocols (see *The Jini Technology Core Platform Specification,* "Discovery and Join"). The methods of this interface define how an entity accesses or modifies the set of groups whose members are lookup services that the entity is interested in discovering through group discovery.

The `DiscoveryLocatorManagement` interface defines methods related to the management of the set of lookup services that are to be discovered using the unicast discovery protocol (as defined in the *Jini Discovery and Join Specification*). The methods of this interface define how an entity accesses or modifies the contents of the set of `LookupLocator` objects corresponding to the specific lookup services the entity has targeted for locator discovery.

Although each interface defines semantics for methods involved in the management of the discovery process, the individual roles each interface plays in that process are independent of each other. Because of this independence, there may be scenarios where it is desirable to implement some subset of these interfaces.

For example, a class may wish to implement the functionality defined in `DiscoveryManagement`, but may not wish to allow entities to modify the groups and locators associated with the lookup services to be discovered. Such a class may have a "hard-coded" list of the groups and locators that it internally registers with the discovery process. For this case, the class would implement only `DiscoveryManagement`.

Alternatively, another class may not wish to allow the entity to register more than one listener with the discovery event mechanism; nor may it wish to allow the entity to terminate discovery. It may simply wish to allow the entity to modify the sets of lookup services that will be discovered. Such a class would implement both `DiscoveryGroupManagement` and `DiscoveryLocatorManagement`, but not `DiscoveryManagement`.

A specific example of a class that implements only a subset of the set of interfaces specified here is the `LookupDiscovery` utility class defined later in this specification. That class implements both the `DiscoveryManagement` and `DiscoveryGroupManagement` interfaces, but not the `DiscoveryLocatorManagement` interface.

Throughout this discussion of the discovery management interfaces, the phrase *implementation class* refers to any concrete class that implements one or more of those interfaces. The phrase *implementation object* should be understood to mean an instance of such an implementation class. Additionally, whenever a description refers to the *discovering entity* (or simply, the *entity),* that phrase is intended to be interpreted as the object (the client or service) that has created an implementation object, and which wishes to use the public methods specified by these interfaces and provided by that object.

DU.2.2 Other Types

The types defined in the specification of the discovery management interfaces are in the `net.jini.discovery` package. The following additional types may also be referenced in this specification. Whenever referenced, these object types will be referenced in unqualified form:

```
net.jini.core.discovery.LookupLocator
net.jini.core.lookup.ServiceRegistrar
net.jini.discovery.DiscoveryEvent
net.jini.discovery.DiscoveryListener
net.jini.discovery.DiscoveryChangeListener
net.jini.discovery.LookupDiscovery
net.jini.discovery.LookupDiscoveryManager
java.io.IOException
java.security.Permission
java.util.EventListener
java.util.EventObject
java.util.Map
```

DU.2.3 The `DiscoveryManagement` Interface

The public methods specified by the `DiscoveryManagement` interface are:

```
package net.jini.discovery;

public interface DiscoveryManagement {
    public void addDiscoveryListener
                                (DiscoveryListener listener);
    public void removeDiscoveryListener
                                (DiscoveryListener listener);
    public ServiceRegistrar[] getRegistrars();
    public void discard(ServiceRegistrar proxy);
    public void terminate();
}
```

DU.2.3.1 The Semantics

The `DiscoveryManagement` interface defines methods related to the discovery event mechanism and discovery process termination. Through this interface, an entity can register or un-register `DiscoveryListener` objects to receive discovery events (instances of `DiscoveryEvent`), retrieve proxies to the currently discovered lookup services, discard a lookup service so that it is eligible for re-discovery, or terminate the discovery process.

Implementation classes of this interface may impose additional semantics on any method. For example, such a class may choose to require that rather than simply terminate discovery processing, the `terminate` method additionally should cancel all leases held by the implementation object and terminate all lease management being performed on behalf of the entity.

For information on any additional semantics imposed on a method of this interface, refer to the specification of the particular implementation class.

The `DiscoveryEvent`, `DiscoveryListener`, and `DiscoveryChangeListener` classes are defined later in this specification.

The `addDiscoveryListener` method adds a listener to the set of objects listening for discovery events. This method takes a single argument as input: an instance of `DiscoveryListener` corresponding to the listener to add to the set.

Once a listener is registered, it will be notified of all lookup services discovered to date, and will then be notified as new lookup services are discovered or existing lookup services are discarded.

If the added listener is also an instance of `DiscoveryChangeListener` (a subclass of `DiscoveryListener`), then in addition to receiving events related to discovered and discarded lookup services, that listener will also be notified of group membership changes that occur in any of the lookup services targeted for at least group discovery.

If `null` is input to this method, a `NullPointerException` is thrown. If the listener input to this method duplicates (using the `equals` method) another element in the set of listeners, no action is taken.

Implementations of the `DiscoveryManagement` interface must guarantee reentrancy with respect to `DiscoveryListener` objects registered through this method. Should the instance of `DiscoveryManagement` invoke a method on a registered listener (a local call), calls from that method to any method of the `DiscoveryManagement` instance are guaranteed not to result in a deadlock condition.

The `removeDiscoveryListener` method removes a listener from the set of objects listening for discovery events. This method takes a single argument as input: an instance of `DiscoveryListener` corresponding to the listener to remove from the set.

If the listener object input to this method does not exist in the set of listeners maintained by the implementation class, then this method will take no action.

The `getRegistrars` method returns an array consisting of instances of the `ServiceRegistrar` interface. Each element in the returned set is a proxy to one of the currently discovered lookup services. Each time this method is invoked, a new array is returned. If no lookup services have been discovered, an empty array is returned. This method takes no arguments as input.

The discard method removes a particular lookup service from the managed set of lookup services, and makes that lookup service eligible to be re-discovered. This method takes a single argument as input: an instance of the ServiceRegistrar interface corresponding to the proxy to the lookup service to discard.

If the proxy input to this method is null, or if it matches (using the equals method) none of the lookup services in the managed set, this method takes no action.

Currently, there exist utilities such as the LookupDiscovery and LookupDiscoveryManager helper utilities that will, on behalf of a discovering entity, automatically discard a lookup service upon determining that the lookup service has become unreachable or uninteresting. Although most entities will typically employ such a utility to help with both its discovery as well as its discard duties, it is important to note that if the entity itself determines that the lookup service is unavailable, it is the responsibility of the entity to invoke the discard method. This scenario usually happens when the entity attempts to interact with a lookup service, but encounters an exceptional condition (for example, a communication failure). When the entity actively discards a lookup service, the discarded lookup service becomes eligible to be re-discovered. Allowing unreachable lookup services to remain in the managed set can result in repeated and unnecessary attempts to interact with lookup services with which the entity can no longer communicate. Thus, the mechanism provided by this method is intended to provide a way to remove such "stale" lookup service references from the managed set.

Invoking the discard method defined by the DiscoveryManagement interface will result in the flushing of the lookup service from the appropriate cache, ultimately causing a discard notification—referred to as a *discarded event*—to be sent to all listeners registered with the implementation object. When this method completes successfully, the lookup service is guaranteed to have been removed from the managed set, and the lookup service is then said to have been "discarded". No such guarantee is made with respect to when the discarded event is sent to the registered listeners. That is, the event notifying the listeners that the lookup service has been discarded may or may not be sent asynchronously.

The terminate method ends all discovery processing being performed on behalf of the entity. This method takes no input arguments.

After this method has been invoked, no new lookup services will be discovered, and the effect of any new operations performed on the current implementation object are undefined.

Any additional termination semantics must be defined by the implementation class.

DU.2.4 The DiscoveryGroupManagement Interface

The public methods specified by the DiscoveryGroupManagement interface are as follows:

```
package net.jini.discovery;

public interface DiscoveryGroupManagement {
    public static final String[] ALL_GROUPS = null;
    public static final String[] NO_GROUPS = new String[0];

    public String[] getGroups();
    public void addGroups(String[] groups) throws IOException;
    public void setGroups(String[] groups) throws IOException;
    public void removeGroups(String[] groups);
}
```

DU.2.4.1 The Semantics

The DiscoveryGroupManagement interface defines methods and constants related to the management of the set containing the names of the groups whose members are the lookup services that are to be discovered using the multicast discovery protocols; that is, lookup services that are discovered by way of group discovery. The methods of this interface define how an entity retrieves or modifies the managed set of groups to discover, where phrases such as "the groups to discover" or "discovering the desired groups" refer to the discovery of the lookup services that are members of those groups.

The methods that modify the managed set of groups each take a single input parameter: a String array, none of whose elements may be null. Each of these methods throws a NullPointerException when at least one element of the input array is null.

The empty set is denoted by an empty array, and "no set" is indicated by null. Invoking any of these methods with an input array that contains duplicate group names is equivalent to performing the invocation with the duplicates removed from the array.

The ALL_GROUPS and the NO_GROUPS constants are defined for convenience, and represent no set and the empty set respectively.

The getGroups method returns an array consisting of the names of the groups in the managed set; that is, the names of the groups the implementation object is currently configured to discover.

If the managed set of groups is empty, this method will return an empty array. If there is no managed set of groups, then `null` (`ALL_GROUPS`) is returned, indicating that any lookup service within range—even those that have no group affiliation—are to be discovered.

If an empty array is returned, that array is guaranteed to be referentially equal to the `NO_GROUPS` constant; that is, the array returned from that method and the `NO_GROUPS` constant can be tested for equality using the == operator.

This method takes no arguments as input and, provided the managed set of groups currently exists, will return a new array upon each invocation.

The `addGroups` method adds a set of group names to the managed set. The array input to this method contains the group names to be added to the set.

This method throws `IOException` because an invocation of this method may result in the re-initiation of the discovery process, which can throw `IOException` when socket allocation occurs.

This method throws an `UnsupportedOperationException` if there is no managed set of groups to augment, and it throws a `NullPointerException` if `null` (`ALL_GROUPS`) is input. If an empty array (`NO_GROUPS`) is input, the managed set of groups will not change.

The `setGroups` method replaces all of the group names in the managed set with names from a new set. The array input to this method contains the group names with which to replace the current names in the managed set.

Once a new group name has been placed in the managed set, no event will be sent to the entity's listener for the lookup services belonging to that group that have already been discovered, although attempts to discover all (as yet) undiscovered lookup services belonging to that group will continue to be made.

If `null` (`ALL_GROUPS`) is input to `setGroups`, then attempts will be made to discover all (as yet) undiscovered lookup services located within the *multicast radius (*Section DU.3, "`LookupDiscovery` Utility"*)* of the implementation object, regardless of group membership.

If an empty array (`NO_GROUPS`) is input to `setGroups`, then group discovery will be halted until the managed set of groups is changed—through a subsequent call to this method or to `addGroups`—to a set that is either a non-empty set of group names or `null` (`ALL_GROUPS`).

This method throws `IOException`. This is because an invocation of this method may result in the re-initiation of the discovery process, a process that can throw `IOException` when socket allocation occurs.

The `removeGroups` method deletes a set of group names from the managed set of groups. The array input to this method contains the group names to be removed from the managed set.

This method throws an UnsupportedOperationException if there is no managed set of groups from which to remove elements. If null (ALL_GROUPS) is input to removeGroups, a NullPointerException will be thrown.

If any element of the set of groups to be removed is not contained in the managed set, removeGroups takes no action with respect to that element. If an empty array (NO_GROUPS) is input, the managed set of groups will not change.

Once a new group name is added to the managed set as a result of an invocation of either addGroups or setGroups, attempts will be made—using the multicast request protocol—to discover all (as yet) undiscovered lookup services that are members of that group. If there are no responses to the multicast requests, the implementation object will stop sending multicast requests, and will simply listen for multicast announcements containing the new groups of interest.

Any already discovered lookup service that is a member of one or more of the groups removed from the managed set as a result of an invocation of either setGroups or removeGroups will be discarded and will no longer be eligible for discovery, but only if that lookup service satisfies both of the following conditions:

- the lookup service is not a member of any group in the new managed set that resulted from the invocation of setGroups or removeGroups, and
- the lookup service is not currently eligible for discovery through other means (such as locator discovery).

DU.2.5 The DiscoveryLocatorManagement Interface

The public methods specified by the DiscoveryLocatorManagement interface are as follows:

```
package net.jini.discovery;

public interface DiscoveryLocatorManagement {
    public LookupLocator[] getLocators();
    public void addLocators(LookupLocator[] locators);
    public void setLocators(LookupLocator[] locators);
    public void removeLocators(LookupLocator[] locators);
}
```

DU.2.5.1 The Semantics

The `DiscoveryLocatorManagement` interface defines methods related to the management of the set of `LookupLocator` objects corresponding to the specific lookup services that are to be discovered using the unicast discovery protocol; that is, lookup services that are discovered by way of locator discovery. The methods of this interface define how an entity retrieves or modifies the managed set of locators to discover. Phrases such as "the locators to discover" and "discovering the desired locators" refer to the discovery of the lookup services that are associated with those locators.

The methods that modify the managed set of locators each take a single input parameter: an array of `LookupLocator` objects, none of whose elements may be `null`. Each of these methods throws a `NullPointerException` when at least one element of the input array is `null`.

Invoking any of these methods with an input array that contains duplicate locators (as determined by `LookupLocator.equals`) is equivalent to performing the invocation with the duplicates removed from the array.

The `getLocators` method returns an array containing the set of `LookupLocator` objects in the managed set of locators; that is, the locators of the specific lookup services that the implementation object is currently interested in discovering.

The returned set includes both the set of locators corresponding to lookup services that have already been discovered and the set of those that have not yet been discovered.

If the managed set is empty, this method returns an empty array. This method takes no arguments as input, and returns a new array upon each invocation.

The `addLocators` method adds a set of locators to the managed set. The array input to this method contains the set of `LookupLocator` objects to add to the managed set.

If `null` is input to `addLocators`, a `NullPointerException` will be thrown. If an empty array is input, the managed set of locators will not change.

The `setLocators` method replaces all of the locators in the managed set with `LookupLocator` objects from a new set. The array input to this method contains the set of `LookupLocator` objects with which to replace the current locators in the managed set.

If `null` is input to `setLocators`, a `NullPointerException` will be thrown.

If an empty array is input to `setLocators`, then locator discovery will be halted until the managed set of locators is changed—through a subsequent call to this method or to `addLocators`—to a set that is non-`null` and non-empty.

The `removeLocators` method deletes a set of locators from the managed set. The array input to this method contains the set of `LookupLocator` objects to remove from the managed set.

If `null` is input to `removeLocators`, a `NullPointerException` will be thrown.

If any element of the set of locators to remove is not contained in the managed set, `removeLocators` takes no action with respect to that element. If an empty array is input, the managed set of locators will not change.

Any already discovered lookup service, corresponding to a locator that is a member of the set of locators removed from the managed set as a result of an invocation of either `setLocators` or `removeLocators`, will be discarded and will no longer be eligible for discovery; but only if it is not currently eligible for discovery through other means (such as group discovery).

DU.2.6 Supporting Interfaces and Classes

Discovery management depends on the interfaces `DiscoveryListener` and `DiscoveryChangeListener`, and on the concrete class `DiscoveryEvent`.

DU.2.6.1 The `DiscoveryListener` Interface

The public methods specified by the `DiscoveryListener` interface are as follows:

```
package net.jini.discovery;

public interface DiscoveryListener extends EventListener {
    public void discovered(DiscoveryEvent e);
    public void discarded(DiscoveryEvent e);
}
```

When an entity employs an object that implements one or more of the discovery management interfaces to perform and manage the entity's discovery duties, the entity often will want that object—generally referred to as a *discovery utility*—to notify the entity when a desired lookup service is either discovered or discarded. The `DiscoveryListener` interface defines a mechanism through which an entity may receive such notifications from a discovery utility. When an entity registers interest in these notifications, an implementation of this interface must be provided to the discovery utility being employed. Through this registered listener, the entity may then receive instances of the `DiscoveryEvent` class, which encapsulate the required information associated with the desired notifications.

The Semantics

The events received by listeners implementing the `DiscoveryListener` interface can be the result of either group discovery or locator discovery. These events contain the discovered or discarded registrars, as well as the set of member groups corresponding to each registrar (see the specification of the `DiscoveryEvent` class).

The `discovered` method is called whenever a new lookup service is discovered or a discarded lookup service is re-discovered.

The `discarded` method is called whenever a previously discovered lookup service is discarded because the lookup service was determined to be either unreachable or no longer interesting to the entity, and the discard process was initiated by either the entity itself (an *active* discard) or the discovery utility employed by the entity (a *passive* discard).

This interface makes the following concurrency guarantee. For any given listener object that implements this interface or any sub-interface, no two methods (either the same two methods or different methods) defined by the interface (or sub-interface) can be invoked at the same time. For example, the `discovered` method must not be invoked while the invocation of another listener's `discarded` method is in progress.

DU.2.6.2 The `DiscoveryChangeListener` Interface

The `DiscoveryChangeListener` interface specifies only one public method:

```
package net.jini.discovery;

public interface DiscoveryChangeListener
                 extends DiscoveryListener
{
    public void changed(DiscoveryEvent e);
}
```

In addition to being notified when a desired lookup service is discovered or discarded, some entities may also wish to be notified when a lookup service experiences changes in its group membership. The `DiscoveryChangeListener` interface defines an extension to the `DiscoveryListener` interface, providing a mechanism through which an entity may receive these additional notifications—

referred to as *changed events*. As with the `DiscoveryListener` interface, when an entity wishes to receive changed events in addition to discovered and discarded events, an implementation of this interface must be provided to the discovery utility being employed. It is through that registered listener that the entity receives the desired notifications encapsulated in instances of the `DiscoveryEvent` class.

The Semantics

When the entity receives a `DiscoveryEvent` object through an instance of the `DiscoveryChangeListener` interface, the event contains the discovered, discarded, or changed registrars, as well as the set of member groups corresponding to each registrar. In the case of a changed event, each set of groups referenced in the event contains the new groups in which the corresponding registrar is a member.

The `changed` method is called whenever the discovery utility encounters changes in the set of groups in which a previously discovered lookup service is a member.

It is important to note that instances of this interface are eligible to receive changed events for only those lookup services that the entity has requested be discovered by (at least) group discovery. That is, if the entity requests that *only* locator discovery be used to discover a specific lookup service, the listener will receive no changed events for that lookup service. This is because the semantics of this interface assume that since the entity expressed no interest in *discovering* the lookup service through its group membership, it must also have no interest in any *changes* in that lookup service's group membership. Thus, if an entity wishes to receive changed events for one or more lookup services, the entity must request that those lookup services be discovered by either group discovery alone, or by both group and locator discovery.

DU.2.6.3 The `DiscoveryEvent` Class

The public methods provided by the `DiscoveryEvent` class are as follows:

```
package net.jini.discovery;

public class DiscoveryEvent extends EventObject {
    public DiscoveryEvent(Object source, Map groups) {...}
    public DiscoveryEvent(Object source,
                          ServiceRegistrar[] regs) {...}
```

```
    public Map getGroups() {...}
    public ServiceRegistrar[] getRegistrars() {...}
}
```

The `DiscoveryEvent` class provides an encapsulation of event information that discovery utilities can use to notify an entity of the occurrence of an event involving one or more `ServiceRegistrar` objects (lookup services) in which the entity has registered interest. Discovery utilities pass an instance of this class to the entity's discovery listener(s) when one of the following events occurs:

- Each lookup service referenced in the event has been discovered for the first time, or re-discovered after having been discarded.
- Each lookup service referenced in the event has been either actively or passively discarded.
- For each lookup service referenced in the event, the set of groups in which the lookup service is a member has changed.

The `DiscoveryEvent` class is a subclass of `EventObject`, adding the following additional items of abstract state: a set of `ServiceRegistrar` instances (*registrars*) referencing the affected lookup services, and a mapping from each of those registrars to their current set of member groups. Methods are defined through which this additional state may be retrieved upon receipt of an instance of this class.

The Semantics

The `equals` method for this class returns `true` if and only if two instances of this class refer to the same object. That is, `x` and `y` are equal instances of this class if and only if `x == y` has the value `true`.

The constructor for this class has two forms, where both forms expect two input parameters. Each form of the constructor takes, as its first input parameter, a reference to the source of the event; that is, the discovery utility object that created the event instance and sent it to the entity's listener(s) through the invocation of the `discovered`, `discarded`, or `changed` method on each listener. Note that neither form of the constructor makes a copy of the second parameter. That is, the reference input to the second parameter is shared with the invoking entity.

Depending on the constructor employed, the second parameter is one of the following:

- A `Map` instance in which each element of the map's key set is a `ServiceRegistrar` instance that references one of the lookup services to be associated with the event being constructed. Each element of the map's value set is a `String` array, containing the names of the groups in which the corresponding lookup service is a member.
- An array of `ServiceRegistrar` instances in which each element references one of the lookup services to be associated with the event being constructed.

  It is important to note that when this form of the constructor is used to construct a `DiscoveryEvent`, although the resulting event contains a `non-null` registrars array, the registrars-to-groups map is `null`. Therefore, discovery utilities should no longer use this constructor to instantiate the events they send.

The `getGroups` method returns the mapping from each registrar referenced by the event to the registrar's current set of member groups. If the event was instantiated using the constructor whose second parameter is an array of `ServiceRegistrar` instances, this method will return `null`.

The returned map's key set is made up of `ServiceRegistrar` instances corresponding to the lookup services for which the event was constructed and sent. Each element of the returned map's value set is a `String` array, containing the names of the member groups of the corresponding lookup service.

On each invocation of this method, the same `Map` object is returned; that is, a copy is not made.

The `getRegistrars` method returns an array of `ServiceRegistrar` instances, in which each element references one of the lookup services for which the event was constructed and sent.

On each invocation of this method, the same array is returned; that is, a copy is not made.

DU.2.7 Serialized Forms

Class	`serialVersionUID`	Serialized Fields
`DiscoveryEvent`	5280303374696501479L	`ServiceRegistrar[] regs` `Map groups`

DU.3 LookupDiscovery Utility

In a Jini application environment the multicast discovery protocols are often collectively referred to as multicast discovery or group discovery. The entities that participate in the multicast discovery protocol are a *discovering entity* (Jini client or service) and a Jini lookup service, which acts as the entity that is to be discovered. When the discovering entity starts, it uses the multicast request protocol to announce its interest in finding lookup services within range. After a specified amount of time, the entity stops sending multicast requests, and simply listens for multicast announcements from any lookup services within range that may be broadcasting their availability. Through either of these protocols, the discovering entity can obtain references to lookup services belonging to member group in which the entity is interested. For the details of the multicast discovery protocols, refer to the *The Jini Technology Core Platform Specification,* "Discovery and Join".

The LookupDiscovery helper utility in the package net.jini.discovery encapsulates the functionality required of an entity that wishes to employ multicast discovery to discover a lookup service located within the entity's *multicast radius* (roughly, the number of hops beyond which neither the multicast requests from the entity, nor the multicast announcements from the lookup service, will propagate). This utility provides an implementation that makes the process of acquiring lookup service instances, based on no information other than group membership, much simpler for both services and clients.

DU.3.1 Other Types

The types defined in the specification of the LookupDiscovery utility class are in the net.jini.discovery package. The following additional types may also be referenced in this specification. Whenever referenced, these object types will be referenced in unqualified form:

```
net.jini.core.discovery.LookupLocator
net.jini.discovery.DiscoveryManagement
net.jini.discovery.DiscoveryGroupManagement
net.jini.discovery.DiscoveryPermission
java.io.IOException
java.io.Serializable
java.security.Permission
```

DU.3.2 The Interface

The public methods provided by the LookupDiscovery class are as follows:

```
package net.jini.discovery;

public class LookupDiscovery
                        implements DiscoveryManagement,
                                   DiscoveryGroupManagement
{
    public static final String[] ALL_GROUPS
                      = DiscoveryGroupManagement.ALL_GROUPS;
    public static final String[] NO_GROUPS
                      = DiscoveryGroupManagement.NO_GROUPS;

    public LookupDiscovery(String[] groups)
                                      throws IOException {...}
}
```

DU.3.3 The Semantics

The only new public method of the LookupDiscovery helper utility class is the constructor. All other public methods implemented by this class are specified in the DiscoveryManagement and the DiscoveryGroupManagement interfaces.

Each instance of the LookupDiscovery class must behave as if it operates independently of all other instances.

The equals method for this class returns true if and only if two instances of this class refer to the same object. That is, x and y are equal instances of this class if and only if x == y has the value true.

For convenience, this class defines the constants ALL_GROUPS and NO_GROUPS, which represent no set and the empty set respectively. For more information on these constants, refer to the specification of the DiscoveryGroupManagement interface.

The constructor of the LookupDiscovery class takes a single input parameter: a String array, none of whose elements may be null. If at least one element of the input array is null, a NullPointerException is thrown.

Constructing this class using an input array that contains duplicate group names is equivalent to constructing the class using an array with the duplicates removed.

If null (ALL_GROUPS) is input to the constructor, then attempts will be made to discover all lookup services located within the current multicast radius, regardless of group membership.

Although discovery events will not be sent by this class until a listener is added through an invocation of the addListener method, discovery processing usually starts as soon as an instance of this class is constructed. However, if an empty array (NO_GROUPS) is passed to the constructor, discovery will not be started until the addGroups or setGroups method is called to change the initial empty set of groups to either a non-empty set, or null (ALL_GROUPS).

The constructor can throw an IOException because the creation of a LookupDiscovery object causes the initiation of the discovery process, a process that can throw IOException when socket allocation occurs.

DU.3.4 Supporting Interfaces and Classes

The LookupDiscovery helper utility class depends on the interfaces DiscoveryManagement and DiscoveryGroupManagement, and on the concrete class DiscoveryPermission.

DU.3.4.1 The DiscoveryManagement Interfaces

The LookupDiscovery class implements both the DiscoveryManagement and the DiscoveryGroupManagement interfaces, which together define methods related to the coordination and management of all group discovery processing. See Section DU.2, “The Discovery Management Interfaces” for more information on those interfaces.

DU.3.4.2 Security and Multicast Discovery: The DiscoveryPermission Class

When an instance of the LookupDiscovery class is constructed, the entity that creates the instance must be granted appropriate discovery permission. For example, if the instance of LookupDiscovery is currently configured to discover a non-empty, non-null set of groups, then the entity that created the instance must have permission to attempt discovery of each of the groups in that set. If the set of groups to discover is null (ALL_GROUPS), then the entity must have permission to attempt discovery of all possible groups. If appropriate permissions are not granted, the constructor of LookupDiscovery, as well as the methods addGroups and setGroups, will throw a java.lang.SecurityException.

Discovery permissions are controlled in security policy files using the permission class DiscoveryPermission. The public methods provided by the DiscoveryPermission class are as follows:

```
package net.jini.discovery;

public final class DiscoveryPermission extends Permission
                                         implements Serializable
{
    public DiscoveryPermission(String group) {...}
    public DiscoveryPermission(String group,
                               String actions) {...}
}
```

The DiscoveryPermission class is a subclass of Permission, adding no additional items of abstract state.

The Semantics

The equals method for this class returns true if and only if two instances of this class have the same group name.

The constructor for this class has two forms: one form expecting one input parameter, the other form expecting two input parameters. Each form of the constructor takes, as its first input parameter, a String representing one or more group names for which to allow discovery.

The second parameter of the second form of the constructor is a String value that is currently ignored because there are no actions associated with a discovery permission.

`DiscoveryPermission` Examples

A number of examples that illustrate the use of this permission are presented. Note that each example represents a line in a policy file.

`permission net.jini.discovery.DiscoveryPermission "*";`
Grant the entity permission to attempt discovery of all possible groups

`permission net.jini.discovery.DiscoveryPermission "";`
Grant the entity permission to attempt discovery of only the "public" group

`permission net.jini.discovery.DiscoveryPermission "foo";`
Grant the entity permission to attempt discovery of the group named "foo"

`permission net.jini.discovery.DiscoveryPermission "*.sun.com";`
Grant the entity permission to attempt discovery of all groups whose names end with the substring ".sun.com"

Each of the above declarations grants permission to attempt discovery of one name. A name does not necessarily correspond to a single group. That is, the following should be noted:

- The name "`*`" grants permission to attempt discovery of *all* possible groups.
- A name beginning with "`*.`" grants permission to attempt discovery of all groups that match the *remainder* of that name; for example, the name `"*.example.org"` would match a group named `"foonly.example.org"` and also a group named `"sf.ca.example.org"`.
- The empty name `""` denotes the *public* group.
- All other names are treated as individual groups and must match exactly.

Finally, it is important to note that a restriction of the Java platform security model requires that appropriate `DiscoveryPermission` be granted to the Jini technology infrastructure software codebase itself, in addition to any codebases that may use Jini technology infrastructure software classes.

DU.3.5 Serialized Forms

Class	`serialVersionUID`	Serialized Fields
`DiscoveryPermission`	–3036978025008149170L	*none*

DU.4 The `LookupLocatorDiscovery` Utility

DU.4.1 Overview

THE *The Jini Technology Core Platform Specification,* "Discovery and Join", states that the "unicast discovery protocol is a simple request-response protocol." In a Jini application environment, the entities that participate in this protocol are a discovering entity (Jini client or service) and a Jini lookup service that acts as the entity to be discovered. The discovering entity sends unicast discovery requests to the lookup service, and the lookup service reacts to those requests by sending unicast discovery responses to the interested discovering entity.

The `LookupLocatorDiscovery` helper utility (belonging to the package `net.jini.discovery`) encapsulates the functionality required of an entity that wishes to employ the unicast discovery protocol to discover a lookup service. This utility provides an implementation that makes the process of finding specific instances of a lookup service much simpler for both services and clients.

Because the `LookupLocatorDiscovery` helper utility class will participate in only the unicast discovery protocol, and because the unicast discovery protocol imposes no restriction on the physical location of a service or client relative to a lookup service, this utility can be used to discover lookup services running on hosts that are located far from, or near to, the hosts on which the service is running. This lack of a restriction on location brings with it a requirement that the discovering entity supply specific information about the desired lookup services to the `LookupLocatorDiscovery` utility; namely, the location of the device(s) hosting each lookup service. This information is supplied through an instance of the `LookupLocator` utility, defined in *The Jini Technology Core Platform Specification,* "Discovery and Join".

It may be of value to note the difference between `LookupLocatorDiscovery` and the `LookupDiscovery` helper utility for group discovery (defined earlier). Although both are non-remote utility classes that entities can use to discover at least one lookup service, the `LookupLocatorDiscovery` utility is designed to provide discovery capabilities that satisfy different needs than those satisfied by the `LookupDiscovery` utility. These two utilities differ in the following ways:

- Whereas the `LookupLocatorDiscovery` utility is used to discover lookup services by their *locators*, employing the unicast discovery protocol, the `LookupDiscovery` utility uses the multicast discovery protocols to discover lookup services by the *groups* to which the lookup services belong.
- Whereas the `LookupLocatorDiscovery` utility requires that the discovering entity supply the specific location—or address—of the desired lookup service(s) in the form of a `LookupLocator` object, the `LookupDiscovery` utility imposes no such restriction on the discovering entity.
- Whereas the `LookupLocatorDiscovery` utility can be used by a discovering entity to discover lookup services that are both "near" and "far," the `LookupDiscovery` utility can be used to discover only those lookup services that are located within the same multicast radius as that of the discovering entity.

DU.4.2 Other Types

The types defined in the specification of the `LookupLocatorDiscovery` utility class are in the `net.jini.discovery` package. The following additional types may also be referenced in this specification. Whenever referenced, these object types will be referenced in unqualified form:

```
net.jini.core.discovery.LookupLocator
net.jini.discovery.DiscoveryManagement
net.jini.discovery.DiscoveryLocatorManagement
```

DU.4.3 The Interface

The public methods provided by the `LookupLocatorDiscovery` class are as follows:

```
package net.jini.discovery;

public class LookupLocatorDiscovery
                        implements DiscoveryManagement
                                   DiscoveryLocatorManagement
{
    public LookupLocatorDiscovery
                              (LookupLocator[] locators) {...}
```

```
        public LookupLocator[] getDiscoveredLocators() {…}
        public LookupLocator[] getUndiscoveredLocators() {…}
    }
```

DU.4.4 The Semantics

Including the constructor, the LookupLocatorDiscovery helper utility class defines three new public methods. All other public methods are inherited from the DiscoveryManagement and DiscoveryLocatorManagement interfaces.

Each instance of the LookupLocatorDiscovery class must behave as if it operates independently of all other instances.

The equals method for this class returns true if and only if two instances of this class refer to the same object. That is, x and y are equal instances of this class if and only if x == y has the value true.

The constructor of the LookupLocatorDiscovery class takes a single input parameter: a set of locators represented as an array of LookupLocator objects, none of whose elements may be null. Each element in the input set corresponds to a specific lookup service the discovering entity wishes to be discovered. Although it is acceptable to input null, if a non-null array containing at least one null element is input, a NullPointerException will be thrown.

Invoking the constructor with an input array that contains duplicate locators (as determined by LookupLocator.equals) is equivalent to performing the invocation with the duplicates removed from the array.

Although discovery events will not be sent by this class until a listener is added through an invocation of the addListener method, discovery processing usually starts as soon as an instance of this class is constructed. However, if null or an empty array is passed to the constructor, discovery will not be started until the addLocators or setLocators method is called to change the managed set of locators to a set of locators that is non-null and non-empty.

The getDiscoveredLocators method returns the set of LookupLocator objects representing the desired lookup services that are currently discovered. If the set is empty, this method will return an empty array. This method takes no arguments as input, and will return a new array upon each invocation.

The getUndiscoveredLocators method returns the set of LookupLocator objects representing the desired lookup services that have not yet been discovered. If the set is empty, this method will return an empty array. This method takes no arguments as input, and will return a new array upon each invocation.

DU.4.5 Supporting Interfaces

The LookupLocatorDiscovery helper utility class depends on the following interfaces: DiscoveryManagement and DiscoveryLocatorManagement.

DU.4.5.1 The DiscoveryManagement Interfaces

The LookupLocatorDiscovery class implements the DiscoveryManagement and DiscoveryLocatorManagement interfaces, which together define methods related to the coordination and management of all locator discovery processing. See Section DU.2, "The Discovery Management Interfaces" for more information on those interfaces.

DU.5 The LookupDiscoveryManager Utility

DU.5.1 Overview

ALTHOUGH the goals of any well-behaved Jini client or service are application-specific, the goals of such entities with respect to their interaction with Jini lookup services generally begin with employing the Jini discovery protocols (defined in *The Jini Technology Core Platform Specification,* "Discovery and Join") to obtain a reference to at least one lookup service. Because the discovery duties performed by such entities may require the management of significant amounts of state information, those duties can become quite tedious.

The LookupDiscoveryManager is a helper utility class (belonging to the package net.jini.discovery) that organizes and manages all discovery-related activities on behalf of a Jini client or service. Rather than providing its own facility for coordinating and maintaining all of the necessary state information related to group names, LookupLocator objects, and DiscoveryListener objects, such an entity can employ this class to provide those facilities on its behalf.

DU.5.2 Other Types

The types defined in the specification of the LookupDiscoveryManager utility class are in the net.jini.discovery package. The following additional types may also be referenced in this specification. Whenever referenced, these object types will be referenced in unqualified form:

```
net.jini.core.discovery.LookupLocator
net.jini.discovery.DiscoveryEvent
net.jini.discovery.DiscoveryListener
net.jini.discovery.DiscoveryManagement
net.jini.discovery.DiscoveryGroupManagement
net.jini.discovery.DiscoveryLocatorManagement
java.io.IOException
```

DU.5.3 The Interface

The only new public method of the LookupDiscoveryManager helper utility class is the constructor. All other public methods implemented by this class are specified in the discovery management interfaces.

```
package net.jini.discovery;

public class LookupDiscoveryManager
                         implements DiscoveryManagement,
                                    DiscoveryGroupManagement,
                                    DiscoveryLocatorManagement
{
    public LookupDiscoveryManager(String[] groups,
                                  LookupLocator[] locators,
                                  DiscoveryListener listener)
                                       throws IOException {…}
}
```

DU.5.4 The Semantics

The equals method for this class returns true if and only if two instances of this class refer to the same object. That is, x and y are equal instances of this class if and only if x == y has the value true.

The constructor for the LookupDiscoveryManager takes the following arguments as input:

- A String array, none of whose elements may be null, in which each element is the name of a group whose members are lookup services the entity wishes to be discovered through group discovery
- An array of LookupLocator objects, none of whose elements may be null, in which each element corresponds to a specific lookup service the entity wishes to be discovered through locator discovery
- A reference to an instance of DiscoveryListener that will be notified when a targeted lookup service is discovered, is discarded, or—under certain conditions—has experienced a change in its group membership

The LookupDiscoveryManager will, on behalf of any entity that constructs an instance of this utility, employ the Jini discovery protocols defined in *The Jini Technology Core Platform Specification,* "Discovery and Join" to attempt to find all lookup services that satisfy the criteria set forth by the contents of the first two arguments, and it will maintain and manage any lookup services that it does discover.

If the constructor is invoked with a set of group names and a set of locators in which either or both sets contain duplicate elements (where duplicate locators are determined by `LookupLocator.equals`), the invocation is equivalent to constructing this class with no duplicates in either set.

If `null` (`DiscoveryGroupManagement.ALL_GROUPS`) is input to the `groups` argument, then attempts will be made through group discovery to discover all lookup services located within the multicast radius of the entity, regardless of group membership.

Typically, group discovery is initiated as soon as an instance of this class is created. However, if an empty array (`DiscoveryGroupManagement.NO_GROUPS`) is passed to the `groups` argument of the constructor, no lookup service will be discovered through group discovery until the `addGroups` or `setGroups` method is called to change the managed set of groups to either a non-empty set, or `null` (`DiscoveryGroupManagement.ALL_GROUPS`).

If at least one element of the `groups` argument is `null`, a `NullPointerException` is thrown.

Typically, locator discovery processing is initiated as soon as an instance of this class is constructed. However, if an empty or `null` array is input to the `locators` argument, no attempt will be made to discover specific lookup services through locator discovery until the `addLocators` or `setLocators` method is called to change the managed set of locators to a set of locators that is non-`null` and non-empty.

If at least one element of the `locators` argument is `null`, a `NullPointerException` is thrown.

The last argument to the constructor is a reference to a listener object that will be registered to receive discovery event notifications. If a `null` reference is input to this argument, then the entity will receive no discovery events until `addDiscoveryListener` is invoked with a non-`null` instance of `DiscoveryListener`.

Once a listener is registered with the `LookupDiscoveryManager`, it will be notified of all lookup services discovered through either group or locator discovery, and will be notified whenever those lookup services are discarded. Thus, if an entity wishes to receive discovered and discarded events from the `LookupDiscoveryManager`, it is the responsibility of the entity to provide an implementation of the `DiscoveryListener` (or the `DiscoveryChangeListener`) interface; an implementation that defines the actions to take upon the receipt of those types of events.

If a listener registered with the `LookupDiscoveryManager` is also an instance of `DiscoveryChangeListener`, then in addition to receiving events related to discovered and discarded lookup services, that listener will also be notified of group membership changes that occur in any of the lookup services targeted for at least group discovery. That is, although such listeners are *eligible* to receive changed events, they will receive no changed events for lookup services for which the entity has requested *only* locator discovery.

Note that if an entity wishes to receive changed events in addition to the discovered and discarded events it receives from the LookupDiscoveryManager, the entity must provide an implementation of DiscoveryChangeListener that defines the actions to take upon the receipt of any of the three possible discovery event types. That is, if the entity provides only an implementation of DiscoveryListener, the entity will receive no changed events for any of the discovered lookup services, regardless of the discovery mechanism employed for those lookup services.

The constructor throws IOException. This is because construction of a LookupDiscoveryManager may initiate the multicast discovery process, which can throw IOException.

Once a lookup service is discovered, there is no longer any need to perform discovery processing with respect to that lookup service. This means that if a lookup service becomes unreachable after it has been discovered, the LookupDiscoveryManager will not know when the lookup service becomes reachable again until that lookup service is discarded.

Although the LookupDiscoveryManager will monitor the multicast announcements for indications of unavailability, it will discard only those unreachable lookup services for which the entity requested discovery through at least group discovery. That is, if the LookupDiscoveryManager determines that a previously discovered lookup service has become unreachable, but the entity requested that it be discovered by locator discovery alone, then the LookupDiscoveryManager will not discard the lookup service.

Thus, whenever the entity itself determines that a previously discovered lookup service has become unreachable, it should not rely on the LookupDiscoveryManager to discard the lookup service. Instead, the entity should inform the LookupDiscoveryManager—through the invocation of the discard method—that the previously discovered lookup service is no longer available, and that attempts should be made to re-discover that lookup service. Typically, an entity determines that a lookup service is unavailable when the entity attempts to use the lookup service but receives an exception or error (RemoteException, for example) as a result of the attempt.

DU.5.5 Supporting Interfaces and Classes

The LookupDiscoveryManager helper utility class depends on the interfaces DiscoveryManagement, DiscoveryGroupManagement, and DiscoveryLocatorManagement, and on the concrete class DiscoveryPermission.

DU.5.5.1 The DiscoveryManagement Interfaces

The LookupDiscoveryManager class implements the DiscoveryManagement, the DiscoveryGroupManagement, and the DiscoveryLocatorManagement interfaces, which together define methods related to the coordination and management of all group and locator discovery processing. See Section DU.2, "The Discovery Management Interfaces" for more information on those interfaces.

DU.5.5.2 Security and Multicast Discovery: The DiscoveryPermission Class

As is the case for the LookupDiscovery class, when an instance of the LookupDiscoveryManager class is constructed, the entity that creates the instance must be granted appropriate discovery permission to perform the group discovery duties that instance attempts to perform on behalf of the entity. If appropriate permissions are not granted, the constructor of LookupDiscoveryManager, as well as the methods addGroups and setGroups, will throw a java.lang.SecurityException.

Discovery permissions are controlled in security policy files using the permission class DiscoveryPermission. The specification of that class, as well as useful examples related to that class, are presented in the specification of the LookupDiscovery utility (see Section DU.2, "The Discovery Management Interfaces").

DU.6 Low-Level Discovery Protocol Utilities

THE utilities presented in this section of the specification are useful when implementing higher-level utilities or other entities or components that will be involved in the Jini discovery process. These utilities encapsulate functionality that allow one to exercise more control when interacting with the Jini discovery protocols. Anyone wishing to provide their own implementation of the Jini lookup service or their own implementation of the discovery utilities presented previously in this specification, may find the utilities presented in this section useful when creating those alternate implementations.

DU.6.1 The `Constants` Class

DU.6.1.1 Overview

The `Constants` class provides easy access to defined constants that may be useful when participating in the discovery process.

DU.6.1.2 Other Types

The types defined in the specification of the `Constants` class are in the `net.jini.discovery` package. The following additional types may also be referenced in this specification. Whenever referenced, these object types will be referenced in unqualified form:

```
java.net.InetAddress
java.net.UnknownHostException
```

DU.6.1.3 The Class Definition

The public constants defined by the `Constants` class are as follows:

```
package net.jini.discovery;

public class Constants {
    public static final short discoveryPort = 4160;
    public static final InetAddress getRequestAddress()
        throws UnknownHostException {...}
    public static final InetAddress getAnnouncementAddress()
        throws UnknownHostException {...}
}
```

DU.6.1.4 The Semantics

The `Constants` class cannot be instantiated. This class has one public variable and two public accessor methods; each is static and final. The constant value associated with the variable, as well as the values returned by the methods, may be useful in the discovery process.

The value of the `discoveryPort` constant serves two purposes:

- The UDP port number over which the multicast request and announcement protocols operate
- The TCP port number over which the unicast discovery protocol operates by default

The `getRequestAddress` method returns an instance of `InetAddress` that contains the address of the multicast group over which the multicast request protocol takes place.

The `getAnnouncementAddress` method returns an instance of `InetAddress` that contains the address of the multicast group over which the multicast announcement protocol takes place.

Note that either `getRequestAddress` or `getAnnouncementAddress` may throw an `UnknownHostException` if called in a circumstance under which multicast address resolution is not permitted.

DU.6.2 The `OutgoingMulticastRequest` Utility

DU.6.2.1 Overview

The `OutgoingMulticastRequest` class provides facilities for marshalling multicast discovery requests into a form suitable for transmission over a network for the purposes of announcing one's interest in discovering a lookup service. This class is useful when building components that participate in the multicast request protocol as part of a group discovery mechanism. This utility should be viewed from the perspective of an entity that wishes to transmit multicast requests in order to discover a lookup service belonging to a set of groups in which the entity is interested.

DU.6.2.2 Other Types

The types defined in the specification of the `OutgoingMulticastRequest` utility class are in the `net.jini.discovery` package. The following additional types may also be referenced in this specification. Whenever referenced, these object types will be referenced in unqualified form:

```
net.jini.core.discovery.ServiceID
java.io.IOException
java.net.DatagramPacket
java.net.InetAddress
```

DU.6.2.3 The Interface

The public methods provided by the `OutgoingMulticastRequest` class are as follows:

```
package net.jini.discovery;

public class OutgoingMulticastRequest {
    public static DatagramPacket[] marshal(int port,
                                           String[] groups,
                                           ServiceID[] heard)
            throws IOException {...}
}
```

DU.6.2.4 The Semantics

The `OutgoingMulticastRequest` class cannot be instantiated. This class has only one public method, which is static.

The `marshal` method takes as input the following arguments, none of which may be `null`:

- The port to which respondents should connect in order to start unicast discovery
- A `String` array, none of whose elements may be `null`, in which each element is the name of a group the requesting entity is interested in discovering
- An array of `ServiceID` objects, none of whose elements may be `null`, in which each element corresponds to a lookup service the requesting entity has already heard from

Since implementations are not required to check for duplicated elements, the arguments represented as arrays must not contain such elements.

The `marshal` method returns an array whose elements are instances of `DatagramPacket`. The array returned will always contain at least one element, and will contain more if the request is not small enough to fit in a single packet. The array returned by this method is fully initialized; it contains a multicast request as payload and is ready to send over the network.

In the event of error, the `marshal` method may throw an `IOException` if marshalling fails. In some instances the exception thrown may be a more specific subclass of that exception.

DU.6.3 The `IncomingMulticastRequest` Utility

DU.6.3.1 Overview

The `IncomingMulticastRequest` class provides facilities that are useful when a requesting entity's announced interest in discovering a lookup service is received. The facilities provided by this class encapsulate the details of the process of unmarshalling such received multicast discovery requests into a form in which the individual parameters of the request may be easily accessed. This class is useful when building components that participate in the multicast request protocol as part of a group discovery mechanism, where an entity that uses such a component wishes to receive multicast requests in order to be discovered through its group membership; for example, an entity such as a lookup service.

DU.6.3.2 Other Types

The types defined in the specification of the `IncomingMulticastRequest` utility class are in the `net.jini.discovery` package. The following additional types may also be referenced in this specification. Whenever referenced, these object types will be referenced in unqualified form:

```
net.jini.core.discovery.ServiceID
java.io.IOException
java.net.DatagramPacket
java.net.InetAddress
```

DU.6.3.3 The Interface

The public methods provided by the `IncomingMulticastRequest` class are as follows:

```
package net.jini.discovery;

public class IncomingMulticastRequest {
    public IncomingMulticastRequest(DatagramPacket dgram)
        throws IOException {...}
    public InetAddress getAddress() {...}
    public int getPort() {...}
    public String[] getGroups() {...}
    public ServiceID[] getServiceIDs() {...}
}
```

DU.6.3.4 The Semantics

Including the constructor, the `IncomingMulticastRequest` class defines five new public methods.

The `equals` method for this class returns `true` if and only if two instances of this class have the same address, port, groups, and service ID values.

The constructor of the `IncomingMulticastRequest` class takes a single input parameter: an instance of `DatagramPacket`. The payload of this parameter is assumed to contain nothing but a marshalled discovery request.

If the marshalled request contained in the input parameter is corrupt, an `IOException` or a `ClassNotFoundException` will be thrown. In some such instances, a more specific subclass of either exception may be thrown that will give more detailed information.

The getAddress method returns an instance of InetAddress that represents the address of the host to contact in order to start unicast discovery.

The getPort method returns an int value that is the port number to connect to on the remote host in order to start unicast discovery.

The getGroups method returns an array consisting of the names of the groups in which the requesting entity (the originator of this request) is interested. The array returned by this method may be of zero length, none of its elements will be null, and elements in the returned array may or may not be duplicated. Furthermore, the set reflected in the returned array may not be complete, but other incoming packets should contain the rest of the set.

The getServiceIDs method returns an array of ServiceID instances in which each element of the array corresponds to a lookup service from which the requesting entity has already heard. The array returned by this method may be of zero length, none of its elements will be null, and elements in the returned array may or may not be duplicated. Furthermore, the set returned by this method may not be complete. That is, there may be more lookup services from which the requesting entity has already heard, but the set returned by this method will not exceed the capacity of a packet.

DU.6.4 The OutgoingMulticastAnnouncement Utility

DU.6.4.1 Overview

The OutgoingMulticastAnnouncement class encapsulates the details of the process of marshalling multicast discovery announcements into a form suitable for transmission over a network for the purposes of announcing the availability of a lookup service to interested parties. This class is useful when building components that participate in the multicast announcement protocol as part of a group discovery mechanism. This utility should be viewed from the perspective of an entity that wishes to transmit multicast announcements in order to be discovered as a lookup service belonging to a set of groups in which other discovering entities may be interested.

DU.6.4.2 Other Types

The types defined in the specification of the OutgoingMulticastAnnouncement utility class are in the net.jini.discovery package. The following additional types may also be referenced in this specification. Whenever referenced, these object types will be referenced in unqualified form:

```
net.jini.core.discovery.LookupLocator
net.jini.core.discovery.ServiceID
java.io.IOException
java.net.DatagramPacket
```

DU.6.4.3 The Interface

The public methods provided by the `OutgoingMulticastAnnouncement` class are as follows:

```
package net.jini.discovery;

public class OutgoingMulticastAnnouncement {
    public static DatagramPacket[] marshal(ServiceID id,
                                           LookupLocator loc,
                                           String[]groups)
        throws IOException {…}
}
```

DU.6.4.4 The Semantics

The `OutgoingMulticastAnnouncement` class cannot be instantiated. This class has only one public method, which is static.

The `marshal` method takes as input the following arguments, none of which may be `null`:

- The instance of `ServiceID` that corresponds to the lookup service being advertised
- The instance of `LookupLocator` through which the lookup service being advertised may be discovered through unicast discovery
- A non-`null` `String` array, none of whose elements may be `null`, in which each element is the name of a group in which the lookup service being advertised is a member

The `marshal` method returns an array whose elements are instances of `DatagramPacket`, the contents of which represents a marshalled multicast announcement. The packets created by this method, as represented by the elements of the returned array, are guaranteed to contain all of the groups in which the lookup service being advertised is a member. Note that the set of groups reflected in the returned collection of datagram packets may be distributed among those packets.

Each element of the array returned by this method is initialized such that it is ready for transmission to the appropriate multicast address and UDP port.

In the event of error, the `marshal` method may throw an `IOException` if marshalling fails. In some instances, the exception thrown may be a more specific subclass of that exception.

DU.6.5 The `IncomingMulticastAnnouncement` Utility

DU.6.5.1 Overview

The `IncomingMulticastAnnouncement` class encapsulates the details of the process of unmarshalling multicast discovery announcements into a form in which the individual parameters of the announcement may be easily accessed. This class is useful when building components that participate in the multicast announcement protocol as part of a group discovery mechanism. This utility should be viewed from the perspective of an entity that wishes to receive multicast announcements in order to discover a lookup service belonging to a set of groups in which the entity is interested.

DU.6.5.2 Other Types

The types defined in the specification of the `IncomingMulticastAnnouncement` utility class are in the `net.jini.discovery` package. The following additional types may also be referenced in this specification. Whenever referenced, these object types will be referenced in unqualified form:

```
net.jini.core.discovery.LookupLocator
net.jini.core.discovery.ServiceID
java.io.IOException
java.net.DatagramPacket
```

DU.6.5.3 The Interface

The public methods provided by the `IncomingMulticastAnnouncement` class are as follows:

```
package net.jini.discovery;

public class IncomingMulticastAnnouncement {
    public IncomingMulticastAnnouncement(DatagramPacket p)
        throws IOException {...}
    public ServiceID getServiceID() {...}
    public LookupLocator getLocator() {...}
    public String[] getGroups() {...}
}
```

DU.6.5.4 The Semantics

Including the constructor, the `IncomingMulticastAnnouncement` class defines four new public methods.

The `equals` method for this class returns `true` if and only if two instances of this class have the same service ID values.

The constructor of the `IncomingMulticastAnnouncement` class takes a single input parameter: an instance of `DatagramPacket`. The constructor attempts to unmarshal the input parameter, storing the results in the various fields of this class.

If the contents of the datagram packet cannot be successfully unmarshalled, either an `IOException` or a `ClassNotFoundException` is thrown. In some such instances, a more specific subclass of either exception may be thrown that will give more detailed information.

The `getServiceID` method returns the `ServiceID` instance corresponding to the lookup service that sent the announcement.

The `getLocator` method returns the `LookupLocator` instance corresponding to the lookup service that sent the announcement. It is through the object returned by this method that the lookup service may be discovered via unicast discovery.

The `getGroups` method returns an array consisting of the names of the groups in which the lookup service that sent the announcement is a member. The array returned by this method is never `null`, will contain no `null` elements, or may be empty. Additionally, elements in the returned array may or may not be duplicated.

DU.6.6 The OutgoingUnicastRequest Utility

DU.6.6.1 Overview

The OutgoingUnicastRequest class encapsulates the details of the process of marshalling unicast discovery requests into a form suitable for transmission over a network to attempt discovery of a specific lookup service. This class is useful when building components that participate in the unicast request protocol as part of either a group or a locator discovery mechanism. This utility should be viewed from the perspective of an entity that wishes to transmit unicast requests in order to discover a specific lookup service in which the entity is interested.

DU.6.6.2 Other Types

The types defined in the specification of the OutgoingUnicastRequest utility class are in the net.jini.discovery package. The following additional types may also be referenced in this specification. Whenever referenced, these object types will be referenced in unqualified form:

```
java.io.IOException
java.io.OutputStream
```

DU.6.6.3 The Interface

The public methods provided by the OutgoingUnicastRequest class are as follows:

```
package net.jini.discovery;

public class OutgoingUnicastRequest {
    public static void marshal(OutputStream str)
        throws IOException {…}
}
```

DU.6.6.4 The Semantics

The OutgoingUnicastRequest class cannot be instantiated. This class has only one public method, which is static.

The marshal method takes only one parameter as input: an instance of OutputStream, which is the stream to which the unicast request is written. After the unicast request is written to the stream, the stream is flushed.

In the event of error, the `marshal` method may throw an `IOException` if writing to the stream fails. In some instances, the exception thrown may be a more specific subclass of that exception.

DU.6.7 The `IncomingUnicastRequest` Utility

DU.6.7.1 Overview

The `IncomingUnicastRequest` class encapsulates the details of the process of unmarshalling unicast discovery requests into a form in which the individual parameters of the request may be easily accessed. This class is useful when building components that participate in the unicast request protocol as part of either a group or a locator discovery mechanism. This utility should be viewed from the perspective of an entity—such as a lookup service—that wishes to receive unicast requests in order to be discovered through direct, unicast communication.

DU.6.7.2 Other Types

The types defined in the specification of the `IncomingUnicastRequest` utility class are in the `net.jini.discovery` package. The following additional types may also be referenced in this specification. Whenever referenced, these object types will be referenced in unqualified form:

```
java.io.InputStream
java.io.IOException
```

DU.6.7.3 The Interface

The public methods provided by the `IncomingUnicastRequest` class are as follows:

```
package net.jini.discovery;

public class IncomingUnicastRequest {
    public IncomingUnicastRequest(InputStream str)
        throws IOException {…}
}
```

DU.6.7.4 The Semantics

The only new public method defined by the `IncomingUnicastRequest` class is the constructor.

The constructor of the `IncomingUnicastRequest` class takes a single input parameter: an instance of `InputStream`, which is the stream from which the unicast request is read.

In the event of error, an `IOException` may be thrown if reading from the stream fails. In some instances, the exception thrown may be a more specific subclass of that exception.

DU.6.8 The `OutgoingUnicastResponse` Utility

DU.6.8.1 Overview

The `OutgoingUnicastResponse` class encapsulates the details of the process of marshalling a unicast discovery response into a form suitable for transmission over a network to respond to a unicast discovery request. This class is useful when building components that participate in the unicast request protocol as part of either a group or a locator discovery mechanism. This utility should be viewed from the perspective of a entity—such as a lookup service—that wishes to transmit responses to unicast requests in order to be discovered through direct, unicast communication.

DU.6.8.2 Other Types

The types defined in the specification of the `OutgoingUnicastResponse` utility class are in the `net.jini.discovery` package. The following additional types may also be referenced in this specification. Whenever referenced, these object types will be referenced in unqualified form:

```
net.jini.core.lookup.ServiceRegistrar
java.io.IOException
java.io.OutputStream
```

DU.6.8.3 The Interface

The public methods provided by the OutgoingUnicastResponse class are as follows:

```
package net.jini.discovery;

public class OutgoingUnicastResponse {
    public static void marshal(OutputStream s,
                               ServiceRegistrar reg
                               String[] groups)
                                   throws IOException {...}
}
```

DU.6.8.4 The Semantics

The OutgoingUnicastResponse class cannot be instantiated. This class has only one public method, which is static.

The marshal method takes as input the following arguments, none of which may be null:

- An instance of OutputStream, which is the stream to which the unicast response is written.
- An instance of ServiceRegistrar that references the proxy to the lookup service that will be marshalled and written to the stream.
- A non-null String array, none of whose elements may be null, in which each element is the name of a group in which the lookup service referenced by the reg parameter is a member. Note that duplicate elements are allowed in this parameter.

The marshal method marshals the reg parameter and writes the result to the stream. It then writes each element of the groups parameter to the stream. After the complete unicast response is written to the stream, the stream is flushed.

This method may throw an IOException if a failure occurs while marshalling or writing to the stream. In some instances, the exception thrown may be a more specific subclass of that exception.

DU.6.9 The IncomingUnicastResponse Utility

DU.6.9.1 Overview

The IncomingUnicastResponse class encapsulates the details of the process of unmarshalling a unicast discovery response into a form in which the individual parameters of the request may be easily accessed. This class is useful when building components that participate in the unicast request protocol as part of either a group or a locator discovery mechanism. This utility should be viewed from the perspective of an entity that wishes to receive unicast responses in order to discover lookup services through direct, unicast communication.

DU.6.9.2 Other Types

The types defined in the specification of the IncomingUnicastResponse utility class are in the net.jini.discovery package. The following additional types may also be referenced in this specification. Whenever referenced, these object types will be referenced in unqualified form:

```
net.jini.core.lookup.ServiceRegistrar
java.io.InputStream
java.io.IOException
```

DU.6.9.3 The Interface

The public methods provided by the IncomingUnicastResponse class are as follows:

```
package net.jini.discovery;

public class IncomingUnicastResponse {
    public IncomingUnicastResponse(InputStream s)
        throws IOException, ClassNotFoundException {...}
    public ServiceRegistrar getRegistrar() {...}
    public String[] getGroups() {...}
}
```

DU.6.9.4 The Semantics

Including the constructor, the IncomingUnicastResponse class defines three new methods.

The `equals` method for this class returns `true` if and only if two instances of this class reference the same lookup service proxy (registrar).

The constructor of the `IncomingUnicastResponse` class takes a single input parameter: an instance of `InputStream`, which is the stream from which the contents of the unicast response is read.

An `IOException` may be thrown if reading from the stream fails. A `ClassNotFoundException` may be thrown if failure occurs while unmarshalling the proxy to the lookup service contained in the unicast response. In some such instances, a more specific subclass of either exception may be thrown that will give more detailed information.

The `getRegistrar` method returns an instance of `ServiceRegistrar` that references the proxy to the lookup service sent in the unicast response.

The `getGroups` method returns an array consisting of the names of the groups in which the lookup service referenced in the response is a member. The array returned by this method is never `null`, will contain no `null` elements, or may be empty. Additionally, elements in the returned array may or may not be duplicated.

THE JINI ENTRY UTILITIES SPECIFICATION defines exactly one utility: the `AbstractEntry` class, which is a useful—but not required—superclass for `Entry` classes. This class uses the standard properties for `Entry` classes to provide default implementations of common methods, such as `equals` and `hashCode`.

EU

Jini Entry Utilities Specification

EU.1 Entry Utilities

ENTRIES are designed to be used in distributed algorithms for which exact-match lookup semantics are useful. An entry is a typed set of objects, each of which may be tested for exact match with a template. The details of entries and their semantics are discussed in *The Jini Technology Core Platform Specification,* "Entry".

When designing entries, certain tasks are commonly done in similar ways. This specification defines a utility class for such common tasks.

EU.1.1 AbstractEntry

The class `net.jini.entry.AbstractEntry` is a specific implementation of `Entry` that provides useful implementations of `equals`, `hashCode`, and `toString`:

```
package net.jini.entry;

public abstract class AbstractEntry implements Entry {
    public boolean equals(Object o) {...}
    public int hashCode() {...}
    public String toString() {...}
    public static boolean equals(Entry e1, Entry e2) {...}
    public static int hashCode(Entry entry) {...}
    public static String toString(Entry entry) {...}
}
```

The static method `AbstractEntry.equals` returns `true` if and only if the two entries are of the same class and for each field *F*, the two objects' values for *F* are either both `null` or the invocation of `equals` on one object's value for *F* with the other object's value for *F* as its parameter returns `true`. The static method `hashCode` returns zero XOR the `hashCode` invoked on each non-`null` field of the entry. The static method `toString` returns a string that contains each field's name and value. The non-static methods `equals`, `hashCode`, and `toString` return a result equivalent to invoking the corresponding static method with `this` as the first argument.

EU.1.2 Serialized Form

Class	`serialVersionUID`	Serialized Fields
`AbstractEntry`	5071868345060424804L	*none*

THE JINI LEASE UTILITIES SPECIFICATION The Jini™ lease utilities encapsulate functionality that provides for the coordination, systematic renewal, and overall management of a set of leases associated with some object on behalf of another object.

JINI™

LM

Jini Lease Utilities Specification

LM.1 Introduction

THIS specification defines helper utility classes, along with supporting interfaces and classes, that encapsulate functionality which provides for the coordination, systematic renewal, and overall management of a set of leases associated with some object on behalf of another object. Currently, this specification defines only one helper utility class:

- The `LeaseRenewalManager` helper utility

LM.2 The LeaseRenewalManager

THE LeaseRenewalManager class (belonging to the package net.jini.lease) encapsulates functionality that provides for the systematic renewal and overall management of a set of leases associated with one or more remote entities on behalf of a local entity.

The concept of leased resources is fundamental to the Jini technology programming model. Providing a leasing mechanism helps to prevent the accumulation of outdated and unwanted resources in time-based distributed systems, such as the Jini technology infrastructure. The leasing model for Jini network technology (Jini technology), defined in *The Jini Technology Core Platform Specification,* "Leasing and Distributed Systems", requires renewed proof of interest to continue the existence of a leased resource. Thus, any Jini technology-enabled client (Jini client) or Jini technology-enabled service (Jini service) that requests the use of the leased resources provided by another Jini service may be granted access to those resources for a negotiated period of time, and must continue to request renewal of the lease on each resource for as long as the client or service wishes to have access to the resource.

For example, the Jini lookup service leases two resources: residency in its database and registration with its event notification mechanism. Thus, if a service that is registered with a Jini lookup service wishes to continue its residency beyond the length of the current lease, the service must request a lease renewal from that lookup service. This renewal process must be repeated for as long as the service wishes to maintain its residency in the lookup service. Similarly, if a client has requested that a lookup service notify it of events of interest, then prior to the expiration of the lease on the event registration, the client must request that the lookup service continue to send such events. As with residency in the lookup service, these renewal requests must be repeated for as long as the client wishes to receive event notifications.

Another example of a Jini service providing leased resources would be a service that implements *The Jini Technology Core Platform Specification,* "Transaction" to manage transactions on behalf of registered participants. That specification requires that a transaction must be a leased resource. Therefore, any entity that creates such a transaction object is required to negotiate (with an entity

referred to as a *transaction manager*) a lease on that object, repeatedly requesting lease renewals prior to the lease's expiration, for as long as the transaction is to remain in effect.

The LeaseRenewalManager class is designed to be a simple mechanism that provides for the systematic renewal and overall management of leases granted on resources that are provided by Jini services and for which a Jini client or service has registered interest. The LeaseRenewalManager is a utility class, not a remote service. In order to use this utility, an entity must create, in its own address space, an instance of the LeaseRenewalManager to manage the entity's leases locally.

LM.2.1 Other Types

The types defined in the specification of the LeaseRenewalManager utility class are in the net.jini.lease package. The following types may be referenced in this specification. Whenever referenced, these types will be referenced in unqualified form:

```
net.jini.core.lease.Lease
net.jini.core.lease.UnknownLeaseException
net.jini.core.lease.LeaseDeniedException
java.rmi.RemoteException
java.rmi.NoSuchObjectException
java.util.EventObject
java.util.EventListener
```

LM.3 The Interface

THE public methods provided by the LeaseRenewalManager class are:

```
package net.jini.lease;

public class LeaseRenewalManager
{
    public LeaseRenewalManager() {…}
    public LeaseRenewalManager(Lease lease,
                               long desiredExpiration,
                               LeaseListener listener) {…}
    public void renewUntil(Lease lease,
                           long desiredExpiration,
                           long renewDuration,
                           LeaseListener listener) {…}
    public void renewUntil(Lease lease,
                           long desiredExpiration,
                           LeaseListener listener) {…}
    public void renewFor(Lease lease,
                         long desiredDuration,
                         long renewDuration,
                         LeaseListener listener) {…}
    public void renewFor(Lease lease,
                         long desiredDuration,
                         LeaseListener listener) {…}
    public long getExpiration(Lease lease)
        throws UnknownLeaseException {…}
    public void setExpiration(Lease lease,
                              long  desiredExpiration)
        throws UnknownLeaseException {…}
    public void remove(Lease lease)
        throws UnknownLeaseException {…}
    public void cancel(Lease lease)
```

```
        throws UnknownLeaseException, RemoteException {…}
    public void clear() {…}
}
```

LM.4 The Semantics

THE term *client* is used in this specification to refer to the local entity that is using the LeaseRenewalManager to manage a collection of leases on its behalf. This collection is referred to as the *managed set*.

The LeaseRenewalManager distinguishes between two time values associated with lease expiration: the *desired expiration* time for the lease and the *actual expiration* time granted when the lease is created or last renewed. The desired expiration represents when the client would like the lease to expire. The actual expiration represents when the lease is going to expire if it is not renewed. Both time values are absolute times, not relative time durations. The desired expiration time can be retrieved using the renewal manager's getExpiration method, which is described below. The actual expiration time of a lease object can be retrieved by invoking the getExpiration method directly on the lease (see the Lease interface defined in *The Jini Technology Core Platform Specification,* "Distributed Leasing").

Each lease in the managed set also has two other associated attributes: a *renewal duration* and a *remaining desired duration*. The remaining desired duration is always the desired expiration less the current time. The renewal duration is usually a positive number and is the new duration that will be requested when the renewal manager renews the lease, unless the renewal duration is greater than the remaining desired duration. If the renewal duration is greater than the remaining desired duration, then the remaining desired duration will be requested when renewing the lease. One exception is that when the desired expiration is Lease.FOREVER, the renewal duration may be Lease.ANY, in which case Lease.ANY will be requested when renewing the client lease, regardless of the value of the remaining desired duration.

For example, if the renewal duration associated with a given lease is 360,000 milliseconds, then when the renewal manager renews the lease, it will ask for a new duration of 360,000 milliseconds—unless the lease is going to reach its desired expiration in less than 360,000 milliseconds. If the lease's desired expiration is within 360,000 milliseconds, the renewal manager will ask for the difference between the current time and the desired expiration. If the renewal duration

had been `Lease.ANY`, the renewal manager would have asked for a new duration of `Lease.ANY`.

The term *definite exception* is used to refer to exceptions that result from operations on a lease (such as a renewal attempt) that are indicative of a permanent failure of the lease. For the purposes of this document, all bad object exceptions, bad invocation exceptions, and `LeaseExceptions` are considered to be definite exceptions (see *Introduction to Helper Utilities and Services*, Section US.2.6, "What Exceptions Imply about Future Behavior").

The `LeaseRenewalManager` generates two kinds of local events. The first kind is a *renewal failure event* that is generated when the renewal manager finds that it can't renew a lease. The second kind is a *desired expiration reached event,* which is generated when a lease's desired expiration is reached. Each event signals that the renewal manager has removed a lease from the managed set without an explicit request by the client. When placing a lease in the managed set, the client can provide either a `LeaseListener` object that will receive any renewal failure events associated with the lease, or a `DesiredExpirationListener` (a subinterface of `LeaseListener`) object that will receive both renewal failure and desired expiration reached events associated with the lease. Both kinds of event are represented by `LeaseRenewalEvent` objects.

The `LeaseRenewalManager` makes a concurrency guarantee. When the `LeaseRenewalManager` makes a remote call (for example, when requesting the renewal of a lease), any invocations made on the methods of the `LeaseRenewalManager` will not be blocked. Because of these concurrency guarantees, it is not possible for the various methods that remove leases from the managed set (for example, `remove`, `cancel`, and `clear`) to guarantee that the renewal manager will not attempt to renew leases that have just been removed. Similarly, it is not possible for the methods that change the desired expiration or renewal duration associated with a lease (for example, `renewUntil`, `renewFor`, and `setExpiration`) to guarantee that the next renewal of the lease will request a duration that is consistent with the new desired expiration and/or renewal duration (it will be consistent with either the old pair or the new pair). However, implementations should keep the window where such renewals could occur as small as possible.

The `LeaseRenewalManager` makes a similar reentrancy guarantee with respect to `LeaseListener` and `DesiredExpirationListener` objects registered with the `LeaseRenewalManager`. Should the `LeaseRenewalManager` invoke a method on a registered listener (a local call), calls from that method to any method of the `LeaseRenewalManager` are guaranteed not to result in a deadlock condition. One implication of this guarantee is that the delivery of events is asynchronous with respect to any call (or sequence of calls) made on the renewal manager after the event occurs; this allows events to be delivered after they have been made moot by intervening calls on the renewal manager. For example, the renewal manager may deliver events regarding leases that were removed from the managed set after the calls that removed the leases in question completed. Implementations should keep the window where such notifications could occur as small as possible.

The `equals` method for this class returns `true` if and only if two instances of this class refer to the same object. That is, `x` and `y` are equal instances of this class if and only if `x == y` has the value `true`.

The constructor has two forms:

- The first form of the constructor takes no arguments. This form of the constructor instantiates a `LeaseRenewalManager` object that initially manages no leases.
- The second form of the constructor creates a `LeaseRenewalManager` that initially manages a single lease. This form of the constructor requires that a reference to the initial lease be supplied as an argument. This form of the constructor also takes a `desiredExpiration` argument that represents the desired expiration time for the lease and a reference to a `LeaseListener` object that should receive notifications of events associated with the lease.

Creating a `LeaseRenewalManager` using the second form of the constructor is equivalent to invoking the no-argument constructor followed by an invocation of the three-argument form of the `renewUntil` method (described later).

The `renewUntil` method adds a lease to the set of leases being managed by the `LeaseRenewalManager`. There are two versions of this method: a four-argument form that allows the client to specify the renewal duration directly, and a three-argument form that infers the renewal duration from the desired expiration argument. The four-argument form will be described first.

This method takes as arguments: a reference to the lease to manage, the desired expiration time of the lease, the renewal duration time for the lease, and a reference to the `LeaseListener` object that will receive notification of events associated with this lease. The `LeaseListener` argument may be `null`.

If `null` is passed as the `lease` parameter, a `NullPointerException` will be thrown. If the `desiredExpiration` parameter is `Lease.FOREVER`, the `renewDuration` parameter may be `Lease.ANY` or any positive value; otherwise, the `renewDuration` parameter must be a positive value. If the `renewDuration` parameter does not meet these requirements, an `IllegalArgumentException` will be thrown.

If the lease passed to this method is already in the set of managed leases, the listener object, the desired expiration, and the renewal duration associated with

that lease will be replaced with the new listener, desired expiration, and renewal duration.

A lease will remain in the set of managed leases until one of the following occurs:

- The lease's desired expiration time is reached; this will generate a desired expiration reached event.
- An explicit removal of the lease from the set is requested via a `cancel`, `clear`, or `remove` call on the renewal manager.
- The lease's actual expiration time is reached before its desired expiration; this will generate a renewal failure event.
- The renewal manager tries to renew the lease and gets a definite exception; this will generate a renewal failure event.

The `renewUntil` method interprets the value of the `desiredExpiration` parameter as the *desired* absolute system time after which the lease is no longer valid. This argument provides the ability to indicate an expiration time that extends beyond the actual expiration of the lease. If the value passed for this argument does indeed extend beyond the lease's actual expiration time, then the lease will be systematically renewed at appropriate times until one of the conditions listed above occurs. If the value is less than or equal to the actual expiration time, nothing will be done to modify the time when the lease actually expires. That is, the lease will *not* be renewed with an expiration time that is less than the actual expiration time of the lease at the time of the call.

The `renewDuration` parameter is interpreted as the renewal duration, in milliseconds, to associate with the lease.

If a non-`null` object reference is passed in as the `LeaseListener` parameter, this object will receive notification of exceptional conditions occurring upon a renewal attempt of the lease. In particular, exceptional conditions include the reception of a definite exception or the lease's actual expiration being reached before its desired expiration. If the listener implements the interface `DesiredExpirationListener` it will also receive notification if the lease's desired expiration is reached while the lease is still in the set.

If a definite exception occurs during a lease renewal request, the exception will be wrapped in an instance of the `LeaseRenewalEvent` class (described later) and sent to the listener's `notify` method.

If an indefinite exception (see *Introduction to Helper Utilities and Services*, Section US.2.6, "What Exceptions Imply about Future Behavior") occurs during a renewal request for a particular lease, renewal requests will continue to be made for that lease until: the lease is renewed successfully, a renewal attempt results in a definite exception, or the lease's actual expiration time has been exceeded. If the lease cannot be successfully renewed before its actual expiration is reached, the exception associated with the most recent renewal attempt will be wrapped in an instance of the `LeaseRenewalEvent` class and sent to the listener's `notify` method.

If the lease's actual expiration is reached before the lease's desired expiration time and either (1) the last renewal attempt succeeded or (2) there have been no renewal attempts, a `LeaseRenewalEvent` containing a `null` exception will be sent to the listener's `notify` method. Case 1 can occur if the extension granted by the last renewal was very short. Case 2 can occur if the client adds a lease that has already expired (or is about to) to the managed set of leases.

If `null` is passed as the value of the `LeaseListener` parameter, then no notifications will be delivered.

Calling the three-argument form of `renewUntil` with a `desiredExpiration` of `Lease.ANY` is equivalent to making the following call:

```
renewUntil(lease, Lease.FOREVER, Lease.ANY, listener);
```

Otherwise, the three-argument form is equivalent to:

```
renewUntil(lease, desiredExpiration, Lease.FOREVER,
           listener);
```

Usage Note: Unless an application has a good reason for doing otherwise, it should use `Lease.ANY` or `Lease.FOREVER` for the renewal duration of a given lease. Using these values gives the grantor of the lease the most flexibility in the length of time for which it grants renewals. In most cases, the grantor of a lease is in a better position than the lease holder to make trade-offs between renewal frequency and the risk of holding on to resources longer than necessary. Specifying a value for the renewal duration of a lease might make sense if the holder of the lease has more information on the value of the leased resource than the grantor, or if the holder needs to ensure that there is an upper bound on how long the lease will remain valid.

The `renewFor` method adds a lease to the set of leases being managed by the `LeaseRenewalManager`. Like `renewUntil` this method has both three- and four-argument forms. The four-argument form of this method takes as parameters: `lease`, a reference to the lease to manage; `desiredDuration`, a `long` representing the desired duration of `lease`; `renewDuration`, a `long` representing the renewal duration; and `listener`, a reference to a `LeaseListener` object that will receive notifications of events associated with this lease. Both `desiredDuration` and `renewDuration` are expressed in milliseconds.

The semantics of the four-argument form of `renewFor` are similar to those of the four-argument form of `renewUntil`, with `desiredDuration` + current time

being used for the value of the desiredExpiration parameter of renewUntil. The only exception is that, in the context of renewFor, the value of the renewDuration parameter may be Lease.ANY only if the value of the desiredDuration parameter is *exactly* Lease.FOREVER.

This method tests for arithmetic overflow in the desired expiration time computed from the value of desiredDuration parameter (desiredDuration + current time). Should such overflow be present, a value of Lease.FOREVER is used to represent the lease's desired expiration time.

The three-argument form of this method is equivalent to the following call:

```
renewFor(lease, desiredDuration, Lease.FOREVER,
         listener);
```

Note that for both versions of renewFor, a value of Lease.ANY for the desiredDuration parameter does not have any special semantics associated with it. Calling either version of renewFor with a desiredDuration of Lease.ANY will result in the lease having a desired expiration one millisecond in the past, causing the lease to be immediately dropped from the managed set. The method will not throw an exception in this circumstance. A renewal failure event will be generated if the actual expiration is before the desired expiration; otherwise a desired expiration reached event will be generated.

The getExpiration method returns the current *desired* expiration time requested for a particular lease, not the actual expiration that was granted when the lease was created or last renewed. The only argument to this method is the reference to the lease object. If the lease is not in the set of managed leases, an UnknownLeaseException will be thrown.

The setExpiration method replaces the current desired expiration of a given lease contained in the set of managed leases with a new desired expiration time. The only arguments to this method are the reference to the lease object and the new expiration time.

An invocation of this method with a lease that is currently a member of the managed set is equivalent to an invocation of the renewUntil method with the lease's current listener input to the listener parameter. In particular, if the value of the expiration parameter is less than or equal to the lease's current actual expiration, this method takes no action.

An invocation of this method with a lease that is not in the set of managed leases will result in an UnknownLeaseException.

The remove method removes a given lease from the set of managed leases. The only argument to this method is the reference to the lease object. If the lease is not in the set of managed leases, an UnknownLeaseException will be thrown.

Note that this method does not cancel the given lease; activities such as lease cancellation are left the for the client to manage.

The `cancel` method both removes a given lease from the set of managed leases and cancels the given lease. The only argument to this method is the reference to the lease object. If the lease is not in the set of managed leases, an `UnknownLeaseException` will be thrown.

Any exception (definite or otherwise) occurring during the cancellation of the lease will have no effect on the removal of the lease from the managed set. That is, even if an exception occurs during the `cancel` operation, the lease will have been removed from the managed set upon return from this method.

Any exception thrown by the `cancel` method of the lease object itself may also be thrown by this method.

The `clear` method removes all leases from the set of managed leases. It does not request the cancellation of those leases. This method takes no arguments.

LM.5 Supporting Interfaces and Classes

THE LeaseRenewalManager utility class depends on the interfaces LeaseListener and DesiredExpirationListener. Both of these interfaces reference one class, LeaseRenewalEvent.

LM.5.1 The LeaseListener Interface

The public methods specified by the LeaseListener interface are as follows:

```
package net.jini.lease;

public interface LeaseListener extends EventListener
{
    void notify(LeaseRenewalEvent e);
}
```

The LeaseListener interface defines the mechanism through which the client receives notification of renewal failure events generated by the renewal manager. These events are delivered using the notify method. Renewal failure events are generated when the LeaseRenewalManager has failed to renew one of the leases that it is managing. Such renewal failures typically occur because one of the following conditions is met:

- After successfully renewing a lease any number of times and experiencing no failures, the LeaseRenewalManager determines—prior to the next renewal attempt—that the actual expiration time of the lease has passed; implying that any further attempt to renew the lease would be fruitless.
- An indefinite exception occurs during each attempt to renew a lease from the point that the first such exception occurs until the point when the LeaseRenewalManager determines that lease's actual expiration time has passed.
- A definite exception occurs during a lease renewal attempt.

It is the responsibility of the client to pass into the LeaseRenewalManager a reference to an object that implements the LeaseListener interface, which defines the actions to take upon receipt of a renewal failure event notification. When one of the above conditions occurs, the LeaseRenewalManager will send an instance of LeaseRenewalEvent to that listener object.

LM.5.1.1 The Semantics

The notify method is invoked by the LeaseRenewalManager when it fails to renew a lease because one of the conditions described above has occurred. This method takes one parameter, an instance of the LeaseRenewalEvent class, which contains information about the lease on which the failed renewal attempt was made and information on what caused the failure.

Note that prior to invoking the notify method, the LeaseRenewalManager removes the lease that could not be renewed from the managed set of leases. Note also that because of the reentrancy guarantee made by the LeaseRenewalManager, new leases can be added safely from within the notify method.

LM.5.2 The DesiredExpirationListener Interface

The public methods specified by the DesiredExpirationListener interface are as follows:

```
package net.jini.lease;

public interface DesiredExpirationListener
    extends LeaseListener
{
    void expirationReached(LeaseRenewalEvent e);
}
```

The expirationReached method receives desired expiration reached events. These are generated when the LeaseRenewalManager removes a lease from the managed set because the lease's desired expiration has been reached. Note that any object that has been registered to receive desired expiration reached events will also receive renewal failure events.

It is the responsibility of the client to pass into the LeaseRenewalManager a reference to an object that implements the DesiredExpirationListener interface, which defines the actions to take upon receipt of a desired expiration reached event notification.

LM.5.2.1 The Semantics

The `expirationReached` method is invoked by the `LeaseRenewalManager` when a lease in the managed set reaches its desired expiration. This method takes one parameter: an instance of the `LeaseRenewalEvent` class, which contains information about the lease who's desired expiration has been reached.

Note that prior to invoking the `expirationReached` method, the `LeaseRenewalManager` removes the affected lease from the managed set of leases. Note also that because of the reentrancy guarantee made by the `LeaseRenewalManager`, callbacks into the renewal manager can be made safely from within the `expirationReached` method.

LM.5.3 The `LeaseRenewalEvent` Class

This class defines the local event that is sent by the `LeaseRenewalManager` to the client's registered listener when the `LeaseRenewalManager` generates a renewal failure event or desired expiration reached event. As previously stated, a renewal failure event typically occurs because the actual expiration time of a lease has been reached before a successful renewal request could be made, or a renewal request resulted in a definite exception. A desired expiration reached event occurs when a lease reaches its desired expiration time at or before its actual expiration. The `LeaseRenewalEvent` class encapsulates information about the lease on which such an event occurs and, if it is a renewal failure, the cause.

```
package net.jini.lease;

public class LeaseRenewalEvent extends EventObject
{
    public LeaseRenewalEvent(LeaseRenewalManager source,
                             Lease lease,
                             long expiration,
                             Throwable ex) {...}
    public Lease getLease() {...}
    public long getExpiration() {...}
    public Throwable getException() {...}
}
```

The `LeaseRenewalEvent` class is a subclass of the `EventObject` class, adding the following additional items of abstract state: a reference to the associated `Lease` object; a `long` value representing the desired expiration of the lease; and the exception (if any) that caused the event to be sent. In addition to the methods of the `EventObject` class, this class defines methods through which this additional state may be retrieved.

LM.5.3.1 The Semantics

The constructor of the `LeaseRenewalEvent` class takes the following parameters as input:

- A reference to the instance of the `LeaseRenewalManager` that generated the event
- The lease associated with this event
- The desired expiration time of the lease
- The `Throwable` associated with the last renewal attempt (if any)

The `getLease` method returns a reference to the `Lease` object associated with the event. This method takes no arguments.

The `getExpiration` method returns a `long` value representing the desired expiration of the `Lease` object associated with the event. This method takes no arguments.

The `getException` method returns the exception, if any, that is associated with the event. This method takes no arguments. If the `LeaseRenewalEvent` represents a desired expiration reached event this method will return `null`.

If the `LeaseRenewalEvent` represents a renewal failure event the `getException` method will return the exception that caused the event to be sent. The conditions under which a renewal failure event may be sent, and the related values returned by this method, are as follows:

- When any lease in the managed set has passed its actual expiration time, and either the most recent renewal attempt was successful or there have been no renewal attempts, the `LeaseRenewalManager` will cease any further attempts to renew the lease, and will send a `LeaseRenewalEvent` with no associated exception. In this case, invoking this method will return `null`.
- For any lease from the managed set for which the most recent renewal attempt was unsuccessful because of the occurrence of a indefinite exception, the `LeaseRenewalManager` will continue to attempt to renew the

affected lease at the appropriate times until: the renewal succeeds, the lease's actual expiration time has passed, or a renewal attempt throws a definite exception. If a definite exception is thrown or the lease expires, the `LeaseRenewalManager` will cease any further attempts to renew the lease, and will send a `LeaseRenewalEvent` containing the exception associated with the last renewal attempt.

- If, while attempting to renew a lease from the managed set, a definite exception is encountered, the `LeaseRenewalManager` will cease any further attempts to renew the lease, and will send a `LeaseRenewalEvent` containing the particular exception that occurred.

LM.5.4 Serialized Forms

Class	`serialVersionUID`	Serialized Fields

`LeaseRenewalEvent`	-6263993416463483O2L	`Lease lease`
		`long expiration`
		`Throwable ex`

THE JINI JOIN UTILITIES SPECIFICATION The Jini join utilities encapsulate functionality that can help Jini services demonstrate good behavior in their discovery and registration related interactions with Jini lookup services.

In particular, the Jini join utilities perform functions related to lookup service discovery and registration (joining), as well as lease renewal and attribute management, which the Jini technology programming model requires of a well-behaved Jini technology-enabled service.

JINI™

JU
Jini Join Utilities Specification

JU.1 Introduction

THIS specification defines helper utility classes, along with supporting interfaces and classes, that encapsulate functionality that can help Jini services demonstrate good behavior in their discovery and registration related interactions with Jini lookup services. In particular, the Jini join utilities perform functions related to lookup service discovery and registration (joining), as well as lease renewal and attribute management, which the Jini technology programming model requires of a well-behaved Jini technology-enabled service. Currently, this specification defines only one helper utility class:

- The `JoinManager` helper utility

JU.2 The JoinManager

THE goal of any well-behaved Jini technology-enabled service (Jini service), implemented within the bounds defined by the Jini technology programming model, is to advertise the service it provides by requesting residency within at least one Jini lookup service. Making such a request of a Jini lookup service is known as registering with, or *joining*, a lookup service. To demonstrate this good behavior, a service must comply with both the multicast discovery protocol and the unicast discovery protocol to discover the lookup services it is interested in joining. The service must also comply with the join protocol to register with the desired lookup services. The details of the discovery and join protocols are described in, *The Jini Technology Core Platform Specification,* "Discovery and Join".

For the service to maintain its residency in the lookup services it has joined, the service must provide for the coordination, systematic renewal, and overall management of all leases on that residency. In addition to handling all discovery and join duties, as well as managing all leases on lookup residency, the service must provide for the coordination and management of any attribute sets with which it may have registered.

With respect to the duties described above, a Jini service may perform all but the attribute set management duties by using the helper utility classes `LookupDiscoveryManager` and `LeaseRenewalManager`. (For information on these classes, refer to *The Jini Technology Core Platform Specification,* "Discovery and Join" and *Jini Lease Renewal Service Specification*).

Rather than writing a service to use these classes in a coordinated fashion (in addition to providing for attribute management), the service may be written to employ the `JoinManager` class from the `net.jini.lookup` package. This utility class performs all of the functions related to discovery, joining, service lease renewal, and attribute management that the Jini technology programming model requires of a well-behaved Jini service. Each of these activities is intimately involved with the maintenance of a service's residency in one or more lookup services (the service's *join state*), hence the name `JoinManager`.

The `JoinManager` class provides an implementation of the functionality described above. The use of this class in a wide variety of services can help minimize the work resulting from having to repeatedly implement this required functionality in each service.

The JoinManager is a utility class, not a remote service. Jini services that wish to use this utility will create an instance of the JoinManager in the service's address space to manage the entity's join state locally.

Note that when the term *service* is used, it refers to the object that has created an instance of the JoinManager and avails itself of the public methods of that utility class.

JU.2.1 Other Types

The types defined in the specification of the JoinManager utility class are in the net.jini.lookup package. The following types may be referenced in this chapter. Whenever referenced, these object types will be referenced in unqualified form:

```
net.jini.core.lease.Lease
net.jini.core.entry.Entry
net.jini.core.lookup.ServiceID
net.jini.core.lookup.ServiceRegistrar
net.jini.core.lookup.ServiceRegistration
net.jini.discovery.DiscoveryListener
net.jini.discovery.DiscoveryManagement
net.jini.lookup.entry.ServiceControlled
net.jini.lease.LeaseRenewalManager
net.jini.discovery.LookupLocatorDiscovery
net.jini.discovery.LookupDiscoveryManager
java.io.IOException
java.rmi.MarshalledObject
java.util.EventListener
```

JU.3 The Interface

THE public methods provided by the JoinManager class are as follows:

```
package net.jini.lookup;

public class JoinManager {
    public JoinManager(Object obj,
                       Entry[] attrSets,
                       ServiceIDListener callback,
                       DiscoveryManagement discoveryMgr,
                       LeaseRenewalManager leaseMgr)
                                     throws IOException {...}
    public JoinManager(Object obj,
                       Entry[] attrSets,
                       ServiceID serviceID,
                       DiscoveryManagement discoveryMgr,
                       LeaseRenewalManager leaseMgr)
                                     throws IOException {...}

    public DiscoveryManagement getDiscoveryManager() {...}
    public LeaseRenewalManager getLeaseRenewalManager() {...}
    public ServiceRegistrar[]  getJoinSet() {...}

    public Entry[] getAttributes(){...}
    public void addAttributes(Entry[] attrSets) {...}
    public void addAttributes(Entry[] attrSets,
                              boolean checkSC) {...}
    public void setAttributes(Entry[] attrSets) {...}
    public void modifyAttributes(Entry[] attrSetTemplates,
                                 Entry[] attrSets) {...}
    public void modifyAttributes(Entry[] attrSetTemplates,
                                 Entry[] attrSets,
```

```
                                      boolean checkSC) {…}
    public void terminate() {…}
}
```

JU.4 The Semantics

THE JoinManager helper utility class defines a number of public methods in addition to the constructor. This utility defines an accessor method that allows the entity to retrieve the set of lookup services with which the entity has been registered (by the JoinManager), as well as methods that allow the entity to retrieve references to the objects the JoinManager uses for discovery management and lease renewal management. Additionally, the JoinManager class defines methods the entity may use to manage the attributes associated with the entity, and a method that allows the entity to terminate the join processing being performed on its behalf.

The equals method for the JoinManager class returns true if and only if two instances of this class refer to the same object. That is, x and y are equal instances of this class if and only if x == y has the value true.

The constructor of the JoinManager class has two forms. Each form of the constructor throws IOException because construction of a JoinManager may initiate the multicast discovery process, which can throw IOException.

The first form of the constructor takes the following parameters as input:

- A reference to the service requesting the services of the JoinManager
- An array containing the service's attributes
- A reference to an object that implements the ServiceIDListener interface (belonging to the package net.jini.lookup)
- A reference to an object that implements the DiscoveryManagement interface
- An instance of the LeaseRenewalManager utility class

Passing null as the value of the attrSets parameter is equivalent to passing an empty Entry array.

The assignment of a service ID to the service will result in an event notification being sent to the listener object that was passed as the ServiceIDListener argument (callback). If a null value is passed in through this argument, then no such notification will be sent.

To use the JoinManager, the service supplies an object through which notifications that indicate a lookup service has been discovered or discarded will be received. At a minimum, this object must satisfy the contract defined in the DiscoveryManagement interface. That is, this object must provide the JoinManager with the ability to set discovery listeners and to discard previously discovered lookup services when they are found to be unavailable.

The DiscoveryManagement argument may be set to a value of null. If null is the value of this argument, then an instance of the LookupDiscoveryManager utility class will be constructed to listen for events announcing the discovery of only those lookup services that are members of the public group.

The LeaseRenewalManager argument may be set to a value of null. If null is the value of this argument, an instance of the LeaseRenewalManager class will be created, initially managing no Lease objects. This feature allows a service that employs the JoinManager either to use a single entity to manage all of its leases, or to use separate entities: one to manage the leases unrelated to the join process, and one to manage the leases that result from the join process and that are accessible only within the JoinManager.

The first form of the constructor is typically used by services that have not yet been assigned a service ID, but that have been pre-configured to join lookup services that the service identifies through the initialization of a discovery manager.

The second form of the constructor takes the same arguments as the first, except that an instance of the ServiceID replaces an instance of the ServiceIDListener interface. Note that the ServiceID class is defined in *The Jini Technology Core Platform Specification,* "Lookup Service", and the ServiceIDListener interface is described later.

The second form of the constructor applies the same semantics to the attrSets, discoveryMgr, and leaseMgr arguments as is applied by the first form of the constructor.

The second form of the constructor should be used by services that have already been assigned a service ID (possibly by the service provider or as a result of a prior registration with some lookup service), and that may or may not have been pre-configured to join lookup services identified by group or by specific location.

The getDiscoveryManager method returns the instance of DiscoveryManagement that was either passed into the constructor by the entity or that was created as a result of null being passed as that parameter. This method takes no arguments as input.

The object returned by this method encapsulates the mechanism by which either the JoinManager or the entity itself can set discovery listeners and discard previously discovered lookup services when they are found to be unavailable.

The getLeaseRenewalManager method returns an instance of the LeaseRenewalManager class. This method takes no arguments as input.

The object returned by this method manages the leases requested and held by the JoinManager. Although it may also manage leases unrelated to the join process that are requested and held by the service itself, the leases with which the JoinManager is concerned are the leases that correspond to the service registration requests the JoinManager has made with each lookup service the service wishes to join.

The getJoinSet method returns an array of ServiceRegistrar objects, each corresponding to a lookup service with which the service is currently registered (joined). If there are no lookup services with which the service is currently registered, this method returns the empty array. This method takes no arguments as input and will return a new array upon each invocation.

The getAttributes method returns an array containing the set of attributes currently associated with the service. If the service is not currently associated with an attribute set, this method returns the empty array. This method takes no arguments as input and will return a new array upon each invocation.

Note that although a new array is returned by getAttributes, the elements of that array are *not* copies. Thus, it important that the elements of the array returned by getAttributes not be modified; doing so could cause the state of the JoinManager to become corrupted or inconsistent. This potential for corruption or inconsistency is why the effects of modifying the elements of the array returned by getAttributes are undefined.

The addAttributes method associates a new set of attributes with the service, in addition to the service's current set of attributes. The association of this new set of attributes with the service will be propagated to each lookup service with which the service is registered. This propagation must be performed asynchronously, so there is no guarantee that the propagation of the attributes to all lookup services with which the service is registered will have completed upon return from this method.

The set of attributes consisting of the union of the new set with the old set will be associated with the service in all future join processing.

There are two forms of the addAttributes method. Both forms of this method take as input an argument (attrSets) representing the set of attributes to associate with the service. This set is represented as an array of Entry objects, none of whose elements may be null. If at least one element of this input set is null, a NullPointerException is thrown.

An invocation of either form of this method with duplicate elements in the `attrSets` parameter (where duplication means attribute equality as defined by calling the `MarshalledObject.equals` method on field values) is equivalent to performing the invocation with the duplicates removed from that parameter. If `null` is passed in as the value of this parameter, a `NullPointerException` will be thrown.

The second form of this method also takes as input a flag indicating whether or not this method should determine if the attributes in the input set are instances of the `ServiceControlled` interface, which is a marker interface that is used to control which entities may modify a service's attribute set. For more information on this interface, refer to *Jini Lookup Attribute Schema Specification*, Section LS.4.1, "Indicating User Modifiability". If the value of this flag is `true` and at least one of the attributes to be added is an instance of the `ServiceControlled` interface, a `SecurityException` will be thrown and propagated through this method.

Note that because there is no guarantee that attribute propagation will have completed upon return from this method, services that invoke this method must take care not to modify the contents of the input array. Doing so could cause the service's attribute state to be corrupted or inconsistent on a subset of the lookup services with which the service is registered as compared with the state reflected on the remaining lookup services. It is for this reason that the effects of modifying the contents of the input array, after this method is invoked, are undefined.

The `setAttributes` method replaces the service's current set of attributes with the given new set of attributes. This method takes a single argument as input: an array of `Entry` objects, none of whose elements may be `null`, which represents the set of attributes that will replace the current set of attributes. If at least one element of this input set is `null`, a `NullPointerException` is thrown.

The replacement of the service's current set of attributes with the new set of attributes will be propagated to each lookup service with which the service is registered. This propagation must be performed asynchronously, so there is no guarantee that the propagation of the attributes to all lookup services with which the service is registered will have completed upon return from this method.

The service's new set of attributes will be associated with the service in all future join processing.

An invocation of this method with duplicate elements in the `attrSets` parameter (where duplication means attribute equality as defined by calling the `MarshalledObject.equals` method on field values) is equivalent to performing the invocation with the duplicates removed from that parameter. If `null` is input to `setAttributes`, a `NullPointerException` will be thrown.

For the same reason as noted above in the description of the addAttributes method, the effects of modifying the contents of the input array after the method setAttributes is invoked, are undefined.

The modifyAttributes method changes the service's current set of attributes using the same semantics as the modifyAttributes method of the class ServiceRegistration (see *The Jini Technology Core Platform Specification,* "Lookup Service"). This method has two forms. The first form takes two arguments, the second form takes three arguments. Both forms will take an array of templates in the first argument and an array of attributes in the second argument. The templates are used to identify which elements to modify from the service's current set of attributes. The attribute array contains the actual modifications to be made. The additional argument in the signature of the second form of modifyAttributes is a flag indicating whether or not this method should determine if the attributes in the input set are instances of the ServiceControlled interface, which is a marker interface used to control which entities may modify a service's attribute set (see *Jini Lookup Attribute Schema Specification*, Section LS.4.1, "Indicating User Modifiability"). If the value of this flag is true and at least one of the attributes to be modified is an instance of the ServiceControlled interface, a SecurityException will be thrown and propagated through this method.

The association of the new set of attributes with the service will be propagated to each lookup service with which the service is registered. This propagation must be performed asynchronously. Because of this asynchronous behavior, there is no guarantee that the propagation of the attributes to all lookup services with which the service is registered will have completed upon return from this method.

The set of attributes that results after the modifications have been applied will be associated with the service in all future join processing.

The modifyAttributes method throws an IllegalArgumentException if one of the following conditions is satisfied:

- The length of the array containing the templates does not equal the length of the array containing the attributes
- Any element of either array is not an instance of a valid Entry class (for example, the class is not public, does not contain a no-arg constructor, or has at least one public field which is a non-static, non-final primitive)
- The class of attrSets[*i*] is neither the same as, nor a super class of, the class of attrSetsTemplate[*i*]

For the same reason as that noted above in the description of the addAttributes method, the effects of modifying the contents of the attrSets parameter, after modifyAttributes is invoked, are undefined.

The terminate method performs cleanup duties related to the termination of the lookup service discovery event mechanism, as well as to the lease and thread management performed by the JoinManager. This method will cancel all of the service's managed leases that were granted by the lookup services with which the service is registered, and will terminate all threads that have been created.

If the discovery manager employed by the JoinManager was created by the JoinManager itself, this method will terminate *all* discovery processing being performed by that manager object on behalf of the service; otherwise, the discovery manager supplied by the service is still valid.

Whether an instance of the LeaseRenewalManager class was supplied by the service or created by the JoinManager itself, any reference to that object obtained by the service prior to termination will still be valid after termination.

The JoinManager makes certain concurrency guarantees with respect to an invocation of the terminate method while other method invocations are in progress. The termination process described above will not begin until completion of all invocations of the methods defined in the public interface of the JoinManager. Upon completion of the termination process, the semantics of all current and future method invocations on the current instance of the JoinManager are undefined, although the reference to the LeaseRenewalManager object employed by the JoinManager is still valid.

JU.5 Supporting Interfaces and Classes

THE JoinManager class depends on the interfaces DiscoveryManagement and ServiceIDListener discussed below.

JoinManager also references the concrete classes LookupDiscoveryManager and LeaseRenewalManager, each described in a separate specification.

JU.5.1 The DiscoveryManagement Interface

Although it is not necessary for the JoinManager itself to execute the discovery process, it does need to be notified when one of the lookup services it wishes to join is discovered or discarded. Thus, at a minimum, the JoinManager requires access to the discovery events sent to the listeners registered with the discovery process' event mechanism. The instance of DiscoveryManagement that is passed as an argument to the constructor of the JoinManager provides a mechanism for acquiring access to those events. For a complete description of the semantics of the methods of this interface, refer to the *Jini Discovery Utilities Specification*.

One noteworthy item about the semantics of the JoinManager is the effect that invocations of the discard method of DiscoveryManagement will have on any discovery listeners created by the JoinManager. The DiscoveryManagement interface specifies that the discard method will remove a particular lookup service from the managed set of lookup services that have already been discovered, allowing that lookup service to be rediscovered. Invoking this method will result in the flushing of the lookup service from the appropriate cache, ultimately causing a discard notification to be sent to all DiscoveryListener objects registered with the event mechanism of the discovery process, including all listeners registered by the JoinManager.

The receipt of an event notification indicating that a lookup service has been discarded ultimately results in the removal (but not cancellation) of the registration lease granted by the discarded lookup service, and that is managed by the LeaseRenewalManager on behalf of the JoinManager. After removal occurs, the lease will eventually expire.

JU.5.2 The ServiceIDListener Interface

The ServiceIDListener interface defines the methods used by a service to register a request for notification from the JoinManager upon the assignment of a serviceID by a lookup service. It is the responsibility of the service to create and pass into the JoinManager an object that implements this interface. That implementation must provide the definition of the actions to take upon receipt of the notification. Typically, the action taken will be to persist the assigned serviceID reference.

```
package net.jini.lookup;

public interface ServiceIDListener extends EventListener {
    public void serviceIDNotify(ServiceID serviceID);
}
```

The intent of this interface is to allow the entity to receive the ServiceID instance assigned to it by the lookup service. It is not part of the semantics of the call that the return from the ServiceIDNotify method can be delayed while the recipient of the call processes the information delivered by the method. Thus, it is highly recommended that implementations of this interface avoid time consuming operations, and return from the method as quickly as possible. For example, one strategy might be to simply notify a separate thread, operating asynchronously, which is designed to place the ServiceID instance in persistent storage.

THE JINI SERVICE DISCOVERY UTILITIES SPECIFICATION defines discovery utilities that encapsulate functionality an entity can exploit to help in its search for, and acquisition of, services of interest. In particular, the service discovery utilities provide mechanisms for caching discovered services, service discovery event management, filtering, and standard service lookup.

SD

Jini Service Discovery Utilities Specification

SD.1 Introduction

THIS specification defines helper utility classes, along with supporting interfaces and classes, that encapsulate functionality that can help a Jini technology-enabled service or client (*Jini service* or *Jini client*) in acquiring services of interest that are registered with the various lookup services with which the service or client wishes to interact. Currently, the service discovery utilities specification defines only one helper utility class:

- The `ServiceDiscoveryManager` helper utility

SD.2 The ServiceDiscoveryManager

THE interactions of an entity that operates in a client-like fashion within a Jini application environment are generally distinguished by the fact that the entity first discovers one or more Jini lookup services, then queries one or more of the discovered lookup services for references to Jini services that the entity may employ in some task. This process, in which Jini services as well as Jini clients may participate, is often referred to as *service discovery*. Since services and clients can perform both *lookup discovery* and *service discovery*, the primary characteristic that distinguishes a Jini service from a client is the service's ability to be registered with a lookup service. Thus, with respect to service discovery, there is no difference between a Jini service and a Jini client.

Because there is no need to make such a distinction, the terms *entity* and *client-like entity* will be used interchangeably throughout this specification to refer to Jini clients or services that create an instance of the `ServiceDiscoveryManager` (from the package `net.jini.lookup`) and use the public methods of that class to perform and manage their service discovery duties.

Once a client-like entity discovers a set of lookup services and retrieves references to desired services from those lookup services, the entity may choose to discontinue query-related discovery processing. That is, having obtained references to all of the services it wishes to employ, the entity may view the references it holds to the lookup services as no longer necessary.

But over the execution life of any such entity, partial failures such as system crashes or network outages may intermittently affect the availability of some of those services of interest. This results in a need to re-query the lookup services to find references to new instances of the service that can replace the unavailable instance. Such scenarios make it desirable for a client-like entity to maintain its references to the lookup services it queries. If an instance of a service is found to be unavailable, the entity can query those lookup services to obtain an instance of the service that is available.

Since a query on a lookup service is a remote call, such calls are much more costly in terms of overhead and failure risk than are local calls. This cost is magnified when an entity must make frequent queries for multiple services, so an entity may find it desirable to cache the services it obtains from the original queries on the lookup services. Furthermore, by populating the cache with multiple instances of the desired services, redundancy in the availability of those services can be provided. Thus, if an instance of a service is found to be unavailable when needed, the entity can execute a local query on the cache rather than one or more remote queries on the lookup services to obtain an instance which is available.

Typically, an entity will request the creation of a separate cache for each service type of interest. The cache provides a method with which the entity can retrieve an element of the cache. In general, the particular service reference that is returned should not matter to the entity. It should only matter that *a* service reference has been returned, not *which* service reference. If for some reason it does matter to an entity which service reference is returned, then the cache also provides a mechanism that will allow the entity to retrieve all elements of the cache. The entity can then iterate through each element, selecting the particular reference it desires.

Although interacting with a local cache of services in this way can be very useful to entities that need frequent access to multiple services, some client-like entities may wish to interact with the cache in a reactive manner. For example, an entity such as a service browser typically wishes to be *notified* of the arrival of new services of interest as well as any changes in the state of the current services in the cache. Polling for such changes is usually viewed as undesirable. If the cache were to also provide an event mechanism with notification semantics, the needs of both types of entity could be satisfied.

From the scenarios discussed above, one could conclude that when acting in a client-like fashion, it is desirable for an entity to maintain, as much as possible, up-to-date knowledge of the availability of the *lookup* services of interest as well as the state information associated with all other types of services in which the entity is interested. By maintaining current service state information, the entity can implement efficient mechanisms for service access and usage.

The `ServiceDiscoveryManager` class is a helper utility class that any entity can use to create and populate a cache such as that described previously, and with which the entity can register for notification of the availability of services of interest. Like the `JoinManager` utility class, this class needs to be notified when a desired lookup service is discovered. For information on the `JoinManager` utility class, refer to the *Jini Join Utilities Specification*.

Unlike the `JoinManager`, the `ServiceDiscoveryManager` does not register the entity as a service with discovered lookup services. Although both the `JoinManager` and the `ServiceDiscoveryManager` perform lookup discovery event handling for the entities that employ them, the `JoinManager` performs *join* processing for Jini services, while the `ServiceDiscoveryManager` performs *service discovery and management* processing both for clients and for services. Thus, typical usage patterns for Jini services wishing to find and use other Jini services generally indicate the employment of both the `JoinManager` and the `ServiceDiscoveryManager` utilities, whereas Jini clients would typically use only the `ServiceDiscoveryManager`.

The `ServiceDiscoveryManager` class can be asked to "discover" services an entity is interested in using, and to cache the references to those services as each is found. The cache can be viewed as a set of service references that the entity can access locally as needed through one of the public, non-remote methods provided in the cache's interface. A service reference added to the cache will be removed from the cache when all of the lookup services with which that service is registered have been discarded.

The `ServiceDiscoveryManager` class also provides a mechanism for an entity to request that it be notified when a service of interest is discovered for the first time or has encountered a state change such as removal from all lookup services or attribute set changes.

For convenience, this class also provides versions of a method named `lookup`, which employs invocation semantics similar to the semantics of the `lookup` method of the `ServiceRegistrar` interface defined in *The Jini Technology Core Platform Specification,* "Lookup Service". This method may be useful to entities that need to find services on an infrequent basis, or when the cost of making a remote call is outweighed by the overhead of maintaining a local cache (for example, because of limited resources).

All three mechanisms described above—local queries on the cache, service discovery notification, and remote lookups—employ the same template matching scheme as that described in *The Jini Technology Core Platform Specification,* "Lookup Service". Additionally, each mechanism allows the entity to supply an object referred to as a *filter.* Such an object is a non-remote object that defines additional matching criteria that the `ServiceDiscoveryManager` applies when searching for the entity's services of interest. This filtering facility is particularly useful to entities that wish to extend the capabilities of the standard template matching scheme.

The `ServiceDiscoveryManager` is a utility class, not a remote service. Client-like entities that wish to use this utility will create an instance of the `ServiceDiscoveryManager` in the entity's address space so as to manage the entity's "lookup state" locally.

SD.2.1 The Object Types

The types defined in the specification of the `ServiceDiscoveryManager` utility class are in the `net.jini.lookup` package. The following types may be referenced in this chapter. Whenever referenced, these object types will be referenced in unqualified form:

```
net.jini.core.discovery.LookupLocator
net.jini.core.lease.Lease
net.jini.core.lookup.ServiceEvent
net.jini.core.lookup.ServiceItem
net.jini.core.lookup.ServiceMatches
net.jini.core.lookup.ServiceRegistrar
net.jini.core.lookup.ServiceTemplate
net.jini.discovery.DiscoveryListener
net.jini.discovery.DiscoveryManagement
net.jini.discovery.LookupDiscoveryManager
net.jini.lease.LeaseRenewalManager
net.jini.lookup.LookupCache
net.jini.lookup.ServiceDiscoveryEvent
net.jini.lookup.ServiceDiscoveryListener
net.jini.lookup.ServiceItemFilter
java.io.IOException
java.rmi.server.UnicastRemoteObject
java.rmi.MarshalledObject
java.rmi.RemoteException
java.util.EventListener
java.util.EventObject
java.util.Set
```

SD.3 The Interface

THE public interface provided by the ServiceDiscoveryManager class defines methods that allow an entity to request that references to services matching criteria defined by the entity be found in discovered lookup services and cached for local retrieval. This interface also defines methods for retrieving the manager objects employed by this utility, and for performing termination processing.

```
package net.jini.lookup;

public class ServiceDiscoveryManager {
    public ServiceDiscoveryManager
                          (DiscoveryManagement discoveryMgr,
                           LeaseRenewalManager leaseMgr)
                                throws IOException {…}
    public LookupCache createLookupCache
                         (ServiceTemplate tmpl,
                          ServiceItemFilter filter,
                          ServiceDiscoveryListener listener)
                                throws RemoteException {…}
    public ServiceItem lookup(ServiceTemplate tmpl,
                              ServiceItemFilter filter) {…}
    public ServiceItem lookup(ServiceTemplate tmpl,
                              ServiceItemFilter filter,
                              long waitDur)
                                throws InterruptedException,
                                       RemoteException {…}
    public ServiceItem[] lookup
                             (ServiceTemplate tmpl,
                              int maxMatches,
                              ServiceItemFilter filter) {…}
    public ServiceItem[] lookup(ServiceTemplate tmpl,
                                int minMatches,
                                int maxMatches,
```

```
                                        ServiceItemFilter filter,
                                        long waitDur)
                                         throws InterruptedException,
                                                RemoteException {…}
    public DiscoveryManagement getDiscoveryManager() {…}
    public LeaseRenewalManager getLeaseRenewalManager() {…}
    public void terminate() {…}
}
```

SD.4 The Semantics

THE `ServiceDiscoveryManager` makes certain concurrency guarantees with respect to the methods it defines. When a method of `ServiceDiscoveryManager` invokes a remote method, although such an invocation may block other remote calls made in the `ServiceDiscoveryManager`, invocations of local methods will not be blocked.

SD.4.1 The Methods

The `ServiceDiscoveryManager` helper utility class defines a number of public methods in addition to its constructor. This utility defines a factory method that allows the entity to create a local cache for storing references to desired services that have been previously discovered. Additionally, this class defines a set of methods that the entity may use to query (remotely) each discovered lookup service for other services that are of interest to the entity.

The `equals` method for the `ServiceDiscoveryManager` class returns `true` if and only if two instances of this class refer to the same object. That is, `x` and `y` are equal instances of this class if and only if `x == y` has the value `true`.

SD.4.1.1 The Constructor

The constructor of the `ServiceDiscoveryManager` takes two arguments: an object that implements the `DiscoveryManagement` interface and a reference to a `LeaseRenewalManager` object. The constructor throws an `IOException` because construction of a `ServiceDiscoveryManager` may initiate the multicast discovery process, a process that can throw `IOException`.

To use the `ServiceDiscoveryManager`, an entity supplies an object through which notifications that indicate a lookup service has been discovered or discarded will be received. At a minimum, this object must satisfy the contract defined in the `DiscoveryManagement` interface. That is, this object must provide the `ServiceDiscoveryManager` with the ability to set discovery listeners and to discard previously discovered lookup services when they are found to be unavailable.

A value of `null` may be passed as the `DiscoveryManagement` argument. If the value of the argument is `null`, an instance of the `LookupDiscoveryManager` utility class will be constructed to discover only those lookup services that are members of the public group.

A value of `null` may be passed as the `LeaseRenewalManager` argument. If the value of the argument is `null`, an instance of the `LeaseRenewalManager` class will be created, initially managing no `Lease` objects.

SD.4.1.2 The `createLookupCache` Method

The `createLookupCache` method allows an entity to request that the `ServiceDiscoveryManager` create a new managed set (or cache) and populate it with services, which match criteria defined by the entity, and whose references are registered with one or more of the lookup services the entity has targeted for discovery.

This method returns an object of type `LookupCache`. Through this return value, the entity can query the cache for services of interest, manage the cache's event mechanism for service discoveries, or terminate the cache. The definition of the `LookupCache` interface is presented later in this specification.

An entity typically uses the object returned by this method to provide *local* storage of, and access to, references to services that it is interested in using. Entities that need frequent access to numerous services will find the object returned by this method quite useful because acquisition of those service references is provided through local method invocations. Additionally, because the object returned by this method provides an event mechanism, it is also useful to entities wishing to simply monitor, in an event-driven manner, the state changes that occur in the services of interest.

The `createLookupCache` method takes three arguments: an instance of `ServiceTemplate`, an instance of `ServiceItemFilter`, and an instance of `ServiceDiscoveryListener`. Both the interfaces `ServiceItemFilter` and `ServiceDiscoveryListener` are presented later in this chapter.

Together, the `tmpl` and the `filter` arguments define the criteria with which service-matching should be performed. The `listener` argument references an object that will receive notifications when services matching the input criteria are discovered for the first time, or have encountered a state change such as removal from all lookup services or attribute set changes. If `null` is input to the `listener` argument for a particular invocation of this method, the cache resulting from that invocation will send no such notifications.

The tmpl argument employs template matching semantics that are identical to the semantics described in *The Jini Technology Core Platform Specification,* "ServiceTemplate and Item Matching") to identify the service(s) to acquire from lookup services in the managed set. The object passed to the filter argument is then used to apply additional matching criteria to any service references found through template matching. The additional matching criteria defined by the filter parameter are application-specific, and therefore must be defined by the client-like entity itself (as described in Section SD.5.2, "The ServiceItemFilter Interface"). Furthermore, once an instance of the cache is created, the filter associated with that instance will not change during the life of that particular cache. If the filter is changed so that its original behavior is modified, the effect on the cache is undefined.

As a convenience, a null reference input to the tmpl argument is treated as equivalent to inputting a ServiceTemplate constructed with all null arguments (all *wildcards*). That is, the cache will attempt to discover all services contained in each lookup service in the managed set. If a null value is passed as the filter argument, then only template matching will be employed to find the desired services.

Entities that invoke this method must take care not to modify the contents of the object input through the tmpl parameter after the cache has been created. Doing so could cause the state of the cache to become corrupted or inconsistent. It is for this reason that the effects of modifying the contents of the tmpl parameter, after this method is invoked, are undefined.

Events and the Cache

To keep its contents up to date, the cache must register with the event mechanism of each lookup service in the managed set. From the point of view of the cache, a service is "discovered" when it receives a remote event from one of those lookup services notifying the cache of the existence of a service matching the input criteria. In addition, whenever one of the cache's discovered services experiences a state change in one of the lookup services in which it is registered, the cache will receive a remote event identifying that state change whenever the change satisfies the matching criteria.

For a number of reasons the cache may receive multiple events corresponding to the same Jini service. For example, a particular Jini service may be registered with more than one lookup service from the managed set. If the cache requests events from each lookup service using a template configured with no restriction along the service ID search axis and little or no restriction along the attribute search axis, the cache will receive a notification each time one of the following events occurs at any of the those lookup services:

- The service, matching the template, is registered with one of the lookup services.
- The lease of the matching service is cancelled or expires.
- An attribute set associated with the matching service is modified in some way.

Just as the cache requests that it be notified of state changes in matching services occurring within each lookup service, an entity may request that the cache deliver events that indicate analogous state changes in the service references stored in the cache.

There are two significant differences in the event mechanism between the lookup services and the cache, and the event mechanism between the cache and the client-like entity. First and foremost, the events sent from the lookup services to the cache are *remote* events, whereas the events sent from the cache to the entity are *local* events. Second, each registration or state-change event sent from the cache to the entity may actually have been a result of multiple corresponding events received by the cache from a set of lookup services. Thus, there is a many-to-one relationship between the events received by the cache and the events sent by the cache.

For many entities that use the cache's event mechanism to interact with the cache's discovered services, knowledge of the number of distinct service references, as well as identification of the lookup services with which those references are registered, is of no interest. Such entities typically are interested only in acquiring *a* reference—not *all* references—to the desired services. Thus, the relationship between the two event mechanisms described previously allows the `ServiceDiscoveryManager` to hide the lookup services with which the cache interacts from the entity. For entities that are interested in the additional information, the cache provides methods separate from the event mechanism for obtaining such information.

To summarize, although the cache may receive *multiple* events signaling a state change related to a particular matching service, the cache will typically send only a *single* corresponding event to the entity. That is, for any matching service:

- The cache will send a *service discovery event* to the entity only once: after the cache acquires the *first* reference to the matching service.
- The cache will send a *service removal event* to the entity only once: after every reference to the service has had its lease expire or cancelled; that is, only after all references to the matching service have been removed from every lookup service in the cache's managed set.

◆ For each set of event(s) notifying the cache that a particular modification has been made to the attribute set associated with one of the service references, one *service modification event* will be sent to the entity, but *only if* the attribute set state reflected in the received event represents an actual change in the service's current attribute set state (as maintained by the cache).

With respect to the state of the attribute sets associated with the service references stored in the cache, the cache should be viewed as maintaining a single attribute set state for each collection of service references that represent the same service. That single state will always be equivalent to the state reflected in the last attribute set modification event received by the cache.

For example, suppose each of three different references to a service that matches the input criteria is registered with three lookup services in the managed set. Suppose the attribute sets associated with each service reference are modified in exactly the same way. For this specific case, the cache would receive three events—one from each lookup service—signaling these modifications. Upon receipt of the first event, the cache modifies its current notion of the service's attribute set state, and then notifies the entity of the change, but only if the state reflected in the event represents a change in the current state. Because the remaining two events received by the cache represent the same state change as that represented in the first event, the cache sends no other notification.

Next, suppose a second modification, different from the first, is made on only two of the service references, and a third unique modification is made on the remaining service reference. In this case, the cache will still receive three events, but how the cache handles the events is dependent on the order of arrival of the events. For simplicity, call the three events e_1, e_2, and e_3. Use s to represent the cache's current notion of the service's attribute set state, and use s_1 and s_2 to represent the states resulting after each attribute modification has occurred. In this example, e_1 and e_2 will be sent to the cache after the each of the service's attribute sets is modified to s_1 in their respective lookup services. Event e_3 is sent after the service's attribute sets are modified to s_2 in the remaining lookup service.

If the order of arrival is e_1, e_2, and then e_3, the cache will change s into s_1 and notify the entity after the arrival of e_1 but will do nothing upon the arrival of e_2. Upon the arrival of e_3, the cache will change s (which is now s_1) into s_2. If the order of arrival of the events is e_1, e_3, and then e_2, the cache will first change s into s_1, then into s_2, and then back into s_1 again. Furthermore, for each state change made, the cache will send a notification to the entity.

Thus, the events generated by the cache's event mechanism and sent by the cache to the entity are more representative of the state changes that occur in the cache than in the lookup services.

An entity may register for events from the cache in one of two ways. The entity may supply an instance of `ServiceDiscoveryListener` to the listener argument of the `createLookupCache` method, or it may invoke a method on the cache to add a listener to the cache. Thus, an entity may register for events from the cache at any time during the execution life of the cache.

Similarly, the cache provides a method that an entity, which is currently registered for events from the cache, may use at any time to unregister with the cache's event mechanism.

SD.4.1.3 The `lookup` Method

The `lookup` method queries each available lookup service in the managed set for service reference(s) that match criteria defined by the entity that invokes this method. Entities typically employ this method when they need infrequent access to services and when the cost of making remote queries is outweighed by the overhead of maintaining a local cache (for example, because of resource limitations).

The `lookup` method has four versions, each version falling into one of two categories: those versions of this method that return a single instance of `ServiceItem` and those versions that return a set of service references as an array of `ServiceItem` objects.

Two arguments are common to all versions of this method: an instance of `ServiceTemplate` and an instance of `ServiceItemFilter`.

Within each category, the versions of `lookup` differ only in whether or not a particular version provides what is referred to as a "wait" (or blocking) feature. That is, each category contains both a non-blocking version of `lookup` which returns immediately when unable to find the desired service, and a blocking version which returns only after waiting a specified amount of time for the desired service to be discovered. The particular version of `lookup` that an entity employs is typically determined by the entity's intended usage pattern.

The descriptions that follow refer to all versions of the `lookup` method, except where explicitly noted.

The `tmpl` argument and the `filter` argument both have semantics identical to that defined for these arguments in the description of the `createLookupCache` method above. In particular,

- A `null` reference value for the `tmpl` parameter is treated as the equivalent of a "wildcarded" `ServiceTemplate`.
- If `null` is the value for the `filter` parameter, only template matching will be employed to find the desired services.

- The effects of modifying the contents of the `tmpl` parameter while the invocation is in progress are unpredictable and undefined.

If no service can be found that matches the desired criteria, then the versions of `lookup` from the first category—those that return a single instance of `ServiceItem`—will return `null`, whereas the versions from the second category—those that return an array of `ServiceItem` instances—will return an empty array.

The versions of `lookup` from the first category can be used in a fashion similar to the first form of the `lookup` method defined in the `ServiceRegistrar` interface described in *The Jini Technology Core Platform Specification,* "Lookup Service". That is, an entity would typically invoke one of these versions of `lookup` when it wishes to find a *single* service reference and the particular lookup service with which that service reference is registered is unimportant to the entity.

Each version of `lookup` defined in the `ServiceDiscoveryManager` differs with the corresponding version of `lookup` in `ServiceRegistrar` in the following ways:

- The versions of `lookup` defined in the `ServiceDiscoveryManager` query *multiple* lookup services (the order in which the lookup services are queried is dependent on the implementation).
- The versions of `lookup` defined in the `ServiceDiscoveryManager` can apply additional matching criteria, in the form of a filter object, when deciding whether a service reference found through standard template matching should be returned to the entity.

The versions of `lookup` that return an array of `ServiceItem` objects can be used in a fashion similar to the second form of `lookup` defined in the `ServiceRegistrar` interface. That is, an entity would typically invoke these versions of `lookup` when it wishes to find *multiple* service references matching the input criteria. Each of the versions of `lookup` that return an array of `ServiceItem` objects takes as one of its arguments an `int` parameter, `maxMatches`, that represents the maximum number of matches that should be returned. The array returned by these methods will contain no more than `maxMatches` service references, although it may contain fewer than that number.

As with the versions of `lookup` that return a single instance of `ServiceItem`, multiple queries and filtering are also notable differences between the second-category versions of this method and their counterpart in `ServiceRegistrar`.

For each version of `lookup`, whenever a lookup service query returns a `null` service reference, the filter is bypassed, and the service reference is excluded from the return object. On the other hand, if the query returns a non-null service reference in which the associated array of attribute contains one or more null elements, the filter is still applied and the service reference is included in the return object.

Each version of lookup may be confronted with duplicate references during a search for a service of interest. This is because the same service may register with more than one lookup service in the managed set. As with the cache, when a set of service references is returned by lookup, each service reference in the return set will be unique with respect to all other service references in the set, as determined by the equals method provided by each reference.

If it is determined that a lookup service is unavailable (due to an exception or some other non-fatal error) while interacting with a lookup service from the managed set, all versions of lookup will invoke the discard method on the instance of DiscoveryManagement being employed by the ServiceDiscoveryManager. Doing so will result in the unavailable lookup service being discarded and made eligible for rediscovery.

Recall that the propagation of modifications to a service's attributes across a set of lookup services typically occurs asynchronously. It is for this reason that while invoking lookup to find a set of matching services, it is possible that the set returned may contain multiple references having the same service ID with different attributes. Note that although this sort of inconsistent state can also occur if the entity employs a cache, the cache will eventually reflect the correct state.

The Blocking Feature of lookup

As noted above, each category contains a version of lookup that provides a feature in which the entity can request that if the number of service references found throughout the available lookup services does not fall into a desired range, the method will wait a finite period of time until either an acceptable minimum number of service references are discovered or the specified time period has passed.

The versions of lookup providing this blocking feature each takes as one of its parameters a value of type long that represents the number of milliseconds to wait for the service to be discovered. In addition to RemoteException, each of these versions of lookup may throw an InterruptedException.

One of these blocking versions of lookup implicitly uses a value of one for both the acceptable minimum and the allowable maximum number of service references to discover. The other blocking version requires that the entity specify the range through the minMatches and maxMatches parameters, respectively.

Prior to blocking, each of these versions of lookup first queries each available lookup service in an attempt to retrieve a satisfactory number of matching services. Whether or not the method actually blocks is dependent on how many matching service references are found during the query process. Blocking occurs only if after querying *all* of the available lookup services, the number of matching services found is less than the acceptable minimum. If the waiting period (measured from when blocking first begins) passes before that minimum number of service references is found, the method will return the service references that have been discovered up to that point. If the waiting period passes and no services have been found, `null` or an empty array (depending on the version of `lookup`) will be returned.

If, after querying all of the available lookup services, the number of matching services found is greater than or equal to the specified minimum but less than the specified maximum, the method will return the currently discovered service references without blocking. If the initial query process produces the desired maximum number of service references, the method will return the results immediately.

The blocking versions of `lookup` are quite useful to entities that cannot proceed until such a service of interest is found. If a non-positive value is input to the `waitDur` argument, then the method will not wait. It will simply query the available lookup services and employ the return semantics described above.

The values of the `minMatches` and `maxMatches` arguments must both be positive, and `maxMatches` must be greater than or equal to `minMatches`; otherwise, an `IllegalArgumentException` will be thrown.

The blocking versions of `lookup` make a concurrency guarantee with respect to the discovery of new lookup services during the wait period. That is, while waiting for matching service reference(s) to be discovered, if one or more of the desired—but previously unavailable—lookup services is discovered and added to the managed set, those new lookup services will also be queried for the service(s) of interest.

In addition, the blocking versions of `lookup` throw `InterruptedException`. When an entity invokes either version with valid parameters, the entity may decide during the wait period that it no longer wishes to wait the entire period for the method to return. Thus, while the method is blocking on the discovery of matching service(s), it may be interrupted by invoking the `interrupt` method from the `Thread` class. The intent of this mechanism is to allow the entity to interrupt a blocking `lookup` in the same way it would a sleeping thread.

SD.4.1.4 The `getDiscoveryManager` Method

The `getDiscoveryManager` method returns an object that implements the `DiscoveryManagement` interface. The object returned by this method provides the `ServiceDiscoveryManager` with the ability to set discovery listeners and to discard previously discovered lookup services when they are found to be unavailable. This method takes no arguments.

SD.4.1.5 The `getLeaseRenewalManager` Method

The `getLeaseRenewalManager` method returns a `LeaseRenewalManager` object. The object returned by this method manages the leases requested and held by the `ServiceDiscoveryManager`. In general, these leases correspond to the registrations made by the `ServiceDiscoveryManager` with the event mechanism of each lookup service in the managed set. This method takes no arguments.

SD.4.1.6 The `terminate` Method

The `terminate` method performs cleanup duties related to the termination of the event mechanism for *lookup service* discovery, the event mechanism for *service* discovery, and the cache management duties of the `ServiceDiscoveryManager`. That is, the `terminate` method will terminate each `LookupCache` instance created and managed by the `ServiceDiscoveryManager`. Additionally, if the discovery manager employed by the `ServiceDiscoveryManager` was created by the `ServiceDiscoveryManager` itself, then the `terminate` method will also terminate that discovery manager.

Note that if the discovery manager was created externally and supplied to the `ServiceDiscoveryManager`, then any reference to that discovery manager held by the entity will remain valid, even after the `ServiceDiscoveryManager` has been terminated. Similarly, if the entity holds a reference to the lease renewal manager employed by the `ServiceDiscoveryManager`, that reference will also remain valid after termination, whether lease renewal manager was created externally or by the `ServiceDiscoveryManager` itself.

The `ServiceDiscoveryManager` makes certain concurrency guarantees with respect to an invocation of `terminate` while other method invocations are in progress. The termination process described above will not begin until completion of all invocations of the public methods defined in the public interface of `ServiceDiscoveryManager`; that is, until completion of invocations of `createLookupCache`, `lookup`, `getDiscoveryManager`, and `getLeaseRenewalManager`.

Upon completion of the termination process, the semantics of all current and future method invocations on the terminated instance of the `ServiceDiscoveryManager` are undefined.

SD.4.2 Defining Service Equality

The ability to accurately determine when two different service references are equal is very important to the ServiceDiscoveryManager in general, and the LookupCache in particular. Any restriction placed on that ability can result in inefficient and undesirable behavior. Storing and managing duplicate service references—that is, proxies that refer to the same version of the same back end service—is usually viewed as undesirable. In other words, when storing and managing service references, it is very desirable to be able to determine not only that two different proxies refer to the same back end service, but if they do refer to the same back end, whether or not the current version of the referenced service has been replaced with a new version.

The mechanism employed by the LookupCache to avoid storing duplicate service references is the equals method provided by the discovered services themselves. This is because an individual well-behaved service of interest will usually register with multiple lookup services, and for each lookup service with which that service registers, the LookupCache will receive a separate event containing a reference to the service. When the LookupCache receives events from multiple lookup services, the service ID (retrieved from the service reference in the event) together with the equals method provided by the service itself, is used to distinguish the service references from each other. In this way, when a new event arrives containing a reference associated with the same service as an already-stored reference, the LookupCache can determine whether the new reference is a duplicate or the service has been replaced with a new version of itself. In the former case, the duplicate would be ignored; in the latter case, the old reference would be replaced with the new reference.

Thus, the LookupCache relies on the provider of each service to override the equals method inherited from the class Object with an implementation that allows for the identification of duplicate service proxies. In addition to the equals method, each service should also provide a proper implementation of the hashCode method. This is because even if an entity never explicitly calls on the equals method to compare service references, those references may still be stored in container classes (for example, Hashtable) where such comparisons are made "under the covers." From the point of view of the ServiceDiscoveryManager and the LookupCache, providing an appropriate implementation for both the equals method and the hashCode method is a key characteristic of good behavior in a Jini service.

Note that there is no need to override either the equals method or the hashCode method if the service is implemented as a purely remote object in which the service proxy is an RMI stub. In this case, appropriate implementations for both methods are already provided in the stub.

SD.4.3 Exporting RemoteEventListener Objects

A subset of the methods on the ServiceDiscoveryManager, when invoked, will result in a request for registration with the event mechanism of one or more lookup services. The methods that result in such a request are createLookupCache and the blocking versions of the lookup method.

Any entity that invokes one of these methods must export, to each lookup service with which a registration occurs, the stub classes of the RemoteEventListener object through which instances of RemoteEvent will be received. Furthermore, each of these methods must throw RemoteException. The reasons that a RemoteException can occur fall into one of the following categories:

- Each of these methods attempts to export a remote object, a process that can throw RemoteException.
- Each of these methods attempts to register with the event mechanism of at least one lookup service, a process that can throw RemoteException.

How each of the affected methods handle the RemoteException is dependent on the reason for the exception. If a RemoteException (or any other non-fatal exception or error) is thrown during an attempt to register for events from a lookup service, that lookup service will be discarded and made eligible for rediscovery. On the other hand, if a RemoteException occurs during an attempt to export the listener, the method from which that attempt is made will re-throw the same exception.

The potential for RemoteException during the export process imposes the following requirement: the *same* instance of the listener must be exported to each lookup service from which events will be requested. Furthermore, the creation and export of the listener must occur prior to the event registration process. This requirement guarantees that should a RemoteException occur after the registration process has begun, the exception will not be propagated and event processing will continue.

To understand the significance of this requirement, consider the scenario in which a different instance of the listener is exported to each lookup service. If a new lookup service is discovered after the event process has begun for the other lookup services in the managed set, a new instance of the listener must be created and exported. Should a RemoteException occur during the export process, the exception will be propagated and all event processing will stop—a result that many entities may view as undesirable.

To facilitate exporting the listener, the entity—whether it is a Jini client or a Jini service—is responsible for providing and advertising a mechanism through which each lookup service will acquire the listener's stub classes.

For example, one implementation of the `ServiceDiscoveryManager` might provide a special JAR file containing only the listener stub classes to optimize download time. By including this JAR file in the entity's `java.rmi.server.codebase` property (in the appropriate format, specifying transport protocol and location), the entity *advertises* the mechanism that lookup services can employ to acquire the stub classes. By executing a process to serve up the JAR file (for example, an HTTP server), the mechanism through which each lookup service acquires those stub classes is *provided.*

It is important to note that should such a mechanism not be made available to each lookup service with which event registration will be requested, a "silent failure" can occur repeatedly. If the mechanism is not available, each lookup service cannot acquire the exported listener. Because each lookup service cannot acquire the exported listener, any attempts to register for events will fail. Whenever an attempt to register for events fails, the associated lookup service will be discarded and made eligible for rediscovery. Upon rediscovery of the discarded lookup service, the cycle repeats when a new attempt to register for events is made.

SD.5 Supporting Interfaces and Classes

THE ServiceDiscoveryManager utility class depends on the following interfaces defined in *The Jini Technology Core Platform Specification,* "Lookup Service": ServiceTemplate, ServiceItem, and ServiceMatches. This class also depends on a number of interfaces, each defined in this section; those interfaces are DiscoveryManagement, ServiceItemFilter, ServiceDiscoveryListener, and LookupCache.

The ServiceDiscoveryManager class references the following concrete classes: LookupDiscoveryManager and LeaseRenewalManager, each described in a separate chapter of this document, and ServiceDiscoveryEvent, which is defined in this chapter.

SD.5.1 The DiscoveryManagement Interface

Although it is not necessary for the ServiceDiscoveryManager itself to execute the discovery process, it does need to be notified when one of the lookup services it wishes to query is discovered or discarded. Thus, at a minimum, the ServiceDiscoveryManager requires access to the instances of DiscoveryEvent sent to the listeners registered with the event mechanism of the discovery process. The instance of DiscoveryManagement passed to the constructor of the ServiceDiscoveryManager provides a mechanism for acquiring access to those events. For a complete description of the semantics of the methods of this interface, refer to the *Jini Discovery Utilities Specification.*

One noteworthy item about the semantics of the ServiceDiscoveryManager is the effect that invocations of the discard method of DiscoveryManagement have on any cache objects created by the ServiceDiscoveryManager. The DiscoveryManagement interface specifies that the discard method will remove a particular lookup service from the managed set of lookup services already discovered, allowing that lookup service to be rediscovered. Invoking this method will result in the flushing of the lookup service from the appropriate cache. This effect ultimately causes a discard notification to be sent to all DiscoveryListener objects registered with the event mechanism of the discovery process (including all listeners registered by the `ServiceDiscoveryManager`).

The receipt of an event notification indicating that a lookup service from the managed set has been discarded must ultimately result in the cancellation and removal of all event leases that were granted by the discarded lookup service and that are managed by the `LeaseRenewalManager` on behalf of the `ServiceDiscoveryManager`.

Furthermore, every service reference stored in the cache that is registered with the discarded lookup service but is not registered with any of the remaining lookup services in the managed set will be "discarded" as well. That is, all previously discovered service references that are registered with only unavailable lookup services will be removed from the cache and made eligible for service rediscovery.

SD.5.2 The `ServiceItemFilter` Interface

The `ServiceItemFilter` interface defines the methods used by an object such as the `ServiceDiscoveryManager` or the `LookupCache` to apply additional matching criteria when searching for services in which an entity has registered interest. It is the responsibility of the entity requesting the application of additional criteria to construct an implementation of this interface that defines the additional criteria, and to pass the resulting object (referred to as a *filter*) into the object that will apply it.

The filtering mechanism provided by implementations of this interface is particularly useful to entities that wish to extend the capabilities of the standard template matching scheme. For example, because template matching does not allow one to search for services based on a range of attribute values, this additional matching mechanism can be exploited by the entity to ask the managing object to find all registered printer services that have a resolution attribute between say, 300 dpi and 1200 dpi.

```
package net.jini.lookup;

public interface ServiceItemFilter {
    public boolean check(ServiceItem item);
}
```

SD.5.2.1 The Semantics

The `check` method defines the implementation of the additional matching criteria to apply to a `ServiceItem` object found through standard template matching. This method takes one argument: the `ServiceItem` object to test against the additional criteria. This method returns `true` if the input object satisfies the additional criteria and `false` otherwise.

Neither a `null` reference nor a `ServiceItem` object containing `null` fields will be passed into this method by the `ServiceDiscoveryManager`.

If the parameter input to this method is a `ServiceItem` object that has non-`null` fields but is associated with attribute sets containing `null` entries, this method must process that parameter in a reasonable manner.

Should an exception occur during an invocation of this method, the semantics of how that exception is handled are undefined.

This method must not modify the contents of the input `ServiceItem` object because it could result in unpredictable and undesirable effects on future processing by the `ServiceDiscoveryManager`. That is why the effects of any such modification to the contents of that input parameter are undefined.

SD.5.3 The `ServiceDiscoveryEvent` Class

The `ServiceDiscoveryEvent` class encapsulates the service discovery information made available by the event mechanism of the `LookupCache`. All listeners that an entity has registered with the cache's event mechanism will receive an event of type `ServiceDiscoveryEvent` upon the discovery, removal, or modification of one of the cache's services, as described previously in "Events and the Cache."

This class is a subclass of the class `EventObject`. In addition to the methods of the `EventObject` class, this class provides two additional accessor methods that can be used to retrieve the additional state associated with the event: `getPreEventServiceItem` and `getPostEventServiceItem`.

The `getSource` method of the `EventObject` class returns the instance of `LookupCache` from which the given event originated.

```
package net.jini.lookup;

public class ServiceDiscoveryEvent extends EventObject {
    public ServiceDiscoveryEvent(Object source,
                                 ServiceItem preEventItem,
                                 ServiceItem postEventItem)
```

```
                                                    {...}

        public ServiceItem getPreEventServiceItem() {...}
        public ServiceItem getPostEventServiceItem() {...}
    }
```

SD.5.3.1 The Semantics

The constructor of `ServiceDiscoveryEvent` takes three arguments:

- An instance of `Object` corresponding to the instance of `LookupCache` from which the given event originated
- A `ServiceItem` reference representing the state of the service (associated with the given event) *prior to* the occurrence of the event
- A `ServiceItem` reference representing the state of the service *after* the occurrence of the event

If `null` is passed as the `source` parameter for the constructor, a `NullPointerException` will be thrown.

Depending on the nature of the discovery event, a `null` reference may be passed as one or the other of the remaining parameters, but never both. If `null` is passed as both the `preEventItem` and the `postEventItem` parameters, a `NullPointerException` will be thrown.

Note that the constructor will not modify the contents of either `ServiceItem` argument. Doing so can result in unpredictable and undesirable effects on future processing by the `ServiceDiscoveryManager`. That is why the effects of any such modification to the contents of either input parameter are undefined.

The `getPreEventServiceItem` method returns an instance of `ServiceItem` containing the service reference corresponding to the given event. The service state reflected in the returned service item is the state of the service *prior* to the occurrence of the event.

If the event is a discovery event (as opposed to a removal or modification event), then this method will return `null` because the discovered service had no state in the cache prior to its discovery.

The `getPostEventServiceItem` method returns an instance of `ServiceItem` containing the service reference corresponding to the given event. The service state reflected in the returned service item is the state of the service *after* the occurrence of the event.

If the event is a removal event, then this method will return `null` because the discovered service has no state in the cache after it is removed from the cache.

Because making a copy can be a very expensive process, neither accessor method returns a copy of the service reference associated with the event. Rather, each method returns the appropriate service reference from the cache itself. Due to this cost, listeners (see Section SD.5.4, "The `ServiceDiscoveryListener` Interface" below) that receive a `ServiceDiscoveryEvent` must not modify the contents of the object returned by these methods; doing so could cause the state of the cache to become corrupted or inconsistent because the objects returned by these methods are also members of the cache. This potential for corruption or inconsistency is why the effects of modifying the object returned by either accessor method are undefined.

SD.5.4 The `ServiceDiscoveryListener` Interface

The `ServiceDiscoveryListener` interface defines the methods used by objects such as a `LookupCache` to notify an entity that events of interest related to the elements of the cache have occurred. It is the responsibility of the entity wishing to be notified of the occurrence of such events to construct an object that implements the `ServiceDiscoveryListener` interface and then register that object with the cache's event mechanism. Any implementation of this interface must define the actions to take upon receipt of an event notification. The action taken is dependent on both the application and the particular event that has occurred.

```
package net.jini.lookup;

public interface ServiceDiscoveryListener {
    public void serviceAdded(ServiceDiscoveryEvent event);
    public void serviceRemoved(ServiceDiscoveryEvent event);
    public void serviceChanged(ServiceDiscoveryEvent event);
}
```

SD.5.4.1 The Semantics

As described previously in the section titled "Events and the Cache," when the cache receives from one of the managed lookup services, an event signaling the *registration* of a service of interest for the *first time* (or for the first time since the service has been discarded), the cache invokes the `serviceAdded` method on all instances of `ServiceDiscoveryListener` that are registered with the cache; doing so notifies the entity that a service of interest has been discovered. The method `serviceAdded` takes one argument: an instance of `ServiceDiscoveryEvent` containing references to the service item corresponding to the event, including representations of the service's state both before and after the event.

When the cache receives, from a managed lookup service, an event signaling the *removal* of a service of interest from the *last* such lookup service with which it was registered, the cache invokes the `serviceRemoved` method on all instances of `ServiceDiscoveryListener` that are registered with the cache; doing so notifies the entity that a service of interest has been discarded. The `serviceRemoved` method takes one argument: a `ServiceDiscoveryEvent` object containing references to the service item corresponding to the event, including representations of the service's state both before and after the event.

When the cache receives, from a managed lookup service, an event signaling the unique *modification* of the attributes of a service of interest (across the attribute sets of all references to the service), the cache invokes the `serviceChanged` method on all instances of `ServiceDiscoveryListener` that are registered with the cache; doing so notifies the entity that the state of a service of interest has changed. The `serviceChanged` method takes one argument: a `ServiceDiscoveryEvent` object containing references to the service item corresponding to the event, including representations of the service's state both before and after the event.

Should an exception occur during an invocation of any of the methods defined by this interface, the semantics of how that exception is handled are undefined.

Each method defined by this interface must not modify the contents of the `ServiceDiscoveryEvent` parameter; doing so can result in unpredictable and undesirable effects on future processing by the `ServiceDiscoveryManager`. It is for this reason that if one of these methods modifies the contents of the parameter, the effects are undefined.

This interface makes the following concurrency guarantee: for any given listener object that implements this interface, no two methods (either the same two methods or different methods) defined by the interface can be invoked at the same time by the same cache. For example, the `serviceRemoved` method must not be invoked while the invocation of another listener's `serviceAdded` method is in progress.

Finally, it should be noted that the intent of the methods of this interface is to allow the recipient of the `ServiceDiscoveryEvent` to be informed that a service has been added to, removed from, or modified in the cache. Calls to these methods are synchronous to allow the entity that makes the call (for example, a thread that interacts with the various lookup services of interest) to determine whether or not the call succeeded. However, it is not part of the semantics of the call that the notification return can be delayed while the recipient of the call reacts to the occurrence of the event. It is therefore highly recommended that implementations of this interface avoid time consuming operations and return from the method as quickly as possible. For example, one strategy might be to simply note the occurrence of the ServiceDiscoveryEvent and perform any time-consuming event handling asynchronously.

SD.5.5 The LookupCache Interface

The LookupCache interface defines the methods provided by the object created and returned by the ServiceDiscoveryManager when an entity invokes the createLookupCache method. Within this object are stored the discovered service references that match criteria defined by the entity. Through this interface the entity may retrieve one or more of the stored service references, register and unregister with the cache's event mechanism, and terminate all of the cache's processing.

```
package net.jini.lookup;

public interface LookupCache {
    public ServiceItem   lookup(ServiceItemFilter filter);

    public ServiceItem[] lookup(ServiceItemFilter filter,
                                int maxMatches);

    public void addListener
                         (ServiceDiscoveryListener listener);
    public void removeListener
                         (ServiceDiscoveryListener listener);

    public void discard(Object serviceReference);

    public void terminate();
}
```

SD.5.5.1 The Semantics

Depending on which version is invoked, the lookup method of the LookupCache interface returns one or more elements—each matching the input criteria—that were stored in the associated cache. The object that is returned is either a single instance of ServiceItem or a set of service references in the form of an array of ServiceItem objects. Each service item that is returned by either form of this method must have been previously discovered both to be registered with one or more of the lookup services in the managed set and to match criteria defined by the entity.

One argument is common to both forms of `lookup`: an instance of `ServiceItemFilter`. The semantics of the `filter` argument are identical to those of the `filter` argument specified for a number of the methods defined in the interface of the `ServiceDiscoveryManager` utility class. This argument is intended to allow an entity to separate its filtering into two steps: an initial filter applied during the discovery phase and then a finer resolution filter applied upon retrieval from the cache. As with the methods of the `ServiceDiscoveryManager`, if `null` is the value of this argument, then no additional filtering will be performed.

The second form of the `lookup` method of the `LookupCache` interface takes an additional argument: a parameter of type `int` that represents the maximum number of matches that should be returned. The array returned by this form of `lookup` will contain no more than the requested number of service references, although it may contain fewer than that number. The value input to this argument must be positive; otherwise, an `IllegalArgumentException` will be thrown.

If the cache is empty, or if no service can be found that matches the input criteria, then the first form of `lookup` will return `null`, whereas the second form of `lookup` will return an empty array. The algorithm used to select the return element(s) from the set of matching service references is implementation dependent.

Neither form of the `lookup` method of the `LookupCache` interface returns a copy of the matching service reference(s) that were selected; rather, each form returns the actual service reference(s) from the cache itself. Because the actual service reference(s) are returned, entities that invoke either form of this method must not modify the contents of the returned reference(s). Modifying the returned service reference(s) could cause the state of the cache to become corrupted or inconsistent. This potential for corruption or inconsistency is why the effects of modifying the service reference(s) returned by either form of `lookup` is undefined.

Typically, an entity will request the creation of a separate cache for each service type of interest. When the entity simply needs a reference to a service of a particular type, the entity should invoke the first form of `lookup` to retrieve one element from the cache; in this case, which particular service reference that is returned will not, in general, matter to the entity. If for some reason it does matter to an entity which service reference is returned, then the entity can invoke the second form of `lookup` requesting that `Integer.MAX_VALUE` service references be returned; doing so will return all elements of the cache that match the input criteria. The entity can then iterate through each element, selecting the desired reference.

The `addListener` method will register a `ServiceDiscoveryListener` object with the event mechanism of a `LookupCache`. This listener object will receive a

ServiceDiscoveryEvent upon the discovery, removal, or modification of one of the cache's services, as described previously in "Events and the Cache." This method takes one argument: a reference to the ServiceDiscoveryListener object to register.

If null is input to the addListener method, a NullPointerException is thrown. If the object input is a duplicate (using the equals method) of another element in the set of listeners, no action is taken.

Once a listener is registered, it will be notified of all service references discovered to date, and will be notified as new services are discovered and existing services are modified or discarded.

The LookupCache makes a reentrancy guarantee with respect to any ServiceDiscoveryListener objects registered with it. Should the LookupCache invoke a method on a registered listener (a local call), any call from that method to a local method of the LookupCache is guaranteed not to result in a deadlock condition.

The removeListener method will remove a ServiceDiscoveryListener object from the set of listeners currently registered with a LookupCache. Once all listeners are removed from the cache's set of listeners, the cache will send no more ServiceDiscoveryEvent notifications. This method takes one argument: a reference to the ServiceDiscoveryListener object to remove.

If the parameter value to removeListener is null, or if the listener passed to this method does not exist in the set of listeners maintained by the implementation class, then this method will take no action.

If an entity determines that a service reference retrieved from the cache is no longer available, the entity should request the removal of that reference from the cache. The mechanism for discarding an unavailable service from the cache is provided by the discard method of the LookupCache interface. The discard method takes one argument: an instance of Object whose reference is the service reference to remove from the cache. If the proxy input to this method is null, or if it matches (using the equals method) none of the service references in the cache, this method takes no action.

The discard method not only deletes the service reference from the cache, but also causes a notification to be sent to all registered listeners indicating that the service has been discarded (see the description of the serviceRemoved method in the section that specifies the ServiceDiscoveryListener interface). The service is guaranteed to have been removed from the cache when this method completes successfully; the service is then said to have been *discarded.* No such guarantee is made with respect to when the discard event is sent to the client's registered listeners. That is, the event that notifies the client that the service has been discarded may or may not be sent asynchronously.

With respect to discarding services, there is a situation that must be handled by all implementations of the LookupCache. Because the LookupCache discovers a service through a lookup service rather than through the service itself, there is a danger that, unless the LookupCache takes action (described below), once a service has been discarded, it may never be rediscovered. This can happen because even though a service may be discarded from the cache, it may not be discarded from the lookup services with which it is registered.

To understand this situation, it might help to first consider the conditions under which a service is normally discarded from the cache and then rediscovered. An entity typically discards a service when the entity determines that the service has become unavailable. Recall that a service usually becomes unavailable to an entity when the service crashes, the service is shut down, or the link between the entity and the service experiences a *network partition*. Under normal circumstances, when a well-defined service becomes unavailable because it has crashed or has been shut down, and the entity—after determining that the service is unavailable—discards the service, the cache will rediscover the service when the service comes back on line. The service is rediscovered because a well-behaved service will typically reregister with each lookup service with which it was registered prior to crashing or shutting down. Note that such a service will reregister even when its original lease with a lookup service is still valid. When the service reregisters with a lookup service, the lookup service notifies the cache's listener that a reregistration has occurred, and the service is then rediscovered.

A special case of the scenario just described involves services that choose to persist their leases. Typically, when a service that persists its leases comes back on line after a crash or a shutdown, the service will *not* reregister with any lookup service for which the associated lease is still valid. If none of the service's leases expire during the period in which the service is down, then when the service comes back on line, it will never reregister with any of the desired lookup services, and the cache will never be notified that the discarded service has become available once again.

Therefore it is important to note that there are conditions that may hinder rediscovering certain types of services that were discarded as a result of a crash or shutdown. This situation should not occur with any frequency because services that persist their leases are expected to be less common than other types of services. However, there is a common scenario in which *any* type of service may be discarded but never rediscovered. This new scenario is characterized not by service crashes or shutdowns, but by communication failures. In this situation, communication failures cause only the entity to view the service as unavailable; that is *each lookup service in the managed set can still communicate with the service*.

As with service crashes or shutdowns, communication failures between the entity and the service can also cause the entity to discard the service. But problems can arise when the communication failures occur between the entity and the service, but not between the service and any of the lookup services in the managed set. Although the service never goes down, it is still discarded by the entity because the inability to communicate with the service causes the entity to view the service as unavailable. But because the service can still communicate with the lookup services, the service will continue renewing its residency in each lookup service. Thus, since none of the service's leases expire, the service never reregisters with any of the lookup services, and the lookup services will never send events to the cache's listener that cause the service to be rediscovered.

To address the scenarios described above, all implementations must do the following when a service is discarded from the cache:

- Place the reference to the discarded service in separate storage, and remove the reference from the cache's storage (to guarantee that subsequent queries of the cache do not return that same unavailable reference).
- Wait an implementation-dependent amount of time that is likely to exceed the typical service lease duration.
- If a `ServiceEvent` with a transition equal to `TRANSITION_MATCH_NOMATCH` is received (indicating that the service's lease has expired), then the service reference that was set aside can be flushed, and the service is then truly discarded.
- If such a `ServiceEvent` is not received (indicating that a transient communication failure probably occurred), the service reference that was set aside should be placed back in the cache's local storage, and if the entity is registered for events from the cache, the appropriate event should be sent to the entity's registered listener.

The `terminate` method performs cleanup duties related to the termination of the processing being performed by a particular instance of `LookupCache`. For that instance, this method cancels all event leases granted by the lookup services that supplied the contents of the cache, and unexports all remote listener objects registered with those lookup services. The `terminate` method is typically called when the entity is no longer interested in the contents of the `LookupCache`. Upon completion of the termination process, the semantics of all current and future method invocations on the current instance of `LookupCache` are undefined.

THE JINI LOOKUP DISCOVERY SERVICE SPECIFICATION allows a third party to perform an entity's discovery duties. For example, to conserve computational resources, an activatable entity may wish to deactivate; thus, such an entity may wish to employ a separate Jini helper service to perform its discovery duties while it is deactivated. The lookup discovery service is a Jini helper service through which other Jini services and clients may request that discovery processing be performed on their behalf.

JINI™

LD
Jini Lookup Discovery Service

LD.1 Introduction

PART of *The Jini Technology Core Platform Specification,* "Discovery and Join" is devoted to defining the discovery requirements for well-behaved Jini clients and services, called *discovering entities*, which are required to participate in the multicast discovery protocols. Discovering entities are required to send multicast discovery requests to lookup services with which the entities wish to interact. In addition, they must continuously listen for and act on announcements from the desired lookup services. Interactions with a discovered lookup service may involve registration with that lookup service, or may simply involve querying the lookup service for services of interest (or both). To find *specific* lookup services, discovering entities also need to be able to participate in the unicast discovery protocol.

Under certain circumstances, a discovering entity may find it useful to allow a third party to perform the entity's discovery duties. For example, an activatable entity that wishes to deactivate may wish to employ a special Jini technology-enabled service (*Jini service*)—referred to as a *lookup discovery service*—to perform discovery duties on its behalf. Such an entity may wish to deactivate for various reasons, one being to conserve computational resources. While the entity is inactive, the lookup discovery service, running on the same or a separate host, would employ the discovery protocols to find lookup services in which the entity has expressed interest and would notify the entity when a previously unavailable lookup service has become available.

The facilities of the lookup discovery service are of particular value in a scenario in which a new lookup service is added to a long-lived djinn containing multiple inactive services. Without the use of a lookup discovery service, the time frame over which the new lookup service is fully populated can be both unpredictable and unbounded.

To understand why this time frame can be unpredictable, consider the fact that an inactive service has no way of discovering a new lookup service. This means that each inactive service in the djinn that wishes to discover and join a new lookup service must first activate. Since activation of a service occurs when some client attempts to use the service, the amount of time that passes between the arrival of the new lookup service and the activation of the service can vary greatly over the range of services in the djinn. Thus, the time frame over which the lookup service becomes fully populated cannot be predicted because it could take arbitrarily long before all of the services activate and then discover and join the new lookup service.

In addition to being unpredictable, the time it takes for the lookup service to fully populate can also be unbounded. This is because there is no guarantee that the lookup service will send multicast announcements between the time the service activates and the time it deactivates. If the timing is right, it is possible that one or more of the services in the djinn may never discover and join the new lookup service. Thus, without the use of the lookup discovery service, the new lookup service may never fully populate.

As another example of a discovering entity that may find it useful to allow a third party to perform the entity's discovery duties, consider an entity that exists in an environment with one of the following characteristics:

- The environment does not support multicast.
- The environment contains no lookup services within the entity's *multicast radius* (roughly, the number of hops beyond which neither the multicast requests from the entity nor the multicast announcements from the lookup service will propagate).
- The environment does contain lookup service(s) within the entity's multicast radius, but at least one service needed by the entity is not registered with any lookup service within that radius.

If such an entity was provided with references to lookup services—located outside of the entity's multicast radius—that contain services needed by the entity, the entity could contact each lookup service and retrieve the desired service references. One way to provide the entity with access to those lookup services might be to configure the entity to find and use a lookup discovery service, operating beyond the entity's range, that can employ multicast discovery to find nearby lookup services belonging to groups in which the entity has expressed interest.

After acquiring references to the targeted lookup services, the lookup discovery service would pass those references to the entity, providing the entity with access to the services registered with each lookup service. In this way, the entity participates in the multicast discovery protocols through a proxy relationship with the lookup discovery service, gaining access not only to lookup services outside of its own range, but also to all of the services registered with those lookup services.

Note that the scenario just described does not come without restrictions. For the lookup discovery service to be able to "link" an entity with lookup services in the way just described, the lookup discovery service must be registered with a lookup service having a location that either is known to the entity or is within the multicast radius of the entity. Furthermore, the lookup discovery service must be running on a host that is located within the multicast radius of the lookup services with which the entity wishes to be linked. That is, the entity must be able to find the lookup discovery service, and the lookup discovery service must be able to find the other desired lookup services.

To address these scenarios, the lookup discovery service participates in both the multicast discovery protocols and the unicast discovery protocol on behalf of a registered discovering entity or *client*. This service will listen for and process multicast announcement packets from Jini lookup services and will, until successful, repeatedly attempt to discover specific lookup services that the client is interested in finding.

Upon discovery of a previously undiscovered lookup service of interest, the lookup discovery service notifies all entities that have requested the discovery of that lookup service that such an event has occurred. The event mechanism employed by the lookup discovery service satisfies the requirements defined in *The Jini Technology Core Platform Specification,* "Distributed Events". Note that the entity that receives such an event notification does not have to be the client of the lookup discovery service; it may be a third-party event-handling service such as an event mailbox service. Once a client is notified of the discovery of a lookup service, it is left to the client to define the semantics of how it interacts with that lookup service. For example, the client may wish to join the lookup service, simply query it for other useful services, or both.

The lookup discovery service must be implemented as a well-behaved Jini service and must comply with all of the policies embodied in the Jini technology programming model. Thus, the resources granted by this service are leased, and implementations of this service must adhere to the distributed leasing model for Jini technology as defined in *The Jini Technology Core Platform Specification,* "Distributed Leasing". That is, the lookup discovery service will grant its services for only a limited period of time without an active expression of continuing interest on the part of the client.

LD.1.1 Goals and Requirements

The requirements of the interfaces and classes specified in this document are:

- To define a service that not only employs the Jini discovery protocols to discover, by way of either group association or `LookupLocator` association, lookup services in which clients have registered interest, but that also notifies its clients of the discovery of those lookup services
- To provide this service in such a way that it can be used by entities that deactivate
- To comply with the policies of the Jini technology programming model

The goals of this document are as follows:

- To describe the lookup discovery service
- To provide guidance in the use and deployment of services that implement the `LookupDiscoveryService` interface and related classes and interfaces

LD.1.2 Other Types

The types defined in the specification of the `LookupDiscoveryService` interface are in the `net.jini.discovery` package. The following object types may be referenced in this chapter. Whenever referenced, these object types will be referenced in unqualified form:

```
net.jini.core.discovery.LookupLocator
net.jini.core.event.EventRegistration
net.jini.core.event.RemoteEventListener
net.jini.core.lease.Lease
net.jini.core.lookup.ServiceID
net.jini.core.lookup.ServiceRegistrar
net.jini.discovery.DiscoveryEvent
net.jini.discovery.DiscoveryGroupManagement
net.jini.discovery.DiscoveryListener
java.io.IOException
java.rmi.MarshalledObject
java.rmi.NoSuchObjectException
java.rmi.RemoteException
java.util.Map
```

LD.2 The Interface

THE `LookupDiscoveryService` interface defines the service—referred to as the *lookup discovery service*—previously introduced in this specification. Through this interface, other Jini services and clients may request that discovery processing be performed on their behalf. This interface belongs to the `net.jini.discovery` package, and any service implementing this interface must comply with the definition of a Jini service. This interface is not a remote interface; each implementation of this service exports a front-end proxy object that implements this interface local to the client, using an implementation-specific protocol to communicate with the actual remote server (the back end). All of the proxy methods must obey normal Java Remote Method Invocation (RMI) remote interface semantics except where explicitly noted. Two proxy objects are equal (using the `equals` method) if they are proxies for the same lookup discovery service.

The one method defined in this interface throws a `RemoteException`, and requires only the default serialization semantics so that this interface can be implemented directly using Java RMI.

```
package net.jini.discovery;

public interface LookupDiscoveryService {
    public LookupDiscoveryRegistration register(
                                  String[] groups,
                                  LookupLocator[] locators,
                                  RemoteEventListener listener,
                                  MarshalledObject handback,
                                  long leaseDuration)
                                         throws RemoteException;
}
```

When requesting a registration with the lookup discovery service, the client indicates the lookup services it is interested in discovering by submitting two sets of objects. Each set may contain zero or more elements. One set consists of the names of the groups whose members are lookup services the client wishes to be discovered. The other set consists of `LookupLocator` objects, each corresponding to a specific lookup service the client wishes to be discovered.

For each successful registration the lookup discovery service will manage both the set of group names and the set of locators submitted. These sets will be referred to as the *managed set of groups* and the *managed set of locators*, respectively. The managed set of groups associated with a particular registration contains the names of the groups whose members consist of lookup services that the client wishes to be discovered through *multicast discovery*. Similarly, the managed set of locators contains instances of `LookupLocator`, each corresponding to a specific lookup service that the client wishes to be discovered through *unicast discovery*. The references to the lookup services that have been discovered will be maintained in a set referred to as the *managed set of lookup services* (or managed set of *registrars*).

Note that when the general term *managed set* is used, it should be clear from the context whether groups, locators, or registrars are being discussed. Furthermore, when the term *group discovery* or *locator discovery* is used, it should be taken to mean, respectively, the employment of either the multicast discovery protocols or the unicast discovery protocol to discover lookup services that correspond to members of the appropriate managed set.

LD.3 The Semantics

To employ the lookup discovery service to perform discovery on its behalf, a client must first register with the lookup discovery service by invoking the `register` method defined in the `LookupDiscoveryService` interface. The `register` method is the only method specified by this interface.

LD.3.1 Registration Semantics

An invocation of the `register` method produces an object—referred to as a *registration object* (or simply a *registration*)—that is mutable. That is, the registration object contains methods through which it may be changed. Because registrations are mutable, each invocation of the `register` method produces a new registration object. Thus, the `register` method is not idempotent.

The `register` method may throw a `RemoteException`. Typically, this exception occurs when there is a communication failure between the client and the lookup discovery service. When this exception does occur, the registration may or may not have been successful.

Each registration with the lookup discovery service is persistent across restarts (or crashes) of the lookup discovery service until the lease on the registration expires or is cancelled.

The `register` method takes the following as arguments:

- A `String` array, none of whose elements may be `null`, consisting of zero or more elements in which each element is the name of a group whose members are lookup services that the client requesting the registration wishes to be discovered via group discovery
- An array of `LookupLocator` objects, none of whose elements may be `null`, consisting of zero or more elements in which each element corresponds to a specific lookup service that the client requesting the registration wishes to be discovered via locator discovery

- A non-null RemoteEventListener object which specifies the entity that will receive events notifying the registration when a lookup service of interest is discovered or discarded
- Either null or an instance of MarshalledObject specifying an object that will be included in the notification event that the lookup discovery service sends to the registered listener
- A long value representing the amount of time (in milliseconds) for which the resources of the lookup discovery service are being requested

The register method returns an object that implements the LookupDiscoveryRegistration interface. It is through this returned object that the client interacts with the lookup discovery service. This interaction includes activities such as group and locator management, state retrieval, and discarding discovered but unavailable lookup services so that they are eligible for rediscovery (see Section LD.4.1, "The LookupDiscoveryRegistration Interface" for definition of the semantics of the methods of the LookupDiscoveryRegistration interface).

The groups argument takes a String array, none of whose elements may be null. Although it is acceptable to specify null (which is equivalent to DiscoveryGroupManagement.ALL_GROUPS) for the groups argument itself, if the argument contains one or more null elements, a NullPointerException is thrown. If the value is null, the lookup discovery service will attempt to discover all lookup services located within the multicast radius of the host on which the lookup discovery service is running. If an empty array (equivalent to DiscoveryGroupManagement.NO_GROUPS) is passed in, then no group discovery will be performed for the associated registration until the client, through the registration's setGroups or addGroups method, changes the contents of the managed set of groups to either a non-empty set of group names or null.

The locators argument takes an array of LookupLocator objects, none of whose elements may be null. If either the empty array or null is passed in as the locators argument, then no locator discovery will be performed for the associated registration until the client, through the registration's addLocators or setLocators method, changes the managed set of locators to a non-empty set of locators. Although it is acceptable to input null for the locators argument itself, if the argument contains one or more null elements, a NullPointerException is thrown.

If the register method is invoked with a set of group names and a set of locators in which either or both sets contain duplicate elements (where duplicate locators are determined by LookupLocator.equals), the invocation is equivalent to constructing this class with no duplicates in either set.

Upon discovery of a lookup service, through either group discovery or locator discovery, the lookup discovery service will send an event, referred to as a *discovered event*, to the listener associated with the registration produced by the call to `register`.

After initial discovery of a lookup service, the lookup discovery service will continue to monitor the group membership state reflected in the multicast announcements from that lookup service. Depending on the lookup service's current group membership, the lookup discovery service may send either a discovered event or an event referred to as a *discarded event*. The conditions under which either a discovered event or a discarded event will be sent are as follows:

- If the multicast announcements from an already discovered lookup service indicate that the lookup service is a member of a new group, a discovered event will be sent to the listener of each registration that has yet to receive a discovered event for that lookup service, but that has previously registered interest in the new group.
- If the multicast announcements from an already discovered lookup service indicate that the lookup service has changed its group membership in such a way that the lookup service is no longer of interest to one or more of the registrations that previously registered interest in the groups of that lookup service, a discarded event will be sent to the listener of each such registration. This type of discarded event is sometimes referred to as a *passive no-interest discarded event* ("passive" because the lookup discovery service, rather than the client, initiated the discard process).
- If the multicast announcements from an already discovered lookup service are no longer being received, a discarded event will be sent to the listener of each registration that previously registered interest in one or more of that lookup service's member groups. This type of discarded event is sometimes referred to as a *passive communication discarded event*.

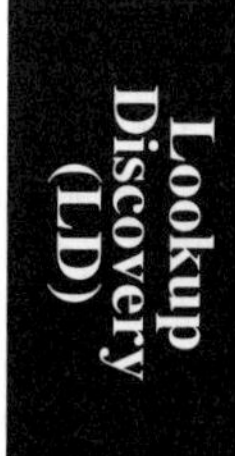

It is important to note that when the lookup discovery service (passively) discards a lookup service, due to group membership changes (lost interest) or unavailability (communication failure), the discarded event will be sent to only the listeners of those registrations that have previously requested that the affected lookup service be discovered through at least group discovery. That is, the listener of any registration that is interested in the affected lookup service through *only* locator discovery will not be sent either type of passive discarded event. This is because the semantics of the lookup discovery service assume that since the client, through the registration request, expressed no interest in discovering the lookup service through its group membership, the client must also have no interest in any group-related changes in that lookup service's state.

A more detailed discussion of the event semantics of the lookup discovery service is presented in Section LD.3.2, "Event Semantics".

A valid parameter must be passed as the `listener` argument of the `register` method. If a `null` value is input to this argument, then a `NullPointerException` will be thrown and the registration fails.

Note that if an indefinite exception occurs while attempting to send a discovered or discarded event to a registration's listener, the lookup discovery service will continue to attempt to send the event until either the event is successfully delivered or the client's lease on that registration expires. If an `UnknownEventException`, a bad object exception, or a bad invocation exception occurs while attempting to send a discovered or discarded event to a registration's listener, the lookup discovery service assumes that the client is in an unknown, possibly corrupt state, and will cancel the lease on the registration and clear the registration from its managed set.

The state information maintained by the lookup discovery service includes the set of group names, locators, and listeners submitted by each client through each invocation of the `register` method, with duplicates eliminated. This state information contains no knowledge of the clients that register with the lookup discovery service. Thus, there is no requirement that a client identify itself during the registration process.

LD.3.2 Event Semantics

For each registration created by the lookup discovery service, an event identifier will be generated that uniquely maps the registration to the listener as well as to the registration's managed set of groups and managed set of locators. This event identifier is returned as a part of the returned registration object and is unique across all other active registrations with the lookup discovery service.

Whenever the lookup discovery service finds a lookup service matching the discovery criteria of one or more of its registrations, it sends an instance of `RemoteDiscoveryEvent` (a subclass of `RemoteEvent`) to the listener corresponding to each such registration. The event sent to each listener will contain the appropriate event identifier.

Once an event signaling the discovery (by group or locator) of a desired lookup service has been sent, no other discovered events for that lookup service will be sent to a registration's listener until the lookup service is discarded (either actively, by the client through the registration, or passively by the lookup discovery service) and then rediscovered. Note that more information about what it means for a lookup service to be discarded is presented in Section LD.3.1, "Registration Semantics" and the section of this specification titled "Discarding Lookup Services".

If, between the time a lookup service is discarded and the time it is rediscovered, a new registration is requested having parameters indicating interest in that lookup service, upon rediscovery of the lookup service an event will also be sent to that new registration's listener.

The sequence numbers for a given event identifier are strictly increasing (as defined in *The Jini Technology Core Platform Specification,* "Distributed Events"), which means that when any two such successive events have sequence numbers that differ by only a value of 1, then no events have been missed. On the other hand, when the set of received events is viewed in order, if the difference between the sequence numbers of two successive events is greater than 1, then one or more events may or may not have been missed. For example, a difference greater than 1 could occur if the lookup discovery service crashes, even if no events are lost because of the crash. When two such successive events have sequence numbers whose difference is greater than 1, there is said to be a *gap* between the events.

When a gap occurs between events, the local state (on the client) related to the discovered lookup services may or may not fall out of sync with the corresponding remote state maintained by the lookup discovery service. For example, if the gap corresponds to a missed event representing the (initial) discovery of a targeted lookup service, the remote state will reflect this discovery, whereas the client's local state will not. To allow clients to identify and correct such a situation, each registration object provides a method that returns a set consisting of the proxies to the lookup services that have been discovered for that registration. With this information the client can update its local state.

When requesting a registration with the lookup discovery service, a client may also supply (as a parameter to the `register` method) a reference to an object, wrapped in a `MarshalledObject`, referred to as a *handback.* When the lookup discovery service sends an event to a registration's listener, the event will also contain a reference to this handback object. The lookup discovery service will not change the handback object. That is, the handback object contained in the event sent by the lookup discovery service will be identical to the handback object registered by the client with the event mechanism.

The semantics of the object input to the `handback` argument are left to each client to define, although `null` may be input to this argument. The role of the `handback` object in the remote event mechanism is detailed in *The Jini Technology Core Platform Specification,* "Distributed Events".

LD.3.3 Leasing Semantics

When a client registers with the lookup discovery service, it is effectively requesting a lease on the resources provided by that service. The initial duration of the lease granted to a client by the lookup discovery service will be less than or equal to the requested duration reflected in the value input to the `leaseDuration` argument. That value must be positive, `Lease.FOREVER`, or `Lease.ANY`. If any other value is input to this argument, an `IllegalArgumentException` will be thrown. The client may obtain a reference to the `Lease` object granted by the lookup discovery service through the associated registration returned by the service (see Section LD.4.1, "The `LookupDiscoveryRegistration` Interface").

LD.4 Supporting Interfaces and Classes

THE lookup discovery service depends on the LookupDiscoveryRegistration interface, as well as on the concrete classes RemoteDiscoveryEvent and LookupUnmarshalException.

LD.4.1 The LookupDiscoveryRegistration Interface

When a client requests a registration with the lookup discovery service, an object that implements the LookupDiscoveryRegistration interface is returned. It is through this interface that the client manages the state of its registration with the lookup discovery service.

```
package net.jini.discovery;

public interface LookupDiscoveryRegistration {
    public EventRegistration getEventRegistration();
    public Lease getLease();
    public ServiceRegistrar[] getRegistrars()
                             throws LookupUnmarshalException,
                                    RemoteException;
    public String[] getGroups() throws RemoteException;
    public LookupLocator[] getLocators()
                                      throws RemoteException;
    public void addGroups(String[] groups)
                                      throws RemoteException;
    public void setGroups(String[] groups)
                                      throws RemoteException;
    public void removeGroups(String[] groups)
                                      throws RemoteException;
    public void addLocators(LookupLocator[] locators)
                                      throws RemoteException;
    public void setLocators(LookupLocator[] locators)
```

```
                                            throws RemoteException;
    public void removeLocators(LookupLocator[] locators)
                                            throws RemoteException;
    public void discard(ServiceRegistrar registrar)
                                            throws RemoteException;
}
```

As with the `LookupDiscoveryService` interface, the `LookupDiscoveryRegistration` interface is not a remote interface. Each implementation of the lookup discovery service exports proxy objects that implement this interface local to the client, using an implementation-specific protocol to communicate with the actual remote server. All of the proxy methods must obey normal Java RMI remote interface semantics except where explicitly noted. Two proxy objects are equal (using the `equals` method) if they are proxies for the same registration created by the same lookup discovery service.

The discovery facility of the lookup discovery service, together with its event mechanism, make up the set of resources clients register to use. Because the resources of the lookup discovery service are leased, access is granted for only a limited period of time unless there is an active expression of continuing interest on the part of the client.

When a client uses the registration process to request that a lookup discovery service perform discovery of a set of desired lookup services, the client is also registered with the service's event mechanism. Because of this implicit registration with the event mechanism, the lookup discovery service "bundles" both resources under a single lease. When that lease expires, both discovery processing and event notifications will cease with respect to the registration that resulted from the client's request.

To facilitate lease management and event handling, the `LookupDiscoveryRegistration` interface defines methods that allow the client to retrieve its event registration information. Additional methods defined by this interface allow the client to retrieve references to the registration's currently discovered lookup services, as well as to modify the managed sets of groups and locators.

If the client's registration with the lookup discovery service has expired or been cancelled, then any invocation of a remote method defined in this interface will result in a `NoSuchObjectException`. That is, any method that communicates with the back end server of the lookup discovery service will throw a `NoSuchObjectException` if the registration on which the method is invoked no longer exists. Note that if a client receives a `NoSuchObjectException` as a result of an invocation of such a method, although the client can assume that the registration no longer exists, the client cannot assume that the lookup discovery service itself no longer exists.

Each remote method of this interface may throw a `RemoteException`. Typically, this exception occurs when there is a communication failure between the client and the lookup discovery service. Whenever this exception occurs as a result of the invocation of one of these methods, the method may or may not have completed its processing successfully.

LD.4.1.1 The Semantics

The methods defined by this interface are organized into a set of accessor methods, a set of group mutator methods, a set of locator mutator methods, and the `discard` method. Through the accessor methods, various elements of a registration's state can be retrieved. The mutator methods provide a mechanism for changing the set of groups and locators to be discovered for the registration. Through the `discard` method, a particular lookup service may be made eligible for rediscovery.

The Accessor Methods

The `getEventRegistration` method returns an `EventRegistration` object that encapsulates the information the client needs to identify a notification sent by the lookup discovery service to the registration's listener. This method is not remote and takes no arguments.

The `getLease` method returns the `Lease` object that controls a client's registration with the lookup discovery service. It is through the `Lease` object returned by this method that the client requests the renewal or cancellation of the registration with the lookup discovery service. This method is not remote and takes no arguments.

Note that the object returned by the `getEventRegistration` method also provides a `getLease` method. That method and the `getLease` method defined by the `LookupDiscoveryRegistration` interface both return the same `Lease` object. The `getLease` method defined here is provided as a convenience to avoid the indirection associated with the `getLease` method on the `EventRegistration` object, as well as to avoid the overhead of making two method calls.

The `getRegistrars` method returns a set of instances of the `ServiceRegistrar` interface. Each element in the set is a proxy to one of the lookup services that have already been discovered for the registration. Additionally, each element in the set will be unique with respect to all other elements in the set, as determined by the `equals` method provided by each element. The contents of the set make up the current remote state of the set of lookup services discovered for the registration. This method returns a new array on each invocation.

This method can be used to maintain synchronization between the set of discovered lookup services making up a registration's local state on the client and the registration's corresponding remote state maintained by the lookup discovery service. The local state can become unsynchronized with the remote state when a gap occurs in the events received by the registration's listener.

According to the event semantics of the lookup discovery service, if there is no gap between two sequence numbers, no events have been missed and the states remain synchronized with each other; if there is a gap, events may or may not have been missed. Therefore, upon finding gaps in the sequence of events, the client can invoke this method and use the returned information to synchronize the local state with the remote state.

To construct its return set, the `getRegistrars` method retrieves from the lookup discovery service the set of lookup service proxies making up the registration's current remote state. When the lookup discovery service sends the requested set of proxies, the set is sent as a set of marshalled instances of the `ServiceRegistrar` interface. The lookup discovery service individually marshals each proxy in the set that it sends because if it were not to do so, *any* deserialization failure on the set would result in an `IOException`, and failure would be declared for the whole deserialization process, not just an individual element. This would mean that all elements of the set sent by the lookup discovery service—even those that were successfully deserialized—would be unavailable to the client. Individually marshalling each element in the set minimizes the "all or nothing" aspect of the deserialization process, allowing the client to recover those proxies that can be successfully unmarshalled and to proceed with processing that might not be possible otherwise.

When constructing the return set, this method attempts to unmarshal each element of the set of marshalled proxy objects sent by the lookup discovery service. When failure occurs while attempting to unmarshal any of those elements, this method throws an exception of type `LookupUnmarshalException` (described later). It is through the contents of that exception that the client can recover any available proxies and perform error handling related to the unavailable proxies. The contents of the `LookupUnmarshalException` provide the client with the following useful information:

- The knowledge that a problem has occurred while unmarshalling at least one of the elements making up the remote state of the registration's discovered lookup services

- The set of proxy objects that were successfully unmarshalled by the `getRegistrars` method
- The set of marshalled proxy objects that could not be unmarshalled by the `getRegistrars` method
- The set of exceptions corresponding to each failed attempt at unmarshalling

The type of exception that occurs when attempting to unmarshal an element of the set sent by the lookup discovery service is typically an `IOException` or a `ClassNotFoundException` (usually the more common of the two). A `ClassNotFoundException` occurs whenever a remote object on which the marshalled proxy depends cannot be retrieved and loaded, usually because the codebase of one of the object's classes or interfaces is currently "down." To address this situation, the client may wish to proceed with its processing using the successfully unmarshalled proxies, and attempt to unmarshal the unavailable proxies (or re-invoke this method) at some later time.

If the `getRegistrars` method returns successfully without throwing a `LookupUnmarshalException`, the client is guaranteed that all marshalled proxies belonging to the set sent by the lookup discovery service have each been successfully unmarshalled; the client then has a snapshot—relative to the point in time when this method is invoked—of the remote state of the lookup services discovered for the associated registration.

The `getGroups` method returns an array consisting of the group names from the registration's managed set; that is, the names of the groups the lookup discovery service is currently configured to discover for the associated registration. If the managed set of groups is empty, this method returns the empty array. If there is no managed set of groups associated with the registration (that is, the lookup discovery service is configured to discover `DiscoveryGroupManagement.ALL_GROUPS` for the registration), then `null` is returned.

The `getLocators` method returns an array consisting of the `LookupLocator` objects from the registration's managed set; that is, the locators of the specific lookup services the lookup discovery service is currently configured to discover for the associated registration. If the managed set of locators is empty, this method returns the empty array.

The Group Mutator Methods

With respect to a particular registration, the groups to be discovered may be modified using the methods described in this section. In each case, a set of groups is represented as a `String` array, none of whose elements may be `null`. If any set of groups input to one of these methods contains one or more `null` elements, a

NullPointerException is thrown. The empty set is denoted by the empty array (DiscoveryGroupManagement.NO_GROUPS), and "no set" is indicated by null (DiscoveryGroupManagement.ALL_GROUPS). No set indicates that all lookup services within the multicast radius should be discovered, regardless of group membership. Invoking any of these methods with an input set of groups that contains duplicate names is equivalent to performing the invocation with the duplicate group names removed from the input set.

The addGroups method adds a set of group names to the registration's managed set. This method takes one argument: a String array consisting of the set of group names with which to augment the registration's managed set.

If the registration has no current managed set of groups to augment, this method throws an UnsupportedOperationException. If the parameter value is null, this method throws a NullPointerException. If the parameter value is the empty array, then the registration's managed set of groups will not change.

The setGroups method replaces all of the group names in the registration's managed set with names from a new set. This method takes one argument: a String array consisting of the set of group names with which to replace the current names in the registration's managed set.

If null is passed to setGroups, the lookup discovery service will attempt to discover any undiscovered lookup services located within range of the lookup discovery service, regardless of group membership.

If the empty set is passed to setGroups, then group discovery will be halted until the registration's managed set of groups is changed—through a subsequent call to this method or to addGroups—to a set that is either a non-empty set of group names or null.

The removeGroups method deletes a set of group names from the registration's managed set. This method takes one argument: a String array containing the set of group names to remove from the registration's managed set.

If the registration has no current managed set of groups from which to remove elements, this method throws an UnsupportedOperationException. If null is input, this method throws a NullPointerException. If the registration does have a managed set of groups from which to remove elements, but either the input set is empty or none of the elements in the input set match any element in the managed set, then the registration's managed set of groups will not change.

Once a new group name has been placed in the registration's managed set as a result of an invocation of either addGroups or setGroups, if there are lookup services belonging to that group that have already been discovered for that registration, no event will be sent to the registration's listener for those particular lookup services. However, attempts to discover any undiscovered lookup services belonging to that group will continue to be made on behalf of the registration.

Any already discovered lookup service that is a member of one or more of the groups removed from the registration's managed set as a result of an invocation of either setGroups or removeGroups will be discarded and will no longer be eligible for discovery (for that registration), but only if that lookup service satisfies both of the following conditions:

- The lookup service is not a member of any group in the registration's new managed set resulting from the invocation of setGroups or removeGroups
- With respect to the registration, the lookup service is not currently eligible for discovery through locator discovery; that is, the lookup service does not correspond to any element in the registration's managed set of locators.

The Locator Mutator Methods

With respect to a particular registration, the set of locators to discover may be modified using the methods described in this section. In each case, a set of locators is represented as an array of LookupLocator objects, none of whose elements may be null. If any set of locators input to one of these methods contains one of more null elements, a NullPointerException is thrown. Invoking any of these methods with a set of locators that contains duplicate locators (as determined by LookupLocator.equals) is equivalent to performing the invocation with the duplicates removed from the input set.

The addLocators method adds a set of LookupLocator objects to the registration's managed set. This method takes one argument: an array consisting of the set of locators with which to augment the registration's managed set.

If null is passed to addLocators, a NullPointerException will be thrown. If the parameter value is the empty array, the registration's managed set of locators will not change.

The setLocators method replaces all of the locators in the registration's managed set with LookupLocator objects from a new set. This method takes one argument: an array consisting of the set of locators with which to replace the current locators in the registration's managed set.

If null is passed to setLocators, a NullPointerException will be thrown.

If the empty set is passed to setLocators, then locator discovery will be halted until the registration's managed set of locators is changed—through a subsequent call to this method or to addLocators—to a set that is non-null and non-empty.

The removeLocators method deletes a set of LookupLocator objects from the registration's managed set. This method takes one argument: an array containing the set of `LookupLocator` objects to remove from the registration's managed set.

If `null` is passed to `removeLocators`, a `NullPointerException` will be thrown. If any element of the set of locators to remove is not contained in the registration's managed set, `removeLocators` takes no action with respect to that element. If the parameter value is the empty array, the managed set of locators will not change.

Whenever a new locator is placed in the managed set as a result of an invocation of one of the locator mutator methods and that new locator equals none of the previously discovered locators (across all registrations), the lookup discovery service will attempt unicast discovery of the lookup service associated with the new locator.

If locator discovery is attempted for a registration, such discovery attempts will be repeated until one of the following events occurs:

- The lookup service is discovered
- The client's lease on the registration expires
- The client explicitly removes the locator from the registration's managed set

Upon discovery of the lookup service corresponding to the new locator, or upon finding a match between the new locator and a previously discovered lookup service, a discovered event will be sent to the registration's listener, unless that lookup service was previously discovered for that registration through group discovery.

Any already discovered lookup service corresponding to a locator that is removed from the registration's managed set as a result of an invocation of either `setLocators` or `removeLocators` will be discarded and will no longer be eligible for discovery, but only if it is not currently eligible for discovery through group discovery—that is, only if the lookup service is not also a member of one or more of the groups in the registration's managed set of groups.

Discarding Lookup Services

When the lookup discovery service removes an already discovered lookup service from a registration's managed set of lookup services, the lookup service is said to be *discarded*.

There are a number of situations in which the lookup discovery service will discard a lookup service:

- In response to a discard request resulting from an invocation of a registration's `discard` method
- In response to a declaration—via an invocation of one of the mutator methods on a registration—that there is no longer any interest in one or more of the registration's already discovered lookup services
- In response to the determination that the multicast announcements from an already discovered lookup service indicate that the lookup service has changed its group membership in such a way that the lookup service is no longer of interest to one or more of the registrations that previously registered interest in the groups of that lookup service
- In response to the determination that the multicast announcements from an already discovered lookup service are no longer being received

For each of these cases, whenever the lookup discovery service discards a lookup service, it will send an event to the registration's listener to notify it that the lookup service has been discarded.

The `discard` method provides a mechanism for registered clients to inform the lookup discovery service of the existence of an unavailable—or *unreachable*—lookup service, and to request that the lookup discovery service discard that lookup service and make it eligible for rediscovery.

The `discard` method takes a single argument: the proxy to the lookup service to discard. This method takes no action if the parameter to this method equals none of the proxies reflected in the managed set (using proxy equality as defined in *The Jini Technology Core Platform Specification,* "Lookup Service". If `null` is passed to `discard`, a `NullPointerException` is thrown.

Although the lookup discovery service monitors the multicast announcements from all discovered lookup services for indications of unavailability, it should be noted that there are conditions under which the lookup discovery service will not discard such a lookup service, even when the lookup service is found to be unreachable. Whether or not the lookup discovery service discards such an unreachable lookup service is dependent on how each registration is configured for discovery with respect to that lookup service. If every registration that is configured to discover the unreachable lookup service is configured to discover it through locator discovery only, the lookup discovery service will not discard the lookup service. In other words, in order for the lookup discovery service to discard a lookup service it has determined is unreachable, at least one registration must be configured for discovery of at least one group in which that lookup service is a member.

Thus, whenever a client determines that a previously discovered lookup service has become unreachable, it should not rely on the lookup discovery service to discard the lookup service. Instead, the client should inform the lookup discovery service—through the invocation of the registration's `discard` method—that the previously discovered lookup service is no longer available and that attempts should be made to rediscover that lookup service for the registration. Typically, a client determines that a lookup service is unavailable when the client attempts to use the lookup service but receives an indefinite exception, a bad object exception, or a bad invocation exception as a result of the attempt.

Note that the lookup discovery service may be acting on behalf of numerous clients that have access to the same lookup service. If that lookup service becomes unavailable, many of those clients may invoke `discard` between the time the lookup service becomes unavailable and the time it is rediscovered. Upon the first invocation of `discard`, the lookup discovery service will re-initiate discovery of the relevant lookup service for the registration of the client that made the invocation. For all other invocations made prior to rediscovery, the registrations through which the invocation is made are sent a discarded event, and added to the list of registrations that will be notified when rediscovery of the lookup service does occur. That is, upon rediscovery of the lookup service, only those registrations through which the `discard` method was invoked will be notified.

Upon successful completion of the `discard` method, the proxy requested to be discarded is guaranteed to have been removed from the managed set of the registration through which the invocation was made. No such guarantee is made with respect to when the discarded event is sent to each such registration's listener. That is, the event notifying the listeners that the lookup service has been discarded may or may not be sent asynchronously.

LD.4.2 The `RemoteDiscoveryEvent` Class

When the lookup discovery service discovers or discards a lookup service matching the criteria established through one of its registrations, the lookup discovery service sends an instance of the `RemoteDiscoveryEvent` class to the `RemoteEventListener` implemented by the client and registered with the lookup discovery service.

```
package net.jini.discovery;

public class RemoteDiscoveryEvent extends RemoteEvent {
    public RemoteDiscoveryEvent(Object source,
                                long eventID,
                                long seqNum,
                                MarshalledObject handback,
                                boolean discarded,
```

```
                                          Map groups)
                                                 throws IOException {…}

    public boolean isDiscarded() {…}
    public ServiceRegistrar[] getRegistrars()
                              throws LookupUnmarshalException {…}
    public Map getGroups() {…}
}
```

The `RemoteDiscoveryEvent` class provides an encapsulation of event information that the lookup discovery service uses to notify a registration of the occurrence of an event involving one or more `ServiceRegistrar` objects (lookup services) in which the registration has registered interest. The lookup discovery service passes an instance of this class to the registration's discovery listener when one of the following events occurs:

- Each lookup service referenced in the event has been discovered for the first time or rediscovered after having been discarded.
- Each lookup service referenced in the event has been either actively or passively discarded.

`RemoteDiscoveryEvent` is a subclass of `RemoteEvent`, adding the following additional items of abstract state:

- A `boolean` indicating whether the lookup services referenced by the event have been discovered or discarded
- A set of marshalled instances of the `ServiceRegistrar` interface having the characteristic that when each element is unmarshalled, the result is a proxy to one of the discovered or discarded lookup services referenced by the event
- A `Map` instance in which the elements of the map's key set are the instances of `ServiceID` that correspond to each lookup service reference returned in the event, and the map's value set contains the corresponding member groups of each lookup service reference

Methods are defined through which this additional state may be retrieved upon receipt of an instance of this class.

Clients need to know not only when a targeted lookup service has been discovered, but also when it has been discarded. The lookup discovery service uses an instance of `RemoteDiscoveryEvent` to notify a registration when either of these events occurs, as indicated by the value of the `boolean` state variable. When the value of that variable is true, the event is referred to as a *discarded event*; when false, it is referred to as a *discovered event*.

LD.4.2.1 The Semantics

The constructor of the RemoteDiscoveryEvent class takes the following parameters as input:

- A reference to the lookup discovery service that generated the event
- The event identifier that maps a particular registration to both its listener and its targeted groups and locators
- The sequence number of the event being constructed
- The client-defined handback (which may be null)
- A flag indicating whether the event being constructed is a discovered event or a discarded event
- A Map whose key set contains the proxies to newly discovered or discarded lookup service(s) the event is to reference, and whose value set contains the corresponding member groups of each lookup service

If the groups parameter is empty, the constructor will throw an IllegalArgumentException. If null is input to the groups parameter, the constructor will throw a NullPointerException. If none of the proxies referenced in the groups parameter can be successfully serialized, the constructor will throw an IOException.

The isDiscarded method returns a boolean that indicates whether the event is a discovered event or a discarded event. If the event is a discovered event, then this method returns false. If the event is a discarded event, true is retuned.

The getRegistrars method returns an array consisting of instances of the ServiceRegistrar interface. Each element in the returned set is a proxy to one of the newly discovered or discarded lookup services that caused a RemoteDiscoveryEvent to be sent. Additionally, each element in the returned set will be unique with respect to all other elements in the set, as determined by the equals method provided by each element. This method does not make a remote call. With respect to multiple invocations of this method, each invocation will return a new array.

When the lookup discovery service sends an instance of RemoteDiscoveryEvent to the listener of a client's registration, the set of lookup service proxies contained in the event consists of marshalled instances of the ServiceRegistrar interface. The lookup discovery service individually marshals each proxy associated with the event because if it were not to do so, *any* deserialization failure on the set would result in an IOException, and failure would be declared for the whole deserialization process, not just an individual element. This would mean that all elements of the set sent in the event—even those that can be successfully deserialized—would be unavailable to the client through this method. Just as with the getRegistrars method defined by the LookupDiscoveryRegistration interface, individually marshalling each element in the set minimizes the "all or nothing" aspect of the deserialization process, allowing the client to recover those proxies that can be successfully unmarshalled and to proceed with processing that might not be possible otherwise.

When constructing the return set, this method attempts to unmarshal each element of the set of marshalled proxy objects contained in the event. When failure occurs while attempting to unmarshal any of the elements of that set, this method throws an exception of type LookupUnmarshalException. It is through the contents of this exception that the client can recover any available proxies and perform error handling with respect to the unavailable proxies.

If the getRegistrars method returns successfully without throwing a LookupUnmarshalException, the client is guaranteed that all marshalled proxies sent in the event have each been successfully unmarshalled during that particular invocation. Furthermore, after the first such successful invocation, no more unmarshalling attempts will be made (because such attempts are no longer necessary), and all future invocations of this method are guaranteed to return an array with contents identical to the contents of the array returned by the first successful invocation.

Note that an array, rather than a single proxy, is returned by the getRegistrars method so that implementations of the lookup discovery service can choose to "batch" the information sent to a registration. With respect to discoveries, batching the information may be particularly useful when a client first registers with the lookup discovery service.

Upon initial registration, multiple lookup services are typically found over a short period of time, providing the lookup discovery service with the opportunity to send all of the initially discovered lookup services in only one event. Afterward, as so-called "late joiner" lookup services are found sporadically, the lookup discovery service may send events referencing only one lookup service.

Note that the event sequence numbers, as defined earlier in Section LD.3.2, "Event Semantics", are strictly increasing, even when the information is batched.

The getGroups method returns a Map in which the elements of the map's key set are the instances of ServiceID that correspond to each lookup service for which the event was constructed and sent. Each element of the returned map's value set is a String array containing the names of the member groups of the associated lookup service whose `ServiceID` equals to the corresponding key. This method does not make a remote call. On each invocation of this method, the same `Map` object is returned; that is, a copy is not made.

The `Map` returned by the `getGroups` method is keyed by the `ServiceID` of each lookup service in the event, rather than by the proxy of each lookup service to avoid the deserialization issues addressed by the `getRegistrars` method. Thus, client's wishing to retrieve the set of member groups corresponding to any element of the array returned by the `getRegistrars` method, must use the `ServiceID` of the desired element from that array as the key to the `get` method of the `Map` returned by this method and then cast to `String[]`.

LD.4.2.2 Serialized Forms

Class	serialVersionUID	Serialized Fields

`RemoteDiscoveryEvent`	-9171289945014585248L	`boolean discarded`
		`ArrayList marshalledRegs`
		`ServiceRegistrar[] regs`
		`Map groups`

LD.4.3 The `LookupUnmarshalException` Class

Recall that when unmarshalling an instance of `MarshalledObject`, one of the following checked exceptions is possible:

- An `IOException`, which can occur while deserializing the object from its internal representation
- A `ClassNotFoundException`, which can occur if, while deserializing the object from its internal representation, either the class file of the object cannot be found, or the class file of an interface or class referenced by the object being deserialized cannot be found. Typically, a `ClassNotFoundException` occurs when the codebase from which to retrieve the needed class file is not currently available

The `LookupUnmarshalException` class provides a mechanism that clients of the lookup discovery service may use for efficient handling of the exceptions that may occur when unmarshalling elements of a set of marshalled instances of the `ServiceRegistrar` interface. When elements in such a set are unmarshalled, the

LookupUnmarshalException class may be used to collect and report pertinent information generated when failure occurs during the unmarshalling process.

```
package net.jini.discovery;

public class LookupUnmarshalException extends Exception {
    public LookupUnmarshalException
                    (ServiceRegistrar[] registrars,
                     MarshalledObject[] marshalledRegistrars,
                     Throwable[] exceptions) {…}
    public LookupUnmarshalException
                    (ServiceRegistrar[] registrars,
                     MarshalledObject[] marshalledRegistrars,
                     Throwable[] exceptions,
                     String message) {…}
    public ServiceRegistrar[] getRegistrars() {…}
    public MarshalledObject[] getMarshalledRegistrars() {…}
    public Throwable[] getExceptions() {…}
}
```


The LookupUnmarshalException class is a subclass of Exception, adding the following additional items of abstract state:

- A set of ServiceRegistrar instances in which each element is the result of a successful unmarshalling attempt
- A set of marshalled instances of ServiceRegistrar in which each element is the result of an unsuccessful unmarshalling attempt
- A set of exceptions (IOException, ClassNotFoundException, or some unchecked exception) in which each element corresponds to one of the unsuccessful unmarshalling attempts

When exceptional conditions occur while unmarshalling a set of marshalled instances of ServiceRegistrar, the LookupUnmarshalException class can be used not only to indicate that an exceptional condition has occurred, but also to provide information that can be used to perform error handling activities such as:

- Determining if it is feasible to continue with processing
- Reporting errors
- Attempting recovery
- Performing debug activities

LD.4.3.1 The Semantics

The constructor of the `LookupUnmarshalException` class has two forms. The first form of the constructor takes the following parameters as input:

- An array containing the set of instances of `ServiceRegistrar` that were successfully unmarshalled
- An array containing the set of marshalled `ServiceRegistrar` instances that could not be unmarshalled
- An array containing the set of exceptions that occurred during the unmarshalling process

The second form of the constructor takes the same arguments as the first and one additional argument: a `String` describing the nature of the exception.

Each element in the `exceptions` parameter should be an instance of `IOException`, `ClassNotFoundException`, or some unchecked exception. Furthermore, there is a one-to-one correspondence between each element in the `exceptions` parameter and each element in the `marshalledRegistrars` parameter. That is, the element of the `exceptions` parameter corresponding to index *i* should be an instance of the exception that occurred while attempting to unmarshal the element at index *i* of the `marshalledRegistrars` parameter.

If the number of elements in the `exceptions` parameter does not equal the number of elements in the `marshalledRegistrars` parameter, the constructor will throw an `IllegalArgumentException`.

The `getRegistrars` method is an accessor method that returns an array consisting of instances of `ServiceRegistrar`, where each element of the array corresponds to a successfully unmarshalled object. Note that the same array is returned on each invocation of this method; that is, a copy is not made.

The `getMarshalledRegistrars` method is an accessor method that returns an array consisting of instances of `MarshalledObject`, where each element of the array is a marshalled instance of the `ServiceRegistrar` interface and corresponds to an object that could not be successfully unmarshalled. Note that the same array is returned on each invocation of this method; that is, a copy is not made.

The `getExceptions` method is an accessor method that returns an array consisting of instances of `Throwable`, where each element of the array corresponds to one of the exceptions that occurred during the unmarshalling process. Each element in the return set is an instance of `IOException`, `ClassNotFoundException`, or some unchecked exception. Additionally, there should be a one-to-one correspondence between each element in the array returned by this method and the array returned by the `getMarshalledRegistrars` method. Note that the same array is returned on each invocation of this method; that is, a copy is not made.

LD.4.3.2 Serialized Forms

Class	`serialVersionUID`	Serialized Fields

`LookupUnmarshalException`	2956893184719950537L	`ServiceRegistrar[] registars`
		`MarshalledObject[] marshalledRegistrars`
		`Throwable[] exceptions`

THE JINI LOOKUP ATTRIBUTE SCHEMA SPECIFICATION defines a set of attributes that a local administrator might choose to place on a service. These are "serving suggestions"—nobody is required to use these attribute definitions, but they give a starting point for people who need such attributes to either use directly or use for inspiration. This also describes the common style for entry design, including the canonical way to present your entry as a JavaBean object.

LS

Jini Lookup Attribute Schema Specification

LS.1 Introduction

THE Jini lookup service provides facilities for services to advertise their availability and for would-be clients to obtain references to those services based on the attributes they provide. The mechanism that it provides for registering and querying based on attributes is centered on the Java platform type system, and is based on the notion of an *entry*.

An entry is a class that contains a number of public fields of object type. Services provide concrete values for each of these fields; each value acts as an attribute. Entries thus provide aggregation of attributes into sets; a service may provide several entries when registering itself in the lookup service, which means that attributes on each service are provided in a set of sets.

The purpose of this document is to provide a framework in which services and their would-be clients can interoperate. This framework takes two parts:

- We describe a set of common predefined entries that span much of the basic functionality that is needed both by services registering themselves and by entities that are searching for services.
- Since we cannot anticipate all of the future needs of clients of the lookup service, we provide a set of guidelines and design patterns for extending, using, and imitating this set in ways that are consistent and predictable. We also construct some examples that illustrate the use of these patterns.

LS.1.1 Terminology

Throughout this document, we will use the following terms in consistent ways:

- *Service*—a service that has registered, or will register, itself with the lookup service
- *Client*—an entity that performs queries on the lookup service, in order to find particular services

LS.1.2 Design Issues

Several factors influence and constrain the design of the lookup service schema.

Matching Cannot Always Be Automated

No matter how much information it has at its disposal, a client of the lookup service will not always be able to find a single unique match without assistance when it performs a lookup. In many instances we expect that more than one service will match a particular query. Accordingly, both the lookup service and the attribute schema are geared toward reducing the number of matches that are returned on a given lookup to a minimum, and not necessarily to just one.

Attributes Are Mostly Static

We have designed the schema for the lookup service with the assumption that most attributes will not need to be changed frequently. For example, we do not expect attributes to change more often than once every minute or so. This decision is based on our expectation that clients that need to make a choice of service based on more frequently updated attributes will be able to talk to whatever small set of services the lookup service returns for a query, and on our belief that the benefit of updating attributes frequently at the lookup service is outweighed by the cost in network traffic and processing.

Humans Need to Understand Most Attributes

A corollary of the idea that matching cannot always be automated is that humans—whether they be users or administrators of services—must be able to understand and interpret attributes. This has several implications:

- We must provide a mechanism to deal with localization of attributes
- Multiple-valued attributes must provide a way for humans to see only one value (see Section LS.2, "Human Access to Attributes")

We will cover human accessibility of attributes soon.

Attributes Can Be Changed by Services or Humans, But Not Both

For any given attribute class we expect that attributes within that class will all be set or modified either by the service, or via human intervention, but not both. What do we mean by this? A service is unlikely to be able to determine that it has been moved from one room to another, for example, so we would not expect the fields of a "location" attribute class to be changed by the service itself. Similarly, we do not expect that a human operator will need to change the name of the vendor of a particular service. This idea has implications for our approach to ensuring that the values of attributes are valid.

Attributes Must Interoperate with JavaBeans Components

The JavaBeans specification provides a number of facilities relating to the localized display and modification of properties, and has been widely adopted. It is to our advantage to provide a familiar set of mechanisms for manipulating attributes in these ways.

LS.1.3 Dependencies

This document relies on the following other specifications:

- *The Jini Technology Core Platform Specification,* "Entry"
- *Jini Entry Utilities Specification*
- *JavaBeans Specification*

LS.2 Human Access to Attributes

LS.2.1 Providing a Single View of an Attribute's Value

CONSIDER the following entry class:

```
public class Foo implements net.jini.core.entry.Entry {
    public Bar baz;
}

public class Bar {
    int quux;
    boolean zot;
}
```

A visual search tool is going to have a difficult time rendering the value of an instance of class Bar in a manner that is comprehensible to humans. Accordingly, to avoid such situations, entry class implementors should use the following guidelines when designing a class that is to act as a value for an attribute:

- Provide a property editor class of the appropriate type, as described in Section 9.2 of the *JavaBeans Specification*.
- Extend the `java.awt.Component` class; this allows a value to be represented by a JavaBeans component or some other "active" object.
- Provide either a non-default implementation of the `Object.toString` method or inherit directly or indirectly from a class that does so (since the default implementation of `Object.toString` is not useful).

One of the above guidelines should be followed for all attribute value classes. Authors of entry classes should assume that any attribute value that does not satisfy one of these guidelines will be ignored by some or all user interfaces.

LS.3 JavaBeans Components and Design Patterns

LS.3.1 Allowing Display and Modification of Attributes

WE use JavaBeans components to provide a layer of abstraction on top of the individual classes that implement the `net.jini.core.entry.Entry` interface. This provides us with several benefits:

- This approach uses an existing standard and thus reduces the amount of unfamiliar material for programmers.
- JavaBeans components provide mechanisms for localized display of attribute values and descriptions.
- Modification of attributes is also handled, via property editors.

LS.3.1.1 Using JavaBeans Components with Entry Classes

Many, if not most, entry classes should have a bean class associated with them. Our use of JavaBeans components provides a familiar mechanism for authors of browse/search tools to represent information about a service's attributes, such as its icons and appropriately localized descriptions of the meanings and values of its attributes. JavaBeans components also play a role in permitting administrators of a service to modify some of its attributes, as they can manipulate the values of its attributes using standard JavaBeans component mechanisms.

For example, obtaining a `java.beans.BeanDescriptor` for a JavaBeans component that is linked to a "location" entry object for a particular service allows a programmer to obtain an icon that gives a visual indication of what that entry class is for, along with a short textual description of the class and the values of the individual attributes in the location object. It also permits an administrative tool to view and change certain fields in the location, such as the floor number.

LS.3.2 Associating JavaBeans Components with Entry Classes

The pattern for establishing a link between an entry object and an instance of its JavaBeans component is simple enough, as this example illustrates:

```
package org.example.foo;

import java.io.Serializable;
import net.jini.lookup.entry.EntryBean;
import net.jini.entry.AbstractEntry;

public class Size {
    public int value;
}

public class Cavenewt extends AbstractEntry {
    public Cavenewt() {
    }
    public Cavenewt(Size anvilSize) {
        this.anvilSize = anvilSize;
    }
    public Size anvilSize;
}

public class CavenewtBean implements EntryBean, Serializable {
    protected Cavenewt assoc;
    public CavenewtBean() {
        super();
        assoc = new Cavenewt();
    }
    public void setAnvilSize(Size x) {
        assoc.anvilSize = x;
    }
    public Size getAnvilSize() {
        return assoc.anvilSize;
    }
    public void makeLink(Entry obj) {
         assoc = (Cavenewt) obj;
    }
    public Entry followLink() {
```

```
        return assoc;
    }
}
```

From the above, the pattern should be relatively clear:

- The name of a JavaBeans component is derived by taking the fully qualified entry class name and appending the string `Bean`; for example, the name of the JavaBeans component associated with the entry class `foo.bar.Baz` is `foo.bar.BazBean`. This implies that an entry class and its associated JavaBeans component must reside in the same package.
- The class has both a public no-arg constructor and a public constructor that takes each public object field of the class and its superclasses as parameter. The former constructs an empty instance of the class, and the latter initializes each field of the new instance to the given parameter.
- The class implements the `net.jini.core.entry.Entry` interface, preferably by extending the `net.jini.entry.AbstractEntry` class, and the JavaBeans component implements the `net.jini.lookup.entry.EntryBean` interface.
- There is a one-to-one link between a JavaBeans component and a particular entry object. The `makeLink` method establishes this link and will throw an exception if the association is with an entry class of the wrong type. The `followLink` method returns the entry object associated with a particular JavaBeans component.
- The no-arg public constructor for a JavaBeans component creates and makes a link to an empty entry object.
- For each public object field *foo* in an entry class, there exist both a `set`*`Foo`* and a `get`*`Foo`* method in the associated JavaBeans component. The `set`*`Foo`* method takes a single argument of the same type as the *foo* field in the associated entry and sets the value of that field to its argument. The `get`*`Foo`* method returns the value of that field.

LS.3.3 Supporting Interfaces and Classes

The following classes and interfaces provide facilities for handling entry classes and their associated JavaBeans components.

```
package net.jini.lookup.entry;

public class EntryBeans {
    public static EntryBean createBean(Entry e)
        throws ClassNotFoundException, java.io.IOException {...}

    public static Class getBeanClass(Class c)
        throws ClassNotFoundException {...}
}

public interface EntryBean {
    void makeLink(Entry e);
    Entry followLink();
}
```

The `EntryBeans` class cannot be instantiated. Its sole method, `createBean`, creates and initializes a new JavaBeans component and links it to the entry object it is passed. If a problem occurs creating the JavaBeans component, the method throws either `java.io.IOException` or `ClassNotFoundException`.

The `createBean` method uses the same mechanism for instantiating a JavaBeans component as the `java.beans.Beans.instantiate` method. It will initially try to instantiate the JavaBeans component using the same class loader as the entry it is passed. If that fails, it will fall back to using the default class loader.

The `getBeanClass` method returns the class of the JavaBeans component associated with the given attribute class. If the class passed in does not implement the `net.jini.core.entry.Entry` interface, an `IllegalArgumentException` is thrown. If the given attribute class cannot be found, a `ClassNotFoundException` is thrown.

The `EntryBean` interface must be implemented by all JavaBeans components that are intended to be linked to entry objects. The `makeLink` method establishes a link between a JavaBeans component object and an entry object, and the `followLink` method returns the entry object linked to by a particular JavaBeans component. Note that objects that implement the `EntryBean` interface should not be assumed to perform any internal synchronization in their implementations of the `makeLink` or `followLink` methods, or in the `setFoo` or `getFoo` patterns.

LS.4 Generic Attribute Classes

WE will now describe some attribute classes that are generic to many or all services and the JavaBeans components that are associated with each. Unless otherwise stated, all classes defined here live in the `net.jini.lookup.entry` package. The definitions assume the following classes to have been imported:

```
java.io.Serializable
net.jini.entry.AbstractEntry
```

LS.4.1 Indicating User Modifiability

To indicate that certain entry classes should only be modified by the service that registered itself with instances of these entry classes, we annotate them with the `ServiceControlled` interface.

```
public interface ServiceControlled {
}
```

Authors of administrative tools that modify fields of attribute objects at the lookup service should not permit users to either modify any fields or add any new instances of objects that implement this interface.

LS.4.2 Basic Service Information

The `ServiceInfo` attribute class provides some basic information about a service.

```
public class ServiceInfo extends AbstractEntry
    implements ServiceControlled
{
    public ServiceInfo() {…}
    public ServiceInfo(String name, String manufacturer,
                       String vendor, String version,
                       String model, String serialNumber) {…}
```

```
    public String name;
    public String manufacturer;
    public String vendor;
    public String version;
    public String model;
    public String serialNumber;
}

public class ServiceInfoBean
    implements EntryBean, Serializable
{
    public String getName() {...}
    public void setName(String s) {...}
    public String getManufacturer() {...}
    public void setManufacturer(String s) {...}
    public String getVendor() {...}
    public void setVendor(String s) {...}
    public String getVersion() {...}
    public void setVersion(String s) {...}
    public String getModel() {...}
    public void setModel(String s) {...}
    public String getSerialNumber() {...}
    public void setSerialNumber(String s) {...}
}
```

Each service should register itself with only one instance of this class. The fields of the `ServiceInfo` class have the following meanings:

- The `name` field contains a specific product name, such as `"Ultra 30"` (for a particular workstation) or `"JavaSafe"` (for a specific configuration management service). This string should not include the name of the manufacturer or vendor.
- The `manufacturer` field provides the name of the company that "built" this service. This might be a hardware manufacturer or a software authoring company.
- The `vendor` field contains the name of the company that sells the software or hardware that provides this service. This may be the same name as is in the `manufacturer` field, or it could be the name of a reseller. This field exists so that in cases in which resellers relabel products built by other companies, users will be able to search based on either name.

- The `version` field provides information about the version of this service. It is a free-form field, though we expect that service implementors will follow normal version-naming conventions in using it.
- The `model` field contains the specific model name or number of the product, if any.
- The `serialNumber` field provides the serial number of this instance of the service, if any.

LS.4.3 More Specific Information

The `ServiceType` class allows an author of a service to deliver information that is specific to a particular instance of a service, rather than to services in general.

```
public class ServiceType extends AbstractEntry
        implements ServiceControlled
{
    public ServiceType() {...}
    public java.awt.Image getIcon(int iconKind) {...}
    public String getDisplayName() {...}
    public String getShortDescription() {...}
}
```

Each service may register itself with multiple instances of this class, usually with one instance for each type of service interface it implements.

This class has no public fields and, as a result, has no associated JavaBeans component.

The `getIcon` method returns an icon of the appropriate kind for the service; it works in the same way as the `getIcon` method in the `java.beans.BeanInfo` interface, with the value of `iconKind` being taken from the possibilities defined in that interface. The `getDisplayName` and `getShortDescription` methods return a localized human-readable name and description for the service, in the same manner as their counterparts in the `java.beans.FeatureDescriptor` class. Each of these methods returns `null` if no information of the appropriate kind is defined.

In case the distinction between the information this class provides and that provided by a JavaBeans component's meta-information is unclear, the class `ServiceType` is meant to be used in the lookup service as one of the entry classes with which a service registers itself, and so it can be customized on a per-service basis. By contrast, the `FeatureDescriptor` and `BeanInfo` objects for all `EntryBean` classes provide only generic information about those classes and none about specific instances of those classes.

LS.4.4 Naming a Service

People like to associate names with particular services and may do so using the Name class.

```
public class Name extends AbstractEntry {
    public Name() {...}
    public Name(String name) {...}

    public String name;
}

public class NameBean implements EntryBean, Serializable {
    public String getName() {...}
    public void setName(String s) {...}
}
```

Services may register themselves with multiple instances of this class, and either services or administrators may add, modify, or remove instances of this class from the attribute set under which a service is registered.

The name field provides a short name for a particular instance of a service (for example, "Bob's toaster").

LS.4.5 Adding a Comment to a Service

In cases in which some kind of comment is appropriate for a service (for example, "this toaster tends to burn bagels"), the Comment class provides an appropriate facility.

```
public class Comment extends AbstractEntry {
    public Comment() {...}
    public Comment(String comment) {...}

    public String comment;
}

public class CommentBean implements EntryBean, Serializable {
    public String getComment() {...}
    public void setComment(String s) {...}
}
```

A service may have more than one comment associated with it, and comments may be added, removed, or edited by either a service itself, administrators, or users.

LS.4.6 Physical Location

The `Location` and `Address` classes provide information about the physical location of a particular service.

Since many services have no physical location, some have one, and a few may have more than one, it might make sense for a service to register itself with zero or more instances of either of these classes, depending on its nature.

The `Location` class is intended to provide information about the physical location of a service in a single building or on a small, unified campus. The `Address` class provides more information and may be appropriate for use with the `Location` class in a larger, more geographically distributed organization.

```
public class Location extends AbstractEntry {
    public Location() {...}
    public Location(String floor, String room,
                    String building) {...}

    public String floor;
    public String room;
    public String building;
}

public class LocationBean implements EntryBean, Serializable {
    public String getFloor() {...}
    public void setFloor(String s) {...}
    public String getRoom() {...}
    public void setRoom(String s) {...}
    public String getBuilding() {...}
    public void setBuilding(String s) {...}
}

public class Address extends AbstractEntry {
    public Address() {...}
    public Address(String street, String organization,
                   String organizationalUnit, String locality,
                   String stateOrProvince, String postalCode,
```

```
                           String country) {…}

        public String street;
        public String organization;
        public String organizationalUnit;
        public String locality;
        public String stateOrProvince;
        public String postalCode;
        public String country;
    }

    public class AddressBean implements EntryBean, Serializable {
        public String getStreet() {…}
        public void setStreet(String s) {…}
        public String getOrganization() {…}
        public void setOrganization(String s) {…}
        public String getOrganizationalUnit() {…}
        public void setOrganizationalUnit(String s) {…}
        public String getLocality() {…}
        public void setLocality(String s) {…}
        public String getStateOrProvince() {…}
        public void setStateOrProvince(String s) {…}
        public String getPostalCode() {…}
        public void setPostalCode(String s) {…}
        public String getCountry() {…}
        public void setCountry(String s) {…}
    }
```

We believe the fields of these classes to be self-explanatory, with the possible exception of the `locality` field of the `Address` class, which would typically hold the name of a city.

LS.4.7 Status Information

Some attributes of a service may constitute long-lived status, such as an indication that a printer is out of paper. We provide a class, `Status`, that implementors can use as a base for providing status-related entry classes.

```
public abstract class Status extends AbstractEntry {
    protected Status() {…}
    protected Status(StatusType severity) {…}
```

```
        public StatusType severity;
    }

    public class StatusType implements Serializable {
        private final int type;
        private StatusType(int t) { type = t; }
        public static final StatusType ERROR =  new StatusType(1);
        public static final StatusType WARNING =
                                                new StatusType(2);
        public static final StatusType NOTICE = new StatusType(3);
        public static final StatusType NORMAL = new StatusType(4);
    }

    public abstract class StatusBean
        implements EntryBean, Serializable
    {
        public StatusType getSeverity() {…}
        public void setSeverity(StatusType i) {…}
    }
```

We define a separate `StatusType` class to make it possible to write a property editor that will work with the `StatusBean` class (we do not currently provide a property editor implementation).

LS.4.8 Serialized Forms

Class	`serialVersionUID`	Serialized Fields
`Address`	2896136903322046578L	*all public fields*
`AddressBean`	4491500432084550577L	`Address asoc`
`Comment`	7138608904371928208L	*all public fields*
`CommentBean`	5272583409036504625L	`Comment asoc`
`Location`	–3275276677967431315L	*all public fields*
`LocationBean`	–4182591284470292829L	`Location asoc`
`Name`	2743215148071307201L	*all public fields*
`NameBean`	–6026791845102735793L	`Name asoc`

Class	serialVersionUID	Serialized Fields
ServiceInfo	–1116664185758541509L	*all public fields*
ServiceInfoBean	8352546663361067804L	ServiceInfo asoc
ServiceType	–6443809721367395836L	*all public fields*
Status	–5193075846115040838L	*all public fields*
StatusBean	–1975539395914887503L	Status asoc
StatusType	–8268735508512712203L	int type

THE JINI LEASE RENEWAL SERVICE SPECIFICATION is a service that can be employed by both Jini technology-enabled clients (Jini clients) and Jini technology-enabled services (Jini services) to perform all lease renewal duties on their behalf. Services that wish to remain inactive until needed may find the lease renewal service quite useful. Such a service can request that the lease renewal service take on the responsibility of renewing the leases granted to the service, and then safely deactivate without risking the loss of access to the resources corresponding to the leases being renewed.

JINI™

LR

Jini Lease Renewal Service Specification

LR.1 Introduction

LEASING is a key concept in the Jini architecture; in general, Jini technology-enabled services (*Jini services*) grant access to a resource only for as long as the clients of those Jini services actively express interest in the resource being maintained. This pattern is in contrast to many other systems, in which access to a resource is granted until the client explicitly releases the resource. Using a leasing model generally makes a distributed system more robust by allowing stale information and services to be cleaned up, but it also places additional requirements on clients and services.

A client of a leased service may run into difficulties if that client deactivates. Unless the client ensures that some other process renews the client's leases while it is inactive, or that the client is activated before its leases begin to expire, the client will lose access to the resources it has acquired. This loss can be particularly dramatic in the case of lookup service registrations. A service's registration with a lookup service is leased—if the service deactivates (maybe to conserve computational resources on its host) and it does not take appropriate steps, its registrations with lookup services will expire, and before long it will be inaccessible. If that service becomes active only when clients invoke its methods, it may never become active again, because at this point new clients may not be able to find it.

The need to renew leases creates a constant load on clients, servers, and the network. Although batching lease renewals can help (see *The Jini Technology Core Platform Specification,* "Distributed Leasing"*)*, a given client is unlikely to have very many leases granted by any one service at any given time, thus reducing the opportunities for meaningful batching.

This additional load may be an especially great burden on clients that always have the ability to access the network but cannot be continuously connected. A cell phone always has the ability to connect; however, being connected all the time will drain its batteries and accumulate airtime charges. One or two leases may not pose a problem, but a large number of leases could force the phone to be on the network all the time.

A lease renewal service can help mitigate these problems. Clients that wish to become inactive can pass the responsibility for renewing the leases they have been granted to a renewal service. Those clients can then deactivate without risk of losing access to the resources that they have acquired. Clients that have continuous access to the network but cannot be continuously connected, such as the cell phone described previously, can also register with a renewal service that can be continuously connected. The renewal service will renew the client's leases, allowing the client to remain disconnected most of the time. Lastly, if multiple clients pass their leases to a given renewal service, more opportunities for batching renewals will be created.

Like other Jini services, the lease renewal service will grant its services for only a limited period of time without an active expression of continuing interest. To break the recursive cycle that would otherwise result, the renewal service provides an optional event that is triggered before the leases that it grants expire. This event gives activatable processes that have deactivated the opportunity to wake up and renew their lease with the renewal service. Although it may seem odd for the lease renewal service to lease its resources, it is very important that it does so. If it did not, then the lease renewal service could be used to subvert the leasing model.

Lease renewal services are likely to grant longer leases than other Jini services. In some cases the lease may be so long that the client will not need to worry about renewing the lease at all. In other cases the lease may be long enough that a client that deactivates will rarely need to reactivate for the sole purpose of renewing its lease with the renewal service. In any case, the leases that the renewal service grants are likely to be sufficiently long such that the actual renewal calls do not place a significant additional load on the client, the renewal service, or the network.

LR.1.1 Goals and Requirements

The requirements of the set of classes and interfaces in this specification are:

- To provide a service for renewing leases

- To provide this service in such a way that it can be used by activatable processes that deactivate
- To provide this service in a way that does not overly weaken the leasing model

The goals of this specification are:

- To describe the lease renewal service
- To provide guidance in the use, deployment, and implementation of the lease renewal service

LR.1.2 Other Types

The types defined in the specification of the `LeaseRenewalService` interface are in the `net.jini.lease` package. The following object types may be referenced in this chapter. Whenever referenced, these object types will be referenced in unqualified form:

```
java.io.IOException
java.rmi.MarshalledObject
java.rmi.RemoteException
java.rmi.NoSuchObjectException
net.jini.core.lease.Lease
net.jini.core.lease.UnknownLeaseException
net.jini.core.event.RemoteEvent
net.jini.core.event.RemoteEventListener
net.jini.core.event.EventRegistration
```

LR.2 The Interface

THE `LeaseRenewalService` (in the `net.jini.lease` package) defines the interface to the renewal service. The interface is not a remote interface; each implementation of the renewal service exports proxy objects that implement the `LeaseRenewalService` interface local to the client, using an implementation-specific protocol to communicate with the actual remote server. All of the proxy methods obey normal RMI remote interface semantics. Two proxy objects are equal (using the `equals` method) if they are proxies for the same renewal service. All the methods of `LeaseRenewalService` throw `RemoteException` and require only the default serialization semantics. Therefore, `LeaseRenewalService` can be implemented directly using RMI.

```
package net.jini.lease;

public interface LeaseRenewalService {
    public LeaseRenewalSet createLeaseRenewalSet(
            long leaseDuration)
        throws RemoteException;
}
```

Clients of the renewal service organize the leases they wish to have renewed into *lease renewal sets* (or *sets,* for short). A method is provided by the `LeaseRenewalService` interface to create these sets. These sets are then populated by methods on the sets themselves. Two leases in the same set need not be granted by the same service or have the same expiration time; in addition, they can be added or removed from the set independently.

Every method invocation on a renewal service (whether the invocation is directly on the service or indirectly on a `set` the service has created) is atomic with respect other invocations.

The term *client lease* is used to refer to a lease that has been placed into a renewal set. Client leases are distinct from the leases that the renewal service grants on renewal sets it has created.

In general, there will be times when an implementation of the renewal service needs to pass one client lease as an argument to a method call on a second client

lease. There is a security risk in doing so, because such actions can let the second client lease "capture" the first. Implementations may want to verify that their clients can be trusted not to place leases in the set that would take such actions. Another alterative is to pass one `Lease` object to another only if they trust each other. Depending on the environment, conservative tests for such trust could include: ensuring the codebases of both leases are constructed from the same set of URLs, or that all of the URLs come from a common set of hosts or host/port pairs.

Each client lease has two expiration related times associated with it: the *desired expiration* time for the lease and the *actual expiration* time granted when the lease is created or last renewed. The desired expiration represents when the client would like the lease to expire. The actual expiration represents when the lease is going to expire if it is not renewed. Both time values are absolute times, not relative time durations. When a client lease's desired expiration arrives, the lease will be removed from the set without further client intervention.

Each client lease also has two other associated attributes: a *renewal duration* and a *remaining desired duration*. The remaining desired duration is always the desired expiration less the current time. The renewal duration is usually a positive number and represents the duration that will be requested when the renewal service renews the client lease, unless the renewal duration is greater than the remaining desired duration. If the renewal duration is greater than the remaining desired duration, then the remaining desired duration will be requested when renewing the client lease. One exception is that when the desired expiration is `Lease.FOREVER`, the renewal duration may be `Lease.ANY`, in which case `Lease.ANY` will be requested when renewing the client lease, regardless of the value of the remaining desired duration.

For example, if the renewal duration associated with a given client lease is 360,000 milliseconds, then when the renewal service renews the client lease, it will ask for a new duration of 360,000 milliseconds—unless the client lease is going to reach its desired expiration in less than 360,000 milliseconds. If the client lease's desired expiration is within 360,000 milliseconds, the renewal service will ask for the difference between the current time and the desired expiration. If the renewal duration had been `Lease.ANY`, the renewal service would have asked for a new duration of `Lease.ANY`.

If a lease's actual expiration is later than the lease's desired expiration, the renewal service will not renew the lease; the lease will remain in the set until its desired expiration is reached, the set is destroyed, or it is removed by the client.

Each set is leased from the renewal service. If the lease on a set expires or is cancelled, the renewal service will destroy the set and take no further action with regard to the client leases in the set. Each lease renewal set has associated with it an expiration warning event that occurs at a client-specified time before the lease *on the set* expires. Clients can register for warning events using methods provided by the set. A registration for warning events does not have its own lease, but instead is covered by the same lease under which the set was granted.

The term *definite exception* is used to refer to an exception that could be thrown by an operation on a client lease (such as a remote method call) that would be indicative of a permanent failure of the client lease. In this specification, all bad object exceptions, bad invocation exceptions, and `LeaseExceptions` are considered to be definite exceptions (see *Introduction to Helper Utilities and Services*, Section US.2.6, "What Exceptions Imply about Future Behavior").

Each lease renewal set has associated with it a renewal failure event that will occur in either of two cases: if any client lease in the set reaches its actual expiration before its desired expiration is reached, or if the renewal service attempts to renew a client lease and gets a definite exception. Clients can register for failure events using methods provided by the set. A registration for failure events does not have its own lease but instead is covered by the same lease under which the set was granted.

Once placed in a set, a client lease will stay there until one or more of the following occurs:

- The lease on the set itself expires or is cancelled, causing destruction of the set.
- The client lease is removed by the client.
- The client lease's desired expiration is reached.
- The client lease's actual expiration is reached; this will generate a renewal failure event.
- A renewal attempt on the client lease results in a definite exception; this will generate a renewal failure event.

Each client lease in a set will be renewed as long as it is in the set. If a renewal call throws an indefinite exception (see *Introduction to Helper Utilities and Services,* Section US.2.6, "What Exceptions Imply about Future Behavior"), the renewal service should retry the lease renewal until the lease would otherwise be removed from the set. The preferred method of cancelling a client lease is for the client to first remove the lease from the set and then call `cancel` on it. It is also permissible for the client to cancel the lease without first removing the lease from the set, although this is likely to result in additional network traffic.

The client creates a set by calling the `createLeaseRenewalSet` method of a `LeaseRenewalService`. The `leaseDuration` argument specifies how long (in milliseconds) the client wants the set's initial lease duration to be. The duration initially granted for the set's lease will be equal to or shorter than this request; it will not be longer. The value of the `leaseDuration` argument must be positive, `Lease.FOREVER`, or `Lease.ANY`; otherwise, an `IllegalArgumentException` will be thrown. Two calls to the `createLeaseRenewalSet` method will never return objects that are equal. The set's lease is obtained through a method provided by the set.

`LeaseRenewalSet` defines the interface to the sets created by the lease renewal service. This interface is not a remote interface. Each implementation of the renewal service exports proxy objects that implement the `LeaseRenewalSet` interface local to the client and use an implementation-specific protocol to communicate with the actual remote server. All of the proxy methods obey normal RMI remote interface semantics except where explicitly noted. The proxy objects for two sets are equal (using the `equals` method) if they are proxies for the same set created by the same renewal service. Any method that communicates with the remote server should throw a `NoSuchObjectException` if the set no longer exists. If a client receives a `NoSuchObjectException` from one of the operations on a lease renewal set, the client can infer that the set has been destroyed; however, it should *not* infer that the renewal service has been destroyed.

```
package net.jini.lease;

public interface LeaseRenewalSet {
    final public static long RENEWAL_FAILURE_EVENT_ID = 0;
    final public static long EXPIRATION_WARNING_EVENT_ID = 1;

    public void renewFor(Lease leaseToRenew,
                         long  desiredDuration,
                         long  renewDuration)
        throws RemoteException;

    public void renewFor(Lease leaseToRenew,
                              long  desiredDuration)
        throws RemoteException;

    public EventRegistration setExpirationWarningListener(
            RemoteEventListener listener,
            long                minWarning,
            MarshalledObject    handback)
        throws RemoteException;

    public void clearExpirationWarningListener()
        throws RemoteException;
```

```
    public EventRegistration setRenewalFailureListener(
            RemoteEventListener listener,
            MarshalledObject    handback)
        throws RemoteException;

    public void clearRenewalFailureListener()
        throws RemoteException;

    public Lease remove(Lease leaseToRemove)
        throws RemoteException;

    public Lease[] getLeases()
        throws LeaseUnmarshalException, RemoteException;

    public Lease getRenewalSetLease();
}
```

Leases can be added to the set through the `renewFor` methods. There are two forms of this method: a three-argument form and a two-argument form. The three-argument form will be described first. The `leaseToRenew` argument specifies the lease to be renewed. An `IllegalArgumentException` will be thrown if the lease has not expired and was granted by the renewal service itself. An `IllegalArgumentException` will also be thrown if the lease is currently a member of another set allocated by the same renewal service. If `leaseToRenew` is `null`, a `NullPointerException` will be thrown.

The `desiredDuration` parameter is the number of milliseconds that the client would like for the client lease to remain in the set. It is used to calculate the client lease's desired expiration by adding `desiredDuration` to the current time (as viewed by the service). If this causes an overflow, a desired expiration of `Long.MAX_VALUE` will be used. Unlike a lease duration, the desired duration is unilaterally specified by the client, not negotiated between the client and the service. Note that a negative value for `desiredDuration` (including `Lease.ANY`) will result in a desired expiration that is in the past. This will cause the client lease to be dropped immediately from the set and will not result in an exception. A renewal failure event will be generated if and only if the client's actual expiration is before its desired expiration.

If the actual expiration time of the client lease being added to the set is before both the current time (as viewed by the renewal service) and the client lease's desired expiration time, the method will return normally. However, the client lease will be dropped from the set, and a renewal failure event will be generated. If the actual expiration time is before the current time and equal to or after the desired expiration time, the method will return normally, the client lease will be dropped from the set, and no event will be generated.

A `desiredDuration` of `Long.MAX_VALUE` does not imply that the client lease will remain in the set forever. The client lease will be ejected from the set if the set is destroyed, the client lease itself expires, the client lease is removed from the set, or the renewal service makes a renewal attempt on the client lease that results in a definite exception.

The `renewDuration` is the renewal duration to associate with the client lease (in milliseconds). If `desiredDuration` is exactly `Long.MAX_VALUE`, the `renewDuration` may be any positive number or `Lease.ANY`; otherwise it must be a positive number. If these requirements are not met, the renewal service will throw an `IllegalArgumentException`.

Calling `renewFor` with a lease that is equivalent to a client lease already in the set will associate the existing client lease in the set with the new desired duration and renew duration. The original copy of the client lease is not replaced with the new one. These semantics also allow `renewFor` to be used in an idempotent fashion.

The two-argument form of `renewFor` is equivalent to

```
renewFor(leaseToRenew, desiredDuration, Lease.FOREVER)
```

Client leases get returned to clients in a number of ways (via `remove` and `getLeases` calls, as components of events, etc.). The serial format of client leases returned to clients may be either `Lease.DURATION` or `Lease.ABSOLUTE`. In particular it may be necessary to use the `Lease.ABSOLUTE` format if the implementation has access to the client lease only in marshalled form and is unable to unmarshal the client lease before sending it to the client.

Whenever a client lease gets returned to a client, its actual expiration should reflect either:

- The result of the last recorded successful renewal of the client lease performed by the renewal service; or
- The expiration time the client lease originally had when it was added to the set, if the renewal service has been unable to successfully renew the client lease and record the result

Although it is impossible for a renewal service to guarantee that all renewal attempts will be recorded, persistent implementations should attempt to keep the interval between the renewal of a client lease and the logging of the result to a minimum.

Client leases are removed from the set by using the `remove` method. Removal from the set will not cause the lease to be cancelled. The method will return the lease that is being removed. If the lease is not in the set, `null` will be returned; and this call will not be blocked by in-progress renewal attempts. As a result, a client lease removed by this method might be renewed after the method has returned. Implementations should keep the window where renewals of removed leases could occur as small as possible.

The `getLeases` method returns all the client leases in the set at the time of the call, as an array of type `Lease`. If one or more of the `Leases` in the array cannot be deserialized, a `LeaseUnmarshalException` is thrown.

```
package net.jini.lease;

public class LeaseUnmarshalException extends Exception {
    public LeaseUnmarshalException(
            Lease[]            leases,
            MarshalledObject[] marshalledLeases,
            Throwable[]        exceptions) {...}
    public LeaseUnmarshalException(
            Lease[]            leases,
            MarshalledObject[] marshalledLeases,
            Throwable[]        exceptions,
            String             message) {...}

    public Lease[] getLeases() {...}
    public MarshalledObject[] getMarshalledLeases() {...}
    public Throwable[] getExceptions() {...}
}
```

The leases that could be successfully deserialized will be returned by the `getLeases` method of the exception. If no leases could be deserialized, a zero-length array will be returned. The leases that could not be deserialized will be returned in the form of `MarshalledObjects` by the `getMarshalledLeases` method of the exception. For each element of the array returned by the `getMarshalledLeases` method, the corresponding element of the array returned by the `getExceptions` method will hold a `Throwable` that indicates why the given lease could not be deserialized.

Throwing a `LeaseUnmarshalException` represents a (possibly transient) failure in the ability to unmarshal one or more client leases in the set; it does not necessarily imply anything about the state of the renewal service or the set that threw the exception.

The `getRenewalSetLease` method of `LeaseSet` returns the lease associated with the set itself. This method does not make a remote call.

LR.2.1 Events

The lease renewal service does not support multiple simultaneous event listener registrations for the same kind of event. Although it would be useful in some limited circumstances, to do so would require event registrations to be leased separately from the set they are associated with. For the average client of the lease renewal service, this ability would increase the number of leases that it would have to manage. Since the renewal service is based on the premise that some clients have difficulty managing their own leases, increasing the number of leases that a client would need to manage could significantly complicate the implementation of those clients. Because there can be at most one listener for each kind of event, a given set provides a `set/clear` interface instead of the more common `addListener/removeListener` or `addListener/lease.cancel` interfaces.

The source field of each event generated by a lease renewal service is the renewal set that the event is associated with. In the case of an expiration warning event, this is the set that is about to expire. In the case of a renewal failure event, this is the set the client lease was in when the event occurred. Note that the value of the source field will in general be a copy of the set in question, the `equals` method will return `true` for any other copies of the set the client has in its possession, but in general it will not be the same object (that is, comparing two sets using == will usually return `false`).

The event ID `LeaseRenewalSet.EXPIRATION_WARNING_EVENT_ID` is used for all expiration warning events. One event ID is used because there is only one kind of expiration warning event. Similarly, all renewal failure events will have the event ID `LeaseRenewalSet.RENEWAL_FAILURE_EVENT_ID`.

Because all of the expiration warning events generated by a given set will have the same source and event ID, the sequence number of any given expiration warning event generated by the set will be different from the sequence number of any other expiration warning event generated by the set. Similarly, the sequence number of any renewal failure event generated by a given set will be different from the sequence number of any other renewal failure event generated by the set. Two different events with the same source and event ID will have different sequence numbers even if different event registration were in effect when each event was generated.

If a `RemoteEventListener` registered for a renewal failure or expiration warning event throws an `UnknownEventException`, this action will only clear the specific event registration. It will not cancel the lease on the renewal set or affect any other event registration on the set. If the listener throws a bad object exception, the renewal service may clear that specific event registration; it will not clear any registration associated with other listeners, nor will it cancel the lease on the associated renewal set.

If an event listener is replaced and one or more event delivery attempts on the original listener failed, implementations may choose to send some or all of these events to the new listener.

Event listeners may receive notification of events that they are no longer registered to receive, if those events occurred before they were unregistered. Implementations should keep the window where such notifications could occur as small as possible.

The `setExpirationWarningListener` method of `LeaseRenewalSet` allows the client to register for notification of the approaching expiration of the *set's* lease. Expiration warning events are not generated for client leases. The `listener` argument specifies which listener should be notified when the set's lease is about to expire. The `minWarning` argument specifies the minimum number of milliseconds before set lease expiration that the first event delivery attempt should be made by the service. The service may also make subsequent delivery attempts if the first and any subsequent attempts resulted in an indefinite exception. The `minWarning` argument must be zero or a positive number; if it is not, an `IllegalArgumentException` must be thrown. If the current expiration of the set's lease is less than `minWarning` milliseconds away, the event will occur immediately (though it will take time to propagate to the handler).

The `handback` argument to `setExpirationWarningListener` specifies an object that will be part of the expiration warning event notification. This mechanism is detailed in *The Jini Technology Core Platform Specification,* "Distributed Events".

The `setExpirationWarningListener` method returns the event registration for this event. The `Lease` object associated with the registration will be equivalent (in the sense of the `equals` method) to the `Lease` on the renewal set. Because the event registration shares a lease with the set, clients that want to just remove their expiration warning registration without destroying the set should use the `clearExpirationWarningListener` method described below, instead of cancelling the registration's lease. The event ID returned with the registration will be `LeaseRenewalSet.EXPIRATION_WARNING_EVENT_ID`. The source of the registration will be the set. The method will throw a `NullPointerException` if the `listener` argument is `null`. If an event handler has already been specified for this event, the current registration is replaced with the new one. Because both registrations are for the same kind of event, the events sent to the new registration must be in the same sequence as the events sent to the old registration.

The clearExpirationWarningListener method of LeaseRenewalSet removes the event registration currently associated with the approaching expiration of the set's lease. It is acceptable to call this method even if there is no active registration.

The setRenewalFailureListener method of LeaseRenewalSet allows the client to register for the event associated with the failure to renew a client lease in the set. These events are generated when a client lease in the set reaches its actual expiration before its desired expiration or when the service attempts to renew a client lease and gets a definite exception. The listener argument specifies the listener to be notified if a client lease could not be renewed.

The handback argument to setRenewalFailureListener specifies an object that will be part of the renewal failure event notification. This mechanism is detailed in *The Jini Technology Core Platform Specification,* "Distributed Events".

The setRenewalFailureListener method returns the event registration for this event. The Lease object associated with the registration will be equivalent (in the sense of the equals method) to the Lease on the renewal set. Because the event registration shares a lease with the set, clients that want to just remove their expiration warning registration without destroying the set should use the clearRenewalFailureListener method (described below) instead of cancelling the registration's lease. The registration ID returned with the registration will be LeaseRenewalSet.RENEWAL_FAILURE_EVENT_ID. The source of the registration will be the set. The method will throw NullPointerException if the listener argument is null. If an event handler has already been specified for this event, the current registration is replaced with the new one. Because both registrations are for the same kind of event, the events sent to the new registration must be in the same sequence as the events sent to the old registration.

The clearRenewalFailureListener method of LeaseRenewalSet removes the event registration currently associated with the failure to renew client leases. It is acceptable to call this method even if there is no active registration.

```
package net.jini.lease;

public class ExpirationWarningEvent extends RemoteEvent {
    public ExpirationWarningEvent(
            LeaseRenewalSet  source,
            long             seqNum,
            MarshalledObject handback) {...}
    public Lease getRenewalSetLease() {...}
}
```

ExpirationWarningEvent objects are passed to the event handlers specified in calls to the LeaseRenewalSet method, setExpirationWarningListener. The ExpirationWarningEvent is a subclass of RemoteEvent and adds no additional state. Because the source of a ExpirationWarningEvent is the set that is about to expire, the lease that needs to be renewed can be obtained by: calling getSource, casting the result to a LeaseRenewalSet and then invoking the set's getRenewalSetLease method. The convenience method getRenewalSetLease in ExpirationWarningEvent uses this technique to retrieve the lease on the set. The Lease object returned will be equivalent (in the sense of the equals method) to other Lease objects associated with the set but may not be the same object. One notable consequence of having two different objects is that the getExpiration method of the Lease object returned by the event's getRenewalSetLease method may return a different time than the getExpiration methods of other Lease objects granted on the same set.

The expiration time associated with the Lease object returned by the getRenewalSetLease method will reflect the expiration the lease had when the event occurred. Renewal calls may have changed the expiration time of the underlying lease between the time when the event was generated and when it was delivered.

Other aspects of the event's state are described in *The Jini Technology Core Platform Specification,* "Distributed Events". Sequence numbers for a given event ID are increasing. If there is no gap between two sequence numbers, no events have been missed; if there is a gap, events might (but might not) have been missed.

```
package net.jini.lease;

public abstract class RenewalFailureEvent
    extends RemoteEvent
{
    public RenewalFailureEvent(LeaseRenewalSet  source,
                               long             seqNum,
                               MarshalledObject handback) {...}
    abstract public Lease getLease()
        throws IOException, ClassNotFoundException;
    abstract public Throwable getThrowable()
        throws IOException, ClassNotFoundException;
}
```

RenewalFailureEvent objects are passed to the event handlers specified in calls to the LeaseRenewalSet method, setRenewalFailureListener. The RenewalFailureEvent is a subclass of RemoteEvent, adding two additional items of abstract state: the client lease that could not be renewed before expiration and the Throwable object that was thrown by the last recorded renewal attempt (if any). The client lease is returned by the getLease method, and the Throwable object is returned by the getThrowable method. If the Throwable object is null, it can be assumed that during the time between the last-recorded, successful renewal (or when the client lease was added to the set if there have been no renewals) and the actual expiration time of the client lease the renewal service was either unable to attempt a renewal of the client lease, or that it attempted a renewal but was unable to record the result.

Both the getLease and getThrowable methods may throw IOException or ClassNotFoundException. This declaration allows implementations to delay unmarshalling this state until it is actually needed. Once either method of a given RenewalFailureEvent object returns normally, future calls on that method must return the same object and may not throw an exception.

If the renewal service was able to renew the client lease and record the result before the event occurred, the expiration time of the Lease object returned by the event's getLease method will reflect the result of the last-recorded successful renewal call. Note that this time may be distorted by clock skew between hosts if it is currently set to use the Lease.ABSOLUTE serial format. If the Lease object is using the Lease.DURATION serial format, and the event only unmarshals the lease when getLease is called, the expiration time may be distorted if a long time has passed between the time the event was generated by the renewal service and when the client called getLease. When a renewal failure event is generated for a given lease, that lease is removed from the set.

The event's other state is described in *The Jini Technology Core Platform Specification,* "Distributed Events". Sequence numbers for a given event ID are increasing. If there is no gap between two sequence numbers, no events have been missed; if there is a gap, events might (but might not) have been missed.

LR.2.2 Serialized Forms

Class	serialVersionUID	Serialized Fields
RenewalFailureEvent	8891457041959329431L	*none*
ExpirationWarningEvent	-2020487536756927350L	*none*
LeaseUnmarshalException	-6736107321698417489L	Lease[]unmarshalledLeases MarshalledObject[] stillMarshalledLeases Throwable[] exceptions

Lease
Renewal
(LR)

THE JINI EVENT MAILBOX SERVICE SPECIFICATION defines a Jini service that can be employed by Jini technology-enabled clients and services to store event notifications on their behalf. When an entity registers with the event mailbox service, that service will collect events intended for the registered entity until the entity initiates delivery of the events. A service such as the event mailbox can be particularly useful to entities that desire more control over the delivery of the events sent to them. Some entities operating in a distributed system may find it undesirable or inefficient to be contacted solely for the purpose of having an event delivered; preferring to defer the delivery to a time that is more convenient, as determined by the entity itself.

JINI™

EM

Jini Event Mailbox Service Specification

EM.1 Introduction

THE *The Jini Technology Core Platform Specification,* "Distributed Events" states the ability to interpose third-party objects, or "agents," into an event notification chain as one of its design goals. This specification also describes a notification mailbox object, which stores and forwards event notifications on behalf of other objects, as an example of a useful third-party agent. These mailbox objects can be particularly helpful for objects that need more control over how and when they receive event notifications.

For example, it would be impossible to send event notifications to a transient entity that has detached itself from a system of Jini technology-enabled services and/or devices (*Jini system*). In such a situation an entity could employ the services of an event mailbox to store event notifications on its behalf before leaving the system. Upon rejoining the Jini system, the entity could then contact the event mailbox to retrieve any collected events that it would otherwise have missed. Similarly, an entity that wishes to deactivate could use an event mailbox to collect event notifications on its behalf while dormant.

Like other Jini technology-enabled services (*Jini services*), the event mailbox service will grant its services only for a limited period of time without an active expression of continuing interest. Therefore, event mailbox clients still need to renew their leases if they intend to maintain the mailbox's services beyond the initially granted lease period. Any resources (for example, remote objects or storage space) associated with a particular client can be freed once the client's lease has expired or been cancelled. In the previous usage scenarios, it might also benefit a transient or deactivatable entity to employ the services of a lease renewal service (see the *Jini Lease Renewal Service Specification)* to help mitigate the issue of lease maintenance.

The remainder of this specification defines the requirements, interfaces, and protocols of the event mailbox service.

EM.1.1 Goals and Requirements

The requirements of the set of interfaces specified in this document are:

- To define a service that is capable of storing event notifications on behalf of its clients and capable of delivering stored event notifications to those clients upon request
- To provide this service in such a way that it can be used by entities that are temporarily unable or unwilling to receive event notifications
- To provide a service that complies with the policies embodied in the Jini technology programming model

The goals of this specification are:

- To describe the event mailbox service
- To provide guidance in the use and deployment of the event mailbox service

EM.1.2 Other Types

The types defined in the specification of the event mailbox service are in the `net.jini.event` package. This specification assumes knowledge of *The Jini Technology Core Platform Specification,* "Distributed Events" and *The Jini Technology Core Platform Specification,* "Distributed Leasing". The following object types may be referenced in this chapter. Whenever referenced, these object types will be referenced in unqualified form:

```
java.rmi.NoSuchObjectException
java.rmi.RemoteException
net.jini.core.event.RemoteEvent
net.jini.core.event.RemoteEventListener
net.jini.core.lease.Lease
net.jini.core.lease.LeaseDeniedException
```

EM.2 The Interface

THE `EventMailbox` defines the interface to the event mailbox service. Through this interface, other Jini services and clients may request that event notification management be performed on their behalf. This interface belongs to the `net.jini.event` package, and any service implementing this interface must comply with the definition of a Jini service. This interface is not a remote interface; each implementation exports a proxy object that implements this interface local to the client, using an implementation-specific protocol to communicate with the actual remote server. All of the proxy methods obey normal Java Remote Method Invocation (RMI) interface semantics and can therefore be implemented directly using RMI (except where explicitly noted). Two proxy objects are equal (using the `equals` method) if they are proxies for the same event mailbox service.

```
package net.jini.event;

public interface EventMailbox
{
    MailboxRegistration register(long leaseDuration)
        throws RemoteException, LeaseDeniedException;
}
```

Event mailbox clients wishing to use the mailbox service first register themselves with the service using the `register` method. Clients then use the methods of the returned `MailboxRegistration` object (a *registration*) in order to:

- Manage the lease for this particular registration
- Obtain a `RemoteEventListener` reference that can be registered with *event generators* (that is, objects that support event notification for changes in their abstract state). This listener will store any received notifications for this particular registration.
- Enable or disable the delivery of any stored notifications for this particular registration

EM.3 The Semantics

To employ the event mailbox service, a client must first register with the event mailbox service by invoking the `EventMailbox` interface's only method, `register`. Each invocation of the `register` method produces a new registration.

The `register` method may throw a `RemoteException` or a `LeaseDeniedException`. Typically, a `RemoteException` occurs when there is a communication failure between the client and the event mailbox service. If this exception does occur, the registration may or may not have been successful. A `LeaseDeniedException` is thrown if the event mailbox service is unable or unwilling to grant the registration request. It is implementation specific as to whether or not subsequent attempts (with or without the same argument) are likely to succeed.

Each registration with the event mailbox service is persistent across restarts or crashes of the event mailbox service, until the lease on the registration expires or is cancelled.

The `register` method takes a single parameter of type `long` that represents the requested initial lease duration for the registration, in milliseconds. This duration value must be positive (except for the special value of `Lease.ANY`). Otherwise, an `IllegalArgumentException` is thrown.

Every method invocation on an event mailbox service (whether the invocation is directly on the service, or indirectly on a `MailboxRegistration` that the service has created) is atomic with respect to other invocations.

EM.4 Supporting Interfaces and Classes

THE `register` method returns an object that implements the interface `MailboxRegistration`. It is through this interface that the client controls its registration and notification management with the event mailbox service.

```
package net.jini.event;

public interface MailboxRegistration
{
    Lease getLease();
    RemoteEventListener getListener();
    void enableDelivery(RemoteEventListener target)
        throws RemoteException;
    void disableDelivery() throws RemoteException;
}
```

The `MailboxRegistration` interface is not a remote interface. Each implementation of the event mailbox service exports proxy objects that implement this interface local to the client. These proxies use an implementation-specific protocol to communicate with the remote server. All of the remote proxy methods obey normal RMI interface semantics and can therefore be implemented using RMI. Two proxy objects are equal (using the `equals` method) if they are proxies for the same registration, created by the same event mailbox service.

Each remote method of this interface may throw a `RemoteException`. Typically, this exception occurs when there is a communication failure between the client and the event mailbox service. Whenever a method invocation results in a `RemoteException`, the method may or may not have successfully completed.

Any invocation of a remote method defined in this interface will result in a `NoSuchObjectException` if the client's registration with the event mailbox service has expired or has been cancelled. Note that upon receipt of a `NoSuchObjectException`, the client can assume that the registration no longer exists; the client cannot assume that the event mailbox service itself no longer exists.

EM.4.1 The Semantics

The `getLease` method returns the `Lease` object associated with the registration. The client can renew or cancel the registration with the mailbox service through the `Lease` object returned by this method (see *The Jini Technology Core Platform Specification,* "Distributed Leasing"). This method is not remote and takes no arguments.

The `getListener` method returns an object that implements the interface `RemoteEventListener`. This object, referred to as a *mailbox listener*, can then be submitted as the `RemoteEventListener` argument to an event generator's registration method(s) (see *The Jini Technology Core Platform Specification,* "Distributed Events"). Subsequent calls to this method will return equivalent objects (in the `equals` sense). Note that mailbox listeners generated by different registrations will not be equal. This method is not remote and takes no arguments.

The valid period of use for a mailbox listener is tied to the associated registration's lease. A `NoSuchObjectException` will be thrown if an attempt is made to invoke the `notify` method on a mailbox listener whose associated lease has terminated.

Mailbox listener references, just like their associated registrations, are persistent across server restarts or crashes until their associated registration's lease terminates.

The `enableDelivery` method allows a client to initiate delivery of event notifications (received on its behalf by this particular registration) to the client-specified listener, referred to as the *target listener.* This method takes a single argument of type `RemoteEventListener`. Subsequent calls to this method simply replace the registration's existing target listener, if any, with the specified target listener. Passing `null` as the listener argument has the same effect as disabling delivery (see below).

Resubmitting a mailbox listener back to the same mailbox service that generated it will result in an `IllegalArgumentException` being thrown. This is necessary to prevent a recursive event notification chain. Therefore, the event mailbox service must keep track of any listener objects that it generates and reject the resubmission of those objects.

Once enabled, event delivery remains enabled until it is disabled. Any events received while delivery is enabled will also be scheduled for delivery.

Event delivery guarantees with respect to exception handling, ordering, and concurrency are implementation specific and are not specified in this document. However, implementations are encouraged to support the following functionality. If an event delivery attempt produces an indefinite exception, then reasonable efforts should be made to successfully redeliver the event until the associated registration's lease terminates. On the other hand, if an event delivery attempt produces a definite exception, then event delivery should be disabled for the associated registration until it is explicitly enabled again.

Also, implementations may concurrently deliver event notifications to the same target listener, which implies that events may be sent in a different order than the order in which they were originally received. Hence, it is the target listener's responsibility to guard against potential concurrent, out-of-order event delivery.

Similarly, implementations are encouraged to support this method's intended semantics regarding listener replacement. That is, a mailbox client can reasonably assume that listener replacement has occurred upon successful return from this method and can therefore safely unexport the previous listener object. This also implies that any in-progress delivery attempts to the previous listener are either successfully cancelled before returning from this method (blocking), or subsequently retried using the replacement listener after returning from this method (non-blocking). Note that the non-blocking case can potentially allow the previous listener to be notified after successfully returning from this method.

The `disableDelivery` method allows the client to cease event delivery to the existing target listener, if any. It is acceptable to call this method even if no target listener is currently enabled. This method takes no arguments.

Again, event delivery guarantees are implementation specific and are not specified in this document. Implementations are encouraged to support the method's intended semantics regarding delivery suspension. That is, a mailbox client can reasonably assume that event delivery has been suspended upon successful return from this method and can therefore safely unexport the previously enabled listener object if desired. This also implies that any in-progress delivery attempts to the previously enabled listener are either successfully cancelled before returning from this method (blocking), or subsequently retried using the next enabled listener after returning from this method (non-blocking). Note that the non-blocking case can potentially allow the previously enabled listener to be notified after successfully returning from this method.

The event mailbox service does not normally concern itself with the attributes of the `RemoteEvents` that it receives. The one circumstance about which it must concern itself is when a target listener throws an `UnknownEventException` during an event delivery attempt. The event mailbox service must maintain a list, on a per-registration basis, of the particular combinations of event identifier and source reference (obtained from the offending `RemoteEvent` object) that produced the exception. The event mailbox must then propagate an `UnknownEventException` back to any event generator that attempts to deliver a `RemoteEvent` with an identifier-source combination held in a registration's unknown exception list. The service will also skip the future delivery of any stored events that have an identifier-source combination held in this list.

A registration's unknown exception list is cleared upon re-enabling delivery with any target listener. This list is persistent across service restarts or crashes, until the associated registration's lease terminates.

Note that the act of comparing event source objects for equality poses a security risk because source objects are potentially given references to other source objects that are currently using the mailbox. If security is a concern, then care should be taken to prevent independent event sources from obtaining information about each other.

Again, although implementation details are not specified in this document, service implementations need to carefully weigh the trade-offs of taking a particular security approach. For example, a low-security implementation could simply compare source objects using the `equals` method. This approach assumes well-behaved `equals` methods that pose no security risk. A more secure implementation might compare only source objects (using `equals`) that have the same codebase on the assumption that classes from the same codebase are trusted. Unfortunately, this approach will not work for services that evolve by changing their codebase (presumably to the location of the upgraded class files).

The event mailbox does not support multiple, concurrent notification targets per registration. As a result, the interface supports only a set/clear model rather than the more common add/remove model.

Event persistence guarantees are not specified in this document because no single policy can cover all the possible design trade-offs between reliability, efficiency, and performance. It is expected that operational parameters—controls for how the event mailbox deals with issues such as persistence guarantees, storage quotas, and low space behavior—will be exposed through an administration interface, which can vary across different event mailbox implementations.

Event
Mailbox
(EM)

THE JAVASPACES SPECIFICATION describes the JavaSpaces service defined in the package `net.jini.javaSpace`*. A JavaSpaces service provides a simple yet powerful persistent coordination tool for transactionally governed cooperation between loosely coupled players in distributed protocols.*

JINI™

JS

JavaSpaces Service Specification

JS.1 Introduction

DISTRIBUTED systems are hard to build. They require careful thinking about problems that do not occur in local computation. The primary problems are those of partial failure, greatly increased latency, and language compatibility. The Java programming language has a remote method invocation system called RMI that lets you approach general distributed computation in the Java programming language using techniques natural to the Java programming language and application environment. This is layered on the Java platform's object serialization mechanism to marshal parameters of remote methods into a form that can be shipped across the wire and unmarshalled in a remote server's Java virtual machine[1] (JVM).

This specification describes the architecture of JavaSpaces technology, which is designed to help you solve two related problems: distributed persistence and the design of distributed algorithms. JavaSpaces services use RMI and the serialization feature of the Java programming language to accomplish these goals.

---

[1] As used in this document, the terms "Java virtual machine" or "JVM" mean a virtual machine for the Java platform.

JS.1.1 The JavaSpaces Application Model and Terms

A JavaSpaces service holds *entries*. An entry is a typed group of objects, expressed in a class for the Java platform that implements the interface `net.jini.core.entry.Entry`. Entries are described in detail in *The Jini Technology Core Platform Specification,* "Entry".

An entry can be *written* into a JavaSpaces service, which creates a copy of that entry in the space[2] that can be used in future lookup operations.

You can look up entries in a JavaSpaces service using *templates,* which are entry objects that have some or all of its fields set to specified *values* that must be matched exactly. Remaining fields are left as *wildcards*—these fields are not used in the lookup.

There are two kinds of lookup operations: *read* and *take*. A *read* request to a space returns either an entry that matches the template on which the read is done, or an indication that no match was found. A *take* request operates like a read, but if a match is found, the matching entry is removed from the space.

You can request a JavaSpaces service to *notify* you when an entry that matches a specified template is written. This is done using the distributed event model contained in the package `net.jini.core.event` and described in *The Jini Technology Core Platform Specification,* "Distributed Events".

All operations that modify a JavaSpaces service are performed in a transactionally secure manner with respect to that space. That is, if a write operation returns successfully, that entry was written into the space (although an intervening take may remove it from the space before a subsequent lookup of yours). And if a take operation returns an entry, that entry has been removed from the space, and no future operation will read or take the same entry. In other words, each entry in the space can be taken at most once. Note, however, that two or more entries in a space may have exactly the same value.

The architecture of JavaSpaces technology supports a simple transaction mechanism that allows multi-operation and/or multi-space updates to complete atomically. This is done using the two-phase commit model under the default transaction semantics, as defined in the package `net.jini.core.transaction` and described in *The Jini Technology Core Platform Specification,* "Transaction".

Entries written into a JavaSpaces service are governed by a lease, as defined in the package `net.jini.core.lease` and described in *The Jini Technology Core Platform Specification,* "Distributed Leasing".

---

[2] The term "space" is used to refer to a JavaSpaces service implementation.

JS.1.1.1 Distributed Persistence

Implementations of JavaSpaces technology provide a mechanism for storing a group of related objects and retrieving them based on a value-matching lookup for specified fields. This allows a JavaSpaces service to be used to store and retrieve objects on a remote system.

JS.1.1.2 Distributed Algorithms as Flows of Objects

Many distributed algorithms can be modeled as a flow of objects between participants. This is different from the traditional way of approaching distributed computing, which is to create method-invocation-style protocols between participants. In this architecture's "flow of objects" approach, protocols are based on the movement of objects into and out of implementations of JavaSpaces technology.

For example, a book-ordering system might look like this:

- A book buyer wants to buy 100 copies of a book. The buyer writes a request for bids into a particular public JavaSpaces service.
- The broker runs a server that takes those requests out of the space and writes them into a JavaSpaces service for each book seller who registered with the broker for that service.
- A server at each book seller removes the requests from its JavaSpaces service, presents the request to a human to prepare a bid, and writes the bid into the space specified in the book buyer's request for bids.
- When the bidding period closes, the buyer takes all the bids from the space and presents them to a human to select the winning bid.

A method-invocation-style design would create particular remote interfaces for these interactions. With a "flow of objects" approach, only one interface is required: the `net.jini.space.JavaSpace` interface.

In general, the JavaSpaces application world looks like this:

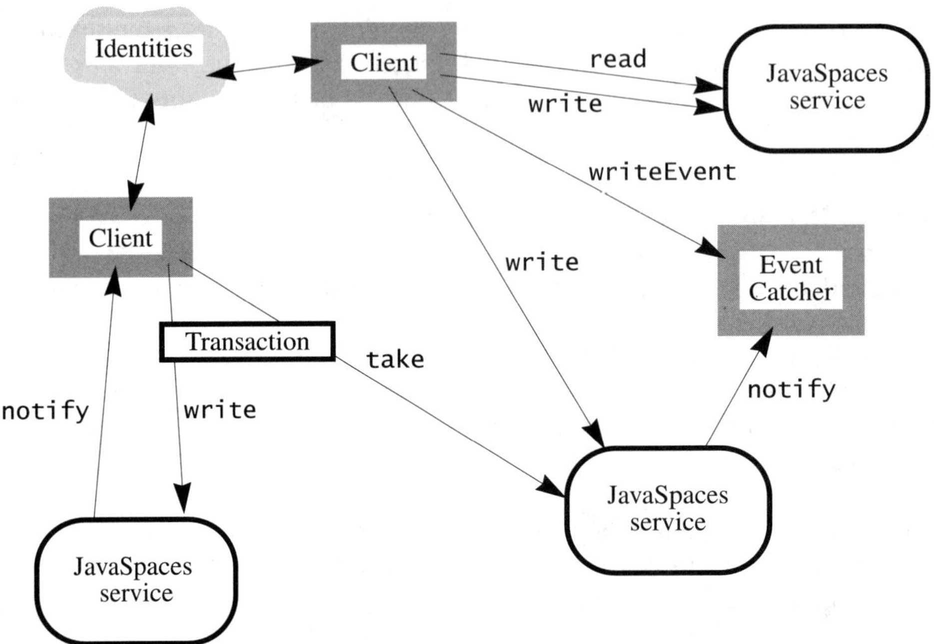

Clients perform operations that map entries or templates onto JavaSpaces services. These can be singleton operations (as with the upper client), or contained in transactions (as with the lower client) so that all or none of the operations take place. A single client can interact with as many spaces as it needs to. Identities are accessed from the security subsystem and passed as parameters to method invocations. Notifications go to event catchers, which may be clients themselves or proxies for a client (such as a store-and-forward mailbox).

JS.1.2 Benefits

JavaSpaces services are tools for building distributed protocols. They are designed to work with applications that can model themselves as flows of objects through one or more servers. If your application can be modeled this way, JavaSpaces technology will provide many benefits.

JavaSpaces services can provide a reliable distributed storage system for the objects. In the book-buying example, the designer of the system had to define the protocol for the participants and design the various kinds of entries that must be passed around. This effort is akin to designing the remote interfaces that an equivalent customized service would require. Both the JavaSpaces system solution and the customized solution would require someone to write the code that presented requests and bids to humans in a GUI. And in both systems, someone would have to write code to handle the seller's registrations of interest with the broker.

The server for the model that uses the JavaSpaces API would be implemented at that point.

The customized system would need to implement the servers. These servers would have to handle concurrent access from multiple clients. Someone would need to design and implement a reliable storage strategy that guaranteed the entries written to the server would not be lost in an unrecoverable or undetectable way. If multiple bids needed to be made atomically, a distributed transaction system would have to be implemented.

All these concerns are solved in JavaSpaces services. They handle concurrent access. They store and retrieve entries atomically. And they provide an implementation of the distributed transaction mechanism.

This is the power of the JavaSpaces technology architecture—many common needs are addressed in a simple platform that can be easily understood and used in powerful ways.

JavaSpaces services also help with data that would traditionally be stored in a file system, such as user preferences, e-mail messages, and images. Actually, this is not a different use of a JavaSpaces service. Such uses of a file system can equally be viewed as passing objects that contain state from one external object (the image editor) to another (the window system that uses the image as a screen background). And JavaSpaces services enhance this functionality because they store objects, not just data, so the image can have abstract behavior, not just information that must be interpreted by some external application(s).

JavaSpaces services can provide distributed *object* persistence with objects in the Java programming language. Because code written in the Java programming language is downloadable, entries can store objects whose behavior will be transmitted from the writer to the readers, just as in an RMI using Java technology. An entry in a space may, when fetched, cause some active behavior in the reading client. This is the benefit of storing objects, not just data, in an accessible repository for distributed cooperative computing.

JS.1.3 JavaSpaces Technology and Databases

A JavaSpaces service can store persistent data which is later searchable. But a JavaSpaces service is not a relational or object database. JavaSpaces services are designed to help solve problems in distributed computing, not to be used primarily as a data repository (although there are many data storage uses for JavaSpaces applications). Some important differences are:

- Relational databases understand the data they store and manipulate it directly via query languages. JavaSpaces services store entries that they understand only by type and the serialized form of each field. There are no general queries in the JavaSpaces application design, only "exact match" or "don't care" for a given field. You design your flow of objects so that this is sufficient and powerful.
- Object databases provide an object oriented image of stored data that can be modified and used, nearly as if it were transient memory. JavaSpaces systems do not provide a nearly transparent persistent/transient layer, and work only on copies of entries.

These differences exist because JavaSpaces services are designed for a different purpose than either relational or object databases. A JavaSpaces service can be used for simple persistent storage, such as storing a user's preferences that can be looked up by the user's ID or name. JavaSpaces service functionality is somewhere between that of a filesystem and a database, but it is neither.

JS.1.4 JavaSpaces System Design and Linda[3] Systems

The JavaSpaces system design is strongly influenced by Linda systems, which support a similar model of entry-based shared concurrent processing. In Section JS.4.1, "Linda Systems", you will find several references that describe Linda-style systems.

No knowledge of Linda systems is required to understand this specification. This section discusses the relationship of JavaSpaces systems with respect to Linda systems for the benefit of those already familiar with Linda programming. Other readers should feel free to skip ahead.

JavaSpaces systems are similar to Linda systems in that they store collections of information for future computation and are driven by value-based lookup. They differ in some important ways:

- Linda systems have not used rich typing. JavaSpaces systems take a deep concern with typing from the Java platform type-safe environment. In JavaSpaces systems, entries themselves, not just their fields, are typed—two different entries with the same field types but with different data types for the

---

[3] "Linda" is the name of a public domain technology originally propounded by Dr. David Gelernter of Yale University. "Linda" is also claimed as a trademark for certain goods by Scientific Computing Associates, Inc. This discussion refers to the public domain "Linda" technology.

Java programming language are different entry types. For example, an entry that had a string and two double values could be either a named point or a named vector. In JavaSpaces systems these two entry types would have specific different classes for the Java platform, and templates for one type would never match the other, even if the values were compatible.

- Entries are typed as objects in the Java programming language, so they may have methods associated with them. This provides a way of associating behavior with entries.
- As another result of typed entries, JavaSpaces services allow matching of subtypes—a template match can return a type that is a subtype of the template type. This means that the read or take may return more states than anticipated. In combination with the previous point, this means that entry behavior can be polymorphic in the usual object-oriented style that the Java platform provides.
- The fields of entries are objects in the Java programming language. Any object data type for the Java programming language can be used as a template for matching entry lookups as long as it has certain properties. This means that computing systems constructed using the JavaSpaces API are object-oriented from top to bottom, and behavior-based (agent-like) applications can use JavaSpaces services for co-ordination.
- Most environments will have more than one JavaSpaces service. Most Linda tuple spaces have one tuple space for all cooperating threads. So transactions in the JavaSpaces system can span multiple spaces (and even non-JavaSpaces system transaction participants).
- Entries written into a JavaSpaces service are leased. This helps keep the space free of debris left behind due to system crashes and network failures.
- The JavaSpaces API does not provide an equivalent of "eval" because it would require the service to execute arbitrary computation on behalf of the client. Such a general compute service has its own large number of requirements (such as security and fairness).

On the nomenclature side, the JavaSpaces technology API uses a more accessible set of terms than the traditional Linda terms. The term mappings are "entry" for "tuple," "value" for "actual," "wildcard" for "formal," "write" for "out," and "take" for "in." So the Linda sentence "When you 'out' a tuple make sure that actuals and formals in 'in' and 'read' can do appropriate matching" would be translated to "When you write an entry make sure that values and wildcards in take and read can do appropriate matching."

JS.1.5 Goals and Requirements

The goals for the design of JavaSpaces technology are:

- Provide a platform for designing distributed computing systems that simplifies the design and implementation of those systems.
- The client side should have few classes, both to keep the client-side model simple and to make downloading of the client classes quick.
- The client side should have a small footprint, because it will run on computers with limited local memory.
- A variety of implementations should be possible, including relational database storage and object-oriented database storage.
- It should be possible to create a replicated JavaSpaces service.

The requirements for JavaSpaces application clients are:

- It must be possible to write a client purely in the Java programming language.
- Clients must be oblivious to the implementation details of the service. The same entries and templates must work in the same ways no matter which implementation is used.

JS.1.6 Dependencies

This document relies upon the following other specifications:

- *Jini Entry Utilities Specification*,
- *Java Object Serialization Specification*
- *Java Remote Method Invocation Specification*
- *Jini Technology Core Platform Specification*,
  - Section "Entry"
  - Section "Distributed Events"
  - Section "Distributed Leasing"
  - Section "Transaction"

JS.2 Operations

THERE are four primary kinds of operations that you can invoke on a JavaSpaces service. Each operation has parameters that are entries, including some that are templates, which are a kind of entry. This chapter describes entries, templates, and the details of the operations, which are:

- `write`: Write the given entry into this JavaSpaces service.
- `read`: Read an entry from this JavaSpaces service that matches the given template.
- `take`: Read an entry from this JavaSpaces service that matches the given template, removing it from this space.
- `notify`: Notify a specified object when entries that match the given template are written into this JavaSpaces service.

As used in this document, the term "operation" refers to a single invocation of a method; for example, two different `take` operations may have different templates.

JS.2.1 Entries

The types `Entry` and `UnusableEntryException` that are used in this specification are from the package `net.jini.core.entry` and are described in detail in *The Jini Technology Core Platform Specification,* "Entry". In the terminology of that specification `write` is a store operation; `read` and `take` are combination search and fetch operations; and `notify` sets up repeated search operations as entries are written to the space.

JS.2.2 net.jini.space.JavaSpace

All operations are invoked on an object that implements the JavaSpace interface. For example, the following code fragment would write an entry of type AttrEntry into the JavaSpaces service referred to by the identifier space:

```
JavaSpace space = getSpace();
AttrEntry e = new AttrEntry();
e.name = "Duke";
e.value = new GIFImage("dukeWave.gif");
space.write(e, null, 60 * 60 * 1000);// one hour
// lease is ignored -- one hour will be enough
```

The JavaSpace interface is:

```
package net.jini.space;

import java.rmi.*;
import net.jini.core.event.*;
import net.jini.core.transaction.*;
import net.jini.core.lease.*;

public interface JavaSpace {
    Lease write(Entry e, Transaction txn, long lease)
        throws RemoteException, TransactionException;
    public final long NO_WAIT = 0; // don't wait at all
    Entry read(Entry tmpl, Transaction txn, long timeout)
        throws TransactionException, UnusableEntryException,
               RemoteException, InterruptedException;
    Entry readIfExists(Entry tmpl, Transaction txn,
                       long timeout)
        throws TransactionException, UnusableEntryException,
               RemoteException, InterruptedException;
    Entry take(Entry tmpl, Transaction txn, long timeout)
        throws TransactionException, UnusableEntryException,
               RemoteException, InterruptedException;
    Entry takeIfExists(Entry tmpl, Transaction txn,
                       long timeout)
        throws TransactionException, UnusableEntryException,
               RemoteException, InterruptedException;
    EventRegistration notify(Entry tmpl, Transaction txn,
              RemoteEventListener listener, long lease,
```

```
                 MarshalledObject handback)
            throws RemoteException, TransactionException;
        Entry snapshot(Entry e) throws RemoteException;
    }
```

The Transaction and TransactionException types in the above signatures are imported from net.jini.core.transaction. The Lease type is imported from net.jini.core.lease. The RemoteEventListener and EventRegistration types are imported from net.jini.core.event.

In all methods that have the parameter, txn may be null, which means that no Transaction object is managing the operation (see Section JS.3, "Transactions").

The JavaSpace interface is not a remote interface. Each implementation of a JavaSpaces service exports proxy objects that implement the JavaSpace interface locally on the client, talking to the actual JavaSpaces service through an implementation-specific interface. An implementation of any JavaSpace method may communicate with a remote JavaSpaces service to accomplish its goal; hence, each method throws RemoteException to allow for possible failures. Unless noted otherwise in this specification, when you invoke JavaSpace methods you should expect RemoteExceptions on method calls in the same cases in which you would expect them for methods invoked directly on an RMI remote reference. For example, invoking snapshot might require talking to the remote JavaSpaces server, and so might get a RemoteException if the server crashes during the operation.

The details of each JavaSpace method are given in the sections that follow.

JS.2.2.1 InternalSpaceException

The exception InternalSpaceException may be thrown by a JavaSpaces service that encounters an inconsistency in its own internal state or is unable to process a request because of internal limitations (such as storage space being exhausted). This exception is a subclass of RuntimeException. The exception has two constructors: one that takes a String description and another that takes a String and a nested exception; both constructors simply invoke the RuntimeException constructor that takes a String argument.

```
package net.jini.space;

public class InternalSpaceException extends RuntimeException {
    public final Throwable nestedException;
    public InternalSpaceException(String msg) {...}
    public InternalSpaceException(String msg, Throwable e) {...}
```

```
        public printStackTrace() {...}
        public printStackTrace(PrintStream out) {...}
        public printStackTrace(PrintWriter out) {...}
    }
```

The `nestedException` field is the one passed to the second constructor, or `null` if the first constructor was used. The overridden `printStackTrace` methods print out the stack trace of the exception and, if `nestedException` is not `null`, print out that stack trace as well.

JS.2.3 write

A `write` places a copy of an entry into the given JavaSpaces service. The `Entry` passed to the `write` is not affected by the operation. Each `write` operation places a new entry into the specified space, even if the same `Entry` object is used in more than one `write`.

Each `write` invocation returns a `Lease` object that is `lease` milliseconds long. If the requested time is longer than the space is willing to grant, you will get a lease with a reduced time. When the lease expires, the entry is removed from the space. You will get an `IllegalArgumentException` if the lease time requested is negative.

If a `write` returns without throwing an exception, that entry is committed to the space, possibly within a transaction (see Section JS.3, "Transactions"). If a `RemoteException` is thrown, the `write` may or may not have been successful. If any other exception is thrown, the entry was not written into the space.

Writing an entry into a space might generate notifications to registered objects (see Section JS.2.7, "`notify`").

JS.2.4 readIfExists and read

The two forms of the `read` request search the JavaSpaces service for an entry that matches the template provided as an `Entry`. If a match is found, a reference to a copy of the matching entry is returned. If no match is found, `null` is returned. Passing a `null` reference for the template will match any entry.

Any matching entry can be returned. Successive read requests with the same template in the same JavaSpaces service may or may not return equivalent objects, even if no intervening modifications have been made to the space. Each invocation of read may return a new object even if the same entry is matched in the JavaSpaces service.

A `readIfExists` request will return a matching entry, or `null` if there is currently no matching entry in the space. If the only possible matches for the template have conflicting locks from one or more other transactions, the `timeout` value specifies how long the client is willing to wait for interfering transactions to settle before returning a value. If at the end of that time no value can be returned that would not interfere with transactional state, `null` is returned. Note that, due to the remote nature of JavaSpaces services, `read` and `readIfExists` may throw a `RemoteException` if the network or server fails prior to the timeout expiration

A `read` request acts like a `readIfExists` except that it will wait until a matching entry is found or until transactions settle, whichever is longer, up to the timeout period.

In both read methods, a timeout of `NO_WAIT` means to return immediately, with no waiting, which is equivalent to using a zero timeout. An `IllegalArgumentException` will be thrown if a negative timeout value is used.

JS.2.5 takeIfExists and take

The `take` requests perform exactly like the corresponding `read` requests (see Section JS.2.4, "`readIfExists` and `read`"), except that the matching entry is removed from the space. Two `take` operations will never return copies of the same entry, although if two equivalent entries were in the JavaSpaces service the two `take` operations could return equivalent entries.

If a `take` returns a non-`null` value, the entry has been removed from the space, possibly within a transaction (see Section JS.3, "Transactions"). This modifies the claims to once-only retrieval: A `take` is considered to be successful only if all enclosing transactions commit successfully. If a `RemoteException` is thrown, the `take` may or may not have been successful. If an `UnusableEntryException` is thrown, the `take` removed the unusable entry from the space; the contents of the exception are as described in *The Jini Technology Core Platform Specification,* "Entry". If any other exception is thrown, the `take` did not occur, and no entry was removed from the space.

With a `RemoteException`, an entry can be removed from a space and yet never returned to the client that performed the `take`, thus losing the entry in between. In circumstances in which this is unacceptable, the `take` can be wrapped inside a transaction that is committed by the client when it has the requested entry in hand.

JS.2.6 snapshot

The process of serializing an entry for transmission to a JavaSpaces service will be identical if the same entry is used twice. This is most likely to be an issue with templates that are used repeatedly to search for entries with `read` or `take`. The client-side implementations of `read` and `take` cannot reasonably avoid this duplicated effort, since they have no efficient way of checking whether the same template is being used without intervening modification.

The `snapshot` method gives the JavaSpaces service implementor a way to reduce the impact of repeated use of the same entry. Invoking `snapshot` with an `Entry` will return another `Entry` object that contains a *snapshot* of the original entry. Using the returned snapshot entry is equivalent to using the unmodified original entry in all operations on the same JavaSpaces service. Modifications to the original entry will not affect the snapshot. You can `snapshot` a `null` template; `snapshot` may or may not return `null` given a `null` template.

The entry returned from `snapshot` will be guaranteed equivalent to the original unmodified object only when used with the space. Using the snapshot with any other JavaSpaces service will generate an `IllegalArgumentException` unless the other space can use it because of knowledge about the JavaSpaces service that generated the snapshot. The snapshot will be a different object from the original, may or may not have the same hash code, and `equals` may or may not return `true` when invoked with the original object, even if the original object is unmodified.

A snapshot is guaranteed to work only within the virtual machine in which it was generated. If a snapshot is passed to another virtual machine (for example, in a parameter of an RMI call), using it—even with the same JavaSpaces service—may generate an `IllegalArgumentException`.

We expect that an implementation of JavaSpaces technology will return a specialized `Entry` object that represents a pre-serialized version of the object, either in the object itself or as an identifier for the entry that has been cached on the server. Although the client may cache the snapshot on the server, it must guarantee that the snapshot returned to the client code is always valid. The implementation may not throw any exception that indicates that the snapshot has become invalid because it has been evicted from a cache. An implementation that uses a server-side cache must therefore guarantee that the snapshot is valid as long as it is reachable (not garbage) in the client, such as by storing enough information in the client to be able to re-insert the snapshot into the server-side cache.

No other method returns a snapshot. Specifically, the return values of the `read` and `take` methods are not snapshots and are usable with any implementation of JavaSpaces technology.

JS.2.7 notify

A notify request registers interest in future incoming entries to the JavaSpaces service that match the specified template. Matching is done as it is for read. The notify method is a particular registration method under *The Jini Technology Core Platform Specification,* "Distributed Events". When matching entries are written, the specified RemoteEventListener will eventually be notified. When you invoke notify you provide an upper bound on the lease time, which is how long you want the registration to be remembered by the JavaSpaces service. The service decides the actual time for the lease. You will get an IllegalArgumentException if the lease time requested is not Lease.ANY and is negative. The lease time is expressed in the standard millisecond units, although actual lease times will usually be of much larger granularity. A lease time of Lease.FOREVER is a request for an indefinite lease; if the service chooses not to grant an indefinite lease, it will return a bounded (non-zero) lease.

Each notify returns a net.jini.core.event.EventRegistration object. When an object is written that matches the template supplied in the notify invocation, the listener's notify method is eventually invoked, with a RemoteEvent object whose evID is the value returned by the EventRegistration object's getEventID method, fromWhom being the JavaSpaces service, seqNo being a monotonically increasing number, and whose getRegistrationObject being that passed as the handback parameter to notify. If you get a notification with a sequence number of 103 and the EventRegID object's current sequence number is 100, there will have been three matching entries written since you invoked notify. You may or may not have received notification of the previous entries due to network failures or the space compressing multiple matching entry events into a single call.

If the transaction parameter is null, the listener will be notified when matching entries are written either under a null transaction or when a transaction commits. If an entry is written under a transaction and then taken under that same transaction before the transaction is committed, listeners registered under a null transaction will not be notified of that entry.

If the transaction parameter is not null, the listener will be notified of matching entries written under that transaction in addition to the notifications it would receive under a null transaction. A notify made with a non-null transaction is implicitly dropped when the transaction completes.

The request specified by a successful notify is as persistent as the entries of the space. They will be remembered as long as an untaken entry would be, until the lease expires, or until any governing transaction completes, whichever is shorter.

The service will make a "best effort" attempt to deliver notifications. The service will retry at most until the notification request's lease expires. Notifications may be delivered in any order.

See *The Jini Technology Core Platform Specification,* "Distributed Events" for details on the event types.

JS.2.8 Operation Ordering

Operations on a space are unordered. The only view of operation order can be a thread's view of the order of the operations it performs. A view of inter-thread order can be imposed only by cooperating threads that use an application-specific protocol to prevent two or more operations being in progress at a single time on a single JavaSpaces service. Such means are outside the purview of this specification.

For example, given two threads *T* and *U*, if *T* performs a `write` operation and *U* performs a `read` with a template that would match the written entry, the `read` may not find the written entry even if the `write` returns before the `read`. Only if *T* and *U* cooperate to ensure that the `write` returns before the `read` commences would the `read` be ensured the opportunity to find the entry written by *T* (although it still might not do so because of an intervening `take` from a third entity).

JS.2.9 Serialized Form

Class	`serialVersionUID`	Serialized Fields
`InternalSpaceException`	-4167507833172939849L	*all public fields*

JS.3 Transactions

THE JavaSpaces API uses the package `net.jini.core.transaction` to provide basic atomic transactions that group multiple operations across multiple JavaSpaces services into a bundle that acts as a single atomic operation. JavaSpaces services are actors in these transactions; the client can be an actor as well, as can any remote object that implements the appropriate interfaces.

Transactions wrap together multiple operations. Either all modifications within the transactions will be applied or none will, whether the transaction spans one or more operations and/or one or more JavaSpaces services.

The transaction semantics described here conform to the default transaction semantics defined in *The Jini Technology Core Platform Specification,* "Transaction".

JS.3.1 Operations under Transactions

Any `read`, `write`, or `take` operations that have a `null` transaction act as if they were in a committed transaction that contained exactly that operation. For example, a `take` with a `null` transaction parameter performs as if a transaction was created, the `take` performed under that transaction, and then the transaction was committed. Any `notify` operations with a `null` transaction apply to `write` operations that are committed to the entire space.

Transactions affect operations in the following ways:

- `write`: An entry that is written is not visible outside its transaction until the transaction successfully commits. If the entry is taken within the transaction, the entry will never be visible outside the transaction and will not be added to the space when the transaction commits. Specifically, the entry will not generate notifications to listeners that are not registered under the writing transaction. Entries written under a transaction that aborts are discarded.
- `read`: A `read` may match any entry written under that transaction or in the entire space. A JavaSpaces service is not required to prefer matching entries

written inside the transaction to those in the entire space. When read, an entry is added to the set of entries read by the provided transaction. Such an entry may be read in any other transaction to which the entry is visible, but cannot be taken in another transaction.

- `take`: A `take` matches like a `read` with the same template. When taken, an entry is added to the set of entries taken by the provided transaction. Such an entry may not be read or taken by any other transaction.
- `notify`: A `notify` performed under a `null` transaction applies to `write` operations that are committed to the entire space. A `notify` performed under a non-`null` transaction additionally provides notification of writes performed within that transaction. When a transaction completes, any registrations under that transaction are implicitly dropped. When a transaction commits, any entries that were written under the transaction (and not taken) will cause appropriate notifications for registrations that were made under a `null` transaction.

If a transaction aborts while an operation is in progress under that transaction, the operation will terminate with a `TransactionException`. Any statement made in this chapter about `read` or `take` apply equally to `readIfExists` or `takeIfExists`, respectively.

JS.3.2 Transactions and ACID Properties

The ACID properties traditionally offered by database transactions are preserved in transactions on JavaSpaces systems. The ACID properties are:

- *Atomicity:* All the operations grouped under a transaction occur or none of them do.
- *Consistency:* The completion of a transaction must leave the system in a consistent state. Consistency includes issues known only to humans, such as that an employee should always have a manager. The enforcement of consistency is outside of the transaction—a transaction is a tool to allow consistency guarantees, and not itself a guarantor of consistency.
- *Isolation:* Ongoing transactions should not affect each other. Any observer should be able to see other transactions executing in some sequential order (although different observers may see different orders).
- *Durability:* The results of a transaction should be as persistent as the entity on which the transaction commits.

The timeout values in `read` and `take` allow a client to trade full isolation for liveness. For example, if a `read` request has only one matching entry and that entry is currently locked in a `take` from another transaction, `read` would block indefinitely if the client wanted to preserve isolation. Since completing the transaction could take an indefinite amount of time, a client may choose instead to put an upper bound on how long it is willing to wait for such isolation guarantees, and instead proceed to either abort its own transaction or ask the user whether to continue or whatever else is appropriate for the client.

Persistence is not a required property of JavaSpaces technology implementations. A transient implementation that does not preserve its contents between system crashes is a proper implementation of the `JavaSpace` interface's contract, and may be quite useful. If you choose to perform operations on such a space, your transactions will guarantee as much durability as the JavaSpaces service allows for all its data, which is all that any transaction system can guarantee.

JS.4 Further Reading

JS.4.1 Linda Systems

1. "How to Write Parallel Programs: A Guide to the Perplexed," Nicholas Carriero and David Gelernter, *ACM Computing Surveys*, Sept., 1989.
2. "Generative Communication in Linda," David Gelernter, *ACM Transactions on Programming Languages and Systems,* Vol. 7, No. 1, pp. 80–112 (January 1985).
3. "Persistent Linda: Linda + Transactions + Query Processing," Brian G. Anderson and Dennis Shasha, *Proceedings of the 13th Symposium on Fault-Tolerant Distributed Systems,* 1994.
4. "Adding Fault-tolerant Transaction Processing to LINDA," Scott R. Cannon and David Dunn, *Software—Practice and Experience,* Vol. 24(5), pp. 449–446 (May 1994).
5. *ActorSpaces: An Open Distributed Programming Paradigm,* Gul Agha, Christian J. Callsen, University of Illinois at Urbana-Champaign, UILU-ENG-92-1846.

JS.4.2 The Java Platform

6. *The Java Programming Language, Third Edition,* Ken Arnold, James Gosling, and David Holmes, Addison Wesley, 2000.
7. *The Java Language Specification,* James Gosling, Bill Joy, and Guy Steele, Addison Wesley, 1996.
8. *The Java Virtual Machine Specification, Second Edition,* Tim Lindholm and Frank Yellin, Addison Wesley, 1999.
9. *The Java Class Libraries, Second Edition,* Patrick Chan, Rosanna Lee, and Doug Kramer, Addison Wesley, 1998.

JS.4.3 Distributed Computing

10. *Distributed Systems,* Sape Mullender, Addison Wesley, 1993.

11. *Distributed Systems: Concepts and Design,* George Coulouris, Jean Dollimore, and Tim Kindberg, Addison Wesley, 1998.

12. *Distributed Algorithms,* Nancy A. Lynch, Morgan Kaufmann Publishers, 1997.

Helper
JavaSpaces
Service
(JS)

THE JINI DEVICE ARCHITECTURE SPECIFICATION describes several ways in which a device (or any other service) can participate in a Jini system without the device (or service) being a general Jini service. The possibilities listed are not exhaustive—there could be other interesting models as well. The main point to pay attention to here is that any service can participate in the Jini architecture, even with no modification of the service provider itself. This "device architecture" applies equally well to legacy systems and other software services.

JINI™

DA

Jini Device Architecture Specification

Device Architecture (DA)

DA.1 Introduction

THE Jini technology infrastructure is built around the model of clients looking for services. The notion of a service encompasses access to information, computation, software that performs particular tasks, and in general any component that helps a user accomplish some goal. Services can themselves be clients of other services, and can be grouped together to provide higher-level functionality.

The Jini architecture requires a service to be defined in terms of a data type for the Java programming language that can then be implemented in different ways by different instances of the service. A service can be a member of many different types, allowing a single service instance to provide a variety of functionality to clients. This is a standard practice in object-oriented software. However, the distributed nature of a system of Jini technology-enabled services and/or devices allows data types for the Java programming language to be implemented in a combination of software and hardware in a way that is unique.

The core of the idea that enables this implementation flexibility is quite simple. Services are defined via an interface, and the implementation of a proxy supporting the interface that will be seen by the service client will be uploaded into the lookup service by the service provider. This implementation is then downloaded into the client as part of that client finding the service. This service-specific implementation needs to be code written in the Java programming language (to ensure portability). However, since this code comes from the actual instance of the service being used, it can know in great detail the specifics of the particular service implementation for which it is the proxy. Not only can the code that is downloaded know about the software used to implement the service, the code can know specifics about the hardware on which the service resides. In the limit case of this, the hardware could be all that there is to the service, and the downloaded software could act as a network-level device driver, taking method calls in the Java programming language from the client and generating specific, hard-coded requests to the hardware on the other end of the network wire.

This approach to services requires that there be a piece of code written in the Java programming language that can be downloaded by the client of the service and some hardware that ultimately runs the service. Between these two points, however, there are a number of options concerning the software structure, hardware structure, and location of components that can be chosen by the service provider. These options allow trade-offs to be made in the functionality provided and the cost of the underlying hardware.

In what follows we begin by discussing in more detail the requirements placed on a service to be part of a system of Jini technology-enabled services and/or devices. We then discuss some examples of combinations of software and hardware that can be used to implement Jini technology-capable services once the specialized implementations in hardware begin to play a role.

DA.1.1 Requirements from the Jini Lookup Service

The actual offering of a service places very few requirements on the entity that makes the offer; indeed, it is possible to implement a device using a Jini technology-enabled software services that offers a service in such a way that the code written in the Java programming language that is downloaded by the client transmits bit patterns to the hardware that are directly interpreted. In such cases the amount of intelligence needed for a a Jini technology-enabled device is minimal. The code written in the Java programming language could talk directly to the device controller in much the same way that the device would be talked to if it were on the local computer's bus (with, of course, some modifications for dealing with the network-centric aspects of the communication).

Unfortunately, providing a service is only part of what is needed to be a Jini technology-enabled service. To be part of a system of Jini technology-enabled services and/or devices, a service must also be able to participate in the Jini discovery protocol and register itself into the local Jini lookup service. This is how a service makes itself known to the djinn, and how the service is accessed by other members of the djinn.

These two requirements are intimately connected. The major goal of the Jini discovery protocol is to allow a device or service to obtain a Java Remote Method Invocation (RMI) reference to the local Jini lookup service. Once this reference has been obtained, the service needs to register itself in that Jini lookup service, allowing other participants in the djinn to find and use the service.

The interface to the Jini lookup service is a full RMI interface, and the implementation of that service uses all of the mechanisms of RMI, including the distributed garbage collection and the dynamic downloading of code. As such, there is an implicit assumption that the service that holds a reference to the Jini lookup service lives inside a full Java virtual machine (JVM) that is at least capable of running the full RMI system.

This assumption is most evident if we consider the possibility of alternate implementations of the Jini lookup service, which might support remote interfaces beyond that specified by the Jini lookup service itself (currently the interface `net.jini.core.lookup.ServiceRegistrar`). Such an implementation would have a different RMI proxy than the current implementation, which would be downloaded if the device had a full JVM and RMI runtime. Devices without a full JVM and RMI runtime would need a different way of dealing with such implementations of the service.

In addition to the need to download the stub code for the Jini lookup service, registering with the service requires the creation of an object of type `net.jini.core.lookup.ServiceItem`, which is itself made up of a set of objects in the Java programming language. Maintenance of these entries in the Jini lookup service can require the creation of other objects in the Java programming language of the type `net.jini.core.entry.Entry`. All of these objects are most easily constructed by using a running JVM.

Finally, registrations with the Jini lookup service are leased, with the lease that is returned requiring renewal for the service to continue to be shown in the lookup service. The specification of the lookup service does not include a specification of the lease object that is returned by a registration. All that is specified is an interface written in the Java programming language that must be supported by the (local) object that is returned as the lease. Thus the design of the Jini lookup service requires that the code that implements the class that in turn implements the `net.jini.core.lease.Lease` interface be downloaded into the service that registers so that the lease can be renewed.

DA.2 Basic Device Architecture Examples

Now we will look at three different approaches for implementing a a Jini technology-enabled service in hardware. Each of the approaches will look the same to a client of the service. Each approach takes a different route to interacting with the Jini lookup service and in providing an interface written in the Java programming language to clients of that service. In each case, a different trade-off was made between the complexity of the device, the flexibility of the device, and the directness of the communication between the client wanting to use the service and the device that implements the service.

All but the first of the examples make use of *interposition*, that is, the ability of a service to add a proxy between itself and the client of the service. The service can use this proxy as an agent to the Jini technology infrastructure, off-loading from the service some of the work needed to join the federation of Jini technology-enabled services and/or devices.

The examples given in this chapter are not the only options available to the service designer who wishes to produce a service that includes a hardware component. Rather, the examples are meant to show some samples of the range of implementation possibilities that are open to such designers. In effect, this document is meant to show that, within the overall Jini architecture, there is no single Jini device architecture. Instead, the device space is freed up, allowing different services to have hardware implementations with different price, performance, functionality, and flexibility design points.

DA.2.1 Devices with Resident Java Virtual Machines

An obvious design for a device that can become part of a federation of Jini technology-enabled services and/or devices is one that includes the computing power, memory, and nonvolatile store necessary to have a full JVM and those parts of the Java application environment necessary to support the Jini technology infrastructure (in particular, those parts needed for code loading, RMI, and any required security). This would make the device into a specialized computing entity, with part of the device dedicated to the parts of the Java platform required by the Jini architecture. On this approach, the hardware implementation is abstracted behind a device-local software abstraction, which in turn is abstracted behind the proxy code used by the client to contact the service. This sort of architecture is shown in Figure AR.2.1.

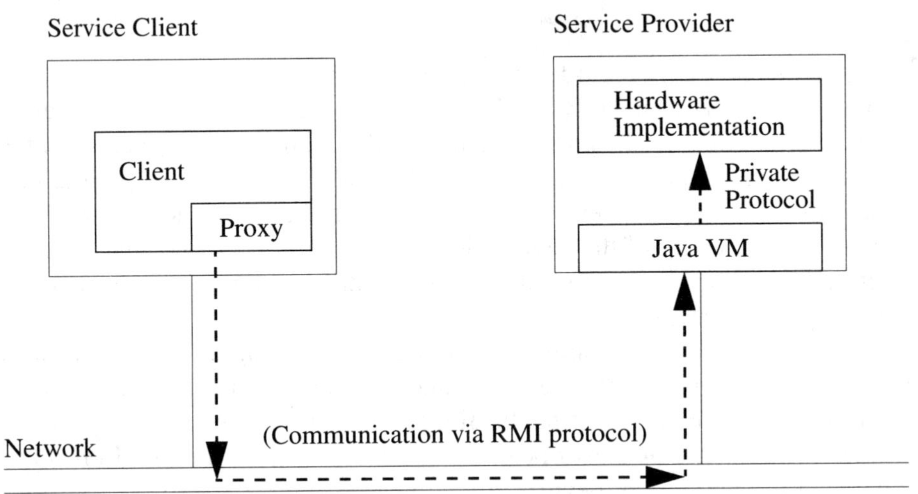

FIGURE DA.2.1: ***A Full Jini Technology-Enabled Device***

Such a device would be able to make full use of Jini technology and Java technology, uploading code that is used to communicate with the device and downloading code that might be needed for the service provided by the device. Such a device can make use of the native RMI protocol for communication over the network, and has a loose tie between the communication protocol and the particular software protocol governing the running of the device itself. On this approach, the device becomes a specialized network appliance offering a particular service (or set of services) via an embedded Java platform.

In effect, this approach uses a hardware implementation for the local implementation of an RMI server, isolating the hardware behind two levels of indirection. The first is that provided by the local proxy code that is uploaded into the Jini lookup service and then downloaded into the client of the service. Additionally, the local JVM and code written in the Java programming language resident on the service device allow mediation between the client proxy and the hardware itself.

A device that took this approach could easily have multiple services implemented on the device in a way that was mediated by the JVM on the device. Further, such a device could be evolved with no impact on the client or the network protocol used between the client and the service, since any change in the hardware would be seen only by the JVM and any server-side code that talked directly to the hardware.

While simple and flexible, this approach does add some cost to the device. In particular, the device would need to have a microprocessor capable of running the JVM, some memory in which to create and store classes, and some nonvolatile store (either disk or NVRAM) from which to load the JVM and Java class files. All of these are in addition to the hardware needed to implement the a Jini technology-enabled service that the device provides. This extra hardware will increase the cost of producing the device.

Meeting these requirements does not call for a hosted version of the JVM or a full version of the Java platform running on the device. The JVM could run on any form of microkernel or directly on the hardware of the device. Further, there are large parts of the Java platform that would not be required for the minimal device—such things as the graphics and user interface classes, which form a significant chunk of the current release, would not be needed. Other parts of that release could also be dropped, allowing a stripped-down Java platform to suffice for Jini technology-enabled devices. It would be worthwhile to determine the exact definition of such a subset of the Java platform and size that component; it would be something close to the definition of embedded Java technology with the additional classes needed to support RMI.

What is important for this kind of approach is for the device to be able to download any code written in the Java programming language (although whether that code is run could depend on the local security manager), utilize the RMI communication system, and handle the requirements of a general virtual machine. By presenting a standard JVM, the device gets full membership in a federation of Jini technology-enabled services and/or devices and complete flexibility in the ways in which the machine communicates between the proxy it provides other members of the federation and the device itself.

DA.2.2 Devices Using Specialized Virtual Machines

We can lower the barrier to entry for a device manufacturer if that manufacturer is willing to give up some of the flexibility provided by the Jini architecture. This can be done by allowing the device to become part of a Jini system of services and/or devices using Jini technology with a specialized virtual machine that is tuned to allow only those operations needed by the Jini discovery protocol and Jini lookup service.

To do this, the device manufacturer would need to implement the interfaces to the Jini discovery and Jini lookup service in the device itself, include specialized knowledge of the kind of leases that are handed out by the Jini lookup service and be able to renew those leases directly, and have sufficient functionality to download and use the stubs for these services. This is a particular set of functionalities that is considerably smaller than that required by the whole of the JVM, and should be possible to implement in much less code. For example, such a JVM would not need to contain a security manager, a code verifier, or a number of the other components that are required for a full JVM.

Such a device would contain a JVM specialized for the application environment for Jini technology, allowing the Jini discovery and Jini lookup services to be accessed and leases of a particular sort to be renewed. This would limit the flexibility of such a device, as the device would not be able to have software changes made over time to the protocol used by the proxy for the device. The specialized knowledge of the kind of lease that is handed out by the lookup service would also tie such a device to a particular implementation of the lookup service. However, this penalty in serviceability might not outweigh the simplicity of the overall device.

DA.2.3 Clustering Devices with a Shared Virtual Machine (Physical Option)

A third approach uses a full JVM, but amortizes the cost of the JVM (both software and hardware) over a number of different devices. In this approach, a group of devices each uses a physically co-located JVM as an intermediate layer between the device and the system of services and/or devices using Jini technology. The device loads code written in the Java programming language into this local virtual machine, allowing that local machine to interact with the device, and then delegates to the local JVM the requirements of interacting with the Jini lookup service, Jini discovery, and Jini leasing.

This approach is very much like the first one discussed in this section, except that the JVM used by the devices is shared. It is still a full JVM, allowing the downloading of code and complete Java platform functionality. However, the most likely implementation of such a device would allow multiple (and perhaps different) kinds of physical devices to be plugged into the overall device to get the sharing of the Java application environment.

Such a device might best be thought of as a "Jini device bay." This bay could provide power, a network connection, and a processor running a JVM and appropriate parts of the Java platform. Physical devices that are used to provide a particular kind of Jini technology-enabled service could be plugged into the device bay and announce themselves to the bay in whatever way the two decided was appropriate. This could be using a proprietary protocol (allowing a device manufacturer to produce both the basic device or devices and the device bay) or some other industry standard, local-device identification scheme.

As part of the local announcement, a new device would tell the device bay where to find the code written in the Java programming language that is needed by a client of the service, and (possibly) where to find code that would allow the device bay to interact with the device. This allows devices to carry their own "drivers," both for the local machine and at the network level.

Upon detection of the new local device, the Jini technology-enabled device bay would register the services provided by the new device (previously known by the device bay) with the Jini lookup service. It would be the role of the device bay to renew leases on the Jini lookup service entries, and to detect removal of any of the devices for which it was acting as proxy. The device bay would provide the Jini lookup service with the code handed to it by the device so that service clients could download that code.

The client of the device service would believe that it is talking to the device registered in the Jini lookup service, but would actually be talking to the device bay. The device bay would act as a dispatcher to the particular device for which it was acting as a proxy, along with any translation of protocol between the network protocol used by the service proxy and the protocol used between the device bay and the actual device. Graphically, the architecture of such an approach is shown in Figure AR.2.2.

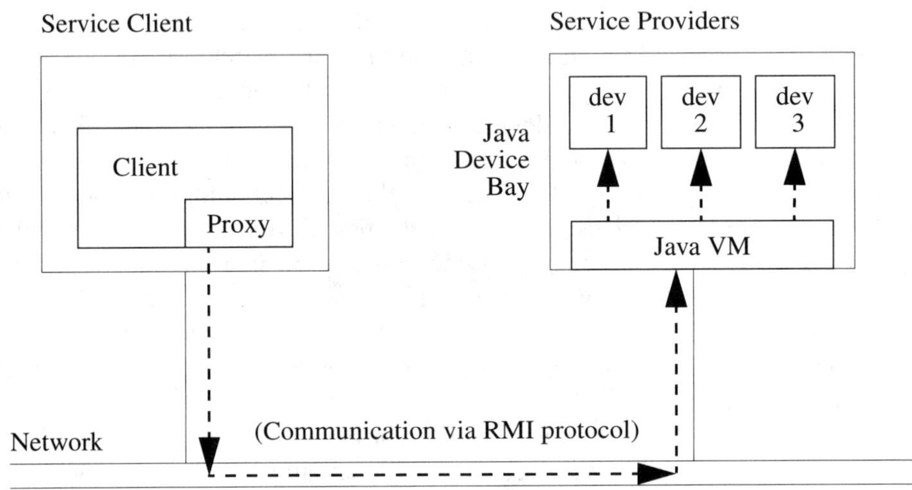

FIGURE DA.2.2: ***Clustering Multiple Devices With a Single Proxy in One Device***

The savings for the device manufacturer in this case comes from the ability of multiple physical devices to share a device bay, which contains the intelligence, memory, and perhaps other components (such as the power supply). By sharing these resources among multiple devices, the extra cost and engineering needed to interact with a system of services and/or devices using Jini technology can be amortized over a large number of devices.

The cost of this approach to the device manufacturers is that the protocol between the device acting as the Jini technology-enabled device bay and the devices that are placed in that bay must be defined in advance and cannot change over time. Because there is no way of introducing dynamic behavior in the particular devices, the pairing of device and Jini technology-enabled device bay must be controlled and known beforehand.

It should be noted that the Jini technology-enabled device bay itself is a Jini technology-enabled device, which can be thought of as providing services to those devices housed within it. As such, it could be a revenue item in its own right. Variations in the implementation could be provided to support various internal announcement protocols (device bay, jetsend, etc.) or hardware buses (including network-like buses such as firewire).

DA.2.4 Clustering Devices with a Shared Virtual Machine (Network Option)

A variation on the device bay approach uses the network rather than a physical enclosure and backplane. On this alternative, a proxy for the JVM used by the various service devices would exist on the network. Service devices could be added to the network, discover the existence of such a proxy device, and register with that proxy. Such a registration could include the code written in the Java programming language needed by a client of the device (either directly or as a URL to use to obtain the code) and code needed by the proxy to communicate with the service device.

When a service device registers with such a network proxy, the proxy device would register with the Jini lookup service on behalf of the service device, thus allowing the service device to become a part of the federation of Jini technology-enabled services and/or devices. Requests to the new service would go first to the proxy for that device, which could then forward the requests (after appropriate protocol translation) to the particular service device. In addition, the proxy could handle the Jini technology-specific tasks such as renewing leases for the service. This alternative is shown in Figure AR.2.3.

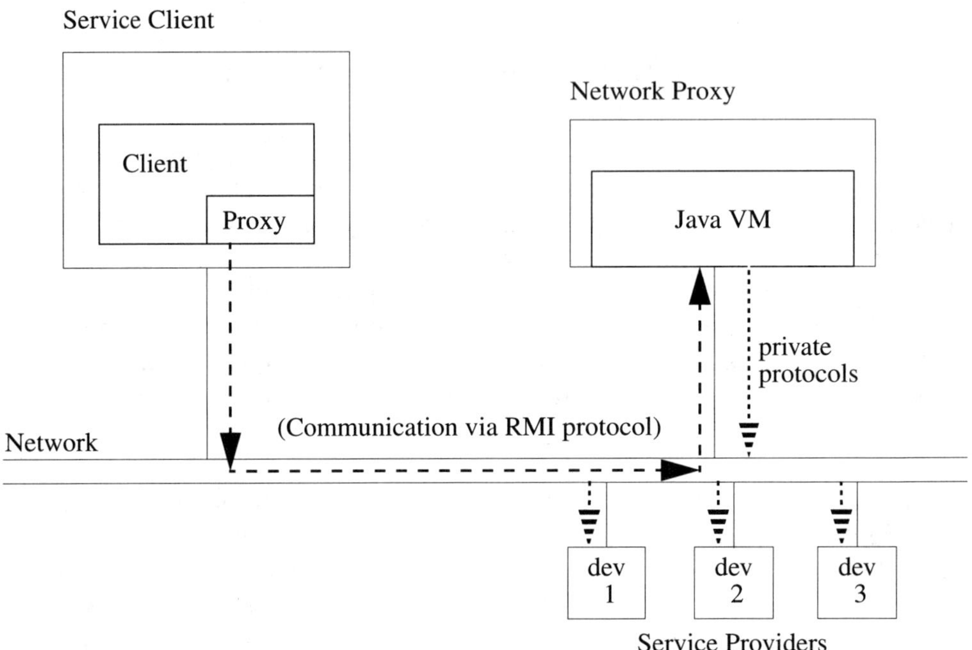

FIGURE DA.2.3: ***Clustering Devices With a Jini Technology-Enabled Proxy on the Network***

This alternative requires somewhat more hardware for the individual device, as it requires each service device using such a proxy to be able to be placed on the network and have its own power supply and network connection. However, the devices would not need individual CPUs, memory, or persistent store; all of that would be provided by the networked proxy for the Jini technology-enabled device.

Devices using this option would need to have a protocol parallel to the Jini discovery protocol between the individual service devices and the network proxy for those devices. This could be a specialized code on the network, known in advance, that the devices can use to identify themselves to the network proxy. This will have to be particular to the device and the proxy for that device. However, once this protocol has been decided upon, no other intelligence needs to be built into the device. All of the intelligence can be built into the network proxy, perhaps uploaded into the proxy by the service device (which could easily carry code written in the Java programming language, even though it cannot execute that code). The protocol the network proxy uses to talk to the devices for which it is a proxy also needs to be statically defined in advance and cannot be changed. However, it can be any protocol the particular device needs.

In this approach, the individual devices will be more complex than they would be in the Jini technology-enabled device bay approach. However, the number of devices that can be served by a network available proxy is not limited by the physical constraints of the proxy device. Nor is there any requirement that the devices and the proxy device be co-located, which is a requirement on the physical clustering scheme.

This is also the approach that can be taken to build "gateways" between the Jini technology-enabled devices and other network-managed devices. Such devices, which already speak a particular protocol, can be spliced into the system of Jini technology-enabled services and/or devices by providing a network proxy that speaks the Jini technology protocols on behalf of such devices, and the existing specialized protocol to such devices. This is the approach that can be used to add consumer electronic devices, factory controls, or home environment controls into the system of Jini technology-enabled services and/or devices.

DA.2.5 Jini Technology-Enabled Software Services over the Internet Inter-Operability Protocol

A final method for connecting devices or services that are not purely based on Java technology software into a system of Jini technology-enabled services and/or devices, centers on using the Object Management Group (OMG)'s Internet Inter-Operability Protocol (IIOP). This protocol defines a standard for data transmission that will be supported by a subset of RMI.

This approach relies on the ability of a device to read an IIOP stream directly, either because the device includes an implementation of a Common Object Request Broker Architecture (CORBA) Object Request Broker (ORB) or because the device knows what IIOP streams to expect and can interpret streams of these known forms directly.

This approach requires the Jini lookup service to supply implementations of its interfaces over both the native RMI protocol and the IIOP protocol. This is supported by RMI over IIOP as long as the interfaces conform to any subsetting requirements established by the OMG. At the present time it appears that the Jini lookup service interfaces are in conformance with the RMI over IIOP subset.

Devices that contain a CORBA ORB could directly interact with the Jini lookup service using the IIOP protocol. The fact that the Jini lookup service generated this protocol via RMI would be transparent to the service itself, and the fact that the service was using a method other than RMI to reply to the Jini lookup service (to renew leases, for example) would be transparent to the Jini lookup service. Current differences between the RMI programming model and the CORBA programming model would need to be dealt with by the device itself; for example, the device would not be able to download the implementation of the stub for the Jini lookup service, and would need an implementation of the `Lease` class used by the Jini lookup service.

Devices that do not include a CORBA ORB could directly interpret the IIOP stream and attempt to interact with the Jini lookup service. This approach requires very little software support on the side of the device (since the bitstream from the wire is being directly interpreted). However, it is an approach that will work only with known versions of the Jini lookup service that exports known implementations of a lease. Any alteration of either the lease implementation or the protocol used by the Jini lookup service, even those that would be invisible to other clients of the service, would make it impossible for the device directly interpreting the IIOP protocol to interact with the new version of the service. Hence this alternative, while lowest in cost with respect to the hardware and software needed by the device, is also the least reliable in the face of implementations that can change over time or that are open to alternate implementations.

PART 3
Supplemental Material

Jini Technology Glossary

activation

The process of transforming a passive object into an active object. Activation requires that an object be associated with a Java virtual machine (JVM)[1], which may entail loading the class for that object into a JVM and the object restoring its persistent state (if any). (*Java Remote Method Invocation Specification,* Section 7.1.1)

activatable service

A Jini service that has a back end implemented with the ability to activate and deactivate. (*Introduction to Helper Utilities and Services,* Section US.2.9, "Activation") (See also *Jini technology-enabled service (Jini service)*)

activation descriptor

A class instance that holds an activatable object's group identifier (specifies the JVM in which it is activated), the object's class name, a location from where to load the object's class code, and object-specific initialization data in marshalled form. (*Java Remote Method Invocation Specification,* Section 7.2)

activation group

The entity that receives a request to activate an object in the JVM and returns the activated object back to the activator. (*Java Remote Method Invocation Specification,* Section 7.2) A separate JVM is spawned for each activation group. (Section 7.4.7)

---

[1] The terms "Java virtual machine" or "JVM" mean a virtual machine for the Java platform.

activator

The entity that supervises activation by being both (1) a database of information that maps activation identifiers to the information necessary to activate an object and (2) a manager of JVMs, that starts up a JVM (when necessary) and forwards requests for object activation (along with the necessary information) to the correct activation group inside a remote JVM. There is usually only one activator per host, started by `rmid`. (*Java Remote Method Invocation Specification,* Section 7.2)

active discard

The process of an entity itself discarding a reference to lookup service. (*Jini Discovery Utilities Specification*, Section DU.2.5.1, "The Semantics") (See also *passive discard*)

active object

A remote object that is instantiated and exported in a JVM on some system.(*Java Remote Method Invocation Specification,* Section 7.1.1)

ancestor transaction

A transaction that is the parent of a specific nested transaction (a transaction in which all its operations are contained, or executed, from within another transaction), or the parent of such a parent, recursively (a grandparent, a great-grandparent, and so on). (*The Jini Technology Core Platform Specification,* Section TX.3.5 "Semantics")

attribute set

A strongly-typed set of fields in a service item (represented by a `net.jini.core.entry.Entry`) that describes the service or provide secondary interfaces to the service. A single attribute is a public field of an `Entry`. (*The Jini Technology Core Platform Specification,* Section LU.1.2 "Attributes")

back end, back-end server

See *remote object.*

bad invocation exception

An exception that implies that any retries of the *same* method with the *same* arguments that are expected to return the *same* value will also fail. For a list of exceptions that fall into this category, please see *Introduction to Helper Utilities and Services*, Section US.2.6, "What Exceptions Imply about Future Behavior".

bad object exception
An exception that implies that any further operations on that object will also fail. For a list of exceptions that fall into this category, please see *Introduction to Helper Utilities and Services*, Section US.2.6, "What Exceptions Imply about Future Behavior".

changed event
An event related to the discarded event that notifies the entity of changes in the contents of the member groups of one or more of the lookup services in the managed set. (*Jini Discovery Utilities Specification*, Section DU.2.6.2, "The `DiscoveryChangeListener` Interface") (See also *discarded event*)

channel
The abstraction for a conduit between two address spaces in the RMI transport layer. As such, it is responsible for managing connections between the local address space and the remote address space for which it is a channel. (*Java Remote Method Invocation Specification,* Section 3.5)

client-like entity
A term that may be used, in general, when referring to Jini clients and Jini services that act as clients. (*Introduction to Helper Utilities and Services*, Section US.2.2, "Jini Clients and Services") (See also *Jini technology-enabled client (Jini client)*)

connection
The stream-oriented (*Java Remote Method Invocation Specification,* Section 3.4) abstraction for transferring data (performing input/output) in the RMI transport layer. (Section 3.5)

deactivation
The process of transforming an active object into a passive object. (*Introduction to Helper Utilities and Services*, Section US.2.9, "Activation") (See also *activation*)

definite exception
An exception that is indicative of a permanent failure. (*Jini Lease Utilities Specification*, Section LM.4, "The Semantics")

desired expiration

A value (in milliseconds) that represents when the client would like the lease to expire. (*Jini Lease Utilities Specification*, Section LM.4, "The Semantics") (See also *remaining desired duration*)

desired expiration reached event

An event that is generated when a lease's desired expiration is reached, which signals that the lease renewal manager has removed a lease from the managed set without an explicit request by the client. (*Jini Lease Utilities Specification*, Section LM.4, "The Semantics") (See also *renewal failure event*)

discarded lookup service

A lookup service is said to be discarded when an already discovered lookup service is removed from the managed set of lookup services. (*Introduction to Helper Utilities and Services*, Section US.2.8, "Discarding a Lookup Service") (See also *discarded event*)

discarded event

An event sent to notify all of an entity's discovery listeners, whenever a lookup service is discarded by a utility employed by the entity. (*Introduction to Helper Utilities and Services*, Section US.2.8, "Discarding a Lookup Service") (See also *changed event*) (See also *active discard*) (See also *discovered event*)

discovered event

An event sent from a lookup discovery service to a registered listener upon discovery of a lookup service. (*Jini Lookup Discovery Service) (See also discarded event*)

discovering entity

One or more cooperating objects in the Java programming language on the same host that are about to start, or are in the process of, obtaining references to one or more Jini lookup services. (*The Jini Technology Core Platform Specification,* Section DJ.1.1 "Terminology") (See also *group discovery*)

discovery utility

An object that implements one or more of the discovery management interfaces to perform and manage the entity's discovery duties. (*Jini Discovery*

Utilities Specification, Section DU.2.6.1, "The `DiscoveryListener` Interface")

distributed event adapter

An event adapter in which the event generator and the event listener instances may exist in different virtual machines, possibly on different hosts. The distributed event adapter is at least a remote event listener, but may also be a remote event generator (see *local event, remote event*). (*The Jini Technology Core Platform Specification,* Section EV.3 "Third-Party Objects")

djinn *(pronounced "gin")*

The group of devices, resources, and users joined by the Jini technology infrastructure. (*The Jini Technology Core Platform Specification,* Section LU.1.1 "The Lookup Service Model") This group, controlled by the Jini technology infrastructure, agrees on basic notions of trust, administration, identification, and policy.

dynamic class loading

The capability of the Java application environment to download files (classes for the Java platform, audio, and images) from an HTTP server at runtime if they are not already available to the client JVM. Dynamic class loading may be used by the RMI runtime to download: stub classes; skeleton classes; classes that are passed as subtypes of declared method parameters; and classes that are passed as subtypes of declared method return types. (See *dynamic stub loading*)

dynamic stub loading

A subset of dynamic class loading, used to support client-side stubs that implement the same set of remote interfaces as a remote object itself. (*Java Remote Method Invocation Specification,* Section 3.1)

endpoint

The abstraction used to denote an address space or JVM in the RMI transport layer. In the implementation an endpoint can be mapped to its transport. That is, given an endpoint, a specific transport instance can be obtained. (*Java Remote Method Invocation Specification,* Section 3.5)

entity

A general term that may refer to a discovering entity, a joining entity, a client-like entity, a service, or some combination of these types of entities. It should be clear from the context what type of entity is being discussed. (*Introduction to Helper Utilities and Services*, Section US.2.2, "Jini Clients and Services")

entry

A typed group of object references, expressed as a class for the Java platform that implements the `net.jini.core.entry.Entry` interface. Entry fields must all be references to `Serializable` objects. (*Jini Entry Specification,* Section EN.1) An entry is a class that contains a number of public fields of object type. Services provide concrete values for each of these fields; each value acts as an attribute. Entries thus provide aggregation of attributes into sets; a service may provide several entries when registering itself in the lookup service, which means that attributes on each service are provided in a set of sets. (*Jini Lookup Attribute Schema Specification*, Section LS.1, "Introduction" LS.1)

event

Something that happens in an object, corresponding to some change in the abstract state of the object. Events are abstract occurrences that are not directly observed outside of an object, and may not correspond to a change in the actual state of the object that advertises the ability to register interest in the event. (*The Jini Technology Core Platform Specification,* Section EV.2.1 "Entities Involved")

event generator

An object that has some kinds of abstract state changes that might be of interest to other objects and allows other objects to register interest in those events. This is the object that will generate notifications when events of this kind occur, sending those notifications to the event listeners that were indicated as targets in the calls that registered interest in that kind of event. (*The Jini Technology Core Platform Specification,* Section EV.2.1 "Entities Involved")

event listener

An object that has an interest in being notified when a particular event type occurs. The event listener (1) implements the appropriate interface and (2) registers with an event generator. (See also *remote event listener*)

event mailbox service

A helper service that can be employed by entities to store event notifications on their behalf. When an entity registers with the event mailbox service, that service will collect events intended for the registered entity until the entity initiates delivery of the events. (*Introduction to Helper Utilities and Services*, Section US.4.3, "The Event Mailbox Service") (See also *notification mailbox*)

export, -ed, -ing

The process of making a remote object available to accept incoming calls on a specific port. An object can be exported (1) if the object is a subclass of `java.rmi.server.UnicastRemoteObject`, through the constructor; (2) if the object is a subclass of `java.rmi.activation.Activatable`, through the constructor; (3) by passing the object to the static `exportObject` method of `UnicastRemoteObject` (*Java Remote Method Invocation Specification,* Section 5.3.1); or (4) by passing the object to the static `exportObject` method of `Activatable`. (Section 7.3)

faulting remote reference

A faulting remote reference to a remote object, sometimes referred to as a fault block, "faults in" the active object's reference upon the first method invocation to the object executed via the faulting reference. Each faulting reference, contained in the remote object's stub, holds both a persistent object handle (a `java.rmi.activation.ActivationID`) and a transient remote reference to the target remote object. (*Java Remote Method Invocation Specification,* Section 7.1.2)

filter

A non-remote object that defines additional matching criteria that will be applied when searching for the entity's services of interest. This filtering facility is particularly useful to entities that wish to extend the capabilities of the standard template-matching scheme. (*Introduction to Helper Utilities and Services*, Section US.3.4.1, "The `ServiceDiscoveryManager` Helper Utility")

front end, front-end proxy

See *proxy*.

group

An organization of lookup services into a logical set. A lookup service is said to be a member of (or to belong to) a group, while a service may advertise itself to one or more groups. (*Introduction to Helper Utilities and Services*, Section US.2.1, "Terms Related to Discovery and Join") (See also *locator*)

group discovery

The discovery process in which a discovering entity employs the multicast discovery protocol to discover lookup services that are members of one or more groups belonging to a set of groups. (*Introduction to Helper Utilities and Services*, Section US.2.1, "Terms Related to Discovery and Join") (See also *locator discovery*)

helper service

A Jini service that can be registered with any number of lookup services and whose methods can execute on remote hosts. In general, a helper service should be of use to more than one type of entity participating in the Jini application environment and should provide a significant reduction in development complexity for developers of such entities. A helper service consists of an interface or set of interfaces and associated implementation that encapsulates behavior that is either required or highly desirable in services that adhere to the Jini technology programming model. (*Introduction to Helper Utilities and Services*, Section US.2.3, "Helper Service")

helper utility

Helper utilities are programming components that can be used during the construction of Jini services and/or clients. Helper utilities are *not* remote and do not register with a lookup service. Helper utilities are instantiated locally by entities wishing to employ them. (*Introduction to Helper Utilities and Services*, Section US.2.4, "Helper Utility")

host

A hardware device that may be connected to one or more networks. An individual host may house one or more JVMs. (*The Jini Technology Core Platform Specification,* Section DJ.1.2 "Host Requirements")

idempotent

A method that is idempotent can be called multiple times and produce only the result as though it were called only a single time.

indefinite exception

An exception that implies no new assertions can be made about the probability of success of any future invocation of that method, regardless of the arguments used or return value expected, nor can any new assertions be made about the probability of success of any *other* operation on the same object. For a list of exceptions that fall into this category, please see the

Introduction to Helper Utilities and Services, Section US.2.6, "What Exceptions Imply about Future Behavior".

inferior transaction
The inverse of the transactional ancestor relationship: Transaction T_i is an inferior of T_a if and only if T_a is an ancestor of T_i. (*The Jini Technology Core Platform Specification,* Section TX.3.5 "Semantics")

Jini technology-enabled client (Jini client)
A discovering entity that can retrieve a service (or a remote reference to a service) registered with a discovered lookup service, and invoke the methods of the service to meet the entity's requirements. An entity that acts only as a client never registers with (requests residency in) a lookup service. (*Introduction to Helper Utilities and Services*, Section US.2.2, "Jini Clients and Services")

Jini technology-enabled service (Jini service)
Both a discovering and a joining entity containing methods that may be of use to some other Jini client or service, and that registers with discovered lookup services to provide access to those methods. Note that a Jini service can also act as a Jini client. (*Introduction to Helper Utilities and Services*, Section US.2.2, "Jini Clients and Services") (See also *back end, back-end server*)

joining entity
One or more cooperating objects in the Java programming language on the same host that have just received a reference to the Jini lookup service and are in the process of obtaining services from, and possibly exporting services to, a djinn. (*The Jini Technology Core Platform Specification,* Section DJ.1.1 "Terminology")

join protocol
The protocol that allows entities to start communicating usefully with services in a djinn, through the Jini lookup service. (*The Jini Technology Core Platform Specification,* Section DJ.1.3 "Protocol Overview")

JVM
A common abbreviation for "Java virtual machine."

lazy activation

The activation mechanism that the RMI system uses, which defers activating an object until a client's first use (that is, the first method invocation). Lazy activation of remote objects is implemented using a *faulting remote reference*. (*Java Remote Method Invocation Specification,* Section 7.1.1)

lease

A grant to use a resource, offered by one object in a distributed system, to another object in that system for a certain period of time. The duration of the lease is negotiated by the two objects when access to the resource is first requested and given. (*The Jini Technology Core Platform Specification,* Section LE.1 "Introduction") A lease ensures that the lease holder will have access to some resource for a period of time. During the period of a lease, a lease can be cancelled by the entity holding the lease. A lease holder can request that a lease be renewed, or a lease can expire. (*The Jini Technology Core Platform Specification,* Section LE.2.1 "Characteristics of a Lease") In the current implementation of RMI, a lease term is not negotiated, as described by *The Jini Technology Core Platform Specification,* "Distributed Leasing"; the lease term is mandated by the implementation server. Another difference is that in RMI there is no notion of explicit lease cancellation; lease cancellation is implicit when a remote reference becomes unreferenced by a specific client. (*Java Remote Method Invocation Specification,* Section 9.1)

lease grantor

The object granting access to a resource for some period of time. (*The Jini Technology Core Platform Specification,* Section LE.2 "Basic Leasing Interfaces")

lease holder

The object asking for the leased resource. (*The Jini Technology Core Platform Specification,* Section LE.2 "Basic Leasing Interfaces")

lease renewal set

Clients of the renewal service organize the leases they wish to have renewed into lease renewal sets. A method is provided by the `LeaseRenewalService` interface to create these sets. These sets are then populated by methods on the sets themselves. (*Jini Lease Renewal Service Specification*, Section LR.2, "The Interface")

lease renewal service

A helper service that can be employed by both Jini clients and services to perform all lease renewal duties on their behalf. (*Introduction to Helper Utilities and Services*, Section US.4.2, "The Lease Renewal Service")

live reference

The concrete representation of a remote object reference (in the RMI transport layer), which consists of an endpoint and an object identifier. Given a live reference for a remote object, a transport can use the endpoint to set up a connection to the address space in which the remote object resides. On the server side, the transport uses the object identifier to look up the target of the remote call. (*Java Remote Method Invocation Specification,* Section 3.5)

local event

An event object that is fired from an event generator to an event listener, where both the generator and the listener instances exist in the same virtual machine. (See *event, remote event*) (*The Jini Technology Core Platform Specification,* Section EV.1.1 "Distributed Events and Notifications")

locator

An instance of the class `net.jini.core.discovery.LookupLocator`, as defined in the *Jini Discovery and Join Specification.* (*Introduction to Helper Utilities and Services*, Section US.2.1, "Terms Related to Discovery and Join") (See also *group*)

locator discovery

The discovery process in which a discovering entity employs the unicast discovery protocol to discover specific lookup services, each corresponding to an element in a set of locators. (*Introduction to Helper Utilities and Services*, Section US.2.1, "Terms Related to Discovery and Join") (See also *group discovery*)

lookup discovery protocol

The protocol that governs the acquisition of a reference to one (or more) instances of the Jini lookup service. (*The Jini Technology Core Platform Specification,* Section DJ.1.3 "Protocol Overview")

lookup discovery service

A helper service that employs the Jini discovery protocols to find lookup services in which an entity has expressed interest and to notify the entity when a previously unavailable lookup service becomes available. (*Introduction to Helper Utilities and Services*, Section US.4.1, "The Lookup Discovery Service")

lookup service

The Jini lookup service provides a central registry of service items, representing services, available within the djinn. This Jini lookup service is a primary means for programs to find services within the djinn, and is the foundation for providing user interfaces through which users and administrators can discover and interact with services in the djinn. (*The Jini Technology Core Platform Specification,* Section LU.1 "Introduction")

lookup service group

See *group.*

manged set

When the general term *managed set* is used, it should be clear from the context whether groups, locators, lookup services, or leases are being discussed. (*Introduction to Helper Utilities and Services*, Section US.2.5, "Managed Sets")

managed set of groups

Each element of the managed set of groups is a name of a group whose members are lookup services that the entity wishes to be discovered through group discovery. The managed set of groups is typically represented as a `String` array or a `Collection` of `String` elements. (*Introduction to Helper Utilities and Services*, Section US.2.5, "Managed Sets")

managed set of locators

Each element of the managed set of locators corresponds to a specific lookup service that the entity wishes to be discovered via locator discovery. Typically, this set is represented as an array of locators or some other `Collection` type whose elements are locators. (*Introduction to Helper Utilities and Services*, Section US.2.5, "Managed Sets")

managed set of lookup services

References to discovered lookup services. (*Introduction to Helper Utilities and Services*, Section US.2.5, "Managed Sets")

marshal streams

Input/output streams, used by the RMI remote reference layer, that employ *object serialization* to enable objects in the Java programming language to be transmitted between address spaces. (*Java Remote Method Invocation Specification,* Section 3.3)

marshalled object

A container for an object that allows that object to be passed as a parameter in an RMI call, but postpones deserializing the object at the receiver until the application explicitly requests the object (via a call to the container object). The *serializable* object contained in the `MarshalledObject` is serialized and deserialized (when requested) with the same semantics as parameters passed in RMI calls (*Java Remote Method Invocation Specification,* Section 7.4.8), which means that any remote object in the `MarshalledObject` is represented by a serialized instance of its stub. The object contained by the `MarshalledObject` may be a remote object, a non-remote object, or an entire graph of remote and non-remote objects.

member group

See *group.*

multicast radius

Roughly the number of hops beyond which neither multicast requests from the entity, nor multicast announcements from the lookup service, will propagate. (*Jini Discovery Utilities Specification*, Section DU.2.6.2, "The `DiscoveryChangeListener` Interface")

notification filter

A distributed event adapter that can be used by either the generator of a notification or the recipient to intercept notification calls, do processing on those calls, and act in accord with that processing (perhaps forwarding the notification, or even generating new notifications). (*The Jini Technology Core Platform Specification,* Section EV.3.2 "Notification Filters") This filter may be used as an event multiplexer or demultiplexer.

notification mailbox

A distributed event adapter that can be used to store the notifications sent to an object until such time as the object for which the notifications were intended desires delivery. Such delivery can be in a single batch, with the mailbox storing any notifications received after the request for delivery until the next request is given. Alternatively, a notification mailbox can be viewed as a faucet, with notifications turned on (delivering any that have arrived since the notifications were last turned off) and then delivering any subsequent notifications to an object immediately, until told to hold the notifications. (*The Jini Technology Core Platform Specification,* Section EV.3.3 "Notification Mailboxes") (See also *event mailbox service*)

object serialization

The system that allows a bytestream to be produced from a graph of objects, sent out of the Java application environment (either saved to disk or sent over the network) and then used to re-create an equivalent set of objects with the same state. (*Java Object Serialization Specification,* Section A.1) In RMI, objects transmitted using the object serialization system are passed by copy to the remote address space, unless they are remote objects, in which case they are passed by reference. (*Java Remote Method Invocation Specification,* Section 3.3)

passive discard

The process of a utility discarding a lookup service on behalf of an entity. (See also *discarded event*)

passive object

A remote object that is not yet instantiated (or exported) in a JVM but that can be brought into an active state (See also *active object*). (*Java Remote Method Invocation Specification,* Section 7.1.1)

proxy

An intermediary object through which one entity (the client) may request the invocation of the methods provided by another entity (the remote object or the service). A proxy can be one of a number of different forms: a smart proxy, the stub of a remote object, or a strictly local proxy. (*Introduction to Helper Utilities and Services*, Section US.2.8.6, "Remote Objects, Stubs, and Proxies")

pure transaction

A transaction in which all access to shared mutable state is performed under transactional control. (*The Jini Technology Core Platform Specification,* Section TX.3.5 "Semantics")

reference list

A reference list for a remote object is a list of client JVMs that hold references to that remote object. A client JVM is removed from the object's reference list when that client no longer references that object. (*Java Remote Method Invocation Specification,* Section 9.1)

registrar

See *lookup service*.

registry

A remote object that maps names to remote objects. The `java.rmi.Naming` class provides methods for lookup, binding, rebinding, unbinding, and listing the contents of a registry. A registry can be used in a virtual machine shared with other server classes or in a standalone JVM. The methods of `java.rmi.registry.LocateRegistry` may be used to get a registry operating on a particular host or host and port. (*Java Remote Method Invocation Specification,* Section 6)

remaining desired duration

The desired expiration (of a lease) less the current time. (*Jini Lease Utilities Specification*, Section LM.4, "The Semantics") (See also *desired expiration*)

remote event

An object that is passed from an event generator to a remote event listener to indicate that an event of a particular kind has occurred. The remote event generator and the remote event listener instances may exist in different virtual machines, possibly on different hosts. (*The Jini Technology Core Platform Specification,* Section EV.2.1 "Entities Involved")

remote event generator

An object that is the source of remote events.

remote event listener

An object implementing the `net.jini.core.event.RemoteEventListener` interface, which is interested in the occurrence of remote events in some other object. The major function of a remote event listener is to receive notifications of the occurrence of a remote event in some other object (or set of objects). (*The Jini Technology Core Platform Specification,* Section EV.2.1 "Entities Involved")

remote interface

An interface written in the Java programming language that extends `java.rmi.Remote`, either directly or indirectly, which declares the methods of a remote object. (*Java Remote Method Invocation Specification,* Section 2.1)

remote method invocation (RMI)

The action of invoking a method of a remote interface on a remote object. (*Java Remote Method Invocation Specification,* Section 2.1)

remote object

An object whose methods can be invoked from another JVM, potentially on a different host. An object of this type is described by one or more *remote interfaces.* (*Java Remote Method Invocation Specification,* Section 2.1)

remote reference layer (RRL)

The layer of the RMI system that supports remote reference behavior (such as invocation to a single object or to a replicated object) and carries out the semantics of method invocation. This layer sits between the RMI stub/skeleton layer and the RMI transport layer. Also handled by the remote reference layer are the reference semantics for the server. (*Java Remote Method Invocation Specification,* Section 3.2)

remote server

See *remote object.*

renewal failure event

An event that is generated when the renewal manager finds that it can't renew a lease, which signals that the lease renewal manager has removed a lease from the managed set without an explicit request by the client. (*Jini Lease Utilities Specification*, Section LM.4, "The Semantics") (See also *desired expiration reached event*)

rmic

The stub and skeleton compiler used to generate the appropriate stubs and skeletons for a specific remote object implementation. The compiler is invoked with the package-qualified class name of the remote object class. The class must previously have been compiled successfully. (*Java Remote Method Invocation Specification,* Section 5.11)

rmid

The activation system daemon which provides an implementation of the activation system interfaces. To use activation, you must first run `rmid`. This is the JVM with which activation descriptions get registered. (*Java Remote Method Invocation Specification,* Section 7.2)

rmiregistry

The RMI system command that provides an implementation of the `java.rmi.registry.Registry` interface. The rmiregistry, run on a remote host, can be accessed by calling methods of the `java.rmi.Naming` class.

semantic transaction

A *transaction* with specific, associated semantics, as opposed to the protocol specified by the `TransactionManager` interface, which does not specify transaction semantics. A semantic transaction is contractual in nature and implies a particular usage pattern, so if a program operates within the constraints of the contract, assumptions can be safely made about the transaction's behavior or state. (*The Jini Technology Core Platform Specification,* Section TX.1.1 "Model and Terms")

serializable

Any data type that may be read from `java.io.ObjectInputStreams` and written to `java.io.ObjectOutputStreams`. This includes primitive data types in the Java programming language, remote objects in the Java programming language, and non-remote objects in the Java programming language that implement the `java.io.Serializable` interface. (*Java Remote Method Invocation Specification,* Section 2.6)

service

Something that can be used by a person, a program, or another service. It can be computational, storage, a communication channel to another user, or another service. Examples of services include devices such as printers, displays, disks, software (such as applications or utilities), information (such as databases and files), and users of the system. Services will appear programmatically as objects in the Java programming language, perhaps made up of other objects in the Java programming language. A service will have an interface, which defines the operations that can be requested of that service. The type of the service determines the interfaces that make up that service. (*The Jini Architecture Specification*, Section AR.2.1.1, "Services")

service items

Each service item represents an instance of a service available within the djinn. The item contains the stub (if the service is implemented as a remote object) or serialized object (if the service makes use of a local proxy) that programs use to access the service, and an extensible collection of attribute sets that describe the service or provide secondary interfaces to the service. A new service item is created in the Jini lookup service when a new service is added to the djinn. (*The Jini Technology Core Platform Specification,* Section LU.1.1 "The Lookup Service Model")

service registrar

A synonym for Jini lookup service. (See *lookup service*) (*The Jini Technology Core Platform Specification,* Section LU.2.5 "`ServiceRegistrar`")

skeleton

The server-side entity that reads parameters from incoming method requests and dispatches calls to the actual remote object implementation. Note that in the Java 2 Software Development Kit, Standard Edition, v1.2, skeleton functionality is now handled by the remote object stub, but skeletons may still be used for compatibility with earlier releases of the 1.1 Java Development Kit (JDK). (*Java Remote Method Invocation Specification,* Section 3.3)

smart proxy

A proxy that typically consists of a set of local methods and a set of one or more remote object references (stubs). Clients invoke one or more of the local methods to access the methods of the remote objects referenced in the smart proxy. (*Introduction to Helper Utilities and Services*, Section US.2.8.6, "Remote Objects, Stubs, and Proxies") (See also *proxy*)

store-and-forward agent

A distributed event adapter that enables the object generating a notification to hand the actual notification of those who have registered interest off to a separate object. This agent can implement various policies for reliability. (*The Jini Technology Core Platform Specification,* Section EV.3.1 "Store-and-Forward Agents")

strictly local proxy

A form of a proxy that consists of only local methods, each executing in the client's JVM. Unlike smart proxies, no remote invocations result when any method of a strictly local proxy is invoked. (See also *smart proxy*)

stub

The proxy for a remote object, which implements all the interfaces that are supported by the remote object implementation and forwards method invocations to the actual remote object instance. (*Java Remote Method Invocation Specification,* Section 3.3) The stub is an object local to the client that acts as the "representative" of the remote object. From the point of view of the client, the stub *is* the remote object. When the client invokes a method on the local stub, communication with the remote object occurs, resulting in the execution of the corresponding method in the remote object's JVM.

stub/skeleton layer

The layer of the RMI system that aids in carrying out method invocation. The stub/skeleton layer is the interface between the application layer and the rest of the RMI system. (*Java Remote Method Invocation Specification,* Section 3.3) This layer does not deal with specifics of any transport, but transmits data to the remote reference layer via the abstraction of *marshal streams*. This layer contains client-side stubs (proxies) and server-side skeletons. (Section 3.2)

template

An entry object that has some or all of its fields set to specified *values.* Templates may be used to find matching entries. A template will match an entry if and only if the template's non-`null` public fields match the entry's non-`null` public fields exactly. Remaining fields (those set to `null`) are not used in the matching process but are left as *wildcards*. (*The Jini Technology Core Platform Specification,* Section EN.1.5 "Templates and Matching")

transaction

In general, a transaction is a tool that allows a set of operations to be grouped in such a way as to make them all appear to either all succeed or all fail; further, the operations in the set appear from outside the transaction to occur simultaneously. In the Jini architecture, the concrete representation of a transaction is encapsulated in an object. (*The Jini Technology Core Platform Specification,* Section TX.1.1 "Model and Terms")

transaction client

An object that does either or both of the following: (1) requests that a transaction manager create a transaction, (2) invokes the `commit` or `abort` method to complete a transaction. A single transaction may have more than one client, since the object that completes a transaction may be different from the object that requested its creation. An object that is a transaction client may also be a transaction manager or participant. (*The Jini Technology Core Platform Specification,* Section TX.1.1 "Model and Terms")

transaction manager

An object that (1) services requests from transaction clients to create transactions and (2) tracks and manages the completion state of those transactions by implementing the `TransactionManager` interface. An object that is a transaction manager may also be a transaction client or participant. (*The Jini Technology Core Platform Specification,* Section TX.1.1 "Model and Terms")

transaction participant

An object that executes operations of a transaction and is able to interact with the manager to complete transactions properly. An object providing this service may implement the `TransactionParticipant` interface. An object that is a transaction participant may also be a transaction manager or client. (*The Jini Technology Core Platform Specification,* Section TX.1.1 "Model and Terms")

transport

The abstraction that manages channels in the RMI transport layer. Each channel is a virtual connection between two address spaces. Within a transport, only one channel exists per pair of address spaces (the local address space and a remote address space). Given an endpoint to a remote address space, a transport sets up a channel to that address space. The transport abstraction is also responsible for accepting calls on incoming connections to the address space, setting up a connection object for the call, and dispatching to higher layers in the system. (*Java Remote Method Invocation Specification,* Section 3.5)

transport layer

The layer of the RMI system that is responsible for connection set up, connection management, and remote object tracking. (*Java Remote Method Invocation Specification,* Section 3.2) The transport layer sits below the *remote reference layer.*

weak reference

When a remote object is not referenced by any client, the RMI runtime refers to it using a weak reference. The weak reference allows the JVM's garbage collector to discard the object if no other strong references to the object exist. The distributed garbage collection algorithm interacts with the local JVM's garbage collector in the usual ways by holding normal or weak references to objects; thus, a weak reference allows the RMI runtime to reference a remote object, but not prevent the object from being garbage collected. (*Java Remote Method Invocation Specification,* Section 3.7)

Note on Distributed Computing describes the environment for which the Jini architecture is designed—one of failure characteristics unknown in local computing. The Jini architecture takes these differences into account in its original design principles, which is one reason why the overall Jini architecture works.

This note was originally published as a Sun Microsystems Laboratories technical report (SMLI TR-94-29). The note has been reformatted for this book. Two observations have been added, marked as [A] and [B] in the text, and presented at the end of the note.

JINI™

APPENDIX A

A Note on Distributed Computing

Jim Waldo, Geoff Wyant, Ann Wollrath, and Sam Kendall

A.1 Introduction

MUCH of the current work in distributed, object-oriented systems is based on the assumption that objects form a single ontological class. This class consists of all entities that can be fully described by the specification of the set of interfaces supported by the object and the semantics of the operations in those interfaces. The class includes objects that share a single address space, objects that are in separate address spaces on the same machine, and objects that are in separate address spaces on different machines (with, perhaps, different architectures). On the view that all objects are essentially the same kind of entity, these differences in relative location are merely an aspect of the implementation of the object. Indeed, the location of an object may change over time, as an object migrates from one machine to another or the implementation of the object changes.

It is the thesis of this note that this unified view of objects is mistaken. There are fundamental differences between the interactions of distributed objects and the interactions of non-distributed objects. Further, work in distributed object-oriented systems that is based on a model that ignores or denies these differences is doomed to failure, and could easily lead to an industry-wide rejection of the notion of distributed object-based systems.

A.1.1 Terminology

In what follows, we will talk about local and distributed computing. By *local computing* (local object invocation, etc.), we mean programs that are confined to a single address space. In contrast, we will use the term *distributed computing* (remote object invocation, etc.) to refer to programs that make calls to other address spaces, possibly on another machine. In the case of distributed computing, nothing is known about the recipient of the call (other than that it supports a particular interface). For example, the client of such a distributed object does not know the hardware architecture on which the recipient of the call is running, or the language in which the recipient was implemented.

Given the above characterizations of "local" and "distributed" computing, the categories are not exhaustive. There is a middle ground, in which calls are made from one address space to another but in which some characteristics of the called object are known. An important class of this sort consists of calls from one address space to another on the same machine; we will discuss these later in the paper.

A.2 The Vision of Unified Objects

There is an overall vision of distributed object-oriented computing in which, from the programmer's point of view, there is no essential distinction between objects that share an address space and objects that are on two machines with different architectures located on different continents. While this view can most recently be seen in such works as the Object Management Group's Common Object Request Broker Architecture (CORBA)[1], it has a history that includes such research systems as Arjuna[2], Emerald[3], and Clouds[4].

In such systems, an object, whether local or remote, is defined in terms of a set of interfaces declared in an interface definition language. The implementation of the object is independent of the interface and hidden from other objects. While the underlying mechanisms used to make a method call may differ depending on the location of the object, those mechanisms are hidden from the programmer who writes exactly the same code for either type of call, and the system takes care of delivery.

This vision can be seen as an extension of the goal of remote procedure call (RPC) systems to the object-oriented paradigm. RPC systems attempt to make cross-address space function calls look (to the client programmer) like local function calls. Extending this to the object-oriented programming paradigm allows papering over not just the marshalling of parameters and the unmarshalling of results (as is done in RPC systems) but also the locating and connecting to the target objects. Given the isolation of an object's implementation from clients of the object, the use of objects for distributed computing seems natural. Whether a given object invocation is local or remote is a function of the implementation of the objects being used, and could possibly change from one method invocation to another on any given object.

Implicit in this vision is that the system will be "objects all the way down"; that is, that all current invocations or calls for system services will be eventually converted into calls that might be to an object residing on some other machine. There is a single paradigm of object use and communication used no matter what the location of the object might be.

In actual practice, of course, a local member function call and a cross-continent object invocation are not the same thing. The vision is that developers write their applications so that the objects within the application are joined using the same programmatic glue as objects between applications, but it does not require that the two kinds of glue be implemented the same way. What is needed is a variety of implementation techniques, ranging from same-address-space implementations like Microsoft's Object Linking and Embedding[5] to typical network RPC; different needs for speed, security, reliability, and object co-location can be met by using the right "glue" implementation.

Writing a distributed application in this model proceeds in three phases. The first phase is to write the application without worrying about where objects are located and how their communication is implemented. The developer will simply strive for the natural and correct interface between objects. The system will choose reasonable defaults for object location, and depending on how performance-critical the application is, it may be possible to alpha test it with no further work. Such an approach will enforce a desirable separation between the abstract architecture of the application and any needed performance tuning.

The second phase is to tune performance by "concretizing" object locations and communication methods. At this stage, it may be necessary to use as yet unavailable tools to allow analysis of the communication patterns between objects, but it is certainly conceivable that such tools could be produced. Also during the second phase, the right set of interfaces to export to various clients—such as other applications—can be chosen. There is obviously tremendous flexibility here for the application developer. This seems to be the sort of development scenario that is being advocated in systems like Fresco[6], which claim that the decision to make an object local or remote can be put off until after initial system implementation.

The final phase is to test with "real bullets" (e.g., networks being partitioned, machines going down). Interfaces between carefully selected objects can be beefed up as necessary to deal with these sorts of partial failures introduced by distribution by adding replication, transactions, or whatever else is needed. The exact set of these services can be determined only by experience that will be gained during the development of the system and the first applications that will work on the system.

A central part of the vision is that if an application is built using objects all the way down, in a proper object-oriented fashion, the right "fault points" at which to insert process or machine boundaries will emerge naturally. But if you initially make the wrong choices, they are very easy to change.

One conceptual justification for this vision is that whether a call is local or remote has no impact on the correctness of a program. If an object supports a particular interface, and the support of that interface is semantically correct, it makes no difference to the correctness of the program whether the operation is carried out within the same address space, on some other machine, or off-line by some other piece of equipment. Indeed, seeing location as a part of the implementation of an object and therefore as part of the state that an object hides from the outside world appears to be a natural extension of the object-oriented paradigm.

Such a system would enjoy many advantages. It would allow the task of software maintenance to be changed in a fundamental way. The granularity of change, and therefore of upgrade, could be changed from the level of the entire system (the current model) to the level of the individual object. As long as the interfaces between objects remain constant, the implementations of those objects can be altered at will. Remote services can be moved into an address space, and objects that share an address space can be split and moved to different machines, as local requirements and needs dictate. An object can be repaired and the repair installed without worry that the change will impact the other objects that make up the system. Indeed, this model appears to be the best way to get away from the "Big Wad of Software" model that currently is causing so much trouble.

This vision is centered around the following principles that may, at first, appear plausible:

- There is a single natural object-oriented design for a given application, regardless of the context in which that application will be deployed;
- Failure and performance issues are tied to the implementation of the components of an application, and consideration of these issues should be left out of an initial design; and
- The interface of an object is independent of the context in which that object is used.

Unfortunately, all of these principles are false. In what follows, we will show why these principles are mistaken, and why it is important to recognize the fundamental differences between distributed computing and local computing.

A.3 Déjà Vu All Over Again

For those of us either old enough to have experienced it or interested enough in the history of computing to have learned about it, the vision of unified objects is quite familiar. The desire to merge the programming and computational models of local and remote computing is not new.

Communications protocol development has tended to follow two paths. One path has emphasized integration with the current language model. The other path has emphasized solving the problems inherent in distributed computing. Both are necessary, and successful advances in distributed computing synthesize elements from both camps.

Historically, the language approach has been the less influential of the two camps. Every ten years (approximately), members of the language camp notice that the number of distributed applications is relatively small. They look at the programming interfaces and decide that the problem is that the programming model is not close enough to whatever programming model is currently in vogue (messages in the 1970s[7,8], procedure calls in the 1980s[9,10,11], and objects in the 1990s[1,2]). A furious bout of language and protocol design takes place and a new distributed computing paradigm is announced that is compliant with the latest programming model. After several years, the percentage of distributed applications is discovered not to have increased significantly, and the cycle begins anew.

A possible explanation for this cycle is that each round is an evolutionary stage for both the local and the distributed programming paradigm. The repetition of the pattern is a result of neither model being sufficient to encompass both activities at any previous stage. However, (this explanation continues) each iteration has brought us closer to a unification of the local and distributed computing models. The current iteration, based on the object-oriented approach to both local and distributed programming, will be the one that produces a single computational model that will suffice for both.

A less optimistic explanation of the failure of each attempt at unification holds that any such attempt will fail for the simple reason that programming distributed applications is not the same as programming non-distributed applications. Just making the communications paradigm the same as the language paradigm is insufficient to make programming distributed programs easier, because communicating between the parts of a distributed application is not the difficult part of that application.

The hard problems in distributed computing are not the problems of how to get things on and off the wire. The hard problems in distributed computing concern dealing with partial failure and the lack of a central resource manager. The hard problems in distributed computing concern insuring adequate performance and dealing with problems of concurrency. The hard problems have to do with differences in memory access paradigms between local and distributed entities. People attempting to write distributed applications quickly discover that they are spending all of their efforts in these areas and not on the communications protocol programming interface.

This is not to argue against pleasant programming interfaces. However, the law of diminishing returns comes into play rather quickly. Even with a perfect programming model of complete transparency between "fine-grained" language-level objects and "larger-grained" distributed objects, the number of distributed applications would not be noticeably larger if these other problems have not been addressed.

All of this suggests that there is interesting and profitable work to be done in distributed computing, but it needs to be done at a much higher-level than that of "fine-grained" object integration. Providing developers with tools that help manage the complexity of handling the problems of distributed application development as opposed to the generic application development is an area that has been poorly addressed.

A.4 Local and Distributed Computing

The major differences between local and distributed computing concern the areas of latency, memory access, partial failure, and concurrency.[1] The difference in latency is the most obvious, but in many ways is the least fundamental. The often overlooked differences concerning memory access, partial failure, and concurrency are far more difficult to explain away, and the differences concerning partial failure and concurrency make unifying the local and remote computing models impossible without making unacceptable compromises.

A.4.1 Latency

The most obvious difference between a local object invocation and the invocation of an operation on a remote (or possibly remote) object has to do with the latency of the two calls. The difference between the two is currently between four and five orders of magnitude, and given the relative rates at which processor speed and network latency speeds are changing, the difference in the future promises to be at best no better, and will likely be worse. It is this disparity in efficiency that is often seen as the essential difference between local and distributed computing.

---

[1] We are not the first to notice these differences; indeed, they are clearly stated in [12].

Ignoring the difference between the performance of local and remote invocations can lead to designs whose implementations are virtually assured of having performance problems because the design requires a large amount of communication between components that are in different address spaces and on different machines. Ignoring the difference in the time it takes to make a remote object invocation and the time it takes to make a local object invocation is to ignore one of the major design areas of an application. A properly designed application will require determining, by understanding the application being designed, what objects can be made remote and what objects must be clustered together.

The vision outlined earlier, however, has an answer to this objection. The answer is two-pronged. The first prong is to rely on the steadily increasing speed of the underlying hardware to make the difference in latency irrelevant. This, it is often argued, is what has happened to efficiency concerns having to do with everything from high level languages to virtual memory. Designing at the cutting edge has always required that the hardware catch up before the design is efficient enough for the real world. Arguments from efficiency seem to have gone out of style in software engineering, since in the past such concerns have always been answered by speed increases in the underlying hardware.

The second prong of the reply is to admit to the need for tools that will allow one to see what the pattern of communication is between the objects that make up an application. Once such tools are available, it will be a matter of tuning to bring objects that are in constant contact to the same address space, while moving those that are in relatively infrequent contact to wherever is most convenient. Since the vision allows all objects to communicate using the same underlying mechanism, such tuning will be possible by simply altering the implementation details (such as object location) of the relevant objects. However, it is important to get the application correct first, and after that one can worry about efficiency.

Whether or not it will ever become possible to mask the efficiency difference between a local object invocation and a distributed object invocation is not answerable *a priori.* Fully masking the distinction would require not only advances in the technology underlying remote object invocation, but would also require changes to the general programming model used by developers.

If the only difference between local and distributed object invocations was the difference in the amount of time it took to make the call, one could strive for a future in which the two kinds of calls would be conceptually indistinguishable. Whether the technology of distributed computing has moved far enough along to allow one to plan products based on such technology would be a matter of judgement, and rational people could disagree as to the wisdom of such an approach.

However, the difference in latency between the two kinds of calls is only the most obvious difference. Indeed, this difference is not really the fundamental difference between the two kinds of calls, and that even if it were possible to develop the technology of distributed calls to an extent that the difference in latency between the two sorts of calls was minimal, it would be unwise to construct a programming paradigm that treated the two calls as essentially similar. In fact, the difference in latency between local and remote calls, because it is so obvious, has been the only difference most see between the two, and has tended to mask the more irreconcilable differences.

A.4.2 Memory Access

A more fundamental (but still obvious) difference between local and remote computing concerns the access to memory in the two cases—specifically in the use of pointers. Simply put, pointers in a local address space are not valid in another (remote) address space. The system can paper over this difference, but for such an approach to be successful, the transparency must be complete. Two choices exist: either all memory access must be controlled by the underlying system, or the programmer must be aware of the different types of access—local and remote. There is no inbetween.

If the desire is to completely unify the programming model—to make remote accesses behave as if they were in fact local—the underlying mechanism must totally control all memory access. Providing distributed shared memory is one way of completely relieving the programmer from worrying about remote memory access (or the difference between local and remote). Using the object-oriented paradigm to the fullest, and requiring the programmer to build an application with "objects all the way down," (that is, only object references or values are passed as method arguments) is another way to eliminate the boundary between local and remote computing. The layer underneath can exploit this approach by marshalling and unmarshalling method arguments and return values for intra-address space transmission.

But adding a layer that allows the replacement of all pointers to objects with object references only *permits* the developer to adopt a unified model of object interaction. Such a unified model cannot be *enforced* unless one also removes the ability to get address-space-relative pointers from the language used by the developer. Such an approach erects a barrier to programmers who want to start writing distributed applications, in that it requires that those programmers learn a new style of programming which does not use address-space-relative pointers. In requiring that programmers learn such a language, moreover, one gives up the complete transparency between local and distributed computing.[A]

Even if one were to provide a language that did not allow obtaining address-space-relative pointers to objects (or returned an object reference whenever such a pointer was requested), one would need to provide an equivalent way of making cross-address space reference to entities other than objects. Most programmers use pointers as references for many different kinds of entities. These pointers must either be replaced with something that can be used in cross-address space calls or the programmer will need to be aware of the difference between such calls (which will either not allow pointers to such entities, or do something special with those pointers) and local calls. Again, while this could be done, it does violate the doctrine of complete unity between local and remote calls. Because of memory access constraints, the two *have* to differ.

The danger lies in promoting the myth that "remote access and local access are exactly the same" and not enforcing the myth. An underlying mechanism that does not unify all memory accesses while still promoting this myth is both misleading and prone to error. Programmers buying into the myth may believe that they do not have to change the way they think about programming. The programmer is therefore quite likely to make the mistake of using a pointer in the wrong context, producing incorrect results. "Remote is just like local," such programmers think, "so we have just one unified programming model." Seemingly, programmers need not change their style of programming. In an incomplete implementation of the underlying mechanism, or one that allows an implementation language that in turn allows direct access to local memory, the system does not take care of all memory accesses, and errors are bound to occur. These errors occur because the programmer is not aware of the difference between local and remote access and what is actually happening "under the covers."

The alternative is to explain the difference between local and remote access, making the programmer aware that remote address space access is very different from local access. Even if some of the pain is taken away by using an interface definition language like that specified in [1] and having it generate an intelligent language mapping for operation invocation on distributed objects, the programmer aware of the difference will not make the mistake of using pointers for cross-address space access. The programmer will know it is incorrect. By not masking the difference, the programmer is able to learn when to use one method of access and when to use the other.

Just as with latency, it is logically possible that the difference between local and remote memory access could be completely papered over and a single model of both presented to the programmer. When we turn to the problems introduced to distributed computing by partial failure and concurrency, however, it is not clear that such a unification is even conceptually possible.

A.5 Partial Failure and Concurrency

While unlikely, it is at least logically possible that the differences in latency and memory access between local computing and distributed computing could be masked. It is not clear that such a masking could be done in such a way that the local computing paradigm could be used to produce distributed applications, but it might still be possible to allow some new programming technique to be used for both activities. Such a masking does not even seem to be logically possible, however, in the case of partial failure and concurrency. These aspects appear to be different in kind in the case of distributed and local computing.[2]

Partial failure is a central reality of distributed computing. Both the local and the distributed world contain components that are subject to periodic failure. In the case of local computing, such failures are either total, affecting all of the entities that are working together in an application, or detectable by some central resource allocator (such as the operating system on the local machine).

This is not the case in distributed computing, where one component (machine, network link) can fail while the others continue. Not only is the failure of the distributed components independent, but there is no common agent that is able to determine what component has failed and inform the other components of that failure, no global state that can be examined that allows determination of exactly what error has occurred. In a distributed system, the failure of a network link is indistinguishable from the failure of a processor on the other side of that link.

These sorts of failures are not the same as mere exception raising or the inability to complete a task, which can occur in the case of local computing. This type of failure is caused when a machine crashes during the execution of an object invocation or a network link goes down, occurrences that cause the target object to simply disappear rather than return control to the caller. A central problem in distributed computing is insuring that the state of the whole system is consistent after such a failure; this is a problem that simply does not occur in local computing.

The reality of partial failure has a profound effect on how one designs interfaces and on the semantics of the operations in an interface. Partial failure requires that programs deal with indeterminacy. When a local component fails, it is possible to know the state of the system that caused the failure and the state of the system after the failure. No such determination can be made in the case of a distributed system. Instead, the interfaces that are used for the communication must be designed in such a way that it is possible for the objects to react in a consistent way to possible partial failures.

---

2 In fact, authors such as Schroeder[12] and Hadzilacos and Toueg[13] take partial failure and concurrency to be the defining problems of distributed computing.

Being robust in the face of partial failure requires some expression at the interface level. Merely improving the implementation of one component is not sufficient. The interfaces that connect the components must be able to state whenever possible the cause of failure, and there must be interfaces that allow reconstruction of a reasonable state when failure occurs and the cause cannot be determined.

If an object is co-resident in an address space with its caller, partial failure is not possible. A function may not complete normally, but it always completes. There is no indeterminism about how much of the computation completed. Partial completion can occur only as a result of circumstances that will cause the other components to fail.

The addition of partial failure as a possibility in the case of distributed computing does not mean that a single object model cannot be used for both distributed computing and local computing. The question is not "can you make remote method invocation look like local method invocation?" but rather "what is the price of making remote method invocation identical to local method invocation?" One of two paths must be chosen if one is going to have a unified model.

The first path is to treat all objects as if they were local and design all interfaces as if the objects calling them, and being called by them, were local. The result of choosing this path is that the resulting model, when used to produce distributed systems, is essentially indeterministic in the face of partial failure and consequently fragile and non-robust. This path essentially requires ignoring the extra failure modes of distributed computing. Since one can't get rid of those failures, the price of adopting the model is to require that such failures are unhandled and catastrophic.

The other path is to design all interfaces as if they were remote. That is, the semantics and operations are all designed to be deterministic in the face of failure, both total and partial. However, this introduces unnecessary guarantees and semantics for objects that are never intended to be used remotely. Like the approach to memory access that attempts to require that all access is through system-defined references instead of pointers, this approach must also either rely on the discipline of the programmers using the system or change the implementation language so that all of the forms of distributed indeterminacy are forced to be dealt with on all object invocations.

This approach would also defeat the overall purpose of unifying the object models. The real reason for attempting such a unification is to make distributed computing more like local computing and thus make distributed computing easier. This second approach to unifying the models makes local computing as complex as distributed computing. Rather than encouraging the production of distributed applications, such a model will discourage its own adoption by making all object-based computing more difficult.

Similar arguments hold for concurrency. Distributed objects by their nature must handle concurrent method invocations. The same dichotomy applies if one insists on a unified programming model. Either all objects must bear the weight of concurrency semantics, or all objects must ignore the problem and hope for the best when distributed. Again, this is an interface issue and not solely an implementation issue, since dealing with concurrency can take place only by passing information from one object to another through the agency of the interface. So either the overall programming model must ignore significant modes of failure, resulting in a fragile system; or the overall programming model must assume a worst-case complexity model for all objects within a program, making the production of any program, distributed or not, more difficult.

One might argue that a multi-threaded application needs to deal with these same issues. However, there is a subtle difference. In a multi-threaded application, there is no real source of indeterminacy of invocations of operations. The application programmer has complete control over invocation order when desired. A distributed system by its nature introduces truly asynchronous operation invocations. Further, a non-distributed system, even when multi-threaded, is layered on top of a single operating system that can aid the communication between objects and can be used to determine and aid in synchronization and in the recovery of failure. A distributed system, on the other hand, has no single point of resource allocation, synchronization, or failure recovery, and thus is conceptually very different.

A.6 The Myth of "Quality of Service"

One could take the position that the way an object deals with latency, memory access, partial failure, and concurrency control is really an aspect of the implementation of that object, and is best described as part of the "quality of service" provided by that implementation. Different implementations of an interface may provide different levels of reliability, scalability, or performance. If one wants to build a more reliable system, one merely needs to choose more reliable implementations of the interfaces making up the system.

On the surface, this seems quite reasonable. If I want a more robust system, I go to my catalog of component vendors. I quiz them about their test methods. I see if they have ISO9000 certification, and I buy my components from the one I trust the most. The components all comply with the defined interfaces, so I can plug them right in; my system is robust and reliable, and I'm happy.

Let us imagine that I build an application that uses the (mythical) queue interface to enqueue work for some component. My application dutifully enqueues records that represent work to be done. Another application dutifully dequeues them and performs the work. After a while, I notice that my application crashes due to time-outs. I find this extremely annoying, but realize that it's my fault. My application just isn't robust enough. It gives up too easily on a time-out. So I change my application to retry the operation until it succeeds. Now I'm happy. I almost never see a time-out. Unfortunately, I now have another problem. Some of the requests seem to get processed two, three, four, or more times. How can this be? The component I bought which implements the queue has allegedly been rigorously tested. It shouldn't be doing this. I'm angry. I call the vendor and yell at him. After much fingerpointing and research, the culprit is found. The problem turns out to be the way I'm using the queue. Because of my handling of partial failures (which in my naivete, I had thought to be total), I have been enqueuing work requests multiple times.

Well, I yell at the vendor that it is still their fault. Their queue should be detecting the duplicate entry and removing it. I'm not going to continue using this software unless this is fixed. But, since the entities being enqueued are just values, there is no way to do duplicate elimination. The only way to fix this is to change the protocol to add request IDs. But since this is a standardized interface, there is no way to do this.

The moral of this tale is that robustness is not simply a function of the implementations of the interfaces that make up the system. While robustness of the individual components has some effect on the robustness of the overall systems, it is not the sole factor determining system robustness. Many aspects of robustness can be reflected only at the protocol/interface level.

Similar situations can be found throughout the standard set of interfaces. Suppose I want to reliably remove a name from a context. I would be tempted to write code that looks like:

```
while (true) {
    try {
        context->remove(name);
        break;
    }
    catch (NotFoundInContext) {
        break;
    }
    catch (NetworkServerFaliure) {
        continue;
    }
}
```

That is, I keep trying the operation until it succeeds (or until I crash). The problem is that my connection to the name server may have gone down, but another client's may have stayed up. I may have, in fact, successfully removed the name but not discovered it because of a network disconnection. The other client then adds the same name, which I then remove. Unless the naming interface includes an operation to lock a naming context, there is no way that I can make this operation completely robust. Again, we see that robustness/reliability needs to be expressed at the interface level. In the design of any operation, the question has to be asked: What happens if the client chooses to repeat this operation with the exact same parameters as previously? What mechanisms are needed to ensure that they get the desired semantics? These are things that can be expressed only at the interface level. These are issues that can't be answered by supplying a "more robust implementation" because the lack of robustness is inherent in the interface and not something that can be changed by altering the implementation.

Similar arguments can be made about performance. Suppose an interface describes an object which maintains sets of other objects. A defining property of sets is that there are no duplicates. Thus, the implementation of this object needs to do duplicate elimination. If the interfaces in the system do not provide a way of testing equality of reference, the objects in the set must be queried to determine equality. Thus, duplicate elimination can be done only by interacting with the objects in the set. It doesn't matter how fast the objects in the set implement the equality operation. The overall performance of eliminating duplicates is going to be governed by the latency in communicating over the slowest communications link involved. There is no change in the set implementations that can overcome this. An interface design issue has put an upper bound on the performance of this operation.

A.7 Lessons from NFS

We do not need to look far to see the consequences of ignoring the distinction between local and distributed computing at the interface level. NFS®, Sun's distributed computing file system[14,15] is an example of a non-distributed application programer interface (API) (open, read, write, close, etc.) re-implemented in a distributed way.

Before NFS and other network file systems, an error status returned from one of these calls indicated something rare: a full disk, or a catastrophe such as a disk crash. Most failures simply crashed the application along with the file system. Further, these errors generally reflected a situation that was either catastrophic for the program receiving the error or one that the user running the program could do something about.

NFS opened the door to partial failure within a file system. It has essentially two modes for dealing with an inaccessible file server: soft mounting and hard mounting. But since the designers of NFS were unwilling (for easily understandable reasons) to change the interface to the file system to reflect the new, distributed nature of file access, neither option is particularly robust.

Soft mounts expose network or server failure to the client program. Read and write operations return a failure status much more often than in the single-system case, and programs written with no allowance for these failures can easily corrupt the files used by the program. In the early days of NFS, system administrators tried to tune various parameters (time-out length, number of retries) to avoid these problems. These efforts failed. Today, soft mounts are seldom used, and when they are used, their use is generally restricted to read-only file systems or special applications.

Hard mounts mean that the application hangs until the server comes back up. This generally prevents a client program from seeing partial failure, but it leads to a malady familiar to users of workstation networks: one server crashes, and many workstations—even those apparently having nothing to do with that server—freeze. Figuring out the chain of causality is very difficult, and even when the cause of the failure can be determined, the individual user can rarely do anything about it but wait. This kind of brittleness can be reduced only with strong policies and network administration aimed at reducing interdependencies. Nonetheless, hard mounts are now almost universal.

Note that because the NFS protocol is stateless, it assumes clients contain no state of interest with respect to the protocol; in other words, the server doesn't care what happens to the client. NFS is also a "pure" client-server protocol, which means that failure can be limited to three parties: the client, the server, or the network. This combination of features means that failure modes are simpler than in the more general case of peer-to-peer distributed object-oriented applications where no such limitation on shared state can be made and where servers are themselves clients of other servers. Such peer-to-peer distributed applications can and will fail in far more intricate ways than are currently possible with NFS.

The limitations on the reliability and robustness of NFS have nothing to do with the implementation of the parts of that system. There is no "quality of service" that can be improved to eliminate the need for hard mounting NFS volumes. The problem can be traced to the interface upon which NFS is built, an interface that was designed for non-distributed computing where partial failure was not possible. The reliability of NFS cannot be changed without a change to that interface, a change that will reflect the distributed nature of the application.

This is not to say that NFS has not been successful. In fact, NFS is arguably the most successful distributed application that has been produced. But the limitations on the robustness have set a limitation on the scalability of NFS. Because of the intrinsic unreliability of the NFS protocol, use of NFS is limited to fairly small numbers of machines, geographically co-located and centrally administered. The way NFS has dealt with partial failure has been to informally require a centralized resource manager (a system administrator) who can detect system failure, initiate resource reclamation and insure system consistency. But by introducing this central resource manager, one could argue that NFS is no longer a genuinely distributed application.

A.8 Taking the Difference Seriously

Differences in latency, memory access, partial failure, and concurrency make merging of the computational models of local and distributed computing both unwise to attempt and unable to succeed. Merging the models by making local computing follow the model of distributed computing would require major changes in implementation languages (or in how those languages are used) and make local computing far more complex than is otherwise necessary. Merging the models by attempting to make distributed computing follow the model of local computing requires ignoring the different failure modes and basic indeterminacy inherent in distributed computing, leading to systems that are unreliable and incapable of scaling beyond small groups of machines that are geographically co-located and centrally administered.

A better approach is to accept that there are irreconcilable differences between local and distributed computing, and to be conscious of those differences at all stages of the design and implementation of distributed applications. Rather than trying to merge local and remote objects, engineers need to be constantly reminded of the differences between the two, and know when it is appropriate to use each kind of object.

Accepting the fundamental difference between local and remote objects does not mean that either sort of object will require its interface to be defined differently. An interface definition language such as IDL[B] can still be used to specify the set of interfaces that define objects. However, an additional part of the definition of a class of objects will be the specification of whether those objects are meant to be used locally or remotely. This decision will need to consider what the anticipated message frequency is for the object, and whether clients of the object can accept the indeterminacy implied by remote access. The decision will be reflected in the interface to the object indirectly, in that the interface for objects that are meant to be accessed remotely will contain operations that allow reliability in the face of partial failure.

It is entirely possible that a given object will often need to be accessed by some objects in ways that cannot allow indeterminacy, and by other objects relatively rarely and in a way that does allow indeterminacy. Such cases should be split into two objects (which might share an implementation) with one having an interface that is best for local access and the other having an interface that is best for remote access.

A compiler for the interface definition language used to specify classes of objects will need to alter its output based on whether the class definition being compiled is for a class to be used locally or a class being used remotely. For interfaces meant for distributed objects, the code produced might be very much like that generated by RPC stub compilers today. Code for a local interface, however, could be much simpler, probably requiring little more than a class definition in the target language.

While writing code, engineers will have to know whether they are sending messages to local or remote objects, and access those objects differently. While this might seem to add to the programming difficulty, it will in fact aid the programmer by providing a framework under which he or she can learn what to expect from the different kinds of calls. To program completely in the local environment, according to this model, will not require any changes from the programmer's point of view. The discipline of defining classes of objects using an interface definition language will insure the desired separation of interface from implementation, but the actual process of implementing an interface will be no different than what is done today in an object-oriented language.

Programming a distributed application will require the use of different techniques than those used for non-distributed applications. Programming a distributed application will require thinking about the problem in a different way than before it was thought about when the solution was a non-distributed application. But that is only to be expected. Distributed objects are different from local objects, and keeping that difference visible will keep the programmer from forgetting the difference and making mistakes. Knowing that an object is outside of the local address space, and perhaps on a different machine, will remind the programmer that he or she needs to program in a way that reflects the kinds of failures, indeterminacy, and concurrency constraints inherent in the use of such objects. Making the difference visible will aid in making the difference part of the design of the system.

Accepting that local and distributed computing are different in an irreconcilable way will also allow an organization to allocate its research and engineering resources more wisely. Rather than using those resources in attempts to paper over the differences between the two kinds of computing, resources can be directed at improving the performance and reliability of each.

One consequence of the view espoused here is that it is a mistake to attempt to construct a system that is "objects all the way down" if one understands the goal as a distributed system constructed of the *same kind* of objects all the way down. There will be a line where the object model changes; on one side of the line will be distributed objects, and on the other side of the line there will (perhaps) be local objects. On either side of the line, entities on the other side of the line will be opaque; thus one distributed object will not know (or care) if the implementation of another distributed object with which it communicates is made up of objects or is implemented in some other way. Objects on different sides of the line will differ in kind and not just in degree; in particular, the objects will differ in the kinds of failure modes with which they must deal.

A.9 A Middle Ground

As noted in Section A.2, the distinction between local and distributed objects as we are using the terms is not exhaustive. In particular, there is a third category of objects made up of those that are in different address spaces but are guaranteed to be on the same machine. These are the sorts of objects, for example, that appear to be the basis of systems such as Spring[16] or Clouds[4]. These objects have some of the characteristics of distributed objects, such as increased latency in comparison to local objects and the need for a different model of memory access. However, these objects also share characteristics of local objects, including sharing underlying resource management and failure modes that are more nearly deterministic.

It is possible to make the programming model for such "local-remote" objects more similar to the programming model for local objects than can be done for the general case of distributed objects. Even though the objects are in different address spaces, they are managed by a single resource manager. Because of this, partial failure and the indeterminacy that it brings can be avoided. The programming model for such objects will still differ from that used for objects in the same address space with respect to latency, but the added latency can be reduced to generally acceptable levels. The programming models will still necessarily differ on methods of memory access and concurrency, but these do not have as great an effect on the construction of interfaces as additional failure modes.

The other reason for treating this class of objects separately from either local objects or generally distributed objects is that a compiler for an interface definition language can be significantly optimized for such cases. Parameter and result passing can be done via shared memory if it is known that the objects communicating are on the same machine. At the very least, marshalling of parameters and the unmarshalling of results can be avoided.

The class of locally distributed objects also forms a group that can lead to significant gains in software modularity. Applications made up of collections of such objects would have the advantage of forced and guaranteed separation between the interface to an object and the implementation of that object, and would allow the replacement of one implementation with another without affecting other parts of the system. Because of this, it might be advantageous to investigate the uses of such a system. However, this activity should not be confused with the unification of local objects with the kinds of distributed objects we have been discussing.

A.10 References

[1] The Object Management Group. "Common Object Request Broker: Architecture and Specification." *OMG Document Number 91.12.1* (1991).

[2] Parrington, Graham D. "Reliable Distributed Programming in C++: The Arjuna Approach." *USENIX 1990 C++ Conference Proceedings* (1991).

[3] Black, A., N. Hutchinson, E. Jul, H. Levy, and L. Carter. "Distribution and Abstract Types in Emerald." *IEEE Transactions on Software Engineering* SE-13, no. 1, (January 1987).

[4] Dasgupta, P., R. J. Leblanc, and E. Spafford. "The Clouds Project: Designing and Implementing a Fault Tolerant Distributed Operating System." *Georgia Institute of Technology Technical Report GIT-ICS-85/29. (*1985).

[5] Microsoft Corporation. *Object Linking and Embedding Programmers Reference*. version 1. Microsoft Press, 1992.

[6] Linton, Mark. "A Taste of Fresco." Tutorial given at the *8th Annual X Technical Conference (*January 1994).

[7] Jaayeri, M., C. Ghezzi, D. Hoffman, D. Middleton, and M. Smotherman. "CSP/80: A Language for Communicating Sequential Processes." *Proceedings: Distributed Computing CompCon* (Fall 1980).

[8] Cook, Robert. "MOD—A Language for Distributed Processing." *Proceedings of the 1st International Conference on Distributed Computing Systems (*October 1979).

[9] Birrell, A. D. and B. J. Nelson. "Implementing Remote Procedure Calls." *ACM Transactions on Computer Systems* 2 (1978).

[10] Hutchinson, N. C., L. L. Peterson, M. B. Abott, and S. O'Malley. "RPC in the x-Kernel: Evaluating New Design Techniques." *Proceedings of the Twelfth Symposium on Operating Systems Principles* 23, no. 5 (1989).

[11] Zahn, L., T. Dineen, P. Leach, E. Martin, N. Mishkin, J. Pato, and G. Wyant. *Network Computing Architecture*. Prentice Hall, 1990.

[12] Schroeder, Michael D. "A State-of-the-Art Distributed System: Computing with BOB." In *Distributed Systems*, 2nd ed., S. Mullender, ed., ACM Press, 1993.

[13] Hadzilacos, Vassos and Sam Toueg. "Fault-Tolerant Broadcasts and Related Problems." In *Distributed Systems*, 2nd ed., S. Mullendar, ed., ACM Press, 1993.

[14] Walsh, D., B. Lyon, G. Sager, J. M. Chang, D. Goldberg, S. Kleiman, T. Lyon, R. Sandberg, and P. Weiss. "Overview of the SUN Network File System." *Proceedings of the Winter Usenix Conference* (1985).

[15] Sandberg, R., D. Goldberg, S. Kleiman, D. Walsh, and B. Lyon. "Design and Implementation of the SUN Network File System." *Proceedings of the Summer Usenix Conference (*1985).

[16] Khalidi, Yousef A. and Michael N. Nelson. "An Implementation of UNIX on an Object-Oriented Operating System." *Proceedings of the Winter Usenix Conference* (1993). Also *Sun Microsystems Laboratories, Inc. Technical Report SMLI TR-92-3* (December 1992).

A.11 Observations for this Reprinting

[A] When this note was written, the major system programming languages (C, C++, Modula3, etc.) all allowed direct access, to a greater or lesser degree, to pointers to internal memory. This paragraph points out that adding indirect references to such languages would allow two kinds of reference, one of which was distribution transparent while the other was not. Java, of course, does not have direct access to pointers. Because of the Java use of references within the language, it does provide a platform in which address-space-relative pointers are missing. Thus Java not only permits a unified addressing scheme, it enforces that scheme.

[B] There are actually a number of interface definition languages that are referred to by the initials IDL. When this note was originally written, we were referring to the CORBA interface definition language. However, the other languages that use this name share the characteristics discussed here, so the argument presented would apply equally to them.

APPENDIX B
Example Code

The first rule of magic is simple:
Don't waste your time waving your hands and hoping
when a rock or a club will do.
—McCloctnik the Lucid

THE following pages contain the complete code for the examples used in the introductory chapters of this book. The sources are listed in alphabetical order by the full name, including the package name. For your convenience, here is a mapping from the simple class name to its fully-qualified class name:

You can also find the code at `http://java.sun.com/docs/books/jini/`

```
    package chat;

import java.io.Serializable;

/**
 * A single message in the <CODE>ChatStream</CODE>.  This is the
 * type of <CODE>Object</CODE> returned by <CODE>ChatStream.nextMessage</CODE>.
 *
 * @see ChatStream
 */
public class ChatMessage implements Serializable {
    /**
     * The speaker of the message.
     * @serial
     */
    private String speaker;

    /**
     * The contents of the message.
     * @serial
     */
    private String[] content;

    /**
     * The serial version UID.  Stating it explicitly is good.
     *
     * @see fortune.FortuneTheme#serialVersionUID
     */
    static final long serialVersionUID =
                        -1852351967189107571L;

    /**
     * Create a new <CODE>ChatMessage</CODE> with the given
     * <CODE>speaker</CODE> and <CODE>content</CODE>.
     */
    public ChatMessage(String speaker, String[] content) {
        this.speaker = speaker;
        this.content = content;
    }

    /**
     * Return the speaker of the message.
     */
    public String getSpeaker() { return speaker; }

    /**
     * Return the content of the message.  Each string in the array
     * represents a single line of content.
     */
    public String[] getContent() { return content; }
```

```
    // inherit doc comment from superclass
    public String toString() {
        StringBuffer buf = new StringBuffer(speaker);
        buf.append(": ");
        for (int i = 0; i < content.length; i++)
            buf.append(content[i]).append('\n');
        buf.setLength(buf.length() - 1); // strip newline
        return buf.toString();
    }
}
```

```
    package chat;

import java.io.EOFException;
import java.io.Serializable;
import java.rmi.RemoteException;

/**
 * The client-side proxy for a <CODE>ChatServer</CODE>-based
 * <CODE>ChatStream</CODE> service.  This forwards most requests to the
 * server, remembering the last successfully retrieved message index.
 */
class ChatProxy implements ChatStream, Serializable {
    /**
     * Reference to the remote server.
     * @serial
     */
    private final ChatServer server;

    /**
     * The index of the last entry successfully received.
     * @serial
     */
    private int lastIndex = -1;

    /**
     * Cache of the subject of the chat.
     */
    private transient String subject;

    /**
     * Create a new proxy that will talk to the given server object.
     */
    ChatProxy(ChatServer server) {
        this.server = server;
    }

    // inherit doc comment from ChatStream
    public synchronized Object nextMessage()
        throws RemoteException, EOFException
    {
        ChatMessage msg = server.nextInLine(lastIndex);
        lastIndex++;
        return msg;
    }

    // inherit doc comment from ChatStream
    public void add(String speaker, String[] msg)
        throws RemoteException
    {
        server.add(speaker, msg);
```

```
    }

    // inherit doc comment from ChatStream
    public synchronized String getSubject()
        throws RemoteException
    {
        if (subject == null)
            subject = server.getSubject();
        return subject;
    }

    // inherit doc comment from ChatStream
    public String[] getSpeakers() throws RemoteException {
        return server.getSpeakers();
    }

    public boolean equals(Object other) {
      if (other instanceof ChatProxy)
          return server.equals(((ChatProxy) other).server);
      else
          return false;
    }

    public int hashCode() {
        return server.hashCode() + 1;
    }
}
```

```
    package chat;

import java.io.EOFException;
import java.rmi.Remote;
import java.rmi.RemoteException;

/**
 * The interface used by a <CODE>ChatProxy</CODE> to talk to its server.
 *
 * @see ChatProxy
 */
interface ChatServer extends Remote {
    /**
     * Return the next message after <CODE>lastIndex</CODE>.  This call
     * creates idempotency since repeated invocations with the same
     * value of <CODE>lastIndex</CODE> will always return the same
     * value.  This blocks until a message is available.
     *
     * @see message.MessageStream#nextMessage
     */
    ChatMessage nextInLine(int lastIndex)
        throws EOFException, RemoteException;

    /**
     * Add a new message to end of the stream.  The speaker
     * will be added to the list of known speakers if not already
     * in it.  The resulting message will have the speaker as the
     * first line of the message, with the rest of the message as
     * the remaining lines.
     *
     * @see message.MessageStream#nextMessage
     */
    void add(String speaker, String[] msg)
        throws RemoteException;

    /**
     * Return the subject of the chat.  The subject never changes.
     */
    String getSubject() throws RemoteException;

    /**
     * Return the list of speakers with messages in the stream.
     * The order is not significant.
     */
    String[] getSpeakers() throws RemoteException;
}
```

```
    package chat;

import util.ParseUtil;

import java.io.BufferedInputStream;
import java.io.BufferedOutputStream;
import java.io.File;
import java.io.FileInputStream;
import java.io.FileOutputStream;
import java.io.IOException;
import java.io.ObjectInputStream;
import java.io.ObjectOutputStream;
import java.rmi.activation.Activatable;
import java.rmi.activation.ActivationDesc;
import java.rmi.activation.ActivationException;
import java.rmi.activation.ActivationGroup;
import java.rmi.activation.ActivationGroupDesc.CommandEnvironment;
import java.rmi.activation.ActivationGroupDesc;
import java.rmi.activation.ActivationGroupID;
import java.rmi.activation.ActivationSystem;
import java.rmi.MarshalledObject;
import java.rmi.Remote;
import java.rmi.RemoteException;
import java.util.Properties;

/**
 * The administrative program that creates a new <CODE>ChatServerImpl</CODE>
 * chat stream service.  It's invocation is:
 * <pre>
 *     java [<i>java-options</i>] chat.ChatServerAdmin <i>dir subject</i>
 *             [<i>groups|lookupURL classpath codebase policy-file</i>]
 * </pre>
 * Where the options are:
 * <dl>
 * <dt><i><CODE>java-options</CODE></i>
 * <dd>Options to the Java VM that will run the admin program.  Typically
 * this includes a security policy property.
 * <p>
 * <dt><i><CODE>dir</CODE></i>
 * <dd>The directory in which all the chats in the same group will live.
 * <p>
 * <dt><i><CODE>subject</CODE></i>
 * <dd>The subject of the chat.  This must be unique within the group.
 * <p>
 * <dt><i><CODE>groups</CODE></i>|<i><CODE>lookupURL</CODE></i>
 * <dd>Either a comma-separated list of groups in which all the services
 * in the group will be registered or a URL to a specific lookup service.
 * <p>
 * <dt><i><CODE>classpath</CODE></i>
 * <dd>The classpath for the activated service (<CODE>ChatServerImpl</CODE>
```

```
 * will be loaded from this).
 * <p>
 * <dt><i><CODE>codebase</CODE></i>
 * <dd>The codebase for users of the service (<CODE>ChatProxy</CODE> will
 * be loaded from this).
 * <p>
 * <dt><i><CODE>policy-file</CODE></i>
 * <dd>The policy file for the activated service's virtual machine.
 * </dl>
 * <p>The last four parameters imply creation of a new group.  If any
 * are specified they must all be specified.  If none are specified the
 * new chat stream will be in the same activation group as the others
 * who use the same storage directory, and so will use the same values
 * for the last four parameters.
 */
public class ChatServerAdmin {
    /**
     * The main program for <CODE>ChatServerAdmin</CODE>.
     */
    public static void main(String[] args) throws Exception
    {
        if (args.length != 2 && args.length != 6) {
            usage();              // print usage message
            System.exit(1);
        }

        File dir = new File(args[0]);
        String subject = args[1];

        ActivationGroupID group = null;
        if (args.length == 2)
            group = getGroup(dir);
        else {
            String[] groups = ParseUtil.parseGroups(args[2]);
            String lookupURL =
                (args[2].indexOf(':') > 0 ? args[2] : null);
            String classpath = args[3];
            String codebase = args[4];
            String policy = args[5];
            group = createGroup(dir, groups, lookupURL,
                classpath, codebase, policy);
        }

        File data = new File(dir, subject);
        MarshalledObject state = new MarshalledObject(data);
        ActivationDesc desc =
            new ActivationDesc(group, "chat.ChatServerImpl",
                               null, state, true);
        Remote newObj = Activatable.register(desc);
        ChatServer server = (ChatServer) newObj;
```

```
        String s = server.getSubject(); // force server up
        System.out.println("server created for " + s);
    }

    /**
     * Print a usage message for the user.
     */
    private static void usage() {
        System.out.println("usage: java [java-options] " +
            ChatServerAdmin.class + " dir subject " +
            " [groups|lookupURL classpath codebase policy-file]\n");
    }

    /**
     * Create a new group with the given parameters.
     */
    private static ActivationGroupID
        createGroup(File dir, String[] groups, String lookupURL,
                    String classpath, String codebase,
                    String policy)
        throws IOException, ActivationException
    {
        if (!dir.isDirectory())
            dir.mkdirs();

        Properties props = new Properties();
        props.put("java.rmi.server.codebase", codebase);
        props.put("java.security.policy", policy);
        String[] argv = new String[] { "-cp", classpath };
        CommandEnvironment cmd =
            new CommandEnvironment("java", argv);
        ActivationSystem actSys = ActivationGroup.getSystem();
        ActivationGroupDesc groupDesc =
            new ActivationGroupDesc(props, cmd);
        ActivationGroupID id = actSys.registerGroup(groupDesc);

        FileOutputStream fout =
            new FileOutputStream(groupFile(dir));
        ObjectOutputStream out = new ObjectOutputStream(
            new BufferedOutputStream(fout));
        out.writeObject(id);
        out.writeObject(groups);
        out.writeObject(lookupURL);
        out.flush();            // force bits out of buffer
        fout.getFD().sync();    // force bits to the disk
        out.close();

        return id;
    }
```

```
    /**
     * Return a <CODE>File</CODE> object contains the group description.
     * This assumes that nobody will create a group with the subject
     * <CODE>"grpdesc"</CODE>.  This is probably a bad assumption -- a
     * fully robust implementation should either check this and forbid it
     * or figure out a way to store this someplace that does not conflict
     * with subject names.
     */
    static File groupFile(File dir) {
        return new File(dir, "grpdesc");
    }

    /**
     * Get the ActivationGroupID for the existing group in the given
     * directory.
     */
    private static ActivationGroupID getGroup(File dir)
        throws IOException, ClassNotFoundException
    {
        ObjectInputStream in = null;
        try {
            in = new ObjectInputStream(new BufferedInputStream(
                new FileInputStream(groupFile(dir))));
            return (ActivationGroupID) in.readObject();
        } finally {
            if (in != null)
                in.close();
        }
    }
}
```

```
package chat;

import net.jini.core.discovery.LookupLocator;
import net.jini.core.entry.Entry;
import net.jini.core.lookup.ServiceID;

import net.jini.discovery.DiscoveryManagement;
import net.jini.discovery.LookupDiscoveryManager;
import net.jini.lease.LeaseRenewalManager;
import net.jini.lookup.JoinManager;
import net.jini.lookup.ServiceIDListener;

import com.sun.jini.reliableLog.LogHandler;
import com.sun.jini.reliableLog.ReliableLog;

import java.io.File;
import java.io.FileInputStream;
import java.io.InputStream;
import java.io.IOException;
import java.io.ObjectInputStream;
import java.io.ObjectOutputStream;
import java.io.OutputStream;
import java.rmi.activation.Activatable;
import java.rmi.activation.ActivationID;
import java.rmi.MarshalledObject;
import java.util.ArrayList;
import java.util.HashSet;
import java.util.List;
import java.util.Set;

/**
 * The implementation of <CODE>ChatServer</CODE>.  This runs inside an
 * activation group defined by the persistent state from the activation
 * service.
 *
 * @exclude ReliableLogHandler
 */
public class ChatServerImpl implements ChatServer {
    /**
     * The join manager we're using.
     */
    private JoinManager joinMgr;

    /**
     * Our subject of discussion.
     */
    private String subject;

    /**
     * The set of known speakers.
```

```
 */
private Set speakers = new HashSet();

/**
 * The list of messages.
 */
private List messages = new ArrayList();

/**
 * The list of service attributes.
 */
private List attrs;

/**
 * The service ID (or <CODE>null</CODE>).
 */
private ServiceID serviceID;

/**
 * Our persistent storage.
 */
private ChatStore store;

/**
 * Groups to register with (or an empty array).
 */
private String[] groups = new String[0];

/**
 * URL to specific join manager (or <CODE>null</CODE>).
 */
private String lookupURL;

/**
 * The lease renewal manager for all servers in our group.
 * We share it because this gives it more leases it might be
 * able to compress into single renewal messages.
 */
private static LeaseRenewalManager
    renewer = new LeaseRenewalManager();

/**
 * The storage for a <CODE>ChatServerImpl</CODE>.
 */
class ChatStore extends LogHandler
    implements ServiceIDListener
{
    /**
     * The reliable log in which we store our state.
     */
```

```
    private ReliableLog log;

    /**
     * Create a new <CODE>ChatStore</CODE> object for the given
     * directory.  The directory is the full path for the specific
     * storage for this chat on the subject.  The parent directory
     * is the one for the group.
     */
    ChatStore(File dir) throws IOException {
        // If the directory exists, recover from it.  Otherwise
        // create it as a a new subject.
        if (dir.exists()) {
            log = new ReliableLog(dir.toString(), this);
            log.recover();
        } else {
            subject = dir.getName();
            log = new ReliableLog(dir.toString(), this);
            attrs = new ArrayList();
            attrs.add(new ChatSubject(subject));
            log.snapshot();
        }

        // Read in the lookup groups and lookupURL for our service
        ObjectInputStream in = null;
        try {
            in = new ObjectInputStream(
                new FileInputStream(
                    ChatServerAdmin.groupFile(dir.getParentFile())));
            in.readObject();        // skip over the group ID
            groups = (String[]) in.readObject();
            lookupURL = (String) in.readObject();
        } catch (ClassNotFoundException e) {
            unexpectedException(e);
        } catch (IOException e) {
            unexpectedException(e);
        } finally {
            if (in != null)
                in.close();
        }
    }

    /**
     * Stores the current information in storage.  In our case only
     * the start state is snapshoted -- everything else is added
     * incrementally anyway and so the log of changes is the
     * state.  Part of <CODE>ReliableLogHandler</CODE>.
     */
    public void snapshot(OutputStream out) throws Exception {
        ObjectOutputStream oo = new ObjectOutputStream(out);
        oo.writeObject(subject);
```

```
    oo.writeObject(attrs);
}

/**
 * Recovers the information from storage.  Part of
 * <CODE>ReliableLogHandler</CODE>.
 *
 * @see #snapshot
 */
public void recover(InputStream in) throws Exception {
    ObjectInputStream oi = new ObjectInputStream(in);
    subject = (String) oi.readObject();
    attrs = (List) oi.readObject();
}

/**
 * Apply an update from the log during recovery.  The types
 * of data we add happen to all be distinct so we know exactly
 * what something is based on its type alone (lucky us).  Part
 * of <CODE>ReliableLogHandler</CODE>.
 */
public void applyUpdate(Object update) throws Exception {
    if (update instanceof ChatMessage) {
        messages.add(update);
        addSpeaker(((ChatMessage) update).getSpeaker());
    } else if (update instanceof Entry) {
        attrs.add(update);
    } else if (update instanceof ServiceID) {
        serviceID = (ServiceID) update;
    } else {
        throw new IllegalArgumentException(
            "Internal error: update type " +
            update.getClass().getName() + ", " + update);
    }
}

/**
 * Invoked when the serviceID is first assigned to the service.
 * Part of <CODE>ServiceIDListener</CODE>.
 */
public void serviceIDNotify(ServiceID serviceID) {
    try {
        log.update(serviceID);
    } catch (IOException e) {
        unexpectedException(e);
    }
    ChatServerImpl.this.serviceID = serviceID;
}

/**
```

```
         * Add a new speaker to the persistent storage log.
         */
        synchronized void add(ChatMessage msg) {
            try {
                log.update(msg, true);
            } catch (IOException e) {
                unexpectedException(e);
            }
        }
    }

    /**
     * The activation constructor for <CODE>ChatServerImpl</CODE>.  The
     * <CODE>state</CODE> object contains the directory which is our
     * reliable log directory.
     */
    public ChatServerImpl(ActivationID actID,
                          MarshalledObject state)
        throws IOException, ClassNotFoundException
    {
        File dir = (File) state.get();
        store = new ChatStore(dir);
        ChatProxy proxy = new ChatProxy(this);

        LookupLocator[] locators = null;
        if (lookupURL != null) {
            LookupLocator loc = new LookupLocator(lookupURL);
            locators = new LookupLocator[] { loc };
        }
        DiscoveryManagement dm =
            new LookupDiscoveryManager(groups, locators, null);
        joinMgr = new JoinManager(proxy, getAttrs(), store,
                                  dm, renewer);
        Activatable.exportObject(this, actID, 0);
    }

    /**
     * Return the attributes as an array for use in JoinManager.
     */
    private Entry[] getAttrs() {
        return (Entry[]) attrs.toArray(new Entry[attrs.size()]);
    }

    // inherit doc comment from ChatServer
    public String getSubject() {
        return subject;
    }

    // inherit doc comment from ChatServer
    public String[] getSpeakers() {
```

```
        return (String[]) speakers.toArray(new String[speakers.size()]);
    }

    // inherit doc comment from ChatServer
    public synchronized void add(String speaker, String[] lines)
    {
        ChatMessage msg = new ChatMessage(speaker, lines);
        store.add(msg);
        addSpeaker(speaker);
        messages.add(msg);
        notifyAll();
    }

    /**
     * Add a speaker to the known list.  If the speaker is already
     * known, this does nothing.
     */
    private synchronized void addSpeaker(String speaker) {
        if (speakers.contains(speaker))
            return;
        speakers.add(speaker);
        Entry speakerAttr = new ChatSpeaker(speaker);
        attrs.add(speakerAttr);
        joinMgr.addAttributes(new Entry[] { speakerAttr });
    }

    // inherit doc comment from ChatServer
    public synchronized ChatMessage nextInLine(int index) {
        try {
            int nextIndex = index + 1;
            while (nextIndex >= messages.size())
                wait();
            return (ChatMessage) messages.get(nextIndex);
        } catch (InterruptedException e) {
            unexpectedException(e);
            return null; // keeps the compiler happy
        }
    }

    /**
     * Turn any unexpected exception into a runtime exception reflected
     * back to the client.  These are both unexpected and unrecoverable
     * exception (such as "file system full").
     */
    private static void unexpectedException(Throwable e) {
        throw new RuntimeException("unexpected exception: " + e);
    }
}
```

```
    package chat;

import net.jini.entry.AbstractEntry;
import net.jini.lookup.entry.ServiceControlled;

/**
 * An attribute for the <CODE>ChatStream</CODE> service that marks a
 * speaker as being present in a particular stream.
 *
 * @see ChatStream
 */
public class ChatSpeaker extends AbstractEntry
    implements ServiceControlled
{
    /**
     * The serial version UID.  Stating it explicitly is good.
     *
     * @see fortune.FortuneTheme#serialVersionUID
     */
    static final long serialVersionUID =
                            6748592884814857788L;

    /**
     * The speaker's name.
     * @serial
     */
    public String speaker;

    /**
     * Public no-arg constructor.  Required for all <CODE>Entry</CODE>
     * objects.
     */
    public ChatSpeaker() { }

    /**
     * Create a new <CODE>ChatSpeaker</CODE> with the given speaker.
     */
    public ChatSpeaker(String speaker) {
        this.speaker = speaker;
    }
}
```

```
    package chat;

import message.MessageStream;

import java.rmi.RemoteException;

/**
 * A type of <CODE>MessageStream</CODE> whose contents are a chat
 * session.  The <CODE>nextMessage</CODE> method blocks if there is
 * as yet no next message in the stream.  The messages in the stream
 * are ordered, so <CODE>nextMessage</CODE> must be idempotent -- should
 * the client receive a <CODE>RemoteException</CODE>, the next invocation
 * must return the next message that the client has not yet seen.
 * <p>
 * Each message returned by <CODE>nextMessage</CODE> is a
 * <CODE>ChatMessage</CODE> object that has a speaker and what they
 * said.
 *
 * @see ChatMessage
 * @see ChatSpeaker
 * @see ChatSubject
 */
public interface ChatStream extends MessageStream {
    /**
     * Add a new message to the stream.  If the speaker is previously
     * unknown in the stream, a <CODE>ChatSpeaker</CODE> attribute
     * will be added to the service.
     *
     * @see ChatSpeaker
     */
    public void add(String speaker, String[] message)
        throws RemoteException;

    /**
     * Return the subject of the chat.  This does not change during the
     * lifetime of the service.  This subject will also exist as a
     * <CODE>ChatSubject</CODE> attribute on the service.
     *
     * @see ChatSubject
     */
    public String getSubject() throws RemoteException;

    /**
     * Return the list of speakers currently known in the stream.
     * The order is not significant.
     *
     * @see ChatSpeaker
     */
    public String[] getSpeakers() throws RemoteException;
}
```

```
    package chat;

import net.jini.entry.AbstractEntry;
import net.jini.lookup.entry.ServiceControlled;

/**
 * An attribute for the <CODE>ChatStream</CODE> service that marks the
 * subject of discussion.
 *
 * @see ChatStream
 */
public class ChatSubject extends AbstractEntry
    implements ServiceControlled
{
    /**
     * The serial version UID.  Stating it explicitly is good.
     *
     * @see fortune.FortuneTheme#serialVersionUID
     */
    static final long serialVersionUID =
                        -4036337828321897774L;

    /**
     * The subject of the discussion.
     * @serial
     */
    public String subject;

    /**
     * Public no-arg constructor.  Required for all <CODE>Entry</CODE>
     * objects.
     */
    public ChatSubject() { }

    /**
     * Create a new <CODE>ChatSubject</CODE> with the given subject.
     */
    public ChatSubject(String subject) {
        this.subject = subject;
    }
}
```

```
    package chatter;

import chat.ChatStream;
import chat.ChatMessage;
import client.StreamReader;
import message.MessageStream;

import java.rmi.RemoteException;

/**
 * A client that talks to a <CODE>ChatStream</CODE>, allowing the user
 * to add messages as well as read them.  The user's login name is used
 * as their name in the chat.  The usage is:
 * <pre>
 *      java [java-options] chatter.Chatter args...
 * </pre>
 * The arguments are the same as those for <CODE>client.StreamReader</CODE>
 * except that you cannot specify the <CODE>-c</CODE> option.  The stream
 * used will be at least a <CODE>chat.ChatStream</CODE> service.
 *
 * @see client.StreamReader
 * @see ChatterThread
 */
public class Chatter extends StreamReader {
    /**
     * Start up the service.
     */
    public static void main(String[] args) throws Exception
    {
        String[] fullargs = new String[args.length + 3];
        fullargs[0] = "-c";
        fullargs[1] = String.valueOf(Integer.MAX_VALUE);
        System.arraycopy(args, 0, fullargs, 2, args.length);
        fullargs[fullargs.length - 1] = "chat.ChatStream";
        Chatter chatter = new Chatter(fullargs);
        chatter.execute();
    }

    /**
     * Create a new <CODE>Chatter</CODE>.  The <CODE>args</CODE> are
     * passed to the superclass.
     */
    private Chatter(String[] args) {
        super(args);
    }

    /**
     * Overrides <CODE>readStream</CODE> to start up a
     * <CODE>ChatterThread</CODE> when the stream is found.  The
     * <CODE>ChatterThread</CODE> lets the user type messages, while this
```

```
     * thread continually reads them.
     */
    public void readStream(MessageStream msgStream)
        throws RemoteException
    {
        ChatStream stream = (ChatStream) msgStream;
        new ChatterThread(stream).start();
        super.readStream(stream);
    }

    /**
     * Print out a message, marking the speaker for easy reading.
     */
    public void printMessage(int msgNum, Object msg) {
        if (!(msg instanceof ChatMessage))
            super.printMessage(msgNum, msg);
        else {
            ChatMessage cmsg = (ChatMessage) msg;
            System.out.println(cmsg.getSpeaker() + ":");
            String[] lines = cmsg.getContent();
            for (int i = 0; i < lines.length; i++) {
                System.out.print("    ");
                System.out.println(lines[i]);
            }
        }
    }
}
```

```
package chatter;

import chat.ChatStream;

import java.io.BufferedReader;
import java.io.InputStreamReader;
import java.io.IOException;
import java.rmi.RemoteException;
import java.util.ArrayList;
import java.util.List;

/**
 * The thread that <CODE>Chatter</CODE> uses to let the user type
 * new messages.
 */
class ChatterThread extends Thread {
    /**
     * The stream to which we're adding.
     */
    private ChatStream stream;

    /**
     * Create a new <CODE>ChatterThread</CODE> to write to the given stream.
     */
    ChatterThread(ChatStream stream) {
        this.stream = stream;
    }

    /**
     * The thread's workhorse.  Read what the user types and put it into
     * the stream as messages from the user.  The user's name is read from
     * the <CODE>user.name</CODE> property.  A message consists of a series
     * of lines ending in backslash until one that doesn't.
     */
    public void run() {
        BufferedReader in = new BufferedReader(
            new InputStreamReader(System.in));
        String user = System.getProperty("user.name");
        List msg = new ArrayList();
        String[] msgArray = new String[0];
        for (;;) {
            try {
                String line = in.readLine();
                if (line == null)
                    System.exit(0);

                boolean more = line.endsWith("\\");
                if (more) {     // strip trailing backslash
                    int stripped = line.length() - 1;
                    line = line.substring(0, stripped);
```

```
                }
                msg.add(line);
                if (!more) {
                    msgArray = (String[])
                        msg.toArray(new String[msg.size()]);
                    stream.add(user, msgArray);
                    msg.clear();
                }
            } catch (RemoteException e) {
                System.out.println("RemoteException:retry");
                for (;;) {
                    try {
                        Thread.sleep(1000);
                        stream.add(user, msgArray);
                        msg.clear();
                        break;
                    } catch (RemoteException re) {
                        continue;       // try again
                    } catch (InterruptedException ie) {
                        System.exit(1);
                    }
                }
            } catch (IOException e) {
                System.exit(1);
            }
        }
    }
}
```

```
    package client;

import net.jini.core.discovery.LookupLocator;
import net.jini.core.entry.Entry;
import net.jini.core.lookup.ServiceRegistrar;
import net.jini.core.lookup.ServiceTemplate;
import net.jini.core.lookup.ServiceItem;

import net.jini.lookup.ServiceDiscoveryManager;
import net.jini.lookup.ServiceDiscoveryListener;
import net.jini.discovery.DiscoveryManagement;
import net.jini.discovery.LookupDiscoveryManager;
import net.jini.lookup.ServiceDiscoveryEvent;

import message.MessageStream;

import java.io.BufferedReader;
import java.io.EOFException;
import java.io.InputStreamReader;
import java.io.Reader;
import java.lang.reflect.Constructor;
import java.lang.reflect.InvocationTargetException;
import java.rmi.RemoteException;
import java.rmi.RMISecurityManager;
import java.util.HashSet;
import java.util.LinkedList;
import java.util.List;
import java.util.Set;
import java.util.StringTokenizer;

/**
 * This class provides a client that reads messages from a
 * <code>MessageStream</code> service.  It's use is:
 * <pre>
 *     java [<i>java-options</i>] client.StreamReader [-c <i>count</i>]
 *             <i>groups|lookupURL</i>
 *             [<i>service-type</i>|<i>attribute</i> ...]
 * </pre>
 * Where the options are:
 * <dl>
 * <dt><i><CODE>java-options</CODE></i>
 * <dd>Options to the Java VM that will run the admin program.  Typically
 * this includes a security policy property.
 * <p>
 * <dt><i><CODE>-c <i>count</i></CODE></i>
 * <dd>The number of messages to print.
 * <p>
 * <dt><i><CODE>groups</CODE></i>|<i><CODE>lookupURL</CODE></i>
 * <dd>Either a comma-separated list of groups in which all the services
 * in the group will be registered or a URL to a specific lookup service.
```

```
 * <p>
 * <dt><i><CODE>service-type</CODE></i>|<i><CODE>attribute</CODE></i>
 * <dd>A combination (in any order) of service types and attribute definitions.
 * Service types are specified as types that the service must be an instance of.
 * Attribute definitions are either <CODE>Entry</CODE> type names,
 * which declare that the service must have an attribute of that type,
 * or <CODE>Entry</CODE> type names with a single <CODE>String</CODE>
 * parameter for the constructor, as in
 * <CODE><i>AttributeType</i>:<i>stringArg</i></CODE>.
 * </dl>
 * <p>The lookups are searched for a <CODE>MessageStream</CODE> that
 * supports any additional service types specified and that matches all
 * specified attributes.  If one is found, then <CODE><i>count</i></CODE>
 * messages are printed from it.  If a <CODE>RemoteException</CODE>
 * occurs the <CODE>nextMessage</CODE> invocation is retried up to
 * a maximum number of times.
 * <P>
 * This class is designed to be subclassed.  As an example, see
 * <CODE>chatter.Chatter</CODE>.
 *
 * @see message.MessageStream
 * @see chatter.Chatter
 */
public class StreamReader
    implements ServiceDiscoveryListener
{
    /**
     * The number of messages to print.
     */
    private int count;

    /**
     * The lookup groups (or an empty array).
     */
    private String[] groups = new String[0];

    /**
     * The lookup URL (or <code>null</code>).
     */
    private String lookupURL;

    /**
     * The stream and attribute types.
     */
    private String[] typeArgs;

    /**
     * How long to wait for matches before giving up.
     */
    private final static int MAX_WAIT = 5000;    // five seconds
```

```
    /**
     * Maximum number of retries of <code>nextMessage</code>.
     */
    private final static int MAX_RETRIES = 5;

    /**
     * Run the program.
     *
     * @param args      The command-line arguments
     *
     * @see #StreamReader
     */
    public static void main(String[] args) throws Exception
    {
        StreamReader reader = new StreamReader(args);
        reader.execute();
    }

    /**
     * Create a new <code>StreamReader</code> object from the
     * given command line arguments.
     */
    public StreamReader(String[] args) {
        // parse command into the fields count, groups,
        // lookupURL, and typesArgs...
        if (args.length == 0) {
            usage();
            throw new IllegalArgumentException();
        }

        int start;
        if (!args[0].equals("-c")) {
            count = 1;
            start = 0;
        } else {
            count = Integer.parseInt(args[1]);
            start = 2;
        }

        if (args[start].indexOf(':') < 0)
            groups = util.ParseUtil.parseGroups(args[start]);
        else
            lookupURL = args[start];
        typeArgs = new String[args.length - start - 1];
        System.arraycopy(args, start + 1, typeArgs, 0, typeArgs.length);
    }

    /**
     * Print out a usage message.
```

```
     */
    private void usage() {
        System.err.println("usage: java [java-options] " + StreamReader.class +
            " [-c count] groups|lookupURL [service-type|attribute ...]");
    }

    /**
     * Execute the program by consuming messages.  This spawns a
     * <CODE>ServiceDiscoveryManager</CODE> to watch for services
     * of the right type, trying to read those that are found.  Once
     * the <CODE>ServiceDiscoveryManager</CODE> is listening, this
     * thread sleeps up to the maximum time and then exits with an error,
     * since <CODE>serviceAdded</CODE> will exit first if it succeeds.
     *
     * @see #serviceAdded
     */
    public void execute() throws Exception {
        if (System.getSecurityManager() == null)
            System.setSecurityManager(new RMISecurityManager());

        LookupLocator[] locators = null;
        if (lookupURL != null) {
            LookupLocator loc = new LookupLocator(lookupURL);
            locators = new LookupLocator[] { loc };
        }

        DiscoveryManagement dm =        // lookups to search
            new LookupDiscoveryManager(groups, locators, null);
        ServiceDiscoveryManager sdm =   // services to look for
            new ServiceDiscoveryManager(dm, null);
        ServiceTemplate serviceTmpl = buildTmpl(typeArgs);
        sdm.createLookupCache(serviceTmpl, null, this);

        Thread.sleep(MAX_WAIT);
        exit(1, "No service found");
    }

    /**
     * Invoked by <CODE>ServiceDiscoveryManager</CODE> when it
     * finds a service that matches our template.  We try to
     * use it, exiting successfully if it works.  Otherwise we
     * return and wait for the next service.  This is synchronized
     * so that nobody can exit while we're trying out a service, since
     * <CODE>exit</CODE> is also synchronized.  Otherwise we could be
     * in the middle of reading the stream when the timer in
     * <CODE>execute</CODE> went off.
     *
     * @see #execute
     * @see #exit
     */
```

```
public synchronized void
    serviceAdded(ServiceDiscoveryEvent ev)
{
    ServiceItem si = ev.getPostEventServiceItem();
    try {
        readStream((MessageStream) si.service);
        exit(0, null);
    } catch (RemoteException e) {
        return;     // ignore this one, try for another
    }
}

// stub these out -- we don't need them
public void serviceChanged(ServiceDiscoveryEvent ev) { }
public void serviceRemoved(ServiceDiscoveryEvent ev) { }

/**
 * Build up a <code>ServiceTemplate</code> object for
 * matching based on the types listed on the command line.
 */
private ServiceTemplate buildTmpl(String[] typeNames)
    throws ClassNotFoundException, IllegalAccessException,
           InstantiationException, NoSuchMethodException,
           InvocationTargetException
{
    Set typeSet = new HashSet();    // service types
    Set attrSet = new HashSet();    // attribute objects

    // MessageStream class is always required
    typeSet.add(MessageStream.class);

    for (int i = 0; i < typeNames.length; i++) {
        // break the type name up into name and argument
        StringTokenizer tokens =    // breaks up string
            new StringTokenizer(typeNames[i], ":");
        String typeName = tokens.nextToken();
        String arg = null;          // string argument
        if (tokens.hasMoreTokens())
            arg = tokens.nextToken();
        Class cl = Class.forName(typeName);

        // test if it is a type of Entry (an attribute)
        if (Entry.class.isAssignableFrom(cl))
            attrSet.add(attribute(cl, arg));
        else
            typeSet.add(cl);
    }

    // create the arrays from the sets
    Entry[] attrs = (Entry[])
```

```
            attrSet.toArray(new Entry[attrSet.size()]);
        Class[] types = (Class[])
            typeSet.toArray(new Class[typeSet.size()]);

        return new ServiceTemplate(null, types, attrs);
    }

    /**
     * Create an attribute from the class name and optional argument.
     */
    private Object attribute(Class cl, String arg)
        throws IllegalAccessException, InstantiationException,
               NoSuchMethodException, InvocationTargetException
    {
        if (arg == null)
            return cl.newInstance();
        else {
            Class[] argTypes = new Class[] { String.class };
            Constructor ctor = cl.getConstructor(argTypes);
            Object[] args = new Object[] { arg };
            return ctor.newInstance(args);
        }
    }

    /**
     * Read the required number of messages from the given stream.
     */
    public void readStream(MessageStream stream)
        throws RemoteException
    {
        int errorCount = 0;     // # of errors seen this message
        int msgNum = 0;         // # of messages
        while (msgNum < count) {
            try {
                Object msg = stream.nextMessage();
                printMessage(msgNum, msg);
                msgNum++;               // successful read
                errorCount = 0;         // clear error count
            } catch (EOFException e) {
                System.out.println("---EOF---");
                break;
            } catch (RemoteException e) {
                e.printStackTrace();
                if (++errorCount > MAX_RETRIES) {
                    if (msgNum == 0)    // got no messages
                        throw e;
                    else
                        exit(1, "too many errors");
                }
                try {
```

```
                    Thread.sleep(1000); // wait 1 second, retry
                } catch (InterruptedException ie) {
                    exit(1, "Interrupted");
                }
            }
        }
    }

    private synchronized void exit(int status, String msg) {
        if (msg != null)
            System.err.println(msg);
        System.exit(status);
    }

    /**
     * Print out the message in a reasonable format.
     */
    public void printMessage(int msgNum, Object msg) {
        if (msgNum > 0) // print separator
            System.out.println("---");
        System.out.println(msg);
    }
}
```

```
    package fortune;

import message.MessageStream;

import java.io.DataOutputStream;
import java.io.File;
import java.io.FileOutputStream;
import java.io.IOException;
import java.io.RandomAccessFile;
import java.util.ArrayList;
import java.util.List;

import java.rmi.activation.ActivationException;

/**
 * Administer a <code>FortuneStreamImpl</code>.
 * <pre>
 *      java [<i>java options</i>] fortune.FortuneAdmin <i>database-dir</i>
 * </pre>
 * The database is initialized from the fortune set in the directory's
 * <code>fortunes</code> file, creating a file named <code>pos</code> that
 * contains each fortune's starting position.  The <code>fortunes</code>
 * file must be present.  The <code>pos</code> file, if it exists, will
 * be overwritten.
 *
 * @see FortuneStreamImpl
 */
public class FortuneAdmin {
    /**
     * Run the FortuneAdmin utility.  The class comment describes the
     * possibilities.
     *
     * @param args
     *          The arguments passed on the command line
     *
     * @see FortuneAdmin
     */
    public static void main(String[] args) throws Exception {
        if (args.length != 1)
            usage();
        else
            setup(args[0]);
    }

    /**
     * Set up a directory, reading its <code>fortunes</code> file and
     * creating a correct <code>pos</code> file.
     *
     * @param dir
     *          The fortune database directory.
```

```
     * @throws java.io.IOException
     *          Some error accessing the database files.
     */
    private static void setup(String dir) throws IOException {
        File fortuneFile = new File(dir, "fortunes");
        File posFile = new File(dir, "pos");
        if (posFile.exists() &&
            posFile.lastModified() > fortuneFile.lastModified())
        {
            System.out.println("positions up to date");
            return;
        }

        System.out.print("positions out of date, updating");
        // Open the fortunes file
        RandomAccessFile fortunes =
            new RandomAccessFile(new File(dir, "fortunes"), "r");

        // Remember the start of each fortune
        List positions = new ArrayList();
        positions.add(new Long(0));
        String line;
        while ((line = fortunes.readLine()) != null)
            if (line.startsWith("%%"))
                positions.add(new Long(fortunes.getFilePointer()));
        fortunes.close();

        // Write the pos file
        DataOutputStream pos =
            new DataOutputStream(new FileOutputStream(new File(dir, "pos")));
        int size = positions.size();
        pos.writeLong(size);
        for (int i = 0; i < size; i++)
            pos.writeLong(((Long) positions.get(i)).longValue());
        pos.close();
        System.out.println();
    }

    /**
     * Print out a usage message.
     */
    private static void usage() {
        System.out.println("usage: java [java-options] " + FortuneAdmin.class +
            " database-dir");
    }
}
```

```
    package fortune;

import message.MessageStream;

import java.rmi.Remote;
import java.rmi.RemoteException;

/**
 * A <CODE>FortuneStream</CODE> is a <CODE>MessageStream</CODE> whose
 * <CODE>nextMessage</CODE> method returns a random saying on some theme.
 * The theme is returned by the <CODE>getTheme</CODE> method.
 *
 * @see FortuneTheme
 */
interface FortuneStream extends MessageStream, Remote {
    /**
     * Return the theme of the stream.  This is also represented in the
     * lookup service as a <CODE>FortuneTheme</CODE> object.
     */
    String getTheme() throws RemoteException;
}
```

```
package fortune;

import message.MessageStream;
import util.ParseUtil;

import net.jini.core.discovery.LookupLocator;
import net.jini.core.entry.Entry;

import net.jini.discovery.DiscoveryManagement;
import net.jini.discovery.LookupDiscoveryManager;
import net.jini.lease.LeaseRenewalManager;
import net.jini.lookup.JoinManager;
import net.jini.lookup.ServiceIDListener;

import java.io.BufferedInputStream;
import java.io.DataInputStream;
import java.io.DataOutputStream;
import java.io.EOFException;
import java.io.File;
import java.io.FileInputStream;
import java.io.IOException;
import java.io.RandomAccessFile;
import java.rmi.Remote;
import java.rmi.RMISecurityManager;
import java.rmi.server.UnicastRemoteObject;
import java.util.Random;

/**
 * Implement a <code>MessageStream</code> whose
 * <code>nextMessage</code> method returns ‘‘fortune cookie’’ selected
 * at random.  The stream is an activatable remote object.  It requires
 * no special proxy because there is no client-side state or smarts --
 * the simple RMI stub works perfectly for this use.
 *
 * <code>FortuneStreamImpl</code> objects are created using the
 * <code>create</code>.  It’s only public constructor is designed for
 * use by the activation system itself.  The class
 * <code>FortuneAdmin</code> provides a program that will invoke
 * <code>create</code>.
 *
 * @see FortuneAdmin
 */
public class FortuneStreamImpl implements FortuneStream {
    /**
     * Groups to register with (or an empty array).
     */
    private String[] groups = new String[0];

    /**
     * URL to specific join manager (or <CODE>null</CODE>).
```

```
     */
    private String lookupURL;

    /**
     * The directory we work in.
     */
    private String dir;

    /**
     * The theme of this stream.
     */
    private String theme;

    /**
     * The random number generator we use.
     */
    private Random random = new Random();

    /**
     * The positions of the start of each fortune in the file.
     */
    private long[] positions;

    /**
     * The file that contains the fortunes.
     */
    private RandomAccessFile fortunes;

    /**
     * The join manager does most work required of services in Jini systems.
     */
    private JoinManager joinMgr;

    /**
     * @param args      The command line arguments.
     */
    public static void main(String[] args) throws Exception
    {
        FortuneStreamImpl f = new FortuneStreamImpl(args);
        f.execute();
    }

    /**
     * Create a stream that reads from the given directory.
     *
     * @param dir       The directory name.
     */
    private FortuneStreamImpl(String args[])
        throws IOException
    {
```

```
        // Set the groups, lookupURL, dir, and theme
        // fields...
        if (args.length != 3) {
            usage();
            throw new IllegalArgumentException();
        }
        if (args[0].indexOf(':') < 0)
            groups = util.ParseUtil.parseGroups(args[0]);
        else
            lookupURL = args[0];
        dir = args[1];
        theme = args[2];
    }

    /**
     * Print out a usage message.
     */
    private void usage() {
        System.err.println("usage: java " + FortuneStreamImpl.class +
            " groups|lookupURL database-dir theme");
    }

    /**
     * Export this service as a UnicastRemoteObject for debugging purposes.
     *
     * @see #main
     */
    private void execute() throws IOException {
        System.setSecurityManager(new RMISecurityManager());
        UnicastRemoteObject.exportObject(this);

        // set up the fortune database
        setupFortunes();

        // set our FortuneTheme attribute
        FortuneTheme themeAttr = new FortuneTheme(theme);
        Entry[] initialAttrs = new Entry[] { themeAttr };

        LookupLocator[] locators = null;
        if (lookupURL != null) {
            LookupLocator loc = new LookupLocator(lookupURL);
            locators = new LookupLocator[] { loc };
        }
        DiscoveryManagement dm =
            new LookupDiscoveryManager(groups, locators, null);
        joinMgr = new JoinManager(this, initialAttrs,
            (ServiceIDListener) null, dm, null);
    }

    /**
```

```
     * Called when the database needs to be set up.  This can be called
     * multiple times, for example if the database has been modified while
     * the service is running.
     *
     * @throws java.io.IOException
     *          Some problem occurred accessing the database files.
     */
    private synchronized void setupFortunes() throws IOException {
        // Read in the position of each fortune
        File posFile = new File(dir, "pos");
        DataInputStream in = new DataInputStream(
            new BufferedInputStream(new FileInputStream(posFile)));
        int count = (int) in.readLong();
        positions = new long[count];
        for (int i = 0; i < positions.length; i++)
            positions[i] = in.readLong();
        in.close();

        // Close the fortune file if previously opened
        if (fortunes != null)
            fortunes.close();
        // Open up the fortune file
        fortunes = new RandomAccessFile(new File(dir, "fortunes"), "r");
    }

    /**
     * Return the next message from the stream.  Since messages are
     * selected at random, any message is as good as any other and so
     * this is idempotent by contract: there will be no violation of
     * the contract if the client calls it a second time after getting
     * a <code>RemoteException</code>.  The <CODE>Object</CODE> returned
     * is a <CODE>String</CODE> with embeded newlines, but no trailing
     * newline.
     *
     * @throws java.io.EOFException
     *          The database has been corrupted -- no more messages
     *          from this stream.
     */
    public synchronized Object nextMessage() throws EOFException {
        try {
            int which = random.nextInt(positions.length);
            fortunes.seek(positions[which]);
            StringBuffer buf = new StringBuffer();
            String line;
            while ((line = fortunes.readLine()) != null && !line.equals("%%")) {
                if (buf.length() > 0)
                    buf.append('\n');
                buf.append(line);
            }
            return buf.toString();
```

```
        } catch (IOException e) {
            throw new EOFException("directory not available:" + e.getMessage());
        }
    }

    // inherit doc comment from interface
    public String getTheme() {
        return theme;
    }
}
```

```
    package fortune;

import net.jini.entry.AbstractEntry;
import net.jini.lookup.entry.ServiceControlled;

/**
 * This class is used as an attribute in the lookup system to tell
 * the user what theme of fortunes a stream generates.
 */
public class FortuneTheme extends AbstractEntry
    implements ServiceControlled
{
    /**
     * The serial version UID.  Stating it explicitly allows future
     * evolution with a guaranteed consistency of the UID itself.  It
     * is also more efficient since otherwise the UID must be calculated
     * when the class is serialized.  A good specification should include
     * the serial version UID of each class.
     */
    static final long serialVersionUID =
                            -1696813496901296488L;

    /**
     * The theme of this collection of fortunes.
     *
     * @see fortune.FortuneStream#getTheme
     * @serial
     */
    public String theme;

    /**
     * Public no-arg constructor.  Required for all <CODE>Entry</CODE>
     * objects.
     */
    public FortuneTheme() { }

    /**
     * Create a new <CODE>FortuneTheme</CODE> with the given theme.
     */
    public FortuneTheme(String theme) {
        this.theme = theme;
    }
}
```

```
package message;

import java.io.EOFException;
import java.rmi.RemoteException;

/**
 * This interface defines a message stream service.  Successive
 * invocations of <code>nextMessage</code> return the next message in
 * turn.  Subinterfaces may add methods to rewind the stream or
 * otherwise move around within the stream if appropriate.
 */
public interface MessageStream {
    /**
     * Return the next message in the stream.  Each message is an
     * object whose default method of display is a string returned by
     * its <CODE>toString</CODE> method.  This method is idempotent: if
     * the client receives a <code>RemoteException</code>, the next
     * invocation from the client should return an equivalent message.
     * A service may specify which kinds of messages will be returned.
     *
     * @returns The next message as an <CODE>Object</CODE>.
     * @throws  java.io.EOFException
     *          The end of the stream has been reached.
     * @throws  java.rmi.RemoteException
     *          A remote exception has occurred.
     */
    Object nextMessage()
        throws EOFException, RemoteException;
}
```

```
   package util;

import java.util.HashSet;
import java.util.Set;
import java.util.StringTokenizer;

/**
 * This class holds the static <CODE>parseGroups</CODE> method.
 */
public class ParseUtil {
    /**
     * Break up a comma-separated list of groups into an array of strings.
     *
     * @param groupDesc A comma-separated list of groups.
     * @returns         An array of strings (empty if none were specified).
     */
    public static String[] parseGroups(String groupDesc) {
        if (groupDesc.equals(""))
            return new String[] {""};
        Set groups = new HashSet();
        StringTokenizer strs = new StringTokenizer(groupDesc, ", \t\n");
        while (strs.hasMoreTokens())
            groups.add(strs.nextToken());
        return (String[]) groups.toArray(new String[groups.size()]);
    }
}
```

"In my egotisitcal opinion, most people's C programs should be indented six feet down and covered with dirt!"
—Blair P. Houghton, on C program indentation styles

Index

It's a d–mn poor mind that can only think of one way to spell a word!
—Andrew Jackson

A

B

Index

D

Index

Index

E

Index

G

H

I

Index

J

M

N

Index

Index

P

Q

R

Index

Index

Index

V

W

At some point, you have to jump out of the plane under the assumption that you **can** *get the parachute sewn together in time to deploy it.*
—Jick Rickard

Colophon

__Collaboration__, n.:
A literary partnership based on the false assumption that the other people can spell.

THIS book is set in 11 point Times Roman, with variations of size, angle, and weight for headers, chapter quotes, and diagram labels. All code is set in `Lucida Sans Typewriter` at 83% of the surrounding text size. A few decorations are in Zapf Dingbats. The text was written using FrameMaker on several Sun workstations and two Macintosh laptop computers.

Code examples in the introductory material and its associated appendix were written and compiled on the Solaris systems and then broken into fragments by a Perl script looking for specially formatted comments. Source fragments and generated output were inserted in the book by another Perl script.

NOTE TO TRANSLATORS

The fonts in this book have been chosen carefully. The font for code, when mixed with body text, has the same "x" height and roughly the same weight and "color." `Code` in text looks even—if you read quickly it can seem like body text, but it is nonetheless easy to tell that `code` text *is* different. Please use the fonts that we have used (we would be happy to help you locate any that you do not have) or choose other code and body fonts that are balanced in the same way.

Nasrudin returned to his village from the imperial capital,
and the villagers gathered around to hear what had passed.
"At this time," said Nasrudin, "I only want to say that the King spoke to me."
All the villagers but the stupidest ran off to spread the wonderful news.
The remaining villager asked, "What did the King say to you?"
"What he said—and quite distinctly, for everyone to hear—was 'Get out of my way!'"
The simpleton was overjoyed; he had heard words actually spoken by the King,
and seen the very man they were spoken to.

About The Authors

KEN ARNOLD, of Sun Microsystems, is one of the original architects of Jini™ technology and the original lead architect of JavaSpaces™ technology. He is co-author, with James Gosling and David Holmes, of *The Java™ Programming Language, Third Edition*, and is a leading expert in object-oriented design, Java, C, C++ and distributed computing. He also has a checkered past involving U. C. Berkeley, rogue, curses, and other things too embarrassing to mention.

GARY HOLNESS, currently on-leave pursuing his Ph.D., was among the first few engineers on the research and development team that transformed Jini technology from an interesting concept into a reality. He made many contributions to the internal algorithms of the JavaSpaces service implementation from Sun Microsystems, he was responsible for the design and implementation of the transaction service implementation from Sun Microsystems, and he completed the initial specification and design of the Jini event mailbox service. He enjoys a good cannolie and feeds his passion for robotics by building distributed systems.

JOHN MCCLAIN is a Staff Engineer with Sun Microsystems, where he is the technical lead for JavaSpaces technology. In addition, he is responsible for the LeaseRenewalService and LeaseRenewalManager specifications, as well as the development of the contributed LeaseRenewalService implementation from Sun Microsystems. Before joining Sun, John worked at Lockheed Martin Information Systems in the field of advanced distributed simulation.

BRIAN MURPHY has been a member of the Jini technology development team since joining Sun Microsystems in 1997. In addition to participating in the development of the lookup service, he is the technical lead for the 1.1 release of Jini technology. Prior to joining Sun, Brian worked in the telecommunications, robotics and defense industries developing distributed and client/server systems, as well as developing algorithms in the field of digital signal processing.

BRYAN O'SULLIVAN is a Staff Engineer at BEA Systems, where he is responsible for Java RMI technology. While at Sun Microsystems, he developed the Jini discovery and join protocols.

ZANE PAN is a Staff Engineer with Sun Microsystems, who was responsible for the initial design and implementation of the JoinManager, the LeaseRenewalManager and the ServiceDiscoveryManager. Zane also contributed to the Jini lookup service from Sun Microsystems.

BOB RESENDES has been a member of the Jini technology development team since joining Sun Microsystems in 1998. He has contributed to the JavaSpaces technology service implementation from Sun Microsystems and is responsible for the current specification, design, and implementation of the Jini event mailbox service. Prior to Sun, he worked at the Naval Undersea Warfare Center in the field of distributed simulation.

ROBERT W. SCHEIFLER is a Distinguished Engineer and one of the original architects of Jini technology with Sun Microsystems, where he has been responsible for the design and implementation of the lookup service and the associated discovery protocol and attribute schema. Before joining Sun, he spent nine years as Director and President of the X Consortium, a non-profit organization devoted to the development and evolution of the X Window System. He was chief architect of the X Window System protocol, and created the Consortium originally while a principal research scientist at the MIT Laboratory for Computer Science.

JIM WALDO is a Distinguished Engineer with Sun Microsystems, where he is the lead architect for Jini technology. Within Java Software, Jim's research has included object-oriented programming and systems, distributed computing, and user environments. Before joining Sun, Jim spent eight years at Apollo Computer and Hewlett Packard. While at Hewlett Packard, he led the design and development of the first Object Request Broker, and was instrumental in getting that technology incorporated into the first OMG CORBA specification.

ANN WOLLRATH is a Senior Staff Engineer with Sun Microsystems where she is the architect of the Java Remote Method Invocation (RMI) system and one of the original architects of the Jini technology. Previously, during her tenure at Sun Microsystems Laboratories and at the MITRE Corporation, she researched reliable, large-scale distributed systems and parallel computation.

The Jini™ Technology Series

"Ever since I first saw David Gelernter's Linda programming language almost twenty years ago, I felt that the basic ideas of Linda could be used to make an important advance in the ease of distributed and parallel programming. As part of the fruits of Sun's Jini project, we now have the JavaSpaces technology, a wonderfully simple platform for developing distributed applications that takes advantage of the power of the Java programming language. This important book and its many examples will help you learn about distributed and parallel programming. I highly recommend it to students, programmers, and the technically curious."

—Bill Joy, Chief Scientist and co-founder, Sun Microsystems, Inc.

JavaSpaces™ technology, a powerful Jini™ service from Sun Microsystems, facilitates building distributed applications for the Internet and Intranets. The JavaSpaces model involves persistent object exchange "areas" in which remote Java™ processes can coordinate their actions and exchange data. It provides a necessary ubiquitous, cross-platform framework for distributed computing, emerging as a key technology in this expanding field.

This book introduces the JavaSpaces architecture, provides a definitive and comprehensive description of the model, and demonstrates how to use it to develop distributed computing applications. The book presents an overview of the JavaSpaces design and walks you through the basics, demonstrating key features through examples. Every aspect of JavaSpaces programming is examined in depth: entries, distributed data structures, synchronization, communication, application patterns, leases, distributed events, and transactions. You will find information on the official JavaSpaces specification from Sun Microsystems. ***JavaSpaces Principles, Patterns, and Practice*** also includes two full-scale applications—one collaborative and the other parallel—that demonstrate how to put the JavaSpaces model to work.

The Jini™ Technology Series

From the creators of the Jini™ technology at Sun Microsystems comes the official Series for reference material and programming guides. Written by those who design, implement, and document the technology, these books show you how to use, deploy, and create applications using the Jini architecture. The Series is a vital resource of unique insights for anyone utilizing the power of the Java™ programming language and the simplicity of Jini technology.

...from the Source™

http:/java.sun.com/docs/books/jini

Addison-Wesley